Encyclopaedia of
# GOLF

*By the same author*

Rubs of the Green
In Praise of Golf (*with Tom Scott*)

*Other Encyclopaedias published by Robert Hale*

BY PAT BESFORD
Swimming

BY PETER CARRICK
Motor-Cycle Sport

BY A. N. GAULTON
Rugby League Football

BY MAURICE GOLESWORTHY
Cricket
Boxing
Association Football

BY KEN HAWKES AND GERARD LINDLEY
Bowls

BY J. R. JONES
Rugby Union Football
    (*Second edition by Maurice Golesworthy*)

BY ROGER MORTIMER
Flat Racing
(*New edition by John Hanmer in preparation*)

BY ANTHONY PRITCHARD AND KEITH DAVEY
Motor Racing

BY PATRICIA SMYLY
Steeplechasing

BY CHARLES STRATTON
Show Jumping and Combined Training

BY ANNE SUNNUCKS
Chess

BY WALT UNSWORTH
Mountaineering

BY MELVYN WATMAN
Athletics

# Encyclopaedia of
# GOLF

Compiled by
## WEBSTER EVANS

VI ET ARTE.

**ROBERT HALE · LONDON**

*Copyright © 1971, 1974 and 1980 by Webster Evans*

*First published in Great Britain 1971*

*Second Edition 1974*
*Third Edition 1980*

ISBN 0 7091 7746 1

ROBERT HALE LIMITED
Clerkenwell House
Clerkenwell Green
London EC1R 0HT

Printed in Great Britain by
Bristol Typesetting Co. Ltd.
Barton Manor - St Philips
Bristol

# Introduction

This is the first A to Z Encyclopaedia of Golf, covering all aspects of what may truthfully be called the world's most universal outdoor game: its history, leading personalities, origin and meaning of terms used, evolution of clubs and balls, records, championships and championship courses, details of all countries where golf is played, rules and definitions, other golf-like and kindred games. Particular attention is paid to the game in the United States, the world's leading golfing country.

There are some 1,500 entries, and copious cross references. It is of necessity a big book, for there is a great deal to say on the subject.

My copy of Dr Samuel Johnson's *Dictionary* says baldly that golf is " a game played with a ball and a club or bat ". This is true enough, but what a lot lies between those simple and inadequate words. Later writers have enlarged upon the theme. Lloyd George (a keen but indifferent performer) once wrote: " Golf is the only game where the worse player gets the best of it. He obtains more out of it as regards both exercise and enjoyment, for the good player gets worried over the slightest mistake, whereas the poor player makes too many mistakes to worry over them." A fellow politician, Arthur Balfour, said: " Give me my books, my golf clubs, and leisure, and I would ask for nothing more." Leisure, however, was what he lacked. As he put it in a letter to his friend, the future Lord Curzon of Kedleston: " I find it difficult to squeeze in the claims of both golf and politics into the 24 hours." Notice that he put golf first.

Regarding the actual playing of the game, Horace Hutchinson, a great golfer and golf writer of the late nineteenth and early twentieth centuries, put it succinctly if negatively in his book, *Hints on Golf* (1886): " Golf is not agriculture." The author of the first American golf book, James P. Lee, in *Golf in America* (1895), after saying that " a new game has lately been added to the list of our outdoor sports," assured his readers that " there is no racing or any effort to accomplish a hole in less time than your opponent." It conjures up a nice picture. So does the stop-press report that appeared in a London evening paper after Jack White had done a record 75 in the 1904 Open Championship: " White breaks record at Sandwich, going round in 7 minutes, 5 seconds." And, finally, Sir Henry Rider Haggard, author of *King Solomon's Mines* and *She*, said: " Golf, like Art, is a Goddess whom we would woo in early youth if we would win her." All the same, Walter Travis, the controversial American who won three U.S. Amateur Championships and the 1904 British Amateur Championship, did not take up the game until he was 34.

Golfers will play golf anywhere, at any time, no matter how unpromising the situation. Officers in the prisoner-of-war camp at Sagan, in Poland, made themselves a 9-holes course in a compound 350 by 150 yards, and played enthusiastically with home-made balls and one club between them—a hickory-shafted ladies' mashie. Other Allied airmen, shot down after D-Day and expecting capture or worse while waiting to be picked up from an encampment behind the German lines, created a primitive golf course to help to pass the weary and dangerous hours. A Scottish minister, visiting Cairo in the early 1880s and finding himself on top of the Pyramid of Gizeh with a golf ball in his pocket, teed it up and, using his umbrella as a club, drove off into the blue—the first golf shot played in Egypt.

Even if it was not quite the game we know today, golf has been played in Scotland since the mid-fifteenth century at least. And even earlier there were other vaguely golf-like games. The Romans had a game called Paganica ('The Country Game '), using a club to strike a ball made with a leather cover stuffed with feathers—just like the ' feathery ' ball used in Scotland until the coming of the solid ' gutty ' ball about 1848. In mid-fourteenth-century England there was a rustic game called Cambuca, in which the ball was also a ' feathery '. Later, in France and Belgium, players of Crosse, Chole and Jeu de Mail propelled a ball—a wooden one this time or in the case of Chole sometimes a leather one stuffed with hay or moss—across country with curious clubs. The Dutch enjoyed a game called Kolven—in a special court or sometimes on the ice, as shown in those delightful old paintings. Winston Churchill's friend, the famous Pasha of Marrakesh in the Atlas Mountains of Morocco, before becoming a dedicated golfer played a game in the desert called Takoura, with club and wooden ball. And did not the official Russian paper, *Pravda* (meaning Truth), once report that golf is " a game which the Caucasian shepherds played with enthusiasm about 1,000 years ago "?

Golf is indeed the most widespread of outdoor games. The world's most northerly course is in Lapland, well inside the Arctic Circle; the most southerly is that of the Stanley Club, at Port Stanley in the Falkland Islands, in the South Atlantic some 300 miles east of the Straits of Magellan. St Helena has a course, at Longwood, where

Napoleon died in 1821; Mauritius, that other remote island far out in the Indian Ocean, has a club founded in 1844 and thus older than any club in England apart from Royal Blackheath. The same is true of the club at Pau, in the Basses-Pyrenees, dating from 1856, where some of Wellington's Scottish officers are said to have played during the Peninsular War. The first course in the United States consisted of three holes laid out in 1888 in the cow pasture of a Scottish businessman named John Reid at Yonkers-on-Hudson, New York.

Golf has a language of its own, the terms being used and understood in all countries where the game is played; golf is golf in Abu Dhabi on the Persian Gulf, just as it is in St Andrews, even if the greens are 'browns'. The caddie-boys at the Royal Hong Kong Club, however, in less sophisticated days used—for obvious reasons—to call the game 'Hittee-Ball-Say-Damn'. 'Language' has always been associated with golfers.

The old game has thrown up many rich personalities in its long history. Young Tommy Morris, whose hitting was so terrific that his Scotch bonnet used to fly off, made the original British Open Championship Belt his own by winning it three times running—and after winning it a fourth time died while still only 24. The great 'Triumvirate' of Vardon, Taylor and Braid carried off the British Open 16 times between them in the space of 21 years. Immediately after the First World War the American invaders, Walter Hagen and Bobby Jones, similarly monopolised it seven times between 1922 and 1930. Following them came the studious Henry Cotton and the mechanical Ben Hogan, leading up to the modern 'Big Three' of Palmer, Player and Nicklaus, who have given golf its new look and its legions of hero-worshippers exemplified in 'Arnie's Army'. And now even they are giving way to Billy Casper, Tony Jacklin, Lee Trevino and their peers.

Compiling this book has been a labour of love, in the course of which I have discovered many things I didn't know before. I hope it will prove a valuable and entertaining reference book of a type not attempted before. And perhaps readers can help to solve some of golf's still unsolved mysteries. Why, for instance, do golfers talk about 'driving up the pretty'? Where does 'birdie' come from? There is even some doubt about the origin of the word 'golf' itself!

Richmond, Surrey                                        WEBSTER EVANS


### Introduction to Second Edition

A lot of water has flowed under the bridges—including the bridges over the Swilcan Burn at St Andrews—since the First Edition appeared in September 1971. Golf is always changing, in its personalities, its events, its records, even its language. New contenders for championship honours have arisen and some older champions, including the immortal Bobby Jones, have died. As was right and proper, the one nameless hole on the Old Course at St Andrews—the 10th— has been named 'The Bobby Jones Hole'.

Many letters from readers have reached me, often containing most interesting information. I welcome the opportunity that this Second Edition gives to add in fresh information of all kinds and bring things up to date. I hope readers, including young ones just discovering golf, will continue to find plenty of meat in this Encyclopaedia; and I also hope that they will continue to write to me.

W.E.

## Introduction to Third Edition

Several new faces have appeared on the golf scene since the Second Edition was published in 1974—Severiano Ballesteros and Nick Faldo in particular. 'Sevvy', as he is affectionately known, is the latest of the colourful Spanish professionals—and the most promising. It is a real tonic to watch 'Sevvy' thrashing his way out of knee-deep rough, into which a vast but errant drive has landed him.

Young Nick Faldo comes out of much the same mould. He too shows no mercy to his ball. Yet he has a most delicate touch round the greens.

A young amateur who has made his mark is Peter McEvoy. In a two-year period—1977 and 1978—he picked up two British Amateur titles and an English one; played in the Walker Cup team; indeed looked capable of clearing the amateur decks for years to come. And there's a promising new tournament—the European Open Championship—that might well rival the Big Four.

W.E.

PICTURE CREDITS

H. W. Neale: 3, 5, 7, 11, 14, 17, 43; G. M. Cowie: 9, 15, 19, 22, 30, 33, 38, 40; Topical Press: 16; Frank Gardener: 18; Planet News: 26; Leslie F. Thompson: 27; Central Press: 28, 35; Keystone Press Agency: 32; *Dundee Courier and Advertiser*: 36; Syndication International: 41; Associated Press: 44.

# Illustrations

## AARON, Tommy (b 1937)

Runner-up, U.S. Amateur Championship, 1958. Runner-up, U.S.P.G.A. Championship, 1972. Walker Cup team, 1959. Won U.S. Masters, 1973. Canadian Open Champion, 1969, after tie with Sam Snead. Ryder Cup team, 1969. In the last round of the 1968 U.S. Masters he marked Roberto De Vicenzo's card wrongly, giving him a four instead of a three at the 17th, and so lost him a chance to tie with Bob Goalby, the winner. See WALKER AND RYDER CUPS, PLAYED IN BOTH.

## ABBOTT, Buell Patrick (b 1914)

American. Runner-up, U.S. Amateur Championship, 1938, 1941. U.S. Public Links Champion, 1936.

## ABOVE GROUND

A ball is said to be 'above ground' when it is not in a trap or bunker.

## ABU DHABI, GOLF IN

See TRUCIAL STATES, GOLF IN THE.

## ACE

See HOLE-IN-ONE.

## ADAIR, Rhona (Mrs Cuthell) (b 1878)

One of the first and greatest Irish lady golfers. British Ladies' Champion, 1900, 1903 ; runner-up, 1901. Irish Ladies' Champion, 1900, 1901, 1902, 1903 ; runner-up, 1899. Her rivals and contemporaries were the Hezlet sisters. See HEZLET, MAY.

## ADAMS, James (b 1910)

Belgian Open Champion, 1949. Dutch Open Champion, 1949. Italian Open Champion, 1951. Irish Professional Native Champion, 1933—a remarkable feat for a Scot! Runner-up, British Open Championship, 1936, 1938. Runner-up, British Professional Match Play Championship, 1937, 1946, 1951. Tied Dunlop Masters, with Bobby Locke, 1946. Ryder Cup team, 1947, 1949, 1951, 1953. As a boy caddied for Willie Fernie, the 1883 Open Champion who was professional at the Troon Club until his death in 1924.

## ADDRESSING THE BALL

"A player has 'addressed the ball' when he has taken his stance and has also grounded his club, except that in a hazard a player has addressed the ball when he has taken his stance" (Rules of Golf Definition). A player may not ground his club in a hazard.

## ADEN, GOLF IN

Since Aden became the People's Republic of South Yemen in 1968, after being a British Protectorate for 129 years, golf has continued at the Khormaksar and Little Aden Clubs. Both have 12 holes, with oiled sand 'greens'.

## ADJUSTABLE IRONS

There have been several types of adjustable iron clubs, all banned by the R. and A. One was a propeller-blade iron, the blade of which could be set at different angles so that it could serve the purpose of a No. 3, No. 6 or whatever loft was desired. Needless to say, it was ill-balanced. There was also an adjustable putter with a ratchet setting and cranked shaft, mounted on an adjustable bolt that could be set to various degrees of loft. See REJECTED CLUBS.

## ADVICE

" 'Advice' is any counsel or suggestion which could influence a player in determining his play, the choice of a club, or the method of making a stroke" (Rules of Golf Definition). Information on the Rules or Local Rules is not regarded as advice. See RULES OF GOLF, Rule 9.

## AGRIPPA
A popular make of gutty ball in the 1890s. See BALL, MAKES OF ; GUTTY.

## AIR SHOT
This distressing happening occurs when the player misses the ball altogether, the shot counting in his score for the hole. Also called a 'fresh air shot' or, in the old days, 'missing the globe'. Americans sometimes call it a 'whiff'.

## ALBATROSS
A term for a score three under the par for the hole ; associated with the similar terms 'birdie' (one under par) and 'eagle' (two under par). This comparatively rare happening is usually called by American golfers a 'double eagle' or 'golden eagle'.

## ALGERIA, GOLF IN
Before the Second World War and for some years afterwards, when the country was under French control, Algeria had two golf clubs—one in Algiers and the other in Biskra. Since independence in 1962, however, the game seems to have declined in popularity. See MOROCCO, GOLF IN.

## ALLAN, A. J. Travers (1875-98)
British Amateur Champion, 1897. Jack Allan was one of the most remarkable champions. He was a medical student and had played golf for only five years. He played in the most casual fashion in the clothes and shoes in which he had arrived at Muirfield on a bicycle. It was his first Amateur Championship—and his last, for, having qualified as a doctor, he died less than a year later. In the final he defeated James Robb after an unfortunate incident in which, after hooking his ball at the 11th hole in the second round, it was found in Robb's caddie's pocket, an action that lost his master the hole and generally unsettled him.

## ALL FLAT
A term with the same meaning as 'all square', indicating that the players have finished the hole or match level.

## ALLIANCES, GOLFING
All over the country there are golfing alliances, whose object is to run off-season competitions in which both amateurs and professionals can play, and so keep interest in golf going through the winter months. The originator was the Croydon and District Alliance, founded in 1919 by enthusiasts attached to clubs within a radius of 15 miles of Croydon Town Hall, Surrey, thus taking in certain clubs in Surrey, Kent and Middlesex.
The meetings were so successful that many other alliances were formed to cover either districts or counties.

## ALLISS, Percy (b 1897)
Welsh Professional Champion, 1920, 1921. Runner-up, Canadian Open Championship, 1931. Runner-up, French Open Championship, 1931. German Open Champion, 1926, 1927, 1928, 1929, 1933. German Close Professional Champion, 1928. Italian Open Champion, 1927, 1935. British Professional Match Play Champion, 1933, 1937; runner-up, 1935, 1945. Ryder Cup team, 1933, 1935, 1937. Father of Peter and Alec Alliss.

## ALLISS, Peter (b 1931)
Runner-up, French Open Championship, 1957. Italian Open Champion, 1958. Portuguese Open Champion, 1958. Spanish Open Champion, 1956, 1958. P.G.A. Champion, 1957, 1962, 1965. Ryder Cup team, 1953, 1957, 1959, 1961, 1963, 1965, 1967, 1969. Played for England in World (formerly Canada) Cup, 1954, 1955, 1957, 1958, 1959, 1961, 1962, 1966, 1967. Captain P.G.A., 1962. Author of *Alliss Through the Looking Glass* (1963). A well-known T.V. commentator.

## ALUMINIUM SHAFTS
In recent years club shafts have begun to be made from aluminium (in

America, aluminum) and other alloys instead of steel. See STEEL SHAFTS.

## AMATEUR

"An amateur golfer is one who plays the game solely as a non-remunerative or non-profit-making sport" (Rules of Golf). See AMATEUR STATUS, RULES OF.

## AMATEUR INTERNATIONAL, FIRST

The first Amateur International, between England and Scotland, took place at the Royal Liverpool Club, Hoylake, in 1902. Matches were over 36 holes, reckoned by holes up, and Scotland won by 32 holes to 25. The teams were: *Scotland*—R. Maxwell, J. E. Laidlay, J. Graham, L. Balfour-Melville, J. Robb, S. Mure Fergusson, F. Mackenzie, J. R. Gairdner, E. Blackwell, C. E. Dick. *England*—J. Ball, H. H. Hilton, H. G. Hutchinson, C. Hutchings, J. A. T. Bramston, H. C. Ellis, Hon. O. Scott, B. Darwin, G. F. Smith, S. H. Fry. The England-Scotland matches continued until 1932, when Ireland and Wales came in to make the four-sided international series still played annually.

## AMATEUR SIDE OF THE HOLE

See PROFESSIONAL SIDE OF THE HOLE.

## AMATEUR STATUS, RULES OF

The following are the Rules of Amateur Status as approved by the R. and A.:
### Definition of an amateur golfer
An amateur golfer is one who plays the game solely as a non-remunerative or non-profit making sport.

### Rule 1

#### Forfeiture of amateur status at any age
The following are examples of acts at any age which violate the definition of an amateur golfer and cause forfeiture of amateur status:
1. *Professionalism.*
Receiving payment or compensation for serving as:

a. A professional golfer
b. A teaching or playing assistant to a professional golfer.
2. *Professional Intent.*
Taking any action which clearly indicates the intention of becoming a professional golfer.
3. *Instruction.*
Receiving payment or compensation for giving instruction in playing golf, either orally, in writing, by pictures or by other demonstrations, to either individuals or groups.
Exceptions: Teachers of physical training or other subjects whose duties include instruction in games to pupils of a recognised educational establishment.
4. *Prizes and Testimonials.*
a. *Playing for Prize Money:* Playing for prize money or its equivalent in a match, tournament or exhibition.
b. *Other Prizes and Testimonials.* Acceptance of a prize or testimonial of the following character (this applies to total prizes received for any event or series of events in any one tournament or exhibition, including a hole-in-one contest):
(i) In Great Britain and Ireland, of retail value exceeding £50; elsewhere, of retail value exceeding $200 U.S. or the equivalent, or such lesser figure as may be decided by the Governing Body of Golf in any country; or
(ii) Of a nature which is the equivalent of money or makes it readily convertible into money.
Exceptions:
1. Prizes of only symbolic value (such as metal trophies).
2. More than one testimonial award may be accepted from different donors even though their total retail value exceeds £50 or $200 U.S., provided they are not presented so as to evade such value limit for a single award. (Testimonial awards relate to notable performances or contributions to golf, as distinguished from tournament prizes.)
5. *Lending Name or Likeness.*
Receiving or contracting to receive payment, compensation or personal benefit, directly or indirectly, for allowing one's name or likeness as a

golfer to be used in any way for the advertisement or sale of anything, whether or not used in or appertaining to golf.

*Note: An advertisement can contain a player's name or likeness when it is customary to the business of such player and contains no reference to the game of golf.*

6. *Personal Appearance.*

Because of golf skill or golf reputation, receiving payment or compensation, directly or indirectly, for a personal appearance, whether or not in connection with a golf competition or exhibition. (This includes appearance on radio and television broadcasts, testimonial dinners and the like.)

7. *Writing.*

Because of golf skill receiving or contracting to receive payment or compensation, directly or indirectly, for writing golf articles or books or for allowing one's name to be advertised or published as the author of golf articles or books of which he is not actually the author.

8. *Sale of Golf Merchandise.*

Because of golf skill or golf reputation, receiving payment or compensation, directly or indirectly, for selling or promoting the sale of golf merchandise, at either wholesale or retail. (The term 'golf merchandise' does not include clothing or shoes.)

9. *Golf Equipment.*

Accepting golf balls, clubs, golf merchandise, golf clothing or golf shoes from anyone dealing in such merchandise without payment of current market price.

10. *Membership and Privileges.*

Because of golf skill or golf reputation, accepting membership or privileges in a club or at a golf course without full payment for the class of membership or privileges involved unless such membership or privileges have been awarded as purely and deservedly honorary and in recognition of an outstanding performance or contribution to golf.

11. *Expenses.*

Accepting expenses, in money or otherwise, from any source other than one on whom the player is normally or legally dependent to engage in:

a. A golf competition or exhibition.

b. A personal appearance as a golfer, including radio and television broadcasts, testimonial dinners and the like.

Exceptions:

A player may receive a reasonable amount of expenses as follows:

1. As a player in a golf competition or exhibition limited exclusively to players who have not reached their eighteenth birthday;

or

2. As a representative of his country, county, club or similar body, in team matches, when such expenses are paid by the body he represents, or by the body controlling golf in the territory he is visiting.

*Note 1: A player is not considered to be 'normally or legally dependent' upon an employer, a partner or other vocational source, and acceptance of expenses therefrom is not permissible.*

*Note 2: Business Expenses. It is permissible to play in a golf competition while on a business trip with expenses paid provided that the golf part of the expenses is borne personally and is not charged to business. Further, the business involved must be actual and substantial, and not merely a subterfuge for legitimising expenses when the primary purpose is golf competition.*

*Note 3: Private Transport. Acceptance of private transport furnished or arranged for by a tournament sponsor, directly or indirectly, as an inducement for a player to engage in a golf competition or exhibition shall be considered accepting expenses under Rule 1–11.*

12. *Scholarships.*

Because of golf skill or golf reputation, accepting the benefits of a scholarship or any other consideration as an inducement to be a student in an educational establishment.

13. *Conduct Detrimental to Golf.*

Any conduct, including activities in connection with golf gambling, which is considered detrimental to the best interests of the game.

## Rule 2

### Procedure for enforcement and reinstatement

1. *Decision on Violation.*

Whenever information of a possible violation of the Definition of an Amateur Golfer by a player claiming to be an amateur shall come to the attention of the executive committee of the governing body, the committee, after such investigation as it may deem desirable, shall decide whether a violation has occurred. Each case shall be considered on its merits. The decision of the committee shall be final.

2. *Enforcement.*

Upon a decision that a player has violated the Definition of an Amateur Golfer, the committee may declare the amateur status of the player forfeited or require the player to refrain or desist from specified actions as a condition of retaining his amateur status.

The committee shall notify the player, if possible, and may notify any interested golf association of any action taken under this paragraph.

3. *Reinstatement.*

The committee shall have sole power to reinstate a player to amateur status or to deny reinstatement.

Each application for reinstatement shall be decided on its merits. In considering an application for reinstatement, the committee shall normally be guided by the following principles:

a. *Five-Year Limit.* A player shall not normally be eligible for reinstatement if he was in violation of the Definition of an Amateur Golfer for a calendar period of five years or more.

b. *One Reinstatement.* A player shall not be reinstated more than once.

c. *Probation.* The professional holds an advantage over the amateur by reason of having devoted himself to the game as his profession ; other persons violating the Rules of Amateur Status also obtain advantages not available to the amateur. They do not necessarily lose such advantage merely by deciding to cease violating the rules. Therefore, an applicant for reinstatement to amateur status shall undergo probation as prescribed by the committee. Probation shall start from the date of the player's last violation of the Definition of an Amateur Golfer unless the committee decides that it shall start from the date when the player's last violation became known to the committee.

d. *Probationary Period.* No applicant shall normally be eligible for reinstatement until he has conducted himself in accordance with the Definition of an Amateur Golfer for a probationary period of at least two consecutive years. The committee, however, reserves the right to extend or to shorten such period.

e. *Status During Probation.* During probation an applicant for reinstatement shall conform with the Definition of an Amateur Golfer. He shall not be eligible to enter competitions as an amateur. He may, however, enter competitions solely among members of a club of which he is a member, subject to the approval of the club, but he may not represent such club against other clubs.

*Forms of Application for Countries under the Jurisdiction of the Royal and Ancient Golf Club.*

Each application for reinstatement in England, Scotland, Ireland and Wales shall be submitted on the approved form to the County Union, District Association or Provincial Branch of the area where the applicant wishes to play as an Amateur. The body concerned shall, after making all necessary enquiries, forward it through the National Union and the Professional Golfers' Association, with comments endorsed thereon, to the Royal and Ancient Golf Club of St Andrews. Forms of application for reinstatement may be obtained from the Royal and Ancient Golf Club or from the National or County Unions. The application shall include such information as the Royal and Ancient Golf Club may require from time to time and it shall be signed and certified by the applicant. Any application made elsewhere in countries under the jurisdiction of the Royal and Ancient

Golf Club of St Andrews which is doubtful or which is not covered by the above regulations may be submitted to the Royal and Ancient Golf Club through the governing body of golf in that country.

The decision of the Royal and Ancient Golf Club on an application shall be final.

### R. & A. Policy on Gambling

'The R. & A. considers that the organisation of Auction Sweepstakes at Open Handicap Tournaments can lead to abuses and is not in the best interest of the game.

The R. & A. strongly recommends the elimination of such Sweepstakes and asks Unions and Associations in the U.K. and Overseas to do all they can to achieve this end.'

## AMERICA, EARLY REFERENCES TO GOLF CLUBS IN

See UNITED STATES, EARLY REFERENCES TO GOLF CLUBS IN THE.

## AMERICA, GOLF IN

See UNITED STATES, GOLF IN THE.

## AMERICA, PROFESSIONAL GOLFERS' ASSOCIATION OF

See PROFESSIONAL GOLFERS' ASSOCIATION OF AMERICA.

## AMERICAN TOURNAMENT

A match-play tournament in which each competitor plays all the others, the winner being the one scoring the most victories. Also called a Round Robin tournament.

## AMERICAS CUP MATCHES

The Americas Cup was presented by Mr Jerome P. Bowen for a match every other year between teams of amateurs from the United States, Canada and Mexico, the first match being in 1952. Teams were of not more than seven players, the captain being either playing or non-playing. Matches were six a side and were decided by three four-ball matches in the morning and six singles matches in the afternoon on each of the two days.

The U.S. team proved much too strong and the series were discontinued in 1967.

## ANDERSON, James ('Jamie') (1842-1912)

Born St Andrews, elder son of 'Old Daw' Anderson, a famous caddie who later had a refreshment trolley on the course. One of only four players to win the British Open Championship three times running (1877, 1878 and 1879); his victory in the 1878 Open at Prestwick was helped by a hole-in-one at the last hole but one in the last round. His brother David was also a well known St Andrews professional. See BRITISH OPEN CHAMPION MORE THAN ONCE.

## ANDERSON, Jessie

See VALENTINE, MRS GEORGE.

## ANDERSON, John G. (1884-1933)

American. Runner-up, U.S. Amateur Championship, 1913, 1915. French Open Amateur Champion, 1924, 1926; runner-up, 1911. For some years he was golf correspondent for a New York paper.

## ANDERSON, Mrs John (b 1921)

Born Jean Donald. Runner-up British Ladies' Championship, 1948. Scottish Ladies' Champion, 1947, 1949, 1952; runner-up, 1953. French Ladies' Open Champion, 1947. Curtis Cup team, 1948, 1950, 1952.

## ANDERSON, Peter C. (b 1873)

As a student at St Andrews University, won the 1893 British Amateur Championship, defeating John Laidlay, twice Amateur Champion, in the final. Became a clergyman and went to Australia as a schoolmaster.

## ANDERSON, Willie (1878-1910)

A Scot who emigrated to America in the mid-1890s. He played in his first U.S. Open Championship in 1897 and was runner-up to an English-born pro-

"APPLE TREE GANG". This remarkable photograph shows Harry Holbrook, Alexander Kinnan, John Upham and John Reid playing on the original 3-holes course laid out in John Reid's cow pasture at Yonkers-on-Hudson, New York

(*above left*) BALFOUR, EARL (ARTHUR JAMES). Arthur James Balfour, the Conservative politician, did so much toward spreading the golf idea beyond Scotland that he was called "the father of English golf". (*right*) BALLESTEROS, SEVERIANO. The brilliant young Spanish golfer is putting in the 1978 Spanish Open Championship. He has already won the Opens of Holland, France, Switzerland and Japan

(*above*) BALL, MAKES OF. On the left is a "feathery" ball stamped with the name Gourlay, the famous Edinburgh family of ball-makers. In the centre is an early "gutty", with indentations hammered by hand. On the right is a later machine-marked "gutty". (*left*) BONALLACK, MICHAEL FRANCIS. The leading modern British amateur playing a wedge shot at Saunton, Devon. (*below*) CAMBUCA. A rustic golf-like game called Cambuca was played in England as early as the mid-fourteenth century and a similar game was played on the Continent. This picture of Flemish players is from a Book of Hours (1500-1520)

fessional, Joe Lloyd. He became champion in 1901 after winning a play-off against Alex Smith, who was to win the event in 1906. Then Anderson did the hat-trick by winning in 1903, 1904, 1905. At this time he was professional at the Apawamis Club, Rye, New York, and in 1906 he moved to the Onwentsia Club, Lake Forest, Illinois. See UNITED STATES OPEN CHAMPION MORE THAN ONCE.

## ANGELINI, Alfonso (b 1927)

Italian Native Professional Champion, 1947, 1951, 1952, 1953, 1958, 1959, 1961, 1962, 1964, 1965. Tied Italian Open Championship, 1950, with Ugo Grappasonni, but lost play-off. Portuguese Open Champion, 1962, 1966.

## ANGOLA, GOLF IN

There is a golf course at Luanda, the capital of this former Portuguese West African colony.

## ANSTEY, Veronica

See BEHARRELL, MRS JOHN.

## 'ANY FOOL CAN DO IT THE SECOND TIME'

An old golf saying indicating that it is easy to hole a putt given a second chance.

## AOKI, Isao (b 1942)

An unorthodox Japanese player, but good enough to win the World Match-Play tournament, 1978.

## 'APPLE TREE GANG'

See ST ANDREWS GOLF CLUB OF YONKERS.

## APPROACH SHOT

When the player is comparatively near the green, his stroke towards the hole with an iron club is called an approach shot. Any long putt made with a putter is an approach putt.

## APRON OF THE GREEN

The area immediately in front of a green that is normally cut rather more closely than the surrounding fairway. See GREEN.

B

## ARCHER, George (b 1939)

Won U.S. Masters, 1969.

## ARGENTINA, GOLF IN

Golf is popular in the Argentine Republic, and there are about 65 clubs in various parts of the country, including 16 near Buenos Aires, the capital.

The Argentine Amateur Championship was inaugurated as far back as 1895, the Ladies' Championship in 1904, the Open Championship in 1905.

Argentina's most famous modern professional is Roberto De Vicenzo, and others of international repute include José Jurado, Antonio Cerda, Leopoldo Ruiz, Martin Pose and Antonio Perez.

## ARMOUR, Thomas Dickson ('Tommy') (1895-1968)

Born in Scotland but played for both Great Britain and U.S. While serving in the Tank Corps in the First World War, lost the sight of one eye in a gas attack. Won U.S. Open Championship, 1927; British Open Championship, 1931; U.S.P.G.A. Championship, 1930; Canadian Open Championship, 1927, 1930; French Open Amateur Championship, 1920. Played for Britain in the 1921 match against the United States amateurs that led to the Walker Cup series. Went to America in 1922, turned professional in 1924 and played for United States in the forerunner of the Ryder Cup in 1926. After giving up tournament golf, became one of the best (and most expensive) teachers in America. The colour of his hair gave him his nickname of 'The Silver Scot'. Author of *How to Play Your Best Golf All the Time* (1954); *A Round of Golf with Tommy Armour* (1959); *A.B.Cs of Golf* (1967).

## ARMY CHAMPIONSHIP

Founded 1911. A two-round stroke play event held annually at different clubs. Winners have included Captain (later Brigadier) A. Gordon Barry, winner of the 1905 British Amateur Championship; the Walker Cup players, Colonel A. A. Duncan and Major David Blair ; Second Lieutenant Michael Bonallack, five times Amateur Champion ; and Corporal George Will, the Ryder Cup player.

## 'ARNIE'S ARMY'

See PALMER, ARNOLD.

## ARTISAN GOLFERS' ASSOCIATION

This association, like the National Association of Public Golf Courses, was formed largely through the efforts of J. H. Taylor and F. G. Hawtree, with the support of Lord Riddell (of Walton Heath), the newspaper proprietor. Its main objects were to coordinate the various artisan clubs already in existence and to encourage the formation of new ones throughout the country.

When the association was founded in 1921 there were only about a dozen artisan clubs, including the earliest ones—the Bulwell Forest Artisans' Club, Nottingham (1887) ; the Northam Working Men's Club, Westward Ho! (1888), one of whose members was young J. H. Taylor ; and the Cantelupe Artisan Club, Forest Row, Sussex (1889), where Abe Mitchell was a member when he reached the final of the Amateur Championship in 1912.

By the time the first Artisan Championship was held in 1924, there were some 60 artisan clubs affiliated to the Association and the movement has since grown steadily. Several artisan champions have gone on to make their name in the professional field, including Norman Sutton (1928), Alan Poulton (1935), Douglas Sewell (1956, 1958) and George Evans (1959).

The man who in recent years has done more than anybody else to foster the artisan movement is W. J. (Bill) Gardner, for long Honorary Secretary of the Association. They have a journal called *The Artisan Golfer*.

## ASCENSION ISLAND, GOLF ON

Like St Helena, with which it is connected politically, the South Atlantic island of Ascension has its club —the Ascension Island Golf Club— with a 9-holes course. The island was occupied by the British in 1815 when Napoleon was imprisoned on St Helena.

## ASHBY, Harry (b 1946)

English Amateur Champion, 1972, 1973. Won *Golf Illustrated* Gold Vase, 1972.

## ASHLEY, Jean (Mrs Crawford) (b 1939)

U.S. Ladies' Champion, 1965 ; runner-up, 1960, 1967. Curtis Cup team, 1962, 1966, 1968. Non-playing captain, 1972.

## ATTENBOROUGH, Michael F. (b 1939)

Scandinavian Open Amateur Champion, 1965. As Kent Amateur Champion won County Champions' Championship, 1964. Won Oxford and Cambridge Golfing Society's President's Putter, 1962, 1966 ; runner-up, 1964. Walker Cup team, 1967.

## AUCHTERLONIE, Laurence (b 1875)

Born St Andrews, younger brother of Willie Auchterlonie, British Open Champion, 1893. U.S. Open Champion, 1902, being the first to break 80 in all four rounds for a total of 307.

## AUCHTERLONIE, Laurie (b 1904)

Honorary professional of the R. and A. since 1963, succeeding his father, William Auchterlonie.

## AUCHTERLONIE, William (1872-1963)

Born St Andrews. British Open Champion, 1893. Played in his first Open at 16. Professional to the R. and A., 1935-63 ; succeeded by his son, Laurie. With his brother, Laurence, founded clubmaking firm of L. and W. Auchterlonie. He was made an honorary member of the R. and A. in 1950, and his portrait hangs in the clubhouse, showing him standing near the Road Hole with his bag of seven clubs, the number he carried when winning the Open, although he actually used only five.

## AUGUSTA NATIONAL CLUB
See MASTERS TOURNAMENT.

## AUSTRALIA, GOLF IN
There are over 1,300 clubs, great and small, in Australia, scattered throughout the various states. New South Wales has the largest number and the Northern Territory, because of its terrain, the fewest. In the Australian Capital Territory is Royal Canberra, and besides Canberra other Royal clubs are Adelaide, Fremantle, Melbourne, Perth, Queensland, Sydney and Hobart. The oldest Australian club is Royal Melbourne, founded in 1891.

The Australian Golf Union has as members New South Wales, Queensland, South Australia, Tasmania, Victoria and Western Australia. There is also an Australian Ladies' Golf Union and a Professional Golfers' Association.

The Australian Open Championship dates back to 1904, the first winner being the Hon. Michael Scott, who was then living in Australia; he won the title again in 1907 and became British Amateur Champion 26 years later. The Australian Amateur Championship was founded in 1906 (Michael Scott being the winner in 1907, 1909 and 1910), the Ladies' Championship in 1911 and the Professional Championship in 1924. The professional tournament circuit operates annually from October to January.

Among Australia's famous players are Peter Thomson, Norman Von Nida, Kel Nagle, Eric Cremin, Ossie Pickworth, Jim Ferrier (who settled in America), Bruce Devlin, Bruce Crampton and Frank Phillips. Among the newer stars are David Graham, Graham Marsh, Bill Dunk, Greg Norman and Jack Newton. Among the ladies have been Miss Pat Borthwick, Miss Judith Percy and Miss Gail Corry.

Australia can also claim to have had the only world-famous opera singer, Joan Hammond, who was a good enough golfer to play in the British Ladies' Championship; in the 1948 event she gave the current American champion, Louise Suggs, a hard game. She was an all-round athlete and it was largely through the efforts of other Australian lady golfers that she was sent to Europe to study music in the 1930s.

## AUSTRIA, GOLF IN
Golf in Austria goes back to 1901, when the Golf Club Wien was established on the outskirts of Vienna. The game suffered severely during the First and Second World Wars, but the clubs at Innsbruck, Pertisau, Semmering and Dellach survived, and after 1947 others were formed or re-formed at Badgastein, Bad Ischl, Kitzbuhel, Murhof (Frohnleiten), Linz and Salzburg. The International Country Club at Lainz, some 15 miles from Vienna, unfortunately did not survive the last war. At present there are 15 courses, with others under construction. There is an Austrian Golf Federation.

The Austrian Open Amateur Championship dates from 1909, with gaps between 1914 and 1924 and between 1938 and 1946. The Ladies' Open Championship dates from 1925, with a similar gap from 1937 to 1947. Frau Ruth Richter dominated Austrian ladies' golf between 1947 and 1962.

## AWAY
A player is said to be 'away' when his ball, on or near the putting surface, is further away from the hole than that of his oppenent.

## AYLMER, Colin C.
Runner-up, British Amateur Championship, 1910. Played pre-Walker Cup match at Hoylake, 1921. Walker Cup team, 1922.

## BABY A SHOT

To baby a shot—usually an approach to the green—means to hit the ball so feebly and ineffectively that it finishes yards short of its objective.

## BACHLI, Douglas (b 1922)

British Amateur Champion, 1954; the only Australian winner. Australian Amateur Champion, 1948, 1962. Member of unbeaten Australian team in R. and A. Bi-centenary Commonwealth tournament, St Andrews, 1954, and of the Australian team which won the World Cup (formerly Eisenhower Trophy) at St Andrews, 1958.

## BACK DOOR

If a ball goes into the hole at the extreme side or even, as sometimes happens, at the back, it is said to have gone in by the 'back door'— or 'tradesman's entrance'. Similarly, the front side of the hole is the 'front door'.

## BACK NINE

See FRONT NINE.

## BACKSPIN

See GOLF BALL, VELOCITY OF.

## BACK-SWING

The backward movement of the hands and arms that takes the club back so that it can be brought down again into the hitting area, leading to the follow-through. See FOLLOW-THROUGH.

## BAFFY (OR BAFFING SPOON)

An obsolete term for a wooden club similar to the modern No 3 or 4 wood, intended for lofted shots played off the fairway. So called because the ground was 'baffed', or struck, immediately behind the ball. Also called a 'baffing spoon', although even in the late 1880s this term was seldom used. According to Horace Hutchinson in the Badminton Library *Golf* volume (1890), the baffy was " very short and stiff and with the face very much laid back". See SCLAFF.

## BAHAMAS, GOLF IN THE

The Bahamas, in the Atlantic, consist of some 700 islands, of which 30 are inhabited. Golf is played on five of them. On New Providence are six clubs, near Nassau, the capital of the Bahamas—the Nassau Club, the Coral Harbour Club, the Paradise Island Club, the Lyford Cay Club, the new South Ocean Club, on the western tip of the island, and the 9-holes par-3 Blue Hill Club, which is illuminated for play at night.

On Grand Bahama are five clubs— the Bahamian Country Club (King's Inn), the Lucayan Country Club, the Grand Bahama Hotel and Country Club and the new Bahamas Reef and Shannon Country Clubs.

On Eleuthera, at Rock Sound, is the Cotton Bay Club, designed by the famous American course architect, Robert Trent Jones. On Abaco is the new Treasure Cay Club, while at Great Harbour Cay, in the Berry Islands, another new course has been created.

## BAHRAIN, GOLF IN

The Awali Club, Bahrain, in the Persian Gulf, was founded in 1936 as a private club for the employees of the Bahrain Petroleum Co. It has 18 holes with a length of 6,224 yards. Visitors may play as guests of members. See KUWAIT, GOLF IN; TRUCIAL STATES, GOLF IN THE.

## BAIOCCHI, Hugh (b 1946)
South African British P.G.A. Match Play Champion, 1977. Swiss Open Champion, 1973. Dutch Open Champion, 1975.

## BALDING, Al (b 1924)
Canadian P.G.A. Champion, 1955, 1956, 1963, 1970. Mexican Open Champion, 1963. With George Knudson won World (formerly Canada) Cup, 1968, also winning individual title.

## BALEARIC ISLANDS, GOLF IN THE
SEE IBIZA, GOLF IN ; MAJORCA, GOLF IN ; MENORCA, GOLF IN.

## BALFOUR, Earl (Arthur James) (1848-1930)
The Conservative Prime Minister who did more towards popularising golf in England than any other politician, being called 'the father of English golf'. Of him and golf, G. K. Chesterton said: "It came with a rush over the Border, like the blue bonnets, and grew fashionable largely because Arthur Balfour was the fashion". Captain, R. and A., 1894. He once said: "A tolerable day, a tolerable green, a tolerable opponent supply, or ought to supply, all that any reasonably constituted human should require in the way of entertainment." He also said: "Give me my books, my golf clubs, and leisure, and I would ask for nothing more. My ideal in life is to read a lot, write a little, play plenty of golf, and have nothing to worry about." See 'BIG CRAWFORD'.

## BALFOUR-MELVILLE, Leslie (1854-1937)
Son of James Balfour, author of *Reminiscences of Golf on St Andrews Links* (1887). British Amateur Champion, 1895. Also played cricket and rugby for Scotland and won Scottish Lawn Tennis Championship.

## BALL AT REST
A term used to describe a ball that has been struck in the course of play and has come to a standstill. See RULES OF GOLF, Rule 27.

## BALL DEEMED TO MOVE
"A ball is deemed to have moved if it leave its position and come to rest in any other place" (Rules of Golf Definition).

## BALL, DROPPING THE
To replace a lost ball, or to put into play again a ball that has gone out of bounds or reached an unplayable lie or under various other circumstances in accordance with the Rules, a ball may be 'dropped' in order that the hole may be completed. Rule 22–2a tells you how the player should drop the ball: "He shall face the hole, stand erect and drop the ball behind him over his shoulder." In some cases the ball may be placed on the ground instead of dropped. See RULES OF GOLF, Rule 22.

## BALL HOLED
"A ball is 'holed' when it lies within the circumference of the hole and all of it is below the level of the lip of the hole" (Rules of Golf Definition).

## BALL IN PLAY
"A ball is 'in play' as soon as the player has made a stroke on the teeing ground. It remains in play as his ball until holed out, except when it is out of bounds, lost or lifted, or another ball is substituted in accordance with the Rules or Local Rules" (Rules of Golf Definition).
To 'keep the ball in play'—usually acknowledged to be the first essential in foursomes play—means that each partner should endeavour to keep the ball in bounds, out of unplayable lies and out of hazards—and, if possible, on the fairway.

## BALL, John (1861-1940)
John Ball, Sen, also a good golfer, owned the Royal Hotel, the original clubhouse of the Royal Liverpool Club, and young Ball played at Hoylake from his earliest days, becoming one of the world's greatest amateurs

and leader of the Hoylake school of golfers. He was 15 when he played in his first Open Championship in 1876 at St Andrews, finishing only eight strokes behind the winner, Bob Martin. He won the Open in 1890, the first amateur and first Englishman to do so. He won the British Amateur Championship eight times, 1888, 1890, 1892, 1894, 1899, 1907, 1910, 1912; runner-up, 1887, 1895. He was 60 when he played in his last Amateur in 1921.

One of his most famous matches was the final of the 1899 Amateur Championship, in which he defeated 'Freddie' Tait at the 37th—just before the Boer War in which he served in the Cheshire Yeomanry and in which 'Freddie' Tait was killed.

Of John Ball as a golfer, Bernard Darwin wrote in *Golf Between Two Wars* (1944): "The beauty of any particular player's style must, like his exact place in the golfing firmament, be a matter of individual feeling, and I can only say that I have derived greater aesthetic and emotional pleasure from watching Mr Ball than from any other spectacle in any game."

## BALL LOST

"A ball is 'lost' if (a) It be not found or be not identified as his by the player, within five minutes after the player's side or his or their caddies have begun to search for it; or (b) The player has put another ball into play under the Rules" (Rules of Golf Definition). See RULES OF GOLF, Rules 29, 32, 33.

## BALL, MAKES OF

The old 'feathery' ball, which was in use until about 1848, was made almost exclusively in Scotland, and there were comparatively few makers. When the gutta-percha ball superseded it, however, manufacture was far more widespread and the famous American pioneer golfer, Charles B. Macdonald, said that he had a list of 166 makes of 'gutty'.

When the rubber-cored ball came in about 1902 there were soon many different makes on the market. The original Haskell was followed by such long-vanished balls (in my own collection) as the Kempshall Arlington and Kempshall Flyer, the Thanet Flier, Osprey, Arch Colonel, Saracen, Sunbeam, Victor, Gamage's Ariel, Gordon, Traveler, Spalding Midget, Red Seal Special; others were the Zodiac, Ocobo, Cochrane, Henley, Hawk, Star Challenger, Avon Flier, Springvale Kite, Spalding Red, Black and White Dot, Spalding Bird's Eye, Spalding Bob and the famous Dunlop 31.

Between the two World Wars the varieties of ball lessened, although there were still the Spalding Kro-Flite and Top-Flite, the Silver King (Black, Green, Red and Yellow Dot), North British, Whynot, Bromford, Penfold and Dunlops of various kinds, including the '65'.

Since the Second World War numbers have decreased again until there are now only 15 or 20 principal varieties of ball, British and American, to be found in professionals' shops.

See AGRIPPA; ECLIPSE; FEATHERY; GOLF BALLS, BRAMBLE AND DIMPLE MARKINGS; GOURLAY; GUTTY; HASKELL BALL; KEMPSHALL BALL; ORTOGO SINGER; SILVERTOWN; STOUGHTON.

## BALL MARK

In the Rules of Golf, the term 'ball mark' is used, rather than the more usual 'pitch mark', for the small hole in the surface of a putting green caused by a ball landing. Rule 35-1c states: "The player may repair damage to the putting green caused by the impact of a ball. The ball may be lifted to permit repair and shall be replaced on the spot from which it was lifted."

## BALL MARKER

The note at the end of Rule 35-1 states: "When a ball on the putting green is to be lifted, its position should be marked by placing an object, such as a small coin, immediately behind the ball." Most golfers nowadays use a small plastic disc, made like a thumb-tack in various colours.

## BALL PLAYED AS IT LIES

This is one of the fundamental rules of golf. Rule 10 of the St Andrews Code of 1754 puts it thus: "If a Ball be stop'd by any person, Horse, Dog, or anything else, the Ball so stopped must be played where it lies." This was long before the days of such things as 'unplayable balls' or 'preferred lies'. On many courses—particularly inland courses where water doesn't drain away quickly as it does on a links—what are usually called 'winter rules' may be played for part of the year. These are purely local rules. See RULES OF GOLF (for when a ball may be legally moved); PREFERRED LIES.

## BALL, SIZE OF

In the old 'feathery' days, balls were very light in weight; in the 'gutty' days, weight varied a good deal. When the rubber-cored ball was introduced in 1902, no weight and size specifications were laid down. There were 'floaters' that really did float on the surface of water, and in 1912 Dunlops brought out a heavy, tightly wound ball, the Dunlop 31, that good players could hit further than ordinary balls; other firms followed suit and it looked as though some restriction would be vital.

The First World War, however, intervened, and it was not until 1920 that the R. and A. adopted the following resolution: "On and after 1st May, 1921, the weight of the ball shall not be greater than 1.62 oz avoirdupois, and the size not less than 1.62 in in diameter. The Rules of Golf Committee and the Executive Committee of the United States Golf Association will take whatever steps they think necessary to limit the powers of the ball with regard to distance, should any ball of greater power be introduced."

Nevertheless, several new makes of ball were travelling greater distances and in May 1929 the U.S.G.A. decided to adopt what they called "an easier

and pleasanter ball for the average golfer". From 1st January 1931 to 31st December 1932 the legal ball in America was not less than 1.68 in in diameter and not more than 1.55 oz in weight. The R. and A., however, stuck to its formula, and from 1st January 1933 the U.S.G.A. restored the weight to 1.62 oz, keeping the diameter at 1.68 in.

These slightly different specifications have remained in force, although the British P.G.A. in 1969 instituted a two-year trial period during which the American ball had to be used in all P.G.A. sponsored tournaments. This period has been extended indefinitely.

Canada adopted the American ball in 1948, but Australia, New Zealand and South Africa continue to use the British ball.

## BALLESTEROS, Severiano (b 1957)

Spanish. The most dazzling young player to emerge from Europe. Runner-up in British Open, 1977, and won Dutch, 1976, French, 1977, Swiss, 1977, Japanese, 1977, Opens.

## BALTUSROL

Springfield, New Jersey. Founded 1895, deriving its unusual name from land that was once owned by a farmer of Dutch extraction called Baltus Roll. The original course housed the U.S. Ladies' Championship, 1901, 1911; the U.S. Open Championship, 1903 (won by the club's first professional, Willie Anderson), 1915; the U.S. Amateur Championship, 1904. This course was torn up in 1920, additional land bought and two new 18-holes courses laid out by a well-known golf architect, A. W. Tillinghast. Length (Lower Course): 6,999 yards (Par 72). Also Upper Course (Length 6,674 yards: Par 71). The length of the Lower Course was stretched to 7,022 yards (Par 70) for the 1967 U.S. Open.

## BANGLADESH, GOLF IN

See PAKISTAN, GOLF IN.

## BANNERMAN, Harry (b 1942)

Scottish Professional Champion, 1967, 1972. Ryder Cup team, 1971.

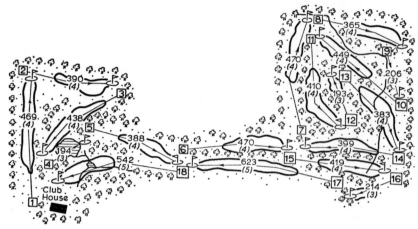

BALTUSROL

## BARBADOS, GOLF IN

As part of the golf boom in the West Indies, the two clubs in Barbados have been founded since the Second World War. They are the 9-holes Sandy Lane Club and the Rockley Country Club, Christ Church, which has 18 holes, made up of the original 9-holes course and a new one. Barbados is about the same size as the Isle of Wight.

## BARBER, Mrs D. N. (b 1939)

Born Sally Bonallack, sister of Michael Bonallack. English Ladies' Champion, 1968; runner-up, 1970. German Ladies' Open Champion, 1958. Curtis Cup team, 1962. See BROTHER AND SISTER GOLFERS.

## BARBER, Jerry (b 1916)

U.S.P.G.A. Champion, 1961, after beating Don January in play-off. At 45 he was the second oldest (after Julius Boros), and at 5 ft 5 ins the smallest winner of the championship. Ryder Cup team, 1955, 1961 (captain).

## BARBER, Miller (b 1931)

One of the steadiest players on the American professional circuit, although he has never won a major championship. Ryder Cup team, 1969, 1971.

## BARNES, Brian W. (b 1945)

British Youths' Champion, 1964. Runner-up, Italian Open Championship, 1971. Dutch Open Champion, 1974. French Open Champion, 1975. Ryder Cup team, 1969, 1971, 1973, 1975, 1977.

## BARNES, James M. 1887-1957)

A Cornishman, he went to America as a professional in 1906 and became one of the few players to win the Open Championships of both countries— U.S. Open in 1921 and British Open in 1925, having been runner-up in 1922. Won the first two U.S.P.G.A. Championships, 1916, 1919; runner-up, 1921, 1924. Because of his height, he was nicknamed 'Long Jim'.

## BARRAS, Olivier (1932-65)

Member of a well-known Swiss golfing family. Swiss National Amateur Champion, 1950, 1951, 1954, 1956, 1958, 1960, 1961, 1962, 1964. Swiss Open Amateur Champion, 1963; runner-up, 1958.

## BARRY, A. Gordon (1886-1942)

British Amateur Champion, 1905,

when a student at St Andrews University; the youngest winner after John Beharrell (1956) and Bobby Cole (1966). He joined the Manchester Regiment and won the Army Championship, 1922, 1925; retired as a brigadier.

## BARRY, Beth (b 1951)
Runner-up, U.S. Ladies' Championship, 1971. Curtis Cup team, 1972.

## BARTON, Pamela (1917-43)
British Ladies' Champion, 1936, 1939; runner-up, 1934, 1935. U.S. Ladies' Champion, 1936. French Ladies' Open Champion, 1934. Played in Curtis Cup team, 1934, 1936. Of British nationality, she was the first player to hold the British and American titles in the same year since Miss Dorothy Campbell did so in 1909. Of Miss Barton, Miss Enid Wilson wrote: "She was a splendid sportswoman, modest, unassuming and thoughtful of others", and Bernard Darwin wrote: "Everybody liked to see her play and everybody liked her simple, modest and friendly character." Author of *A Stroke a Hole* (1937). Killed when a W.A.A.F. officer in air crash at Manston, Kent. See SISTER GOLFERS.

## BASTANCHURY, Jane
See BOOTH, MRS. JANE.

## BAUGH, Laura (b 1955)
U.S. Ladies' Champion, 1971; with Beatrix Hoyt, the youngest winner. Curtis Cup team, 1972. See HOYT, BEATRIX.

## BEARD, Frank (b 1939)
American. Turned professional, 1962. Ryder Cup team, 1969, 1971.

## BECK, John B. (b 1899)
Non-playing captain Walker Cup team, St Andrews, 1938, on first occasion Britain won. Member of team, 1928 and non-playing captain, 1947. Won *Golf Illustrated* Gold Vase, 1925. Won Oxford and Cambridge Golfing Society's President's Putter, 1937. Captain R. and A., 1957.

## BEDDOWS, Mrs Charlotte (1887-1976)
Born Charlotte Stevenson. Scottish Ladies' Champion, 1920, 1921, 1922, 1929; runner-up, 1923, 1950. Veteran Ladies' Champion, 1947, 1949, 1950, 1951. Curtis Cup team, 1932. Represented Scotland in Ladies' Internationals between 1913 and 1951; played in her first Scottish Championship at the age of 17 and was still playing in it in 1970 at 82. Played hockey for Scotland.

## BEHARRELL, John Charles (b 1938)
British Amateur Champion, 1956—at 18 the equal-youngest winner with South African, Bobby Cole, 1966.

## BEHARRELL, Mrs John (b 1937)
Born Veronica Anstey; married to 1956 British Amateur Champion (*above*). During a tour in 1955 by a team of British girl golfers, won both Australian and New Zealand Ladies' Championships. Runner-up, Worplesdon Mixed Foursomes, with her husband, 1960. Curtis Cup team, 1956.

## BELGIUM, GOLF IN
The oldest club in Belgium is Royal Antwerp, founded in 1888 and thus older than most English clubs. Its royal prefix was conferred on it by ex-King Leopold, who similarly honoured eight other Belgian clubs. Altogether there are 13 clubs in Belgium, including two near Brussels—the Royal Club de Belgique and Royal Waterloo.

Ex-King Leopold is, with the late Duke of Windsor, the world's keenest royal golfer. In 1939 he played in the Belgian Open Amateur Championship at Royal Zoute, and in 1949 he reached the last eight in the French Open Amateur Championship at St Cloud. His wife, the Princess de Rethy, is also a keen golfer, and so is his son, the present King Baudouin.

The Belgian Open Amateur Championship started in 1913, but the outbreak of the First World War then caused a gap until 1920. The Belgian Open Championship dates from 1910 (the first winner being the great French professional, Arnaud Massy), the Ladies' Open Championship from 1921 and the Professional Championship from 1922.

Belgium's best known professional is Flory van Donck and among the amateurs are J. de Meulemeester, E. Tavernier, J. Moerman, Mme Pierre Abbeloos and the new star, Mlle Corinne Reybroeck. Golfing affairs are run by the Federation Royale Belge de Golf. See CHOLE ; ROYAL GOLFERS.

## BELT, BRITISH OPEN CHAMPIONSHIP

The original prize for the British Open Championship was a challenge belt, worth approximately £30, presented by the Earl of Eglinton. It was made from red Morocco and was ornamented with massive silver plates, bearing various appropriate devices. The winner held it for a year, but in the event of it being won three times running by the same player, it became his property under the regulations. Tom Morris, Jun, did this in 1868, 1869, 1870, and there was a gap of a year before the new challenge cup was played for in 1872, again being won by young Tommy. The belt remained in his family until his father presented it to the R. and A. It remains in the clubhouse at St Andrews to this day.

The challenge cup was subscribed for by the R. and A. and Prestwick Clubs and the Honourable Company of Edinburgh Golfers. The value was about the same as the belt, none of the clubs being asked to contribute more than £15. See BRITISH OPEN CHAMPIONSHIP ; MORRIS, TOM (JUN).

## BEMAN, Deane R. (b 1938)

U.S. Amateur Champion, 1960, 1963. Joint runner-up, U.S. Open Championship, 1969, having led after two rounds. British Amateur Champion, 1959, while a member of the visiting Walker Cup team ; also in team, 1961, 1963, 1965. World Cup (formerly Eisenhower Trophy) team, 1960, 1962, 1964. Now U.S. P.G.A. tour organiser.

## BEMBRIDGE, Maurice (b 1945)

British Professional Match Play Champion, 1969. Kenya Open Champion, 1968, 1969. Runner-up, New Zealand Open Championship, 1971, 1972. German Open, 1975. Won Dunlop Masters, 1971. Ryder Cup team, 1969, 1971, 1973, 1975.

## BENKA, Peter (b 1946)

British Youths' Champion, 1967 (after tie with Bernard Gallacher), 1968 (after tie with R. A. Durrant). Dutch Amateur Champion, 1972. Walker Cup team, 1969. See TREDINNICK, PAMELA.

## BENTLEY, Arnold L. (b 1911)

English Amateur Champion, 1939. Runner-up, French Open Amateur Championship, 1938. Brother of Harry G. Bentley. See BROTHER GOLFERS.

## BENTLEY, Harry G. (b 1907)

English Amateur Champion, 1936 ; runner-up, 1954. French Open Amateur Champion, 1931, 1932 ; runner-up, 1953. German Open Amateur Champion, 1937, 1938, 1939. Italian Open Amateur Champion, 1954 ; runner-up, 1951. Walker Cup team, 1934, 1936, 1938. See BROTHER GOLFERS.

## BERG, Patricia ('Patty') (b 1918)

U.S. Ladies' Champion, 1938 ; runner-up, 1935, 1937. U.S. Women's Open Champion, 1946, the only year it was decided by match play ; runner-up, 1957. Curtis Cup team, 1936, 1938. Turned professional, 1940.

## BERKSHIRE

Ascot, Berkshire. Founded 1926. Pine and heath country. Length (Red Course): 6,459 yards, S.S.S. 71. Housed English Amateur Championship, 1965. Berkshire Trophy (four rounds stroke play for top amateurs annually). Also Blue Course (6,395 yards, S.S.S. 70).

## BERMUDA, GOLF IN

Golf began in Bermuda in a comparatively modest way before the Second World War, but now it has boomed. There are six clubs: Mid-Ocean (where Archie Compston was the resident professional for some years before his death), Belmont Manor, Castle Harbour, Riddell's Bay, Queen's Park and the St George's Hotel Club. Mid-Ocean, opened in 1922, was designed by Charles B. Macdonald, the famous American amateur.

The Bermuda Amateur Championship began in 1939 and was housed at Riddell's Bay for the first five years, followed by 14 at Mid-Ocean; recently it has also been played for at Belmont and Castle Harbour. Similarly, the Bermuda Ladies Championship was housed at Riddell's Bay in 1939 and 1940, and continued there from 1949-51, but has been at Mid-Ocean since 1957.

## BERNARDINI, Roberto (b 1944)

Italian Native Professional Champion, 1967, 1968, 1973, 1975. Swiss Open Champion, 1968, 1969.

## BERNING, Mrs Susie Maxwell (b 1942)

U.S. Women's Open Champion, 1968, 1972, 1973.

## BEST-BALL

See MATCHES, TYPES OF.

## BEVIONE, Franco (b 1926)

Italian Open Amateur Champion, 1952, 1956, 1957; runner-up, 1953, 1955. Italian Native Amateur Champion, 1946, 1947, 1949, 1950, 1953, 1954, 1955, 1959, 1960, 1961, 1967, 1968; runner-up, 1958, 1966. Husband of Signora Isa Goldschmid-Bevione, many times Italian Ladies' Champion.

## 'BIG CRAWFORD' (Harry Crawford)

Scottish by birth, Harry Crawford, always called 'Big Crawford', was for many years caddie to 'Wee Ben' Sayers at North Berwick. "It was an in-congruous sight", said J. H. Taylor in *Golf: My Life's Work* (1943), "to see the little fellow marching along dwarfed by the huge 17-stone man, whose presence exuded a solemn and masterful dignity." In his later years 'Big Crawford' had a ginger-beer stall near the 8th green at North Berwick and used to fly the Scottish standard on it whenever Arthur Balfour, the politician who was his hero, was playing on the links. See BALFOUR, EARL (ARTHUR JAMES).

## 'BIG THREE', THE MODERN

See NICKLAUS, JACK; PALMER, ARNOLD; PLAYER, GARY.

## BILLIARD CUE, PUTTING WITH A

In the U.S. Amateur Championship at Newport, Rhode Island, in 1895, one player attempted to putt with a billiard cue. The matter, said Charles B. Macdonald in his book, *Scotland's Gift: Golf* (1928), was immediately referred to the United States Golf Association, and they ruled against the billiard cue. According to Macdonald (he won the 1895 U.S. Amateur Championship), there was no further trouble about the make and form of clubs until the controversy about the Schenectady putter in 1909. See SCHENECTADY PUTTER.

## BILLOWS, Raymond E. ('Ray') (b 1915)

Runner-up, U.S. Amateur Championship, 1937, 1939, 1948. Walker Cup team, 1938, 1949.

## BIRDIE

A comparatively modern term for a score one under par for the hole. It spread from America some time between the 1914 and 1939 wars; and the Americans are apt to use it as a verb: thus "He birdied the third." Derivation unknown. See ALBATROSS; BOGEY; EAGLE; PAR.

## BISGOOD, Jeanne (b 1923)

British. English Ladies' Champion, 1951, 1953, 1957. German Ladies'

Champion, 1953. Italian Ladies' Champion, 1953. Norwegian Ladies' Champion, 1955. Portuguese Ladies' Champion, 1954. Swedish Ladies' Champion, 1952. Curtis Cup team, 1950, 1952, 1954 ; non-playing captain, 1970.

## BISHOP, Stanley E. (b 1923)

U.S. Amateur Champion, 1946. Walker Cup team, 1947, 1949.

## BISQUE

A system of handicapping in which the receiver of strokes takes them at the holes of his choice instead of receiving them at the specific holes as laid down on the card of the course. As this choice of strokes is an advantage, the receiver normally gets fewer bisques than he would ordinary strokes ; and, as Horace Hutchinson put it in the Badminton Library volume on *Golf* (1890), "all through the round the giver of points will be playing with a paralysing consciousness of the bisque hanging, like a sword of Damocles, over his head".

The term, of French origin, is also used in real tennis and croquet.

## BLACKWELL BROTHERS

There were four noted St Andrews golfing Blackwells: James, Walter, Edward and Ernley. Sir Ernley Blackwell was Captain of the R. and A., 1933, and Edward, the best golfer, in 1925 ; J. H. Blackwell was Links Convener at St Andrews, 1912-33.

Edward Blackwell (born 1866) was runner-up in the 1904 British Amateur Championship, being beaten in the final by Walter Travis, the first American winner of the title. He was renowned for his driving and is said to have driven from the 18th tee on the Old Course up to the clubhouse steps —and that with a gutty ball. The distance in those days was probably about 340 yards ; in the 1964 Open, when Jack Nicklaus drove the green in each round with a helping wind, the distance was 381 yards. See DRIVES WITH 'GUTTY', LONGEST.

## BLAIR, David A. (b 1917)

Scottish Amateur Champion, 1953 ; runner-up, 1950. Scandinavian Open Amateur Champion, 1961. Army Champion, 1947. Won *Golf Illustrated* Gold Vase, 1955, 1956. Walker Cup team, 1955, 1961. Captain R. & A., 1978.

## BLASTER

The earliest broad-soled bunker clubs were called 'Blasters'. Later the more accepted name became Sand Iron or Sand Wedge. See SAND IRON ; WEDGE.

## BLIND

A shot is played 'blind' if the player cannot see the area in which his ball should land. A hole containing such a situation is called a 'blind hole'. Often the line to be taken is indicated by a direction post. See DIRECTION POST.

## BOBBY JONES HOLE

See ST ANDREWS, NAMES OF HOLES AND BUNKERS AT.

## BOGEY

According to Chambers's Dictionary, "in golf, the score for a given hole, or for the whole course, of an imaginary Colonel Bogey, fixed as a standard ; the bogey score for a course is higher than par". The fullest explanation of the origin of the term is given by the late Henry Leach in his book, *The Spirit of the Links* (1907). Although it has been claimed for the Elie Club, Fife, it is more generally accepted that it originated at the Coventry Club. In December 1890 the club gave to each hole a figure representing the scratch value. This was called the 'ground score', and about six months later a member named Hugh Rotherham offered a prize for a competition in which the entrants played against this ground score, and in the autumn a cup was put up for an annual competition on the same lines.

About this time a party of Coventry members visited the Great Yarmouth Club, where they explained the idea to Dr Thomas Browne, the honorary secretary. He in turn asked various prominent golfers for their views about ground score competitions and received many favourable replies.

A popular music hall song of the day contained the verse:

Hush! Hush! Hush!
Here comes the Bogey man!
So hide your head beneath the clothes,
He'll catch you if he can!

And one day when Dr Browne was playing with a friend, Major Charles Wellman, against the ground score and getting 'caught', as it were, the Major said: "This player of yours is a regular bogey man!" By this chance remark, the name 'bogey' came to be adopted by the Great Yarmouth Club.

A little later Dr Browne went to play at the now-vanished United Service Club at Alverstoke, Hampshire, and told his hosts that he would like to introduce as an honorary member a friend who was a very steady if not brilliant golfer—and explained the 'bogey man' game. They promptly worked out a score for the new member, but before going out to play against him, the honorary secretary, Captain Seely Vidal, said: "Every member of this club has a proper service rank. Our new invisible member, who never makes a mistake, surely ought to be a commanding officer. He must be a colonel." And saluting, he added: "Colonel Bogey, we are delighted to find you on the links, Sir! I couldn't well say see you!"

After that, whenever Dr Browne went, he introduced his imaginary friend as 'Colonel Bogey'. Bogey competitions were reported in the papers and the new scoring system gradually established. Thus, said Henry Leach, the Coventry, Great Yarmouth and United Service Clubs all had a hand in establishing the idea, and he added: "It is quite likely that the golfers of Elie worked out a bogey of their own independently."

Although bogey competitions soon became popular, the R. and A. Rules of Golf Committee stated in April 1900 that they could not take up any questions about bogey competitions because they were not recognised in the Rules of Golf. In 1910, however, the Midland Golf Association asked the Rules of Golf Committee to issue rules for bogey play, and in February 1911 a code was approved for the Midland Association's use and a copy sent to the United States. These rules were considered at a General Meeting of the R. and A. in 1912 and duly approved.

See BOGEY (OR PAR) COMPETITION; PAR; STABLEFORD; STANDARD SCRATCH SCORE.

## BOGEY, AMERICAN USE OF TERM

Originally in Britain the bogey of a hole or course was the score which a scratch player was expected to take for that hole or course. This term has now been superseded by the term par for a hole and Standard Scratch Score for a course. For a time many clubs had a bogey as well as a par score.

In the United States the idea grew that bogey meant one over par at *every* hole and this is how the term is now used. A score of one over par at a hole is a bogey, a score of two over par a double-bogey and so on. Thus in reports on American tournaments you may learn that so-and-so has 'double-bogeyed it'. The American usage is now ousting the British.

See BOGEY; PAR; STANDARD SCRATCH SCORE.

## BOGEY (OR PAR) COMPETITION

In a bogey (or par) competition a player receives three-quarters of his handicap and counts the number of holes he is up or down against the par (originally bogey) of the course. Thus if the par of the first hole, say is four the player puts the sign O, + or — in the appropriate column on the score card, depending on whether his score is equal to, less than or more than four; and so on. It is possible (though improbable) to finish 18 up or 18 down on bogey.

In a bogey or par competition the score taken at every hole halved or won must be recorded. Any hole for which a competitor makes no return must be regarded as a loss.

In all other respects, the rules for stroke play apply. See RULES OF GOLF, Rule 39 ; STABLEFORD.

## BOLD

A word used in such expressions as 'too bold' or 'not bold enough', indicating that the player had either hit the ball too far or not far enough ; or has either taken too much, or not enough, risk in playing a particular shot.

## BOLIVIA, GOLF IN

There are two clubs at La Paz, the capital—the La Paz Club and the Los Pinos Club. Both are good length 18-holes courses. Other Bolivian clubs are at Mallasilla and the mining town of Oruro, the former capital.

There is some doubt about which are the highest golf courses in the world, but the La Paz clubs are some 13,500 feet above sea level and Oruro over 12,000.

## BOLT A PUTT

To bolt a putt means to hit the ball so hard that it is still travelling fast when it goes into the hole. See GOBBLE.

## BOLT, Tommy (b 1918)

U.S. Open Champion, 1958. U.S. Senior Professional Champion, 1969. Ryder Cup team, 1955, 1957. In his earlier days his rather tempestuous character earned him the nickname of 'Thunder Bolt'.

## BOLTON, Mrs S. M. (b 1914)

British. Born Zara Bonner Davis. Runner-up, English Ladies' Championship, 1948. Runner-up, India Ladies' Championship, 1937. Curtis Cup team, 1948 ; non-playing captain, 1956, 1966, 1968.

## BONALLACK, Michael Francis (b 1934)

British Amateur Champion, 1961, 1965, 1968, 1969, 1970. English Amateur Champion, 1962, 1963, 1965,

1967, 1968 ; runner-up, 1959. English Open Amateur Stroke Play Champion, 1964, 1968, 1969, 1971. British Boys' Amateur Champion, 1952. Army Champion, 1955. *Golf Illustrated* Gold Vase, 1961 (tied with D. J. Harrison), 1967 (tied with R. A. Durrant), 1968, 1969 (tied with J. Hayes), 1971. Won Worplesdon Mixed Foursomes, with Mrs Bonallack, 1958. Walker Cup team, 1959, 1961, 1963, 1965, 1967, 1969, 1971 (captain, 1969, 1971). Played for British Isles in World Cup (formerly Eisenhower Trophy) 1960, 1962, 1964, 1966, 1968, 1970. By winning the 1970 Amateur Championship became the first player to win the title three times running. See BROTHER AND SISTER GOLFERS.

## BONALLACK, Mrs Michael (b 1937)

Born Angela Ward. English Ladies' Champion, 1958, 1963 ; runner-up, 1960, 1962. Runner-up, British Ladies' Championship, 1962. Runner-up, French Ladies' Open Championship, 1956. German Ladies' Open Champion, 1955. Portuguese Ladies' Open Champion, 1957. Scandinavian Ladies' Open Champion, 1956. Swedish Ladies' Open Champion, 1955. British Girls' Champion, 1955. Won Worplesdon Mixed Foursomes, with Michael Bonallack, 1958. Curtis Cup team, 1956, 1958, 1960, 1962, 1964, 1966.

## BONALLACK, Sally

See BARBER, MRS D. N.

## BOOMER, Aubrey (b 1897)

Born Jersey. Runner-up, British Open Championship, 1927. French Open Champion, 1921, 1922, 1926, 1929, 1931. Belgian Open Champion, 1922, 1926. Dutch Open Champion, 1924, 1925, 1926. Italian Open Champion, 1932. Ryder Cup team, 1927, 1929.

His brother, Percy (born 1884), was Belgian Open Champion, 1923 ; Dutch Open Champion, 1927 ; Swiss Open Champion, 1924. He was professional at St Cloud, Paris, until the Second World War. See BROTHER GOLFERS.

## BOOTH, Mrs Jane (b 1948)

Born Jane Bastanchury. Curtis Cup team, 1970, 1972.

## BOROS, Julius (b 1920)

U.S. Open Champion, 1952, 1963—at 43 being the second oldest winner, a month younger than Ted Ray was in 1920, the year that Boros was born. He won in 1963 after a tie with Arnold Palmer and Jacky Cupit. U.S.P.G.A. Champion, 1968—the oldest winner. Ryder Cup team, 1959, 1963, 1965, 1967. Author of *How to Play Par Golf* (1953).

## BORROW

To play with 'borrow' means to allow in putting for a slope or, less seldom, for the force of the wind. Hence such phrases as 'too much borrow', 'not enough borrow', etc.

## BORTHWICK, Pat (b 1928)

Australian Ladies' Champion, 1948, 1949, 1953, 1956.

## 'BOSTON SIEGE GUN'

See GUILFORD, JESSE.

## BOURN, T. A. ('Dale') (b 1904)

English Amateur Champion, 1930; runner-up, 1933. Runner-up, British Amateur Championship, 1933. Although his golfing record was not outstanding, Dale Bourn, in Henry Longhurst's words, "will never be forgotten. He was the gay cavalier of golf, a man who would drive into some impenetrable golfing jungle and not only find his ball teed up, but confidently expect to do so." He was killed in the Second World War.

## BOUSFIELD, Kenneth (b 1919)

British Professional Match Play Champion, 1955. Belgian Open Champion, 1958. German Open Champion, 1955, 1959. Portuguese Open Champion, 1960, 1961. Swiss Open Champion, 1958. British Senior Professional Champion, 1972; joint runner-up, 1971. Ryder Cup team, 1949, 1951, 1955, 1957, 1959, 1961. Represented England in World (formerly Canada) Cup matches, 1956, 1957.

## 'BOX' SYSTEM OF SCORING

This system is intended for three-ball match play, instead of playing two separate matches or using the 'points' system. In the 'box' system, the first player to win a hole from the other two players goes into the imaginary 'box'. If he wins the next hole, he gains one point and stays in the 'box'; if he halves the hole, he does not gain a point, but stays in the 'box'; if he loses a hole, he leaves the 'box'. If, however, he wins another hole, he gains another point and stays in the 'box'. See 'POINTS' SYSTEM OF THREE-BALL SCORING.

## BOYD QUAICH TOURNAMENT

This is an invitation tournament at St Andrews open to university students at home and abroad, each competing university being represented by two players. All entrants play two rounds of stroke play over the Old Course, the best 24 then playing a further two rounds, the aggregate for the four rounds deciding the winner.

The Boyd Quaich (a Scottish word for a porridge-bowl or drinking-cup with two handles) was presented by Professor and Mrs David Boyd in memory of their two sons, both St Andrews students, who lost their lives in the Second World War.

## BOYER, Auguste (b 1898)

French Native Professional Champion, 1931, 1933, 1934, 1936. Belgian Open Champion, 1933, 1936. Dutch Open Champion, 1932. German Open Champion, 1930, 1932, 1935, 1936. Italian Open Champion, 1926, 1928, 1930, 1931. Swiss Open Champion, 1930, 1934, 1935. Swiss Professional Champion, 1926.

## BOYLE, Hugh F. (b 1936)

Irish Professional Champion, 1967. Ryder Cup team, 1967.

## BRABAZON OF TARA, LORD (1884-1964)

Born Henry Moore-Brabazon. Pioneer racing motorist and aviator and great all-round sportsman. Captain R. and A., 1952. President, English Golf Union and Professional Golfers' Association. Donor of the E.G.U. Brabazon Trophy, 1947, which from 1957 became the English Open Amateur Stroke Play Championship.

## BRABAZON TROPHY

See ENGLISH OPEN AMATEUR STROKE PLAY CHAMPIONSHIP.

## BRADSHAW, Harry (b 1913)

Tied for British Open Championship, 1949, with Bobby Locke, but lost play-off. Irish Open Champion, 1947, 1949. Irish Native Professional Champion, 1941, 1942, 1943, 1944, 1947, 1950, 1951, 1953, 1954, 1957. Won Dunlop Masters, 1953, 1955. Ryder Cup team, 1953, 1955, 1957. With Christy O'Connor won World (formerly Canada) Cup tournament for Ireland, 1958, at Mexico City.

At the 5th hole in the second round of the 1949 Open at Royal St George's, Sandwich, occurred Harry Bradshaw's famous 'bottle incident'. After cutting his drive slightly, he found his ball lying inside half a broken beer bottle in the rough. He decided to play it where it lay, shattering the bottle and moving the ball 20 or 30 yards. He took six for the hole—normally a comparatively straightforward par-4—and finished the round in 77. This brought him level with Locke on 145 and next day they did similar scores and tied at 283, Locke winning the play-off by 12 strokes.

## BRADY, Mike (b 1888)

American. Runner-up, U.S. Open Championship, 1911, 1919. On the first occasion tied with John J. McDermott and G. C. Simpson (McDermott winning the play-off), and on the second occasion with Walter Hagen, who won the play-off with 77 against 78.

## BRAE BURN

The Brae Burn Country Club, West Newton, Massachusetts. Founded 1897. Length: 6,516 yards (Par 70). Housed U.S. Open Championship, 1919 (when Walter Hagen won his second title); U.S. Amateur Championship, 1928 (when Bobby Jones beat the reigning British champion, Phil Perkins, in the final). Also Curtis Cup match, 1958 (resulting in a tie), 1970. Altered several times by Donald Ross.

## BRAID, James (1870-1950)

Born Earlsferry, Fife. One of the great Triumvirate of Vardon, Taylor and Braid. British Open Champion, 1901, 1905, 1906, 1908, 1910; runner-up, 1897, 1904, 1909. British Professional Match Play Champion, 1903, 1905, 1907, 1911; runner-up, 1913, 1927. French Open Champion, 1910. Took part in several famous challenge matches, partnered by Sandy Herd, Harry Vardon or J. H. Taylor. Professional at Romford and then at Walton Heath, Surrey, for 45 years.

In his younger days Braid was famous for the 'divine fury' of his hitting, yet curiously enough he was not a big hitter when he first came onto the golfing scene. Length came to him suddenly out of the blue. As he put it, "it was just the same as if I went to bed a short driver one night and got up a long driver in the morning. It was then, and is still, the greatest golfing mystery that I have ever come across."

For many years he was a busy golf course architect and among the courses he either designed or restyled are Gleneagles, Carnoustie, Rosemount (Blairgowrie), Royal Blackheath, Wildernesse, Queen's Park (Bournemouth), Buchanan Castle and Forfar. Author of *Golf Guide and How to Play Golf* (1906) and *Advanced Golf* (1908). A biography is Bernard Darwin's *James Braid* (1952).

See TAYLOR, J. H.; VARDON, HARRY.

## BRASSEY

Also Brassy or Brassie. A wooden club with a brass plate covering the

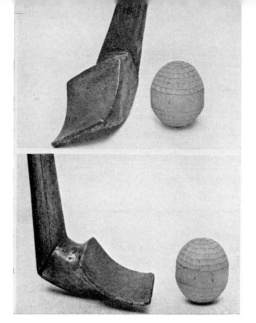

CHOLE. The club and ball used in the ancient French and Belgian game with similarities to golf. The upper picture shows how the club was used for the longer shots and the lower picture how it was turned over for lofting the ball or getting it out of a bad lie

CARR, JOSEPH B. ("JOE"). Ireland's greatest modern amateur. When he finds trouble, as in this picture, he has wonderful powers of recovery

COTTON, THOMAS HENRY. After winning the British Open Championship for the third time, at Muirfield in 1948, Cotton is congratulated by the runner-up, Fred Daly, champion in the previous year

EDINBURGH GOLFERS, HONOURABLE COMPANY OF. In the old days the Edinburgh town crier and his drummers paraded through the streets, carrying the Company's Silver Club, to announce the date of the chief competition to be played on the links of Leith. This drawing is dated 1787

FALDO, NICK. One of the white hopes of British golf, this powerful young man won the English Amateur Championship in 1975 and played in the Ryder Cup team and the World Cup team in 1977 after he had turned professional

(*left*) "FIERY". John Carey—called "Fiery" from the weather-beaten colour of his face—was caddie for many years to Willie Park, Junior, British Open Champion in 1887 and 1889

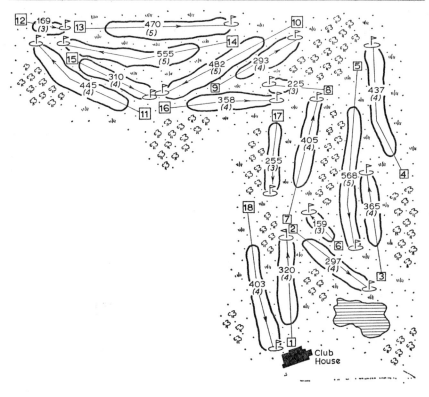

BRAE BURN

sole, corresponding to the modern No 2 wood. The object of the brass plate was to protect the club when playing from a bad lie. Nowadays all wooden clubs are protected with a metal plate of some sort, but old drivers were not. According to Henry Leach's *Spirit of the Links* (1907), "when a Blackheath golfer appeared on a Scottish course, the caddies knew his headquarters at once. 'He comes frae Blackheath', they would say with some depreciation. 'There's naething but gravel pits and stones at Blackheath'." See ROYAL BLACKHEATH.

## BRAZIL, GOLF IN

Golf is not as widespread in Brazil as it is in Argentina. There are 30 clubs, including four near Rio de Janeiro and ten near Sao Paulo. The

C

Brazilian Golf Association has its headquarters in Sao Paulo.

The Brazilian Amateur Championship dates from 1934 and the Open Championship from 1945. Brazil's greatest golfer is Mario Gonzales, who has dominated the championships.

## BREAK-CLUB

Rule 4 of the oldest surviving St Andrews Code, dated 14th May 1754, reads: "You are not to remove Stones, Bones or any Break-club for the sake of playing your Ball, except upon the fair Green, and that only within a Club length of your Ball." A 'break-club' was anything that might cause the club to break while striking at the ball. See RULES, FIRST CODE OF.

## BREWER, Gay (b 1932)

Won U.S. Masters, 1967; tied with Jack Nicklaus and Tommy Jacobs, 1966, but lost play-off. U.S. Junior Amateur Champion, 1949. Canadian Open Champion, 1972. Turned professional, 1956. Ryder Cup team, 1967, 1972. He refers to his somewhat unorthodox swing in the title of his book, *Score Better than You Swing* (1968).

## BREWS, Sidney F. (1900-1972)

Born London. Went to South Africa soon after winning Gloucestershire Championship, 1923. Runnner-up, British Open Championship, 1934. South African Open Champion, 1925, 1927, 1930, 1931, 1933, 1934, 1949, 1952. South African Professional Champion, 1926, 1928, 1933, 1934, 1936, 1952; runner-up, 1938, 1946. Belgian Open Champion, 1929. Dutch Open Champion, 1934, 1935. French Open Champion, 1934, 1935. Lost a famous 36-holes challenge match, with Bobby Locke, against Henry Cotton and Reginald Whitcombe, Walton Heath, 1938, by 2 and 1.

His elder brother, Jock Brews, was South African Open Champion, 1921, 1923, 1926, 1928; runner-up, 1913, 1922, 1924, 1925. See BROTHER GOLFERS.

## BRITISH AMATEUR CHAMPION MORE THAN ONCE

The following players have won the British Amateur Championship more than once:

**Eight times**
John Ball (1888, 1890, 1892, 1894, 1899, 1907, 1910, 1912)

**Five times**
Michael Bonallack (1961, 1965, 1968, 1969, 1970)

**Four times**
Harold Hilton (1900, 1901, 1911, 1913)

**Three times**
Joe Carr (1953, 1958, 1960)

**Twice**
Ernest Holderness (1922, 1924)
Horace Hutchinson (1886, 1887)
John Laidlay (1889, 1891)

Lawson Little (1934, 1935)
Peter McEvoy (1977, 1978)
Robert Maxwell (1903, 1909)
Frank Stranahan (1948, 1950)
Freddie Tait (1896, 1898)
Cyril Tolley (1920, 1929)

## BRITISH AMATEUR CHAMPIONSHIP

If the Prestwick Club was responsible for the British Open Championship, the Royal Liverpool Club, Hoylake, was responsible for the British and English Amateur Championships. In 1885 the club issued invitations for an Open Amateur Tournament, to be held in the week of the Spring Meeting. There were 44 entries and the winner was a Scottish member of the club, Allan F. Macfie, who beat Horace Hutchinson in the final. In 1922 he was recognised as being the first British Amateur Champion, although the first official year of the championship was 1886, it having been inaugurated after the success of the 1885 meeting.

Originally, 24 clubs in England and Scotland helped to promote the championship, which was played in turn at St Andrews, Hoylake and Prestwick until Royal St George's Sandwich, was added to the rota in 1892. Later a number of other courses were brought in, including one non-seaside course—Ganton, near Scarborough (1964).

The handicap limit for the championship is two and it is an all match-play affair; entries are limited to 256 because in the past the numbers have been unwieldy. In 1956 and 1957 the quarter-finals, semi-finals and final were all played over 36 holes, but the present arrangement is for a 36-holes final only.

The first foreigner to win the championship was Australian-born American citizen, Walter J. Travis (1904); the first native-born American winner was Jess Sweetser (1926); the first Irishman was James Bruen (1946); the first Australian was Douglas Bachli (1954):

| Year | Winner | Runner-up | Venue | By |
|------|--------|-----------|-------|-----|
| 1885 | A. F. Macfie | H. G. Hutchinson | R. Liverpool | 7 and 6 |
| 1886 | H. G. Hutchinson | Henry Lamb | St Andrews | 7 and 6 |
| 1887 | H. G. Hutchinson | John Ball | R. Liverpool | 1 hole |
| 1888 | John Ball | J. E. Laidlay | Prestwick | 5 and 4 |
| 1889 | J. E. Laidlay | L. Balfour-Melville | St Andrews | 2 and 1 |
| 1890 | John Ball | J. E. Laidlay | R. Liverpool | 4 and 3 |
| 1891 | J. E. Laidlay | Harold Hilton | St Andrews | 20th |
| 1892 | John Ball | Harold Hilton | R. St George's | 3 and 1 |
| 1893 | Peter Anderson | J. E. Laidlay | Prestwick | 1 hole |
| 1894 | John Ball | S. Mure Fergusson | R. Liverpool | 1 hole |
| 1895 | L. Balfour-Melville | John Ball | St Andrews | 19th |
| 1896 | F. G. Tait | Harold Hilton | R. St George's | 8 and 7 |
| 1897 | A. J. T. Allan | James Robb | Muirfield | 4 and 2 |
| 1898 | F. G. Tait | S. Mure Fergusson | R. Liverpool | 7 and 6 |
| 1899 | John Ball | F. G. Tait | Prestwick | 37th |
| 1900 | Harold Hilton | James Robb | R. St George's | 8 and 7 |
| 1901 | Harold Hilton | John Low | St Andrews | 1 hole |
| 1902 | Charles Hutchings | Sidney Fry | R. Liverpool | 1 hole |
| 1903 | Robert Maxwell | H. G. Hutchinson | Muirfield | 7 and 5 |
| 1904 | W. J. Travis | Edward Blackwell | R. St. George's | 4 and 3 |
| 1905 | A. G. Barry | Hon. O. Scott | Prestwick | 3 and 2 |
| 1906 | James Robb | C. C. Lingen | R. Liverpool | 4 and 3 |
| 1907 | John Ball | C. A. Palmer | St Andrews | 6 and 4 |
| 1908 | E. A. Lassen | H. E. Taylor | R. St George's | 7 and 6 |
| 1909 | Robert Maxwell | C. K. Hutchison | Muirfield | 1 hole |
| 1910 | John Ball | Colin Aylmer | R. Liverpool | 10 and 9 |
| 1911 | Harold Hilton | E. A. Lassen | Prestwick | 4 and 3 |
| 1912 | John Ball | Abe Mitchell | Westward Ho! | 38th |
| 1913 | Harold Hilton | Robert Harris | St Andrews | 6 and 5 |
| 1914 | J. L. C. Jenkins | Charles Hezlet | R. St George's | 3 and 2 |
| 1915-19 | No Championships | | | |
| 1920 | Cyril Tolley | Robert Gardner | Muirfield | 37th |
| 1921 | Willie Hunter | A. J. Graham | R. Liverpool | 12 and 11 |
| 1922 | Ernest Holderness | John Craven | Prestwick | 1 hole |
| 1923 | Roger Wethered | Robert Harris | R. Cinque Ports | 7 and 6 |
| 1924 | Ernest Holderness | E. F. Storey | St Andrews | 3 and 2 |
| 1925 | Robert Harris | K. F. Fradgley | Westward Ho! | 13 and 12 |
| 1926 | Jess Sweetser | A. F. Simpson | Muirfield | 6 and 5 |
| 1927 | Dr W. Tweddell | D. E. Landale | R. Liverpool | 7 and 6 |
| 1928 | T. P. Perkins | Roger Wethered | Prestwick | 6 and 4 |
| 1929 | Cyril Tolley | J. N. Smith | R. St George's | 4 and 3 |
| 1930 | Bobby Jones | Roger Wethered | St Andrews | 7 and 6 |
| 1931 | Eric Martin Smith | John De Forest | Westward Ho! | 1 hole |
| 1932 | John De Forest | Eric Fiddian | Muirfield | 3 and 1 |
| 1933 | Hon. M. Scott | T. A. Bourn | R. Liverpool | 4 and 3 |
| 1934 | W. Lawson Little | James Wallace | Prestwick | 14 and 13 |
| 1935 | W. Lawson Little | Dr W. Tweddell | R. Lytham | 1 hole |
| 1936 | Hector Thomson | Jim Ferrier | St Andrews | 2 holes |
| 1937 | Robert Sweeney | Lionel Munn | R. St George's | 3 and 2 |
| 1938 | Charles Yates | Cecil Ewing | Troon | 3 and 2 |
| 1939 | A. T. Kyle | A. A. Duncan | R. Liverpool | 2 and 1 |
| 1940-45 | No Championships | | | |
| 1946 | James Bruen | Robert Sweeney | R. Birkdale | 4 and 3 |
| 1947 | W. P. Turnesa | Richard Chapman | Carnoustie | 3 and 2 |
| 1948 | Frank Stranahan | Charles Stowe | R. St George's | 5 and 4 |

| Year | Winner | Runner-up | Venue | By |
|------|--------|-----------|-------|-----|
| 1949 | S. M. M'Cready | W. P. Turnesa | Portmarnock | 2 and 1 |
| 1950 | Frank Stranahan | Richard Chapman | St Andrews | 8 and 6 |
| 1951 | Richard Chapman | Charles Coe | R. Porthcawl | 5 and 4 |
| 1952 | E. Harvie Ward | Frank Stranahan | Prestwick | 6 and 5 |
| 1953 | Joe Carr | E. Harvie Ward | R. Liverpool | 2 holes |
| 1954 | Douglas Bachli | W. C. Campbell | Muirfield | 2 and 1 |
| 1955 | J. W. Conrad | Alan Slater | R. Lytham | 3 and 2 |
| 1956 | John Beharrell | L. G. Taylor | Troon | 5 and 4 |
| 1957 | R. Reid Jack | Harold Ridgley | Formby | 2 and 1 |
| 1958 | Joe Carr | Alan Thirlwell | St Andrews | 3 and 2 |
| 1959 | Deane Beman | Bill Hyndman | R. St George's | 3 and 2 |
| 1960 | Joe Carr | R. Cochran | R. Portrush | 8 and 7 |
| 1961 | Michael Bonallack | James Walker | Turnberry | 6 and 4 |
| 1962 | R. D. Davies | John Povall | R. Liverpool | 1 hole |
| 1963 | Michael Lunt | J. G. Blackwell | St Andrews | 2 and 1 |
| 1964 | Gordon Clark | Michael Lunt | Ganton | 39th |
| 1965 | Michael Bonallack | Clive Clark | R. Porthcawl | 2 and 1 |
| 1966 | Bobby Cole | Ronald Shade | Carnoustie | 3 and 2 |
| 1967 | Robert Dickson | Ron Cerrudo | Formby | 2 and 1 |
| 1968 | Michael Bonallack | Joe Carr | Troon | 7 and 6 |
| 1969 | Michael Bonallack | Bill Hyndman | R. Liverpool | 3 and 2 |
| 1970 | Michael Bonallack | Bill Hyndman | R. Co. Down | 8 and 7 |
| 1971 | Steve Melnyk | James Simons | Carnoustie | 3 and 2 |
| 1972 | Trevor Homer | Alan Thirlwell | R. St George's | 4 and 3 |
| 1973 | Richard Siderowf | Peter Moody | R. Porthcawl | 5 and 3 |
| 1974 | Trevor Homer | John Gabrielsen | Muirfield | 2 holes |
| 1975 | Marvin Giles | Mark James | R. Liverpool | 8 and 7 |
| 1976 | Richard Siderowf | John Davies | St Andrews | 37th Hole |
| 1977 | Peter McEvoy | H. M. Campbell | Ganton | 5 and 4 |
| 1978 | Peter McEvoy | Paul McKellar | Royal Troon | 4 and 3 |

## BRITISH BOYS' AMATEUR CHAMPIONSHIP

This championship was founded in 1921, mainly through the efforts of the late Lieutenant-Colonel Thomas South, of Little Aston Hall, Sutton Coldfield, Warwickshire. He remained Honorary Secretary of the Championship Committee until the R. and A. assumed control in 1949.

The chief conditions are that entrants must be under 18 years old and must have senior handicaps of 10 or less, or equivalent junior handicaps. The event is decided by match play, the final being over 36 holes.

The Peter Garner Bowl is awarded to the best 16-year-old competitor.

The Championship has been won by a number of young players who have gone on to make their name in senior golf.

## BRITISH GIRLS' CHAMPIONSHIP

This event—its full name is the British Girls' Open Amateur Championship—was originated by Mr J. S. Wood, of a now vanished paper called *The Gentlewoman*. The first meeting was fixed for the autumn of 1914, but had to be postponed until 1919 because of the outbreak of war. For that year the age limit was raised to 21, next year reduced to 20 and in 1921 finally fixed at under 19 on the last day of the championship. It is open to girls of any nationality.

From 1919 to 1939 all championships were held at the Stoke Poges Club, Bucks, but since the resumption in 1949, after the Second World War, a variety of courses have been used. The first champion was Miss Audrey Croft, and since then many winners have gone on to make their name in senior golf, including Mlle Thion de la Chaume (Mme Lacoste), Miss Enid Wilson, Miss Diana Fishwick (Mrs Critchley), Miss Jessie Anderson (Mrs Valentine), Mlle Lally Vagliano (Mme Patrick Segard), Miss Angela Ward (Mrs Bonallack), Mlle Brigitte Varangot and Miss Ruth Porter.

## BRITISH GOLF SUPPORTERS' ASSOCIATION

A non-profit-making organisation, founded in 1970, with the object of bringing together regular golf spectators and providing them with better facilities at golf's great occasions, arranging parties to go abroad for Ryder and Walker Cup matches, arranging a national tournament sponsorship scheme, and various other activities of interest to golfers.

## BRITISH GUIANA, GOLF IN

See GUYANA, GOLF IN

## BRITISH HONDURAS, GOLF IN

In the capital city, Belize, is the Almond Hill Country Club, founded in 1951. It is a sporting 9-holes course. Formerly there was also the Belize Club.

## BRITISH ISLES, NUMBER OF CLUBS IN THE

There are approximately 2,000 golf clubs, of various sorts and sizes, in the British Isles—approximately 1,125 in England, six in the Channel Islands, 500 in Scotland, 215 in the Republic of Ireland and Northern Ireland, and 100 in Wales.

## BRITISH LADIES' CHAMPIONSHIP

The first Championship was held in June 1893 on the now-vanished 9-holes ladies' course of the Lytham and St Anne's Club, Lancashire. There were nearly two separate 'firsts' because the Wimbledon Club and the Lytham Club both announced an open meeting at much the same time; however, the newly-formed Ladies' Golf Union (largely Wimbledon-inspired) took over the championship, but agreed to hold it at Lytham. The course was not a severe test for the ladies, for the total length of the 18-holes round was only 4,264 yards, the longest hole being 337 yards. There were 38 players, and the winner was the famous Lady Margaret Scott, who beat Miss Issette Pearson, the virtual founder of the L.G.U., in the final by 7 and 5.

These two great ladies met again in the final next year at Littlestone, Kent, this time Lady Margaret winning by 3 and 2. She won again in 1895—and then retired from competitive golf. Littlestone was a much worthier setting for the Ladies' Championship, and thereafter the venue was almost always a famous course of high standard.

In spite of spirited challenges from American golfers as the years went by, British ladies held on to their title until, in 1927, the first foreign winner proved to be Mlle Simone Thion de la Chaume, who later married René Lacoste, the lawn tennis player, and whose daughter is Mlle Catherine Lacoste. In 1928 the title went to another young French golfer, Mlle Manette Le Blan, but the title did not cross the Atlantic until 'Babe' Zaharias won at Gullane in 1947, although Glenna Collett (Mrs Vare) was twice runner-up (1929, 1930). There have been several other French and American victors since, including Mlle Catherine Lacoste (1969), and one Canadian, Marlene Stewart Streit (1953).

The Ladies' Championship has always been decided by match play, the final being over 36 holes since 1913. All entrants have to have amateur status and possess a handicap of eight or under. At present two qualifying rounds are played to reduce the field to manageable proportions.

The following are the winners and runners-up of the championship since its inception:

| Year | Winner | Runner-up | Venue | By |
|------|--------|-----------|-------|-----|
| 1893 | Lady M. Scott | Lena Thomson | Lytham & St Anne's | 7 and 5 |
| 1894 | Lady M. Scott | Edith Lythgoe | Littlestone | 3 and 2 |
| 1895 | Lady M. Scott | Issette Pearson | R. Portrush | 5 and 4 |
| 1896 | Amy Pascoe | Issette Pearson | R. Liverpool | 3 and 2 |
| 1897 | E. C. Orr | Miss Orr | Gullane | 4 and 2 |
| 1898 | Lena Thomson | Elinor Nevile | Yarmouth | 7 and 5 |
| 1899 | May Hezlet | Jessie Magill | Newcastle | 2 and 1 |
| 1900 | Rhona Adair | Elinor Nevile | Westward Ho! | 6 and 5 |
| 1901 | N. Graham | Rhona Adair | Aberdovey | 3 and 1 |
| 1902 | May Hezlet | Elinor Nevile | R. Cinque Ports | 19th |
| 1903 | Rhona Adair | F. Walker-Leigh | R. Portrush | 4 and 3 |
| 1904 | Lottie Dod | May Hezlet | Troon | 1 hole |
| 1905 | Bertha Thomson | M. E. Stuart | R. Cromer | 3 and 2 |
| 1906 | Mrs Kennion | Bertha Thomson | Burnham | 4 and 3 |
| 1907 | May Hezlet | Florence Hezlet | Newcastle | 3 and 1 |
| 1908 | Maud Titterton | Dorothy Campbell | St Andrews | 19th |
| 1909 | Dorothy Campbell | Florence Hezlet | R. Birkdale | 4 and 3 |
| 1910 | Elsie Grant-Suttie | Lily Moore | Westward Ho! | 6 and 4 |
| 1911 | Dorothy Campbell | Violet Hezlet | R. Portrush | 3 and 2 |
| 1912 | Gladys Ravenscroft | Stella Temple | Turnberry | 3 and 2 |
| 1913 | Muriel Dodd | Evelyn Chubb | R. Lytham | 8 and 6 |
| 1914 | Cecil Leitch | Gladys Ravenscroft | Hunstanton | 2 and 1 |
| 1915-19 No Championships | | | | |
| 1920 | Cecil Leitch | Molly Griffiths | Newcastle | 7 and 6 |
| 1921 | Cecil Leitch | Joyce Wethered | Turnberry | 4 and 3 |
| 1922 | Joyce Wethered | Cecil Leitch | Prince's | 9 and 7 |
| 1923 | Doris Chambers | Mrs A. Macbeth | Burnham | 2 holes |
| 1924 | Joyce Wethered | Mrs F. Cautley | R. Portrush | 7 and 6 |
| 1925 | Joyce Wethered | Cecil Leitch | Troon | 37th |
| 1926 | Cecil Leitch | Mrs P. Garon | R. St Davids | 8 and 7 |
| 1927 | Simone de la Chaume | Dorothy Pearson | Newcastle | 5 and 4 |
| 1928 | Manette Le Blan | Sylvia Marshall | Hunstanton | 3 and 2 |
| 1929 | Joyce Wethered | Glenna Collett | St Andrews | 3 and 1 |
| 1930 | Diana Fishwick | Glenna Collett | Formby | 4 and 3 |
| 1931 | Enid Wilson | Wanda Morgan | Portmarnock | 7 and 6 |
| 1932 | Enid Wilson | C. P. R. Montgomery | Saunton | 7 and 6 |
| 1933 | Enid Wilson | Diana Plumpton | Gleneagles | 5 and 4 |
| 1934 | Mrs A. M. Holm | Pamela Barton | R. Porthcawl | 6 and 5 |
| 1935 | Wanda Morgan | Pamela Barton | Newcastle | 3 and 2 |
| 1936 | Pamela Barton | Bridget Newell | Southport | 5 and 3 |
| 1937 | Jessie Anderson | Doris Park | Turnberry | 6 and 4 |
| 1938 | Mrs A. M. Holm | Elsie Corlett | Burnham | 4 and 3 |
| 1939 | Pamela Barton | Mrs T. Marks | R. Portrush | 2 and 1 |
| 1940-45 No Championships | | | | |
| 1946 | Mrs G. Hetherington | Philomena Garvey | Hunstanton | 1 hole |
| 1947 | 'Babe' Zaharias | Jacqueline Gordon | Gullane | 5 and 4 |
| 1948 | Louise Suggs | Jean Donald | R. Lytham | 1 hole |
| 1949 | Frances Stephens | Mrs Val Reddan | R. St David's | 5 and 4 |
| 1950 | Lally de St Sauveur | Mrs G. Valentine | Newcastle | 3 and 2 |
| 1951 | Mrs P. G. MacCann | Frances Stephens | Broadstone | 4 and 3 |
| 1952 | Moira Paterson | Frances Stephens | Troon | 38th |
| 1953 | Marlene Stewart | Philomena Garvey | R. Porthcawl | 7 and 6 |
| 1954 | Frances Stephens | Elizabeth Price | Ganton | 4 and 3 |
| 1955 | Mrs G. Valentine | Barbara Romack | R. Portrush | 7 and 6 |
| 1956 | Margaret Smith | Mary Janssen | Sunningdale | 8 and 7 |

| 1957 | Philomena Garvey | Mrs G. Valentine | Gleneagles | 4 and 3 |
|------|------------------|------------------|------------|---------|
| 1958 | Mrs G. Valentine | Elizabeth Price | Hunstanton | 1 hole |
| 1959 | Elizabeth Price | Belle McCorkindale | Ascot | 37th |
| 1960 | Barbara McIntire | Philomena Garvey | R. St David's | 4 and 2 |
| 1961 | Mrs A. D. Spearman | Diane Robb | Carnoustie | 7 and 6 |
| 1962 | Mrs A. D. Spearman | Mrs M. Bonallack | R. Birkdale | 1 hole |
| 1963 | Brigitte Varangot | Philomena Garvey | Newcastle | 3 and 1 |
| 1964 | Carol Sorenson | Bridget Jackson | Prince's | 37th |
| 1965 | Brigitte Varangot | Mrs I. Robertson | St Andrews | 4 and 3 |
| 1966 | Elizabeth Chadwick | Vivien Saunders | Ganton | 3 and 2 |
| 1967 | Elizabeth Chadwick | Mary Everard | R. St David's | 1 hole |
| 1968 | Brigitte Varangot | Mme C. Rubin | Walton Heath | 20th |
| 1969 | Catherine Lacoste | Ann Irvin | R. Portrush | 1 hole |
| 1970 | Dinah Oxley | Mrs I. Robertson | Gullane | 1 hole |
| 1971 | Michelle Walker | Beverly Huke | Alwoodley | 3 and 1 |
| 1972 | Michelle Walker | Claudine Cros Rubin | Hunstanton | 1 hole |
| 1973 | Ann Irvin | Michelle Walker | Carnoustie | 3 and 2 |
| 1974 | Carol Semple | Mrs Angela Bonallack | R. Porthcawl | 2 and 1 |
| 1975 | Mrs N. Syms | Susan Cadden | St Andrews | 3 and 2 |
| 1976 | Catherine Panton | Miss A. Sheard | Silloth | 1 hole |
| 1977 | Angela Uzielli | Miss V. Marvin | Hillside | 6 and 5 |
| 1978 | Edwina Kennedy | Julia Greenhalgh | Hollinwell | 1 hole |

## BRITISH OPEN CHAMPION MORE THAN ONCE

The following players have won the Open Championship more than once:

### Six times
Harry Vardon (1896, 1898, 1899, 1903, 1911, 1914)

### Five times
James Braid (1901, 1905, 1906, 1908, 1910)

J. H. Taylor (1894, 1895, 1900, 1903, 1909)

Peter Thomson (1954, 1955, 1956, 1958, 1965)

### Four times
Walter Hagen (1922, 1924, 1928, 1929)

Bobby Locke (1949, 1950, 1952, 1957)

Tom Morris, Sen (1861, 1862, 1864, 1867)

Tom Morris, Jun (1868, 1869, 1870, 1872)

Willie Park, Sen (1860, 1863, 1866, 1875)

### Three times
Jamie Anderson (1877, 1878, 1879)
Henry Cotton (1934, 1937, 1948)
Bob Ferguson (1880, 1881, 1882)
Bobby Jones (1926, 1927, 1930)

Jack Nicklaus (1966, 1970, 1978)
Gary Player (1959, 1968, 1974)

### Twice
Harold Hilton (1892, 1897)
Bob Martin (1876, 1885)
Arnold Palmer (1961, 1962)
Willie Park, Jun (1887, 1889)
Lee Trevino (1971, 1972)
Tom Watson (1975, 1977)

## BRITISH OPEN CHAMPIONSHIP

An Open Championship was first suggested at the October meeting of the Prestwick Golf Club, Ayrshire, in 1856, but the famous tournament did not get under way until the autumn of 1860. Play was over three rounds of the 12-holes Prestwick links and there were eight entrants, all professionals of sorts. The winner was Willie Park, senior, of Musselburgh, with a score of 174, and he won the right to hold the Championship Belt for a year. William Steel of Bruntsfield took 232, including 21 shots at one hole.

Several amateurs entered for the 1861 Open, but the winner was Tom Morris, senior. The tournament continued, attracting little except local attention, until 'Young Tommy' Morris made the belt his property by winning the championship three times running, 1868-70.

The championship lapsed for a year, but began again in 1872, the trophy being the now-historic Championship Cup, subscribed for by the Prestwick Club, the R. and A. and the Honourable Company of Edinburgh Golfers. It was now played for at Prestwick, St Andrews and Musselburgh in turn until 1894. The first winner of the cup was 'Young Tommy', who thus established an unbeaten record of four victories in a row; he died on Christmas Day 1875 at the age of 24.

In 1890 the championship was won for the first time by an amateur and an Englishman, John Ball, the famous Hoylake golfer, and now the Open began to be news outside Scotland. In 1892 it was held on the Honourable Company's new course at Muirfield and extended from 36 to 72 holes, the first winner under the new conditions being another Hoylake amateur, Harold Hilton, who was to win again in 1897. In 1894 two English clubs— Royal Liverpool, Hoylake, and Royal St George's, Sandwich—were added to the rota; the winner at Sandwich in 1894 for the first time was an English professional, J. H. Taylor. He won again at St Andrews next year, and in 1896 at Muirfield came the first of Harry Vardon's six victories.

The links of other clubs were added during the ensuing years—Royal Cinque Ports, Deal, Kent (1909); Troon, Ayrshire (1923); Royal Lytham and St Anne's, Lancashire (1926); Carnoustie, Angus (1931) and Royal Birkdale, Southport, Lancashire (1954); Turnberry, Ayrshire (1977). The championship went once (1932) to Prince's, Sandwich, and once to Royal

Portrush, County Antrim (1951).

As the number of entrants increased, various ways were tried of reducing the players in the championship proper to manageable proportions. In 1926 there was a form of regional qualification, in which Bobby Jones, the ultimate winner, had his famous round of 66 at Sunningdale, Berkshire. The present method, however, of exempting certain entrants and making all the others play two qualifying rounds has proved the best. The record number of entries was 528 in 1971.

Entry money was charged for the first time in 1891. In 1919 the R. and A. took over control of the championship from the six clubs over whose courses the event was decided. Gate money was charged for the first time in 1926 at Royal Lytham and St Anne's. Prize money has increased steadily over the years, from the £10 available in 1863 (winner receiving £5) to the £125,000 available in 1978 (winner receiving £12,500). Crowd control has also improved enormously.

The first foreign winner of the championship was a Frenchman, Arnaud Massy (1907); the first American citizen, Scottish-born Jock Hutchison (1921); the first native-born American, Walter Hagen (1922); the first American amateur, Bobby Jones (1926); the first Irishman, Ulster-born Fred Daly (1947); the first South African, Bobby Locke (1949); the first Australian, Peter Thomson (1954); the first New Zealander, Bob Charles (1963); the first Argentinian, Roberto De Vicenzo (1967).

The following are the winners of the Open since its inception:

| Year | Winner | Venue | Score |
|------|--------|-------|-------|
| 1860 | Willie Park Sr | Prestwick | 174 |
| 1861 | Tom Morris Sr | Prestwick | 163 |
| 1862 | Tom Morris Sr | Prestwick | 163 |
| 1863 | Willie Park Sr | Prestwick | 168 |
| 1864 | Tom Morris Sr | Prestwick | 160 |
| 1865 | Andrew Strath | Prestwick | 162 |
| 1866 | Willie Park Sr | Prestwick | 169 |
| 1867 | Tom Morris Sr | Prestwick | 170 |

| Year | Winner | Venue | Score |
|------|--------|-------|-------|
| 1868 | Tom Morris Jr | Prestwick | 154 |
| 1869 | Tom Morris Jr | Prestwick | 157 |
| 1870 | Tom Morris Jr | Prestwick | 149 |
| 1871 | No Championship | | |
| 1872 | Tom Morris Jr | Prestwick | 166 |
| 1873 | Tom Kidd | St Andrews | 179 |
| 1874 | Mungo Park | Musselburgh | 159 |
| 1875 | Willie Park Sr | Prestwick | 166 |
| 1876 | Bob Martin | St Andrews | 176 |
| 1877 | Jamie Anderson | Musselburgh | 160 |
| 1878 | Jamie Anderson | Prestwick | 157 |
| 1879 | Jamie Anderson | St Andrews | 169 |
| 1880 | Bob Ferguson | Musselburgh | 162 |
| 1881 | Bob Ferguson | Prestwick | 170 |
| 1882 | Bob Ferguson | St Andrews | 171 |
| 1883 | Willie Fernie | Musselburgh | 159 |
| 1884 | Jack Simpson | Prestwick | 160 |
| 1885 | Bob Martin | St Andrews | 171 |
| 1886 | David Brown | Musselburgh | 157 |
| 1887 | Willie Park Jr | Prestwick | 161 |
| 1888 | Jack Burns | St Andrews | 171 |
| 1889 | Willie Park Jr | Musselburgh | 155 |
| 1890 | Mr John Ball | Prestwick | 164 |
| 1891 | Hugh Kirkaldy | St Andrews | 166 |
| 1892 | Mr Harold Hilton | Muirfield | 305 |
| 1893 | Willie Auchterlonie | Prestwick | 322 |
| 1894 | J. H. Taylor | R. St George's | 326 |
| 1895 | J. H. Taylor | St Andrews | 322 |
| 1896 | Harry Vardon | Muirfield | 316 |
| 1897 | Mr Harold Hilton | R. Liverpool | 314 |
| 1898 | Harry Vardon | Prestwick | 307 |
| 1899 | Harry Vardon | R. St George's | 310 |
| 1900 | J. H. Taylor | St Andrews | 309 |
| 1901 | James Braid | Muirfield | 309 |
| 1902 | Sandy Herd | R. Liverpool | 307 |
| 1903 | Harry Vardon | Prestwick | 300 |
| 1904 | Jack White | R. St George's | 296 |
| 1905 | James Braid | St Andrews | 318 |
| 1906 | James Braid | Muirfield | 300 |
| 1907 | Arnaud Massy | R. Liverpool | 312 |
| 1908 | James Braid | Prestwick | 291 |
| 1909 | J. H. Taylor | R. Cinque Ports | 295 |
| 1910 | James Braid | St Andrews | 299 |
| 1911 | Harry Vardon | R. St George's | 303 |
| 1912 | Ted Ray | Muirfield | 295 |
| 1913 | J. H. Taylor | R. Liverpool | 304 |
| 1914 | Harry Vardon | Prestwick | 306 |
| 1915-19 | No championships | | |
| 1920 | George Duncan | R. Cinque Ports | 303 |
| 1921 | Jock Hutchison | St Andrews | 296 |
| 1922 | Walter Hagen | R. St George's | 300 |
| 1923 | Arthur Havers | Troon | 295 |
| 1924 | Walter Hagen | R. Liverpool | 301 |
| 1925 | Jim Barnes | Prestwick | 300 |
| 1926 | Mr R. T. Jones | R. Lytham | 291 |

| Year | Winner | Venue | Score |
|------|--------|-------|-------|
| 1927 | Mr R. T. Jones | St Andrews | 285 |
| 1928 | Walter Hagen | R. St George's | 292 |
| 1929 | Walter Hagen | Muirfield | 292 |
| 1930 | Mr R. T. Jones | R. Liverpool | 291 |
| 1931 | Tommy Armour | Carnoustie | 296 |
| 1932 | Gene Sarazen | Prince's | 283 |
| 1933 | Densmore Shute | St Andrews | 292 |
| 1934 | Henry Cotton | R. St George's | 283 |
| 1935 | Alfred Perry | Muirfield | 283 |
| 1936 | Alfred Padgham | R. Liverpool | 287 |
| 1937 | Henry Cotton | Carnoustie | 290 |
| 1938 | Reg Whitcombe | R. St George's | 295 |
| 1939 | Dick Burton | St Andrews | 290 |
| 1940-45 | No championships | | |
| 1946 | Sam Snead | St Andrews | 290 |
| 1947 | Fred Daly | R. Liverpool | 293 |
| 1948 | Henry Cotton | Muirfield | 284 |
| 1949 | Bobby Locke | R. St George's | 283 |
| 1950 | Bobby Locke | Troon | 279 |
| 1951 | Max Faulkner | R. Portrush | 285 |
| 1952 | Bobby Locke | R. Lytham | 287 |
| 1953 | Ben Hogan | Carnoustie | 282 |
| 1954 | Peter Thomson | R. Birkdale | 283 |
| 1955 | Peter Thomson | St Andrews | 281 |
| 1956 | Peter Thomson | R. Liverpool | 286 |
| 1957 | Bobby Locke | St Andrews | 279 |
| 1958 | Peter Thomson | R. Lytham | 278 |
| 1959 | Gary Player | Muirfield | 284 |
| 1960 | Kel Nagle | St Andrews | 278 |
| 1961 | Arnold Palmer | R. Birkdale | 284 |
| 1962 | Arnold Palmer | Troon | 276 |
| 1963 | Bob Charles | R. Lytham | 277 |
| 1964 | Tony Lema | St Andrews | 279 |
| 1965 | Peter Thomson | R. Birkdale | 285 |
| 1966 | Jack Nicklaus | Muirfield | 282 |
| 1967 | Roberto de Vicenzo | R. Liverpool | 278 |
| 1968 | Gary Player | Carnoustie | 289 |
| 1969 | Tony Jacklin | R. Lytham | 280 |
| 1970 | Jack Nicklaus | St Andrews | 283 |
| 1971 | Lee Trevino | R. Birkdale | 278 |
| 1972 | Lee Trevino | Muirfield | 278 |
| 1973 | Tom Weiskopf | Troon | 276 |
| 1974 | Gary Player | R. Lytham | 282 |
| 1975 | Tom Watson | Carnoustie | 279 |
| 1976 | Johnny Miller | R. Birkdale | 279 |
| 1977 | Tom Watson | Turnberry | 268 |
| 1978 | Jack Nicklaus | St Andrews | 281 |

# BRITISH OPEN CHAMPIONSHIP COURSES

The British Open Championship has been (or will be) played on the following courses since 1860:

Carnoustie (Angus): 1931, 1937, 1953, 1968, 1975

Muirfield (East Lothian): 1892, 1896, 1901, 1906, 1912, 1929, 1935, 1948, 1959, 1966, 1972

Musselburgh (Midlothian): 1874,

1880, 1883, 1886, 1889

Prestwick (Ayrshire): 1860-70, 1872, 1875, 1878, 1881, 1884, 1887, 1890, 1893, 1898, 1903, 1908, 1914, 1925

Princes, Sandwich (Kent): 1932

Royal Birkdale (Lancashire): 1953, 1961, 1965, 1971, 1976

Royal Cinque Ports, Deal (Kent): 1909, 1920

Royal Liverpool, Hoylake (Cheshire): 1897, 1902, 1907, 1913, 1924, 1930, 1936, 1947, 1956, 1967

Royal Lytham and St Anne's (Lancashire): 1926, 1952, 1958, 1963, 1969, 1974

Royal Portrush (County Antrim): 1951

Royal St George's, Sandwich (Kent): 1894, 1899, 1904, 1911, 1922, 1928, 1934, 1938, 1949

St Andrews (Fife): 1873, 1876, 1879, 1882, 1885, 1888, 1891, 1895, 1900, 1905, 1910, 1921, 1927, 1933, 1939, 1946, 1955, 1957, 1960, 1964, 1970

Troon (Ayrshire): 1923, 1950, 1962, 1973

Turnberry (Ayrshire): 1977

Musselburgh ceased to be an Open Championship venue when the Honourable Company of Edinburgh Golfers moved their course to Muirfield; Old Prestwick was found too difficult for crowd control after the 1925 Open; and Royal St George's (since 1949), Princes (since 1932) and Royal Cinque Ports (since 1920) have not been used because it is considered that this part of the Kent coast is not sufficiently easy of access to draw a reasonable number of spectators.

## BRITISH OPEN CHAMPIONSHIP, RECORD ENTRY FOR

The record number of entries for the British Open Championship was 528, at Royal Birkdale, 1971—the 100th actual championship. This is small, of course, compared with the U.S. Open Championship entry, which has reached 4,350. The first British Open had eight entrants and the first U.S. Open 11.

## BRITISH PROFESSIONAL MATCH PLAY CHAMPIONSHIP

This famous event began in 1903 as the *News of the World* Tournament, inspired by the two chief proprietors of the paper, Lord Riddell and Sir Emsley Carr, both keen golfers. Although the first two tournaments were held at Sunningdale and Mid-Surrey respectively, it later became closely associated with Walton Heath, the club owned by Lord Riddell (his title was Lord Riddell of Walton Heath) and the Carr family.

In 1946 the tournament was officially recognised as the British P.G.A. Match Play Championship—which in theory it had always been—and the *News of the World* gave £5,025 in prize money every year, the winner receiving £1,250 and the runner-up £500. Unfortunately, 1969 was the last year of this association, but sponsorship has now been continued by the Sun Alliance Co.

Almost all the great British professionals have won this tournament. Although most of the American Ryder Cup team played in 1949, the winner was Dai Rees, and indeed the only non-British winner has been Peter Thomson, champion in 1954, 1961, 1966, 1967.

## BRITISH SOLOMON ISLANDS, GOLF IN THE

Before the Second World War there was a club, with a 9-holes course, at Tulagi, the capital of the British protectorate. It vanished when the Japanese overran the islands, but since 1955 there has been a club at Honiara, where there is an airfield. It has 9 holes, with a two-round length of 6,226 yards.

## BRITISH WOMEN'S OPEN STROKE PLAY CHAMPIONSHIP

After some years' discussion by the Ladies' Golf Union, this new event in the British ladies' calendar was inaugurated in 1969. It comprises 72 holes of scratch stroke play and the first meeting was held at the Northumberland Club, Gosforth Park.

## BRITISH YOUTHS' OPEN AMATEUR CHAMPIONSHIP

This Championship, founded in 1954, is for young men over 18 and under 22 years of age at the time; their handicaps must not exceed six. It is decided by four rounds of stroke play, spread over three days.

Several winners have gone on to make their mark either in the amateur or professional fields, including Alan Bussell (1956), George Will (1957), Alex Caygill (1960), Brian Barnes (1964), Peter Townsend (1965), Peter Oosterhuis (1966), Peter Benka (1967, 1968), John Cook (1969), Baldovino Dassu, an Italian now turned professional (1970), Nick Faldo (1975), Sandy Lyle (1977).

## BRITZ, Teinie (b 1948)

South African Open Champion, 1971. Runner-up, Spanish Open, 1973.

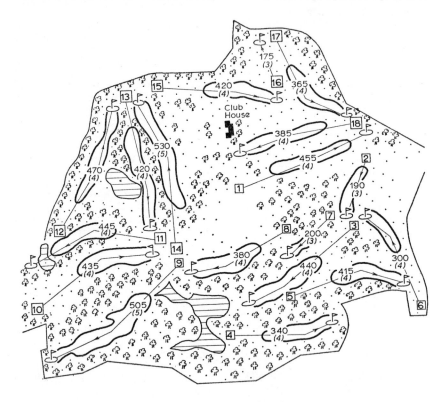

THE COUNTRY CLUB, BROOKLINE

## BROADSTONE

Broadstone, Dorset. Founded 1898. Mainly heathland. Length: 6,219 yards S.S.S. 70. Housed Ladies' Championship, 1951; English Ladies' Championship, 1929.

## BROMLEY-DAVENPORT, Mrs Edward

As Isabella Rieben, Welsh Ladies' Champion, 1932, 1934; as Mrs Nigel Seely, 1948; as Mrs Bromley-Davenport, 1951. Her mother, Mrs Alison

Rieben, who died in 1971, won the title in 1929, 1936; runner-up, 1921, 1928, 1930.

## BROOKLINE

The Country Club, Brookline, Massachusetts. The idea of The Country Club (it is always called just that) was first mooted—as a "Park or Drive", where members "may be free from the annoyances of horse railroads and...meet for pleasure driving and riding"—as long ago as 1860, but the club was not formally established until 1882. Originally the main interests were horse racing and polo, but the first 6 golf holes were laid out in 1892 and the whole course completed in 1909, with an additional 9 holes in 1927. Length: 6,870 yards (Par 71). Housed U.S. Open Championship, 1913 (when Francis Ouimet defeated Harry Vardon and Ted Ray in a dramatic play-off), 1963 (when Julius Boros won a play-off against Arnold Palmer and Jacky Cupit); U.S. Amateur Championship, 1910, 1922, 1934, 1957; U.S. Ladies' Championship, 1941. Also Walker Cup match, 1932, 1973.

## BROTHER AND SISTER GOLFERS

Among the best known brother and sister golfers have been:
Bonallack, Michael and Sally (Mrs Barber)
Craddock-Hartopp, Charles and Gwen (Mrs Morrison)
Cros, Patrick and Claudine (Mme Rubin)
Hezlet, Charles and May, Florence and Violet
Tredinnick, Ivan and Pamela
Wethered, Roger and Joyce (Lady Heathcoat-Amory)

## BROTHER GOLFERS

Among the best known golfing brothers have been the following:
Adams, Jimmy and Harry
Alliss, Peter and Alec
Arana, Javier and Luis
Auchterlonie, William and Laurence
Ballesteros, Manuel and Severiano
Bentley, Harry and Arnold
Blackwell, James, Walter, Edward and Ernley
Boomer, Aubrey and Percy
Brews, Jock and Sidney
Burton, Richard and John
Doleman, John, A. H., William and Frank
Dunn, Willie and Jamie
Dutra, Olin and Mortie
Furgol, Ed and Marty
Gallardo, Angel and Jaimie
Hartley, Rex and Lister
Hebert, Lionel and Jay
Henning, Harold, Graham and Alan
Herd, Sandy and Fred
Horne, Reg and Cyril
Hunt, Bernard and Geoffrey
Kirkaldy, Andrew and Hugh
Lacey, Arthur and Charles
Malik, I. S. and A. S.
Miguel, Sebastian and Angel
Park, Willie and Mungo
Rodrigues, Juan and Jesus
Scott, Michael, Osmund and Denys
Simpson, Jack, Archie, Robert and David
Smith, Alex, Willie and Macdonald
Strath, Andrew, David and George
Toogood, Peter and John
Turnesa, Willie, Jim and Joe
Vardon, Harry, Tom and Fred
Wadkins, Lanny and Bobby
Whitcombe, Charles, Ernest and Reginald

## BROWN, David

British Open Champion, 1886. One of the Musselburgh school of golfers, he was not really a professional, but a slater by trade.

## BROWN, Eric C. (b 1925)

Turned professional after winning Scottish Amateur Championship, 1946. Scottish Professional Champion, 1956, 1957, 1958, 1960, 1962. Irish Open Champion, 1953. Italian Open Champion, 1952. Portuguese Open Champion, 1953. Swiss Open Champion, 1951. Won Dunlop Masters, 1957. Ryder Cup team, 1953, 1955, 1957, 1959, winning all his singles matches; non-playing captain, 1969, 1971.

## BROWN, Mrs Charles S.
The first U.S. Ladies' Champion, 1895, at the Meadowbrook Club, Hempstead, New York. Her score of 132 (69, 63) for the 18 holes was two strokes better than that of the runner-up, Miss N. C. Sargeant. She won a silver pitcher given by Messrs R. D. Winthrop and W. H. Sands. There were 13 competitors. See UNITED STATES LADIES' CHAMPIONSHIP.

## BROWNE, Mary K. (b 1890)
Runner-up, U.S. Ladies' Championship, 1924. In 1911 and 1913 she was U.S. National Lawn Tennis Champion. See DOD, CHARLOTTE ('LOTTIE')

## BROWN, Kenneth (b 1957)
Ryder Cup team, 1977.

## BRUEN, James (1920-72)
British Amateur Champion, 1946. Leading amateur in British Open Championship, 1939. British Boys' Amateur Champion, 1936. Irish Open Amateur Champion, 1938. Irish Close Amateur Champion, 1937, 1938. Walker Cup team, 1938, 1949, 1951. As a young golfer he was famous for his long hitting, his spectacular recovery shots and the 'loop' in his swing. An injury to his right hand and indifferent health prevented him from having an even more dramatic career.

## BRUNEI, GOLF IN
In this British Protected State on the north-west coast of the island of Borneo is the Panaga Club, founded as far back as 1934. It has an 18-holes course, length 6,130 yards.

## BRUNTSFIELD
The Bruntsfield Links Golfing Society dates back to 1761, its old course now being a public park in the middle of Edinburgh. When play became impossible there, the society for some years shared the Musselburgh links with the Musselburgh Club and the Honourable Company of Edinburgh Golfers. Its present home is at Davidson's Mains, on the outskirts of the city. See EDINBURGH GOLFERS, HONOURABLE COMPANY OF; MUSSELBURGH.

## BUCKLEY, James A. (b 1951)
Welsh Amateur Champion, 1968; the youngest to hold the title, having played for Wales in the Amateur Internationals at the age of 15. Welsh Close Champion, 1969. Turned professional, 1969.

## BUDKE, Mary Ann (b 1954)
U.S. Ladies' Champion, 1972.

## BULGARIA, GOLF IN
For the first time a course is being laid out near Sofia, the capital. A Bulgarian enthusiast, M. Savov, came to England in May 1969 to study British courses and to collect information for the architect, who is being assisted by the Romanian professional, Paul Tomita. See TOMITA, PAUL.

## BULGER
An obsolete wooden club with a convex face that was supposed to lessen the likelihood of hitting the ball off the toe or heel. There is some doubt about its inventor. In *Sixty Years of Golf* (1953), Robert Harris says: "The idea was Henry Lamb's, a finalist in the Amateur Championship of 1886...Bob Simpson made it. Freddie Tait, then the rising amateur golfer, undoubtedly popularised it." Horace Hutchinson, in the Badminton Library volume on *Golf* (1890), says that Lamb invented the 'bulger' and had clubs made on this principle by Forgans, but adds that Willie Park (about 1884) "also appears to have once made a club with a bulging face; but he does not appear to have played with it". See FORGAN, ROBERT; LAMB, HENRY; PARK, WILLIE (JUN).

## BULLA, Johnny (b 1914)
American. Runner-up, British Open Championship, 1939, 1946. Runner-up, U.S. Masters, 1949. A representative for a cheaper American ball firm, Bulla was for some years before and after the Second World War in the running for the British Open, although he never really made his mark on the American circuit.

## BUNKER

According to the Rules of Golf, a bunker is "an area of bare ground, often a depression, which is usually covered with sand". It is a Scottish word with several quite different meanings, one of which is a sand-pit. Sir Walter Scott in *Redgauntlet* writes: "They sat cozily nitched into what you might call a bunker—a little sand-pit, dry and snug, and surrounded by its banks, and a screen of whins in full bloom."

The word in its golf meaning goes back in Scotland at least to the mid-seventeenth century, for there is a record of the great Marquess of Montrose (1612-50) incurring expenses at Leith and St Andrews for "Bonker clubis, a irone club, and twa play clubis of my awin", followed by: "For mending bonker club 1s. 6d." He must have encountered some tough bonkers!

The first time the word 'bunker' appeared in the R. and A. Rules was in the code of 1812, where Rule IV reads: "Stones, bones, or any break-club within a club-length of the ball may be removed when the ball lies on grass, but nothing can be removed if it lies on sand, or in a bunker."

See HAZARDS; MONTROSE, MARQUESS OF; TRAP.

## BURGESS, Michael J. (b 1929)

Runner-up, English Amateur Championship, 1955. Tied English Amateur Stroke Play Championship (with Clive Clark and D. J. Millensted), 1965; runner-up, 1964. As Sussex Amateur Champion, won County Champions Championship, 1963. Won Worplesdon Mixed Foursomes, with Miss Bridget Jackson, 1960; runner-up with Signora I. Goldschmid-Bevione, 1963. Leading amateur in Open Championship, 1965.

## BURKE, Billy (b 1902)

American. U.S. Open Champion, 1931, after tie with George Von Elm, the well-known amateur, after the longest play-off in the history of the Open—72 holes, Burke winning by one stroke. Ryder Cup team, 1931, 1933.

## BURKE, Jack (b 1923)

In 1956 won both U.S. Masters and U.S.P.G.A. Championship; runner-up in Masters, 1952. Ryder Cup team, 1951, 1953, 1955, 1957 (captain). Professional at Champions' Club, Houston, Texas, where 1969 U.S. Open was played. Author of *The Natural Way to Better Golf* (1954).

## BURKE, John (b 1900)

Irish Open Amateur Champion, 1947. Irish Amateur Close Champion, 1930, 1931, 1932, 1933, 1936, 1940, 1946, 1947; runner-up, 1935, 1937. South of Ireland Champion, 1928, 1929, 1930, 1931, 1939, 1941, 1942, 1943, 1944, 1945, 1946. West of Ireland Champion, 1933, 1934, 1936, 1938, 1940, 1941. Walker Cup team, 1932.

## BURKEMO, Walter (b 1919)

U.S.P.G.A. Champion, 1953; runner-up, 1951, 1954. Ryder Cup team, 1953.

## BURMA, GOLF IN

In the Republic of the Union of Burma the game has now recovered after the setback of the war against the Japanese. The Rangoon Club in the capital, which goes back to 1905, has an 18-holes course, length 6,680 yards, and there are four other clubs. At Namtu, in the Northern Shan States, the local club has a 9-holes course, and the Moulmein Club, across the Gulf of Martaban from Rangoon, has 12 holes.

At the old club at Rangoon the Burma Amateur Championship was played for every year from 1920-39.

## BURMA ROAD

The nickname given in the years after the Second World War to the West Course of the Wentworth Club, Virginia Water, Surrey, the inference being that its toughness as a test of golf is akin to its infamous namesake where many prisoners of the

Japanese suffered during the war. See WENTWORTH.

## BURNHAM AND BERROW

Burnham-on-Sea, Somerset. Founded 1890. Typical linksland, playing between or over sandhills, menaced by buckthorn. Length: 6,588 yards. S.S.S. 71. Housed Ladies' Championship, 1906, 1938; English Amateur Championship, 1930, 1952, 1963; English Ladies' Championship, 1949, 1960, 1969, E. G. U. Brabazon Trophy, 1956.

## BURNS, George F.

American. Walker Cup team, 1975.

## BURNS, Jack (b 1856)

Born St Andrews. British Open Champion, 1888. After winning, he gave up his occupation as a plasterer and became professional at the Warwick Club. After some years, he returned to St Andrews and worked as a platelayer on the railway. When asked how he was playing, he used to reply: "Never better—I haven't been off the line for years!"

## BURTON, Richard (1907-74)

British Open Champion, 1939. Ryder Cup team, 1935, 1937, 1949. His brother John was British Senior Professional Champion, 1957.

## BURUNDI, GOLF IN

The Republic of Burundi, on the east side of Lake Tanganyika, was a Belgian trusteeship until it was proclaimed an independent state in 1962. There is a 9-holes course at Bujumbura, the capital.

## BUSSELL, Alan Francis (b 1937)

British Boys' Amateur Champion, 1954. British Youths' Open Champion, 1956. Won *Golf Illustrated* Gold Vase, 1959. Walker Cup team, 1957.

## BUSSON, John J. (b 1910)

British Professional Match Play Champion, 1934. Ryder Cup team, 1935.

## BUTLER, Peter J. (b 1932)

French Open Champion, 1968. P.G.A. Champion, 1963. Runner-up, British Professional Match Play Championship, 1964. Ryder Cup team, 1965, 1969, 1971, 1973. Played in Piccadilly World Match Play Championship, 1964, 1965.

## BYE

The holes that are still to be played after a match has been decided. In an 18-holes match, if one player had won by the greatest possible margin —10 up and 8 to play—the bye would consist of those eight holes. It would thus be possible to play what is facetiously called a bye-bye and a bye-bye-bye—and have a bye-bye-bye-bye on the last hole.

Another use of the word occurs in the draw for a match-play competition, when those players not engaged in the first round, because of an uneven number of entries, receive a 'bye' into the second round.

## BYERS, Eben M. (b 1875)

U.S. Amateur Champion, 1906; runner-up, 1902, 1903.

## BYMAN, Bob (b 1955)

American. Dutch Open, 1977, 1978. New Zealand Open, 1977.

## CADDIE

In the Rules of Golf a caddie is "one who carries or handles a player's clubs during play and otherwise assists him in accordance with the Rules". The accepted derivation is from the French *cadet*, a young fellow. The Scots adopted many French words, and a caddie in eighteenth-century Scotland was one who ran errands or acted as a porter; his name was often shortened to 'cad'. In the old days the relationship between a caddie and his master was a unique one, the caddie using the royal (or editorial) 'we' in such phrases as: "We had better take our niblick here." Today the caddie has largely been superseded by the ubiquitous caddie-car or trolley.

In the earlier years of the nineteenth century, the term 'professional golfer' had not been adopted, and a club's senior caddie was player, club-maker and repairer, greenkeeper and ball maker as well as carrier of the clubs of the captain or other distinguished member. The great Allan Robertson (1815-58)—his father was the "Davie, oldest of the cads" of George Fullarton Carnegie's poem, "Golfiana" (1833)—was really the last to combine all these tasks, while Tom Morris senior (1821-1908) could likewise be regarded as the first of the professional golfers.

The Rules of Golf definition dealing with caddies says that "when one caddie is employed by more than one player, he is always deemed to be the caddie of the player whose ball is involved, and equipment carried by him is deemed to be that player's equipment, except when the caddie acts upon specific directions of another player, in which case he is considered to be that player's caddie".

The same definition states that "in threesome, foursome, best-ball and four-ball play, a caddie carrying for more than one player should be assigned to the members of one side". In the United States and some other countries the carrying of more than one bag of clubs by a caddie is fairly common, but rare in Britain.

See CADDIE-CAR ; CADDIES, PAYMENT FOR ; FORECADDIE.

## CADDIE-CAR

Sometimes called a trolley, or in the United States a pull-cart, this is a wheeled contraption, usually made of steel or aluminium, for carrying a player's clubs. In New Zealand they are called 'trundlers'—a nice term—and in the Official Rules of Golf 'Golf Carts'. Previously, a golfer either had a caddie or carried his own clubs in a bag slung over his shoulder. The first caddie-cars came into general use shortly after the Second World War, one of the pioneers being Lord Brabazon of Tara.

The basic idea, however, was considerably older. In the 1920s Starr Wood, the cartoonist, had a drawing in *Punch* showing 'Mr Punch's Patent Caddie Car'; a boy was pushing a trolley containing not only Mr Punch's golf clubs, but a decanter of whisky, a soda-water siphon and two glasses. A 1901 advertisement showed a golf bag with adjustable wheels attached to the side, the description claiming that: "The Rover Golf Caddie relieves the player or his caddie of the entire weight of the clubs ...The carriage (with wooden wheels and rubber tyres) is very easily detached, and the bag can be used separately when so required." The price was 15s. See BRABAZON OF TARA, LORD.

D

## CADDIES, PAYMENT FOR

The question of payment for caddies goes back at least to the seventeenth century. There are records of payment being made by the great Marquess of Montrose in 1628 "to the boy who carried my Lord's clubbes to the field" and by Sir John Foulis, of Ravelstoun: "To the boy who carried my clubs when my Lord Register and Newbyth was at the Links—4s." A Scottish shilling was only a fraction of an English shilling.

In the very old days, payment was a personal matter between master and caddie. At St Andrews, however, as early as 1771 a tariff was agreed on: "Four pence for going the length of the hole called the Hole of Cross, and if they go further than the hole they are to get sixpence—and no more"; to which was added the threat: "Any of the gentlemen of this Society transgressing this rule are to pay two pint bottles of claret at the first meeting they shall attend."

By 1863 at St Andrews a register of regular caddies was formed and a tariff by which caddies over 20 were to receive 1s. 6d. for the first round and 6d. for the second, while those still in their teens were paid 1s. for the first round and 6d. for the second.

At Prestwick in the 1860s and 70s, first-class caddies were paid 6d. a round and second-class ones 4d.

By the 1890s, when golf was growing everywhere, Horace Hutchinson was writing in the Badminton Library volume on *Golf* (1890) that a St Andrews or Musselburgh caddie "can lightly earn seven and sixpence a day by playing two rounds of golf; or, if he does not get an engagement, three and sixpence a day by carrying clubs" —indicating that in those days the term 'caddie' covered a professional player as well as a professional carrier of clubs.

As the cost of living rose and the value of the pound declined, the golfer had to pay more and more for the services—sometimes doubtful—of his caddie. Before the Second World War the normal fee was about 7s. 6d.

a round, plus a tip; caddies were still plentiful, and at busy clubs the caddie-master could guarantee work for 60 or more men and boys on a reasonably fine weekend.

Caddies are now a disappearing race, and when one is available, the fee is usually about £1 or £1.50 a round. In the United States, where a caddie may carry two bags, the fee is positively princely.

When Walter Hagen gave his fee (£75) for winning the 1922 Open Championship to his caddie, Skip Daniels, he started a fashion that has been followed by other famous golfers.

## CADDIE SWING

This phrase is used to describe the absolutely natural, untaught swing that may be seen in caddies swinging a club behind the caddie shed—although, with the decrease in the number of caddies, far less often than in the past.

## 'CADDIE WILLIE'

'Caddie Willie' (William Gunn) was a picturesque character who used to carry the clubs of members of the Royal Burgess Society, Edinburgh, in the early nineteenth century on the Bruntsfield links. A famous portrait of him, wearing a Scots bonnet and a number of coats and waistcoats, painted by an unknown artist, hangs in the Royal Burgess Society's clubhouse. See ROYAL BURGESS GOLFING SOCIETY OF EDINBURGH.

## CAIRNS, Lady Katharine

Runner-up, English Ladies' Championship, 1949. Non-playing captain of the successful British Curtis Cup team, 1952.

## 'CALAMITY JANE'

Bobby Jones's famous putter, named after a character in the old Wild West. With it he won many of his championships, including the British and American Open and Amateur Championships in 1930. It had a slightly lofted blade and a hickory shaft, broken in two places and bound with whipping. Many copies were made of it—including the whipping round the shaft.

There is some doubt about the club's origin. According to Robert Browning, in *A History of Golf* (1955), it was not Bobby who gave the putter its name. What happened was that Bobby had putted badly in the match in which he was rather heavily beaten by Francis Ouimet in the U.S. Amateur Championship of 1921, and on the following day he went over to Nassau, Long Island, to visit Jimmy Maiden, the brother of Stewart Maiden, the professional at Bobby's home club at East Lake. Jimmy presented his visitor with a rusty old putter to which he had given the name of 'Calamity Jane', and with this Bobby holed so many long putts in the course of the day that the thing became a joke.

According to another version, it was not until 1923 that Bobby got the club, already christened 'Calamity Jane', from a young assistant of Jimmy Maiden named Joe Merkel—and went on to win the 1923 U.S. Open with it. According to Robert Harris's *Sixty Years of Golf* (1953), however, Stewart Maiden crossed the Atlantic "carrying with him a putter of mine which was to be the prototype of, if not the original, famous 'Calamity Jane'."

## CALDWELL, Ian (b 1930)

English Amateur Champion, 1961. Runner-up, British Boys' Championship, 1947. Walker Cup team, 1951, 1955.

## CAMBUCA

Also Cambuta. A game played in England at the time of Edward III (mid-fourteenth century). As in Paganica, a crooked stick was used to strike a ball made of leather stuffed with feathers. The ball was presumably propelled towards a mark set up in the ground.

In the famous East Window of Gloucester Cathedral there is a figure in stained glass of a man swinging a club at a yellow-coloured ball on a green ground. It dates from the fourteenth century and, although it has been called 'the golf player', it more likely represents a cambuca player.

See CHOLE ; FEATHERY ; JEU DE MAIL ; PAGANICA ; TAKOURA.

## CAMPBELL, Dorothy

See HURD, MRS DOROTHY CAMPBELL.

## CAMPBELL, Sir Guy (1884-1960)

Well-known golf course architect. The courses he designed or redesigned include Prince's (Sandwich), Ashridge (Hertfordshire), West Sussex (Pulborough), Killarney (County Kerry, Eire). An uncle, Robert Chambers, Jun, laid out with George Morris, a brother of Tom Morris, the original 9 holes in the racecourse at Hoylake that eventually became the links of the Royal Liverpool Club.

## CAMPBELL, William (b 1900)

Runner-up, Scottish Amateur Championship, 1934. Walker Cup team, 1930.

## CAMPBELL, William C. (b 1923)

U.S. Amateur Champion, 1964. Runner-up, British Amateur Championship, 1954. Runner-up, Canadian Amateur Championship, 1952, 1954, 1965. Mexican Amateur Champion, 1956. Walker Cup team, 1951, 1953, 1955 (non-playing captain), 1957, 1965, 1967, 1971.

## CANADA CUP

See WORLD (FORMERLY CANADA) CUP.

## CANADA, GOLF IN

Golf goes back further in Canada than it does in the United States. The first American club—the St Andrews Club, Yonkers, New York—dates from 1888, the Royal Montreal Club from 1873. Neither plays over the original ground. Montreal's earliest golfers played over Fletcher's Fields in Mount Royal Park. Soon, however, they had to move nine miles out to Dixie, a location named by a group of Southern sympathisers who settled there after the American Civil War ended in 1866. The club has had two homes there, the present one providing room for two separate 18-holes courses.

A little over a year after golf began in Montreal, the Royal Quebec Club was founded on what was called 'Cove Fields', near the historic Heights of Abraham. Play continued there until 1917, when the club moved to its present location, where there are two courses of 18 holes. Canada's first inter-club match took place at 'Cove Fields' between these two senior clubs in 1876.

This was the year in which the third oldest club, Toronto, was founded. Here there is an 18 and a 9-holes course. Near Toronto are many fine courses, including the St George's Country Club, where Bob Charles won the 1968 Canadian Open Championship; Pinegrove, scene of the 1969 Open; and the Toronto-Mississsaugua Country Club. Near Montreal are picturesque Laval-sur-le-Lac, the Summerlea Country Club and Richelieu Valley. On the west coast, in British Columbia, are such courses as those of the Capilano Country Club, the Marine Drive Club and the Shaughnessy Country Club, all in the Vancouver neighbourhood.

Altogether Canada has something like 750 clubs, great and small, and a golfing population of something like a million—a percentage that works out about the same as that in the United States. This is remarkable when one remembers that in most of the country—including the provinces of Ontario and Quebec, which contain about 60 per cent of all the courses—the game is confined to the months between May and October; needless to say, golf begins as soon as the snow clears. On the Pacific Coast of British Columbia, on the other hand, with heavy rainfall, but not snowfall, golf is playable almost all the year round, just as it is in Britain and many parts of America.

The Canadian Amateur Championship began in the same year, 1895, as did its American counterpart, but the Canadian Open began nine years later than the American, in 1904, and the Canadian Ladies' Open Championship six years later, in 1901. The Canadian Professional Golfers' Association Championship goes back to 1922 and the Ladies' Close Championship to 1923.

Among Canada's best-known golfers are Charles Ross Somerville (1932 U.S. Amateur Champion), Nick Weslock and Gary Cowan (1968 and 1971 U.S. Amateur Champion) among the amateurs; Mrs Marlene Stewart Streit (British, U.S. and Australian champion as well as Canadian) and the new 21-year-old star, Sandra Post, among the ladies; and Stan Leonard, Al Balding and George Knudson among the professionals.

Golf affairs are run by the Royal Canadian Golf Association, the Canadian Ladies' Golf Union and the Canadian Professional Golfers' Association.

## 'CANADIAN FOURSOME'
See GREENSOME.

## CANARY ISLANDS, GOLF IN THE
The Club de Golf de Las Palmas, Gran Canaria, founded in 1891, is the oldest Spanish club. It has 18 holes and a Standard Scratch Score of 70. Newer—founded in 1968—is the Maspalomas Club. On the neighbouring Atlantic island of Tenerife is the Golf Club de Tenerife, which also has 18 holes.

## CAPE VERDE ISLANDS, GOLF IN THE
This Portuguese group of islands lie in the Atlantic off the west coast of Africa. Like most Portuguese possessions, it has a golf club—the St Vincent Golf and Lawn Tennis Club, at St Vincent (Sao Vicente), on one

of the chief islands. It has a 9-holes course.

## CARNER, Mrs D. R. (b 1939)

Born JoAnne Gunderson. U.S. Ladies' Champion, 1957, 1960, 1962, 1966, 1968; runner-up, 1956, 1964. Curtis Cup team, 1958, 1960, 1962, 1964. U.S. Women's Open Champion, 1971, 1976. Turned professional, 1969. Australian Women's Open Champion, 1975.

## CARNOUSTIE

Carnoustie, Angus. Founded 1842. A long and exceedingly tough and challenging links. Length: 7,252 yards (specially stretched for 1968 Open Championship). S.S.S. 72. Housed Open Championship, 1931, 1937, 1953, 1968. Housed Amateur Championship, 1947, 1966, and Boys' Amateur Championship, 1933, 1939, 1957. Also shorter Burnside Course.

1954, 1956; runner-up, 1947, 1948, 1951. Irish Amateur Close Champion, 1954, 1957, 1963, 1964, 1965, 1967; runner-up, 1951, 1959. Won South, West and East of Ireland Championships many times between 1941 and 1966. Won *Golf Illustrated* Gold Vase, 1951, and many other chief amateur competitions. Leading amateur in the British Open Championship, 1956, 1958. Walker Cup team, 1947, 1949, 1951, 1953, 1955, 1957, 1959, 1961, 1963 (captain), 1965 (non-playing captain), 1967.

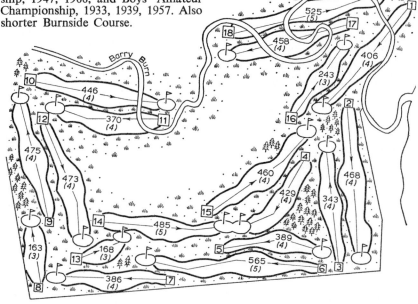

CARNOUSTIE

## CARR, Joseph B. ('Joe') (b 1922)

British Amateur Champion, 1953, 1958, 1960; runner-up, 1968. Irish Open Amateur Champion, 1946, 1950,

## CARR, Roderick J. (b 1950)

Son of Joe Carr (*above*). East of Ireland Champion, 1970; runner-up, 1971. West of Ireland Champion, 1971. Runner-up, North of Ireland Championship, 1970. Walker Cup team, 1971. Turned professional, late 1971.

## 'CARRICK IRON'
This was a primitive broad-faced iron club dating back to the mid-nineteenth century, used for getting the ball out of ruts and bad lies of all kinds See NIBLICK ; PRESIDENT ; RUT IRON.

## CARRIS TROPHY
This tournament was founded by the late Austin F. Carris in 1935. It is for boys under the age of 18 and is decided by 36 holes of stroke play at the Moor Park Club, Hertfordshire, one round each over the High and West Courses. Austin Carris did much for boys' golf and was also one of the founders of the Hazards Golfing Society.

Several winners of the Carris Trophy have gone on to make their name in seniors' golf, including John Langley (1936), R. J. White (1937), Arthur Perowne (1946), Ian Caldwell (1947, 1948), R. T. Walker (1959), D. J. Miller (1961), Peter Townsend (1964), Peter Dawson (1968), Kenneth Brown (1977).

## 'CARRUTHERS CLEEK'
A type of club long out of date. According to the Badminton Library volume on *Golf* (1890), irons were being made with the head thickened and rounded at the back, to give added strength. The 'Carruthers' cleeks and irons "carry the principle of massing the weight behind the point of impact a little further, for in them the shaft runs down right through the 'hose', thus dispensing with some two inches of the length of the 'hose' [the socket into which the shaft fits]."

## CARRY
The distance from the spot where the ball is played to the spot where it lands. Hence 'short carry', 'long carry', 'difficult carry', etc.

## CASPER, William Earl ('Billy') (b 1931)
U.S. Open Champion, 1959, 1966. Won U.S. Masters, 1970, after play-off with Gene Littler. Canadian Open Champion, 1967 (after tie with Art Wall). Runner-up, U.S.P.G.A. Championship, 1958, 1965. Ryder Cup team, 1961, 1963, 1965, 1967, 1969, 1971, 1973, 1975. Author of *Golf Shot-Making With Billy Casper* (1961); *My Million Dollar Shots.*

## CASUAL WATER
"Any temporary accumulation of water which is visible before or after the player takes his stance and which is not a hazard of itself or is not in a water hazard. Snow and ice are casual water or loose impediments, at the option of the player" (Rules of Golf Definition). See RULES OF GOLF, Rule 32.

## CAYGILL, Gordon Alexander ('Alex') (b 1940)
British Youths' Open Champion, 1960, 1962. Ryder Cup team, 1969.

## CENTRE-SHAFTED PUTTER
See SCHENECTADY ; SIMPLEX.

## CERDA, Antonio (b 1921)
Argentinian. Runner-up, British Open Championship, 1951, 1953 (with Frank Stranahan, D. J. Rees, Peter Thomson). Argentine Open Champion, 1948, 1956. Runner-up, Brazilian Open Championship, 1956. Mexican Open Champion, 1958.

## CEYLON, GOLF IN
See SRI LANKA, GOLF IN.

## CHADWICK, Elizabeth (b 1943)
British Ladies' Champion, 1966, 1967. Runner-up, English Ladies' Championship, 1963. Runner-up Italian Ladies' Championship, 1967. Curtis Cup team, 1966. Now Mrs Antony Pook.

## CHAMBERS, Doris E.
British Ladies' Champion, 1923.

Captain Curtis Cup team, 1936, 1948. Represented England in Ladies' Internationals from 1906-25.

## 'CHAMPAGNE TONY'

See LEMA, ANTHONY DAVID.

## CHANNEL ISLANDS, GOLF IN THE

There are three clubs in Jersey— the venerable Royal Jersey Club, founded in 1878, the newer La Moye Club and the 9-holes St Clements Club, on the outskirts of St Helier. Work began on a new course in 1972, designed by Peter Alliss and Dave Thomas. On Guernsey is the Royal Guernsey Club, founded in 1890. A new course, started in 1966, has also been constructed on Alderney. For the many famous golfers who have come from Jersey, see Jersey Golfers. The Channel Islands Amateur Championship dates from 1927 and the Ladies' from 1937, being dominated since 1964 by Mrs A. Lindsay.

## CHAPMAN, Richard D. (b 1911)

U.S. Amateur Champion, 1940. British Amateur Champion, 1951 ; runner-up, 1947, 1950. Canadian Amateur Champion, 1949. French Open Amateur Champion, 1939, 1952. Italian Open Amateur Champion, 1960. Won *Golf Illustrated* Gold Vase, 1948. Walker Cup team, 1947, 1951, 1953.

## CHARACTER BUILDER

An American phrase used to describe those awkward 5 or 6 foot putts—the significance being that the holing of such putts helps to build up a golfer's character, while missing them destroys it.

## CHARLES, Robert J. ('Bob') (b 1936)

This former bank clerk, who plays left-handed, has become one of the best golfers in the world. First British Open Champion from New Zealand, 1963, after tie with Phil Rodgers ; runner-up (with Jack Nicklaus),

1968, 1969. Runner-up, U.S.P.G.A. Championship, 1968. New Zealand Open Champion, 1954, 1966, 1970. New Zealand Professional Champion, 1961. Canadian Open Champion, 1968. Swiss Open Champion, 1962. Won Piccadilly World Match Play Tournament, 1969 ; runner-up, 1968. Author of *Expert Golf Instruction* (1965). See LEFT-HANDED GOLFERS.

## CHEVALIER, Charles (1902-73)

One of many Jersey-born golfers. During his long career he did 30 holes-in-one. He retired in 1969 as professional at Heaton Moor, Stockport, Cheshire, where he got his thirtieth 'ace' in 1962. See HOLES-IN-ONE, GREATEST NUMBER OF.

## CHILE, GOLF IN

The game was established at the Granadilla Country Club, Vina del Mar, as far back as 1895. Other 18-holes clubs are Los Leones, at Santiago, the capital, and the Antofagasta and Iquique Clubs, and altogether there are some 30 clubs.

## CHINA, GOLF IN

It is sad to think that golf, which was established in China as long ago as 1896, is no longer played there. In that year the Shanghai Club was founded, and the China Open Amateur Championship was held there annually from 1924-40. The winner for the last three years was A. Ricketts, entered from the Hungjao Club, Shanghai, and he won again in 1948, the last year of the championship.

The Shanghai Golf Club is no more, but before the Second World War, and until the Chinese took over afterwards, it comprised two courses, Kiangwan and Seekingjao, about 5 miles apart. There were also clubs at Peking, Foochow, Peiping, Tientsin and Tsingtao ; a course in the Hankow racecourse ; and a 9-holes course at Weihaiwei, looking across the Pohai Strait towards Port Arthur.

The North China Championship was held annually between 1925 and

1938, either at Tientsin or Peking; it was a 36-holes stroke-play event. There were rumours in 1971 that a course was being created in Red China, but there were no details. See HONG KONG, GOLF IN ; TAIWAN, GOLF IN.

## CHIP

"A short lofted approach" (Chambers's Dictionary), played with a more lofted club than would be used for a pitch-and-run shot. Also verb—to chip onto the green or up to the hole. May be derived from the usual meaning of the verb to chip—"strike with small sharp cutting blows". See PITCH ; RUN-UP SHOT.

## CHOKING DOWN

Holding the club (usually the shorter irons) lower down the shaft than is customary, the object being to obtain more control in making a delicate shot. A club held in this way is said to be 'choked down'. Also just called 'going down the shaft' or 'down the grip'.

## CHOLE

This ancient Belgian and French game (also called Soule, Choule or Cholle) can best be described as a sort of cross-country golf with peculiar rules of its own. Documentary evidence of Chole goes back to the mid-fourteenth century—about 100 years before the first mention of golf in Scotland. The balls could be made of beechwood or leather stuffed with hay, moss or other material. The clubs had long wooden shafts and iron heads.

A good description of the Belgian game is given by a certain M. Charles Michel in the Badminton Library volume on *Golf* (1890):

The players divide into two parties, after fixing the point on which they are to play, sometimes two or three, or even four leagues distant from the tee. The game is to reach and touch with the ball, say the right-hand pillar of the door of a church in such or such a village. The captains of each side choose a player alternately till all the company are divided into four parties, each under its captain. Then the number of strokes in which the distance is to be covered is, as it were, put up to auction; the side which offers the lowest estimate wins, and strikes off.

Then off they go, across field and meadow, hedge and ditch, the game being usually played in the autumn, when the fields are bare. Each man of the striking-off party swipes at the ball alternately, but when they have had three strokes, a man of the other party *déchole* (hits back). Then the first side plays three more strokes, then comes another *décholade* by the opponents. Thus each of the original strikers has three strikes for one strike by the adversaries. The *décholeurs* try to hit the ball into every kind of hazard. If the ball is hit into an impossible hazard, say over a wall which cannot be climbed, the players settle among themselves where a new ball is to be put down.

As in golf, the Chole ball was teed up for the first stroke and caddies were probably employed to carry spare clubs and balls. A splendid picture of *choleurs* in action, painted by the Flemish artist, Paul Bril, in 1624, is reproduced in *A History of Golf*, by Robert Browning (1955). Emile Zola describes the game as played by French coal-miners in his grim novel, *Germinal*.

See CAMBUCA ; CROSSE ; JEU DE MAIL ; PAGANICA ; TAKOURA.

## CHRISTCHURCH

Shirley, Christchurch, New Zealand. Founded 1873, the second oldest in the country, after Otago (1871). The original course was at Hagley Park, but after 1875 there was a gap until the club was revived in 1891. Hagley Park eventually became unsuitable and after a brief stay at Russley, the present course at Shirley was laid out in 1900. Length (championship tees): 6,533 yards (Course Rating 71).

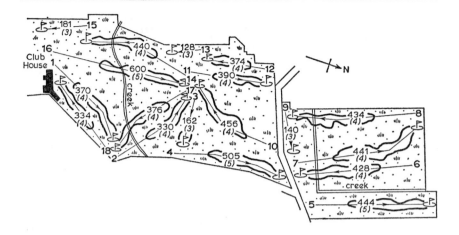

CHRISTCHURCH

## CHRISTMAS ISLAND, GOLF ON

This little island in the eastern part of the Indian Ocean, 12 miles long by 9 wide, has had a 9-holes golf course since 1955. Its length is 2,217 yards, S.S.S. 32. See MALDIVE ISLANDS, GOLF IN THE.

## CHRISTMAS, Martin J. (b 1939)

Runner-up, English Amateur Championship, 1960. Belgian Open Amateur, 1976. Walker Cup team, 1961, 1963.

## CLARK, Clive Anthony (b 1945)

Runner-up, British Amateur Championship and English Amateur Championship, 1965. Won *Golf Illustrated* Gold Vase, 1965. Runner-up, British Boys' Championship, 1961. Runner-up, French Open Championship, 1972. Walker Cup team, 1965.

## CLARK, Gordon James (b 1933)

British Amateur Champion, 1964. Runner-up, English Amateur Championship, 1961. Portuguese Amateur Champion, 1974. Turned professional, 1974. Walker Cup team, 1965.

## CLARK, Howard (b 1954)

Walker Cup team, 1973. Ryder Cup team, 1977.

## CLEEK

A Scottish term for a club, no longer in use, similar to the modern No 2 iron. It usually had rather a narrow face and was used with enormous skill by many golfers of the past. According to H. B. Farnie, who wrote a book called *The Golfer's Manual* (1857), under the pen-name of 'A Keen Hand', there were only three iron clubs—the driving iron, the bunker iron and the 'Cleek or Click'. In the 1890s there were many varieties of the basic cleek, including long cleeks, short cleeks, driving cleeks, lofting cleeks, putting cleeks and 'Carruthers Cleeks'.

The origin is doubtful, but the Oxford Dictionary suggests that it is cognate with the Middle English 'cleche', to clutch; the word, however, also means a hook. See 'CARRUTHERS CLEEK'; NAMES OF IRONS, EQUIVALENT.

## CLUBS, DISTANCE COVERED BY

Each player will, of course, have to find the distance he can cover with the various clubs in his set. Here, however, is a useful guide compiled by Ben Hogan and included in his *Power Golf* (1949):

| | Regular (in yards) | Maximum | Minimum |
|---|---|---|---|
| Driver | 265 | 300 | 235 |
| Brassey | 250 | 270 | 220 |
| No 3 Wood | 235 | 250 | 210 |
| No 4 Wood | 220 | 230 | 200 |
| No 1 Iron | 195 | 220 | 185 |
| No 2 Iron | 185 | 210 | 175 |
| No 3 Iron | 175 | 200 | 165 |
| No 4 Iron | 165 | 190 | 155 |
| No 5 Iron | 155 | 180 | 145 |
| No 6 Iron | 145 | 170 | 135 |
| No 7 Iron | 135 | 160 | 125 |
| No 8 Iron | 125 | 150 | 115 |
| No 9 Iron | 115 | 140 | 105 |
| Pitching Wedge | 50 | 105 | (in to green) |
| Sand Wedge | 25 | 40 | (in to green) |

Allowance would, of course, have to be made for such factors as condition of fairways (affecting run of ball) and of weather (affecting flight of ball).

## CLUBS, LIMITATION OF THE NUMBER OF

See SET.

## CLUB, TOO MUCH

The word club can be used, without the definite or indefinite article, in such phrases as 'too much club' or 'not enough club', to indicate a stroke that is either too strong or not strong enough.

## CLUTCH PUTTER

An expression indicating a player whose putting is so good that he is always clutching a birdie!

## COCKING THE WRISTS

The natural bend (or break) of the wrists that takes place when a club is swung backwards. Some golfers (among them James Adams in Britain and Jerry Barber in America) advocate a deliberate early cocking of the wrists, but the majority prefer the break to come automatically when the hands reach shoulder level.

## COE, Charles R. (b 1924)

U.S. Amateur Champion, 1949, 1958; runner-up, 1959. Runner-up, British Amateur Championship, 1951.

First amateur in U.S. Masters, 1949, 1951. Walker Cup team, 1949, 1951, 1953, 1957 (non-playing captain), 1959 (captain), 1961, 1963.

## COLE, Robert E. ('Bobby') (b 1948)

British Amateur Champion, 1966; the only South African winner and with John Beharrell (1956), the youngest winner of the title. Turned professional, 1967. See YOUNGEST AMATEUR CHAMPIONS.

## COLES, Neil C. (b 1934)

British Professional Match Play Champion, 1964, 1965, 1973; runner-up, 1966. German Open Champion, 1971. Spanish Open Champion, 1973. Runner-up, P.G.A. Championship, 1972. Won first Scottish Open Championship, 1972. Won Dunlop Masters, 1966. Ryder Cup team, 1961, 1963, 1965, 1967, 1969, 1971, 1977. Author of *Neil Coles on Golf* (1965).

## COLLETT, Glenna

See VARE, MRS GLENNA COLLETT.

## COLOMBIA, GOLF IN

There are 20 clubs in Colombia, including three near Bogota, the capital —the Country Club (with two 18-holes courses), the Club Los Lagartos and the San Andres Club. About 150 miles north of Bogota, at Medellin, is a full-length 18-holes course.

In the 1969 World (formerly

Canada) Cup at the Island Club, Singapore, the Colombian pair, A. Bohorquez and R. Gonzales, finished on 575, ahead of all the British teams, South Africa, Canada and many others.

## 'COLOURED' GOLFERS
See NEGRO GOLFERS.

## COLT, Harry Shapland (1869-1951)
Well-known British golf course architect, among the courses he designed or reconstructed being the Eden at St Andrews, the East Course at Wentworth, Berkshire, Moor Park, the New Course at Sunningdale, St George's Hill, Brancepeth Castle, Royal Wimbledon, Longniddry, Stoke Poges, Swinley Forest, Le Touquet, St Cloud, Biarritz, Waterloo (Brussels), Royal Zoute, Zandvoort and a number in the United States, including Pine Valley (with George Crump). From 1901-13 secretary of the Sunningdale Club and for many years a member of the R. and A. Rules of Golf Committee.

## COMMITTEE
"The 'Committee' is the committee in charge of the competition" (Rules of Golf Definition). In its wider sense, a club committee is the duly elected body of men whose duty is to manage the affairs of the club, usually under the chairmanship of the captain and assisted by the secretary. In most clubs the committee is divided into sub-committees responsible for golf and course matters (green committee), the clubhouse and staff (house committee), finance (finance committee) and handicapping (members' handicaps). Many clubs also have a president and vice-presidents, who may as necessary be called on for advice.

The Ladies' section of a club has its own committee or committees for running its own affairs and liaising with the Ladies' Golf Union.

See RULES OF GOLF, Rules 11,36,38.

## COMMONWEALTH TOURNAMENT (LADIES)
This tournament—for a trophy presented by the late Viscountess Astor, a former President of the Ladies' Golf Union—was founded in 1959. It is held every four years for teams of lady golfers from the British Isles and Commonwealth countries. Each match comprises two foursomes and four singles over 18 holes. The first tournament was held at St Andrews and the countries represented were Great Britain, Australia, New Zealand, Canada and South Africa.

## COMPETITOR
"A player in a stroke competition. A 'fellow-competitor' is any player with whom the competitor plays. Neither is the partner of the other. In stroke play foursome and four-ball competitions, where the context so admits, the word 'competitor' or 'fellow-competitor' shall be held to include his partner" (Rules of Golf Definition). See RULES OF GOLF, Rules 37 and 38.

## COMPSTON, Archie (1893-1961)
Runner-up, British Open Championship, 1925. British Professional Match Play Champion, 1925, 1927. Ryder Cup team, 1927, 1929, 1931. In 1928 defeated Walter Hagen in 72 holes challenge match for £500 at Moor Park, Hertfordshire, by 18 and 17. Eventually settled at the Mid-Ocean Club, Bermuda.

## CONCEDE
In match play a player may concede his opponent a putt on the putting green, in which case the opponent is regarded as having holed out with his next stroke. Similarly, he may at any time concede a hole if he considers that he has no chance of winning or halving it, in which case the opponent is regarded as having won the hole without holing out.

## CONGO, GOLF IN REPUBLIC OF
See ZAIRE, GOLF IN REPUBLIC OF.

## CONRAD, Joseph W. (b 1930)

Was British Amateur Champion, 1955, while in England as a member of the 1955 Walker Cup team. In the same year he finished first amateur in the British Open.

## COODY, Charles (b 1937)

Won U.S. Masters, 1971 ; runner-up, 1969. Won World Series, 1971. Ryder Cup team, 1971.

## COOK, John (b 1950)

English Amateur Champion, 1969, being the youngest winner of the title and beating another 19-year-old, Peter Dawson, in the final. British Youths' Champion, 1969. Had a narrow escape from death in Rabat when attempt made on the life of King Hassan of Morocco in July, 1971.

## COOPER, Harry (b 1904)

Went from England to America as a boy and became a professional in 1922. Tied U.S. Open Championship, 1927, with Tommy Armour, but lost play-off ; runner-up, 1936. Canadian Open Champion, 1932, 1937. Runner-up, U.S. Masters, 1936.

In his playing career he was known as 'Light Horse' Harry Cooper, a nickname given to him by Damon Runyon, the sports-columnist and humorist. In a challenge match in 1925, he defeated Walter Hagen by 12 and 11.

## CORFU, GOLF IN

The first club in the Ionian island of Corfu, the Golf and Country Club Ropa Valley, was opened in 1972. Designed by Donald Harradine, it is a full 7,000 yards.

## CORLETT, Elsie (b 1902)

Runner-up British Ladies' Championship, 1938. English Ladies' Champion, 1938 ; runner-up, 1926, 1935. Curtis Cup team, 1932, 1938, 1964 (captain). Veteran Ladies' Champion, 1954.

## CORSICA, GOLF IN

Although golf is not at the moment played on the island that was Napoleon's birthplace, there was a course before the Second World War. Called the Ile-Rousse Club, it had 18 holes.

## COSH, Gordon B. (b 1939)

Scottish Amateur Champion, 1968 ; runner-up, 1965. Walker Cup team, 1965. Played for Britain in World Cup (formerly Eisenhower Trophy), 1966, 1968.

## COSSAR, Simon

Clubmaker, in the second half of the eighteenth century, to the Honourable Company of Edinburgh Golfers. Famous as a maker of both wooden and iron clubs. There are three examples of his work in the R. and A. Club museum—two wooden clubs and a putting cleek. See EDINBURGH GOLFERS, HONOURABLE COMPANY OF.

## COTTON, Thomas Henry (b 1907)

British Open Champion, 1934, 1937, 1948. Belgian Open Champion, 1930, 1934, 1938. French Open Champion, 1946, 1947. German Open Champion, 1937, 1938, 1939 ; runner-up, 1933, 1934, 1935, 1936. Italian Open Champion, 1936. Czechoslovak Open Champion, 1937, 1938. British Professional Match Play Champion, 1932, 1940, 1946 ; runner-up, 1928, 1930, 1949. In challenge matches, beat Horton Smith, 1929, 1930 ; Densmore Shute, 1937 ; with Reginald Whitcombe beat Bobby Locke and Sid Brews, 1938; with Fred Daly beat Bobby Locke and Eric Brown, 1952. Ryder Cup team, 1929, 1937, 1947 (captain), 1953 (non-playing captain).

Henry Cotton turned professional at 17 and at 19 became professional at the Langley Park Club, Beckenham, Kent. Later he was attached to various clubs and has now settled at Penina in the Algarve.

In recent years he has turned to golf-course architecture and has designed courses at, among other places, Abridge, Felixstowe, Canons Brook, Megève (France) and Penina and Vale do Lobo (Portugal).

On P.G.A. committee, 1934-54. A founder and director of the Golf Foundation, to promote golf among the young. Awarded M.B.E. for services to sport, 1946.

Henry Cotton is the only British golfer to have been a successful 'turn' in a music hall. In December 1938 he appeared at the London Coliseum —with Nellie Wallace on the same 'bill'. His 15-minute act consisted mainly in demonstrating shots, on a darkened stage, with shoes, gloves and balls treated with luminous paint and, finally, hitting soft balls into the auditorium with the lights full on.

Author of *Golf* (1932), *This Game of Golf* (1948), *My Swing* (1952), *My Golfing Album* (1959), *Henry Cotton Says* (1962), *Study the Game of Golf with Henry Cotton* (1964), *The Picture World of Golf* (1965). Professional Golf Correspondent of *Golf Illustrated*.

## COUNCIL OF NATIONAL GOLF UNIONS

The C.O.N.G.U. was founded in 1924 following a meeting between the R. and A. Championship Committee and the Golf Unions of England, Ireland, Scotland and Wales. It is made up of two representatives from each union. The chief functions are:

1. To run the Standard Scratch Score and Handicapping Scheme, for which a booklet is issued.

2. To nominate four members of the Board of Management of the Sports Turf Research Institute.

3. To manage the annual Amateur International Matches between the four countries.

4. To arrange dates and prepare a calendar of leading amateur golf events.

## COUNTY CHAMPIONS CHAMPIONSHIP, ENGLISH

This tournament, which began in 1963, brings together all the English county amateur champions for 36-holes of stroke play to decide the 'champion of champions'.

## COURSE

"The whole area within which play is permitted. It is the duty of the authorities in charge of the course to define its boundaries accurately" (Rules of Golf Definition).

Originally the word 'green' was used instead of course, and the modern phrase 'through the green' means "the whole area of the course except (a) Teeing ground and putting green of the hole being played and (b) All hazards on the course" (Rules of Golf Definition). The word 'course' was formerly used to define what we now call 'fairway', as in the Badminton Library volume on *Golf* (1890) definition: "That portion of the links on which the game ought to be played, generally bounded on either side by rough ground or other hazard." Nowadays, of course, the word 'rough' is used to indicate the area bounding the fairway—but not being a hazard. Rough is not recognised in the Rules of Golf.

See FAIRWAY; GREEN, THROUGH THE; LINKS; ROUGH.

## COURSES PLAYED ON, MOST

When he finished a round on the Old Course at St Andrews in 1951, an American golfer named Ralph Kennedy had played on 3,000 different courses in the world. By 1953, when he retired at the age of 71, he had played on 3,615 courses, which is believed to be a record.

## COURSE VALUE

This may be taken into consideration when assessing the Standard Scratch Score of a course and is fully explained in *The Standard Scratch Score and Handicapping Scheme*, prepared by the Council of National Golf Unions:

As the basic Standard Scratch Score is fixed according to the length of the course, in some cases an addition to the basic Standard Scratch Score may require to be made to allow for Course Value. An addition for Course Value will not be made in the case of the normal course, but will be made only for courses with *exceptional* difficulties other than length. In considering Course Value in these cases, there may be taken into account the layout of the course, hazards, whether greens are well guarded or open, whether greens are watered or unwatered, narrowness or width of fairways, nature of rough, and nearness of 'out of bounds' to greens and fairways.

No alterations may be made to the basic Standard Scratch Score for Course Value except with the authority of the National Union concerned. See COUNCIL OF NATIONAL GOLF UNIONS ; STANDARD SCRATCH SCORE.

## COWAN, Gary (b 1940)
U.S. Amateur Champion, 1966, after tie with Deane Beman, 1971. First Canadian winner since C. Ross Somerville, 1932. Canadian Amateur Champion, 1961 ; runner-up, 1959, 1960, 1964, 1968. Member of Canadian team in World Cup (formerly Eisenhower Trophy), 1962, 1964 ; had best individual score, 1962.

## COX, William James (b 1910)
British. Ryder Cup team, 1935, 1937. Well-known teaching professional and television commentator. O.B.E. for services to sport, 1967. Author of *Play Better Golf* (1952) ; *Bill Cox's Golf Companion* (1969).

## CRACK
An old-fashioned term for a first-class golfer, usually one with a handicap of scratch or better. Also used as an adjective—e.g. 'a crack player'.

## CRADDOCK, Tom (b 1931)
Irish Open Amateur Champion, 1958. Irish Amateur Close Champion, 1959 ; runner-up, 1965. Walker Cup team, 1967, 1969.

## CRAMPTON, Bruce (b 1935)
Runner-up, to Jack Nicklaus, U.S. Open Championship and U.S. Masters, 1972. Second in U.S.P.G.A. Cham-

pionship, 1973, 1975. Australian Open Champion, 1956. World (formerly Canada) Cup team, 1972, with Bill Dunk.

## CRAWFORD, Mrs Jean
See ASHLEY, JEAN.

## CRAWLEY, Leonard George (b 1903)
English Amateur Champion, 1931 ; runner-up, 1934, 1937. Won Worplesdon Mixed Foursomes, with Mrs Heppel, 1937 ; with Miss Frances Stephens (Mrs Roy Smith), 1949, 1950. Walker Cup team, 1932, 1934, 1938, 1947. For many years Golf Correspondent of the London *Daily Telegraph*.

## CREAVY, Tom (b 1904)
U.S.P.G.A. Champion, 1931.

## CRENSHAW, Ben (b 1952)
Runner-up, U.S. Masters, 1976. Runner-up U.S. Amateur Championship, 1972.

## CRITCHLEY, Mrs Diana (b 1911)
Born Diana Fishwick, British Ladies' Champion, 1930, defeating Miss Glenna Collett in the final. English Ladies' Champion, 1932, 1949 ; runner-up, 1929. French Ladies' Open Champion, 1932. Dutch Ladies' Champion, 1946. Curtis Cup team, 1932, 1934 ; non-playing captain, 1950.

## CROCE, Alberto (b 1933)
Italian Open Amateur Champion, 1962, 1965. Italian Native Amateur Champion, 1958, 1962, 1966. Italian Native Professional Champion (as amateur), 1960. World (formerly Canada) Cup team, 1972, with Roberto Bernardini.

## CROOME, Arthur (1864-1930)
A county cricketer (for Gloucestershire) and an athlete as well as a golfer. With John L. Low, one of the founders in 1897 of the Oxford and Cambridge Golfing Society, and for some years its secretary. He was also a golf architect, his major creation being the Liphook course, Hampshire.

For many years he wrote about cricket in *The Times* and golf in the *Morning Post*.

## CROQUET STYLE PUTTING

A method of putting in which the player stands astride the line of the putt and swings the putter (usually a centre-shafted club with the shaft at right-angles to the head) in the style adopted by croquet players. This method of putting was banned in the 1968 Code of Rules, Rule 35-IL stating: "The player shall not make a stroke on the putting green from a stance astride, or with either foot touching, the line of the putt or an extension of that line behind the ball."

## CROS, Patrick (b 1939)

French Open Amateur Champion, 1963 ; runner-up, 1966. French Amateur Native Champion, 1959, 1963, 1964, 1965 ; runner-up, 1962, 1967. See BROTHER AND SISTER GOLFERS.

## CROS RUBIN, Mme Claudine (b 1943)

French. Runner-up, British Ladies' Championship, 1968, 1972. French Ladies' Champion, 1960, 1968; runner-up, 1962. French Ladies' Close Champion, 1964, 1965; runner-up, 1962, 1963, 1970. German Ladies' Open Champion, 1961. Runner-up, Italian Ladies' Open Championship, 1960. See BROTHER AND SISTER GOLFERS.

## CROSSE

This old French and Belgian game is, like Chole, a game played with club and ball, across country ; its resemblance to golf is very slight. The French word *crosse* just means a hooked stick or club. In Du Cange's Dictionary the meaning of *crossare* is given as "to play at Crosse or at Chole". As in the case of Chole, the object of Crosse was to hit some object with a ball, not to get it into a hole. See CAMBUCA ; CHOLE ; PAGANICA : TAKOURA.

## CRUICKSHANK, Robert A. (1894-1975)

Born in Scotland. Became a professional in 1921 and went to the United States. Tied for U.S. Open Championship with Bobby Jones, 1923, but lost play-off ; runner-up, 1932.

## CUBA, GOLF IN

It is difficult to discover the present state of golf in Castro's Cuba, but where there were once some ten clubs there now seem to be only two—El Country Club de la Habana, at Havana, and one called Villareal, both of which are mainly used by visiting diplomats and business men.

## CURTIS CUP

Although the first Curtis Cup match took place ten years later than its male counterpart, the Walker Cup, the ladies of Britain and the United States had been playing unofficial matches much longer. As far back as 1905 there were enough American challengers for the British Ladies' Championship at Cromer, Norfolk, to make up a team for a match. Among the visitors were the sisters Harriot and Margaret Curtis, who were to win the U.S. Ladies' Championship four times between them.

Although the Curtis sisters came over for the British Championship again, they did not play in the other unofficial matches in 1911, 1923, 1930. The 1930 match at Sunningdale, however, created so much interest that the sisters offered a trophy for competition and in 1932 the first Curtis Cup match was played. The British team took the whole affair rather lightheartedly and arrived at Wentworth only in time for tea on the day before the match started. The Americans had been practising assiduously, with the result that they won by five matches to three, with one halved, against a team that included Miss Joyce Wethered, Miss Enid Wilson, Miss Wanda Morgan and Miss Molly Gourlay.

The Curtis Cup was presented for

a biennial match and was decided by three 36-holes foursomes and six 36-holes singles, spread over two days, until 1964 when it was changed to three 18-holes foursomes and six 18-holes singles on each of two days. In 1958 the Curtis sisters offered to replace the old Cup with a more resplendent one, but this was happily refused on grounds of sentiment.

The following are the results of the Curtis Cup matches since 1932.

*1932 (Wentworth, Surrey)*
U.S.A. 5 matches; Britain 3 matches; 1 halved.

*1934 (Chevy Chase, Maryland)*
U.S.A. 6 matches; Britain 2 matches; 1 halved.

*1936 (King's Course, Gleneagles)*
U.S.A. 4 matches; Britain 4 matches; 1 halved.

*1938 (Essex Country Club, Mass.)*
U.S.A. 5 matches; Britain 3 matches; 1 halved.

*1948 (Royal Birkdale, Southport)*
U.S.A. 6 matches; Britain 2 matches; 1 halved.

*1950 (Country Club of Buffalo, New York)*
U.S.A. 7 matches; Britain 1 match; 1 halved.

*1952 (Muirfield, East Lothian)*
Britain 5 matches; U.S.A. 4 matches.

*1954 (Merion, Ardmore, Pennsylvania)*
U.S.A. 6 matches; Britain 3 matches.

*1956 (Prince's, Sandwich)*
Britain 5 matches; U.S.A. 4 matches.

*1958 (Brae Burn, Massachusetts)*
Britain 4 matches; U.S.A. 4 matches; 1 halved.

*1960 (Lindrick, Sheffield)*
U.S.A. 6 matches; Britain 2 matches; 1 halved.

*1962 (Broadmoor, Colorado Springs)*
U.S.A. 8 matches; Britain 1 match.

*1964 (Royal Porthcawl, S. Wales)*
U.S.A. 9 matches; Britain 6 matches; 3 halved.

*1966 (Hot Springs, Virginia)*
U.S.A. 11 matches; Britain 3 matches; 4 halved.

*1968 (Royal County Down, N. Ireland)*

U.S.A. 8 matches; Britain 5 matches; 5 halved.

*1970 (Brae Burn, Massachusetts)*
U.S.A. 11 matches; Britain 6 matches; 1 halved.

*1972 (Western Gailes, Ayrshire)*
U.S.A. 9 matches; Britain 7 matches; 2 halved.

*1974 (San Francisco)*
U.S.A. 12 matches; Britain 4 matches; 2 halved.

*1976 (Royal Lytham and St. Anne's)*
U.S.A. 11 matches; Britain 6 matches; 1 halved

*1978 (Apawamis, New York)*
U.S.A. 12 matches; Britain 4 matches; 2 halved.

## CURTIS, Harriot (1878-1975) and Margaret (b 1880)

Donors of the Curtis Cup, Harriot was U.S. Ladies' Champion in 1906 and Margaret in 1907 (beating her sister in the final), 1911 and 1912. Margaret was also runner-up, 1900, 1905. She went on playing in the championship until 1949, when she was 69. See CURTIS CUP.

## CUT-UP SHOT

A type of stroke, more popular in the old days than it is now, in which cut is put on the ball by drawing the club face across it from outside to in (right to left), the ball usually rising abruptly and bouncing to the right on landing. Normally played with one of the steeper-faced irons, but a cut-up shot can also be played with a No 3 or 4 wood or played out of a bunker with a sand-iron.

## CYPRUS, GOLF IN

Unfortunately golf has declined in Cyprus in recent years. Immediately after the Second World War there were three clubs—the Nicosia Club with 18 holes and the Kyrenia and Limassol Clubs with 9 holes. Now the only club open to visitors is the Cyprus Mines Corporation Club, at Pendayia, 35 miles west of Nicosia. The course is open from 1st October to 31st May, and there are 9 holes, with second tees at the 3rd, 8th and

9th holes. Visitors may play there if they have a letter of introduction from their own club. There are British services clubs at Dhekelia and Episkopi in the Sovereign Base areas.

## CZECHOSLOVAKIA, GOLF IN

The story of golf in Czechoslovakia has been one of courage in adversity. Before Germany's annexation in 1939, the game was becoming more and more popular and there were seven courses—at Prague, the capital; Carlsbad; Marienbad; Franzensbad; Pistany; Luhacovice and Trenc Teplice. The Marienbad Club was founded in 1904, partly because King Edward VII's visits to the spa brought many British tourists there; the Carlsbad Club was founded in 1931.

The Czechoslovak Open Amateur and Ladies' Open Championships were held from 1932-38 and the Open Championship from 1935-38, winner in the last two years being Henry Cotton.

Then came the German occupation, followed by the war years and then by the Russian occupation in 1945. By then there were no courses in the country, but in spite of everything golf gradually started up again. Clubs were formed or re-formed, until by 1968 there were 11 of various kinds and the Czechoslovak Open and Ladies' Open Championships have been held again since 1959, either at the Marienbad or Carlsbad Clubs, the winners being Czechoslovaks. It was reported in 1972 that several more courses are coming into being in various parts of the country, including one, designed by Frank Pennink, only ten minutes from the centre of Prague. There is a Czechoslovak Golf Union.

E

**DALLEMAGNE, Marcel (b 1898)**
French Open Champion, 1936, 1937, 1938. French Native Professional Champion, 1930, 1932, 1935, 1937, 1939, 1950. Belgian Open Champion, 1927, 1937. Dutch Open Champion, 1933. Italian Open Champion, 1937. Swiss Open Champion, 1931, 1937.

**DALY, Fred (b 1911)**
British Open Champion, 1947; runner-up, 1948. Irish Open Champion, 1946. Ulster Professional Champion, 1936, 1943, 1946, 1951, 1955-58; runner-up, 1954, 1961, 1962. Irish Native Professional Champion, 1940, 1946, 1952. British Professional Match Play Champion, 1947, 1948, 1952. Ryder Cup team, 1947, 1949, 1951, 1953.

**DARCY, Eamonn (b 1952)**
Ryder Cup team, 1975, 1977. Played for Ireland in World Cup, 1976, 1977.

**DARWIN, Bernard (1876-1961)**
A grandson of Charles Darwin. Captain of the R. and A., 1934. He went to America with the British team as *The Times* correspondent, to cover the first Walker Cup match in 1922, and when Robert Harris, the captain, fell ill, took over the captaincy and played in the match, winning his single against the American captain, William C. Fownes. Won *Golf Illustrated* Gold Vase, 1919; the President's Putter of the Oxford and Cambridge Golfing Society, 1924.

In 1937 he was awarded the C.B.E. for services to literature and sport. He was a delightful writer on golf and many other subjects and was golf correspondent for *The Times* and *Country Life* for many years. He also wrote many of the "Fourth Leaders" in *The Times* and was an authority on the works of Dickens. He was one of the earliest broadcasters on golf.

Among his many books were: *The Golf Courses of Great Britain* (1925), *The Game's Afoot* (1926), *Second Shots* (1930), *Out of the Rough* (1932), *Green Memories* (1933), *Life is Sweet, Brother* (1940), *Pack Clouds Away* (1941), *Golf Between Two Wars* (1944), *Golfing By-Paths* (1946), *Every Idle Dream* (1948), *The World that Fred Made* (1955).

**DASSU, Baldovino (b 1953)**
Italian. British Youths' Champion, 1970; runner-up, 1969. In the Swiss Open in 1971, at Crans-sur-Sierre, he had an 11 under par round of 60, the lowest score in a national Open Championship.

**DAVIES, Edward N. (b 1936)**
Welsh Amateur Champion, 1970, 1972; runner-up 1966, 1969, 1974.

**DAVIES, Pamela (Mrs Large) (b 1930)**
English Ladies' Champion, 1952; runner-up, 1950. British Girls' Champion, 1949.

**DAVIES, Richard D. (b 1930)**
American. British Amateur Champion, 1962. Runner-up, Mexican Amateur Championship, 1957, 1958. Leading amateur, U.S. Open Championship, 1963. Walker Cup team, 1963.

**DEAD**
A ball is said to be dead when it is so near the hole on the putting green that the next shot is a 'dead' certainty. Another use of the word is when the ball falls dead on alighting and doesn't run forward.

## DE BENDERN, Count John (b 1907)

Born John De Forest. British Amateur Champion, 1932; runner-up, 1931. Austrian Open Amateur Champion, 1937. Walker Cup team, 1932. In both British Championships he played very well in spite of suffering, in Bernard Darwin's words, "from the waggling disease in its most aggravated form". See WAGGLE.

## DEEBLE, Peter (b 1954)

English Amateur Champion, 1976. Walker Cup team, 1977.

## DEIGHTON, Dr Frank W. G. (b 1927)

Scottish Amateur Champion, 1956, 1959. Walker Cup team, 1951, 1957.

## DE LA CHAUME, Simone Thion

See LACOSTE, MME RENE.

## DE LAMAZE, Henri (b 1918)

One of France's greatest amateurs. French Open Amateur Champion, 1947, 1948, 1949, 1950, 1954, 1955, 1956, 1957, 1958, 1959, 1960; runner-up, 1951. French Amateur Native Champion, 1947, 1948, 1949, 1950, 1951, 1953, 1955, 1956, 1957, 1958, 1959, 1961, 1962, 1966, 1971; runner-up, 1945, 1952. French Native Professional (Open) Champion, 1952, 1956, 1959. Belgian Amateur Champion, 1953. Italian Open Amateur Champion, 1955, 1958. Spanish Open Champion, 1955. Spanish Open Amateur Champion, 1950, 1951, 1952, Portuguese Open Amateur Champion, 1952.

## DEMARET, James Newton ('Jimmy') (b 1910)

Won U.S. Masters, 1940, 1947, 1950. Argentine Open Champion, 1941. Ryder Cup team, 1947, 1949, 1951; he won all his matches, both singles and foursomes. Famous for his gay clothes and cheerful personality, he was the exact opposite of his friend, Ben Hogan, but they had much success as partners. In his book, *My*

*Partner, Ben Hogan* (1954), he says that "together we formed one of the best four-ball teams golf has ever known".

## DENISON-PENDER, Linda (b 1951)

Runner-up, English Ladies' Championship, 1972. Runner-up French Ladies' Championship, 1972.

## DENMARK, GOLF IN

The game really became established in Denmark between the First and Second World Wars, although the Aalborg Club dates back to 1908. The Copenhagen course is a full-length one of 18 holes, and there are 20 others in the country, including a club on the island of Fano, off the coast of Jutland, and another just opposite on the mainland at Esbjerg. The Danish Golf Union operates from Copenhagen.

The Danish Amateur Open Championship began in 1919 and the Close Championship in 1933; the Ladies' Open Championship in 1931 and the Close Championship in 1933. Both the Close Championships managed to keep going through the German occupation in the Second World War. Since 1949 ladies' golf in Denmark has been almost monopolised by Mrs Tove Palsby.

## DE PRADO, Mme Jaime

See LACOSTE, CATHERINE (MME JAIME DE PRADO).

## DE VICENZO, Roberto (b 1923)

First British Open Champion from Argentina, 1967; runner-up, 1950. Runner-up U.S. Masters, 1968; would have tied but for mistake in score-card. Argentine Open Champion, 1944, 1949, 1951, 1952, 1958, 1967. Argentine Professional Champion, 1944, 1945, 1947, 1948, 1949, 1951, 1952. French Open Champion, 1950, 1960, 1964; runner-up, 1971. Belgian Open Champion, 1950. Dutch Open Champion, 1950. Mexican Open Champion, 1951, 1953, 1955. Spanish Open Champion, 1966; runner-up,

1971. Brazilian Open Champion, 1957, 1960, 1963, 1964; runner-up, 1969, 1970.

## DEVLIN, Bruce W. (b 1937)

Australian Open Champion, 1960; runner-up, 1971. Australian Amateur Champion, 1959. Became professional, 1961. Played for Australia in World Cup (formerly Eisenhower Trophy), 1958, 1960—the winning team, 1958, and runners-up, 1960. Played for Australia in World (formerly Canada) Cup, 1970.

## DICKINSON, Gardner (b 1927)

Ryder Cup team, 1967, 1971.

## DICKSON, Robert B. (b 1944)

American. U.S. and British Amateur Champion in the same year, 1967—the only others to have done so being Harold Hilton (1911), Bobby Jones (1930), Lawson Little (1934, 1935). Walker Cup team, 1967.

## DIEGEL, Leo (1899-1951)

U.S.P.G.A. Champion, 1928, 1929; runner-up, 1926. Canadian Open Champion, 1924, 1925, 1928, 1929. Runner-up to Bobby Jones in British Open Championship, 1930. Ryder Cup team, 1927, 1929, 1931, 1933.

As a golfer, Diegel was famous for his curiously contorted putting style, with his elbows sticking out at right angles to his body—the word 'diegeling' was coined to describe it. His nerves perhaps prevented him from having a better golfing record—in the 1933 British Open at St Andrews he had an air shot on the last green when he had two putts to tie with Densmore Shute and Craig Wood. As he himself put it: "They keep trying to give me a championship, but I won't take it!"

## DILL, Mary Lou (b 1948)

U.S. Ladies' Champion, 1967. Curtis Cup team, 1968.

## DIMPLES IN A GOLF BALL

The average golf ball has 320 dimples. The new hexagonal-dimpled ball has only 252.

## DIRECTION POST

A direction post is put up to indicate the correct line to take if the shot is a blind one to a hidden fairway or green. Sometimes a direction post is put at the back of a green, but more normally the shot is played over it. In the old days blind shots were more common than they are now.

## DIVOT

A Scottish word meaning a piece of turf, cut out by the passage of the club. Hence "Please replace the divot." See ETIQUETTE.

## DOBELL, Mrs Temple (b 1888)

British. Born Gladys Ravenscroft. British Ladies' Champion, 1912; runner-up, 1914. U.S. Ladies' Champion, 1913—the second lady (after Dorothy Campbell) to achieve the double. Runner-up English Ladies' Championship, 1919, and French Ladies' Open Championship, 1912. Her victor in all three championships, when she was runner-up, was Miss Cecil Leitch.

## DOD, Charlotte ('Lottie') (b 1872)

At the age of 15 she won the Ladies' Lawn Tennis Championship at Wimbledon; between 1887 and 1893 she won the title five times. She then retired in favour of golf, becoming British Ladies' Champion in 1904 —the only woman to win both tennis and golf national championships. See BROWNE, MARY K.

## DODD, Muriel (Mrs Macbeth) (b 1891)

British Ladies' Champion, 1913. After the championship Miss Dodd and her friend, Miss Gladys Ravenscroft, crossed the Atlantic, Miss Dodd winning the Canadian Ladies' Championship and Miss Ravenscroft the American. Runner-up, British Ladies'

Championship, 1923, having beaten Miss Joyce Wethered in the semi-final—one of the few times that Miss Wethered failed to reach the final of a tournament for which she had entered.

## DOG-LEG

A hole so laid out that, instead of being straight, it turns sharply either to the right or left at about the place where the second shot has to be played. A double-dog-leg is a hole with two such turnings, one to the right and one to the left, or *vice versa*. In some cases of dog-legs, the corner can be cut by the better golfers, by playing across the angle.

## DOLEMAN FAMILY

They were four Musselburgh brothers, all good golfers—John (1826-1918), A. H. (1836-1914), William (1838-1918), Frank (1848-1929). William was leading amateur in the Open Championship from 1866-70 and played in nearly every Amateur Championship from its inception in 1885 to 1911. A. H. was one of the founders of the Royal Lytham and St Anne's Club and John one of the founders of the Notts Club, Hollinwell.

## DONALD, Jean

See ANDERSON, MRS JOHN.

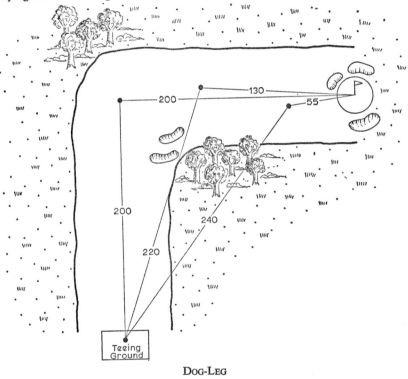

DOG-LEG

## 'DOG LICENCE'

To hand your opponent in a match a 'dog licence' means to beat him by seven and six—once the traditional price of a dog licence in Britain.

## DORMIE (DORMY)

A player is 'dormie' when he is "as many holes up as there are holes remaining to be played" (Rules of Golf Definition). One is always 'dormie up'

—and it is incorrect to speak of being, say, dormie three down. Ernest Weekley, in his *Concise Etymological Dictionary*, gives the derivation from the French *endormi*—"asleep, further exertion being unnecessary". Chambers's Dictionary says: "Conjecturally connected with Latin *dormire*, to sleep ; the player who is 'dormie' cannot lose though he go to sleep."

## DOUBLE BOGEY
The American term for a hole done in two over the par score. See BOGEY ; BOGEY, AMERICAN USE OF TERM ; PAR.

## DOUBLE EAGLE
See ALBATROSS.

## DOUGLAS, Findley S. (b 1866)
Born St Andrews. U.S. Amateur Champion, 1898 ; runner-up, 1899, 1900. A former president of the United States Golf Association.

## DOUGLASS, Dale (b 1936)
Ryder Cup team, 1969.

## DOWNES, Paul (b 1960)
English Amateur Champion, 1978.

## DRAPER, Mrs Marjorie Lilian (b 1905)
Born Marjorie Thomas. Scottish Ladies' Champion (as Mrs R. T. Peel), 1954. Won Worplesdon Mixed Foursomes, with G. W. Mackie, 1952. Curtis Cup team, 1954.

## DRAW
To decide who plays against whom in a match-play competition, or sometimes who plays along with whom in a stroke-play competition, the names of the entrants are 'drawn' (out of a hat, box or other container) and the result published as a list. Used either as a noun or verb. The player whose name is above that of his opponent or fellow-competitor on the draw-sheet has the honour on the first tee. See HONOUR.

## DRAW, PLAYING WITH
A stroke made deliberately so that the ball in flight bends slightly from right to left. This is a type of shot adopted by many top-class golfers. An uncontrolled draw develops into a pull or a full-blooded hook to the left. Also used as a verb. See FADE, CONTROLLED ; PULL ; SLICE.

## DREADNAUGHT
A type of driver that had a brief popularity in the early days of this century. Its main feature was its rather large, clumsy-looking head. It was named after the huge battleships, with big guns, that were then being built for the Navy.

## DREW, Norman V. (b 1932)
One of the only two golfers who have represented Britain in both Walker Cup (1953) and Ryder Cup (1959) matches. Irish Open Amateur Champion, 1952, 1953. Irish Native Professional Champion, 1959. North of Ireland Open Amateur Champion, 1950, 1952. Irish World (formerly Canada) Cup team, 1960, 1961. See WALKER AND RYDER CUPS, PLAYED IN BOTH.

## DRIVE
The word drive, meaning "to play from the tee or with a driver" (Chambers's Dictionary), was used in golf at least in the mid-nineteenth century, but as early as the twelfth century in the expression "driving balls wide over the fields". The golf historian, Robert Browning, thought that golf's 'drive' was probably borrowed from the language of cricket.

## "DRIVE FOR SHOW, PUTT FOR DOUGH"
A saying among professional golfers, indicating that, while driving may be more spectacular, getting the ball into the hole wins the money.

## DRIVER
"A club used in golf to propel the ball from the teeing-ground" (Cham-

bers's Dictionary). The word was used at least as early as the middle of the nineteenth century, for it appears in H. B. Farnie's *The Golfer's Manual* (1857). The golfer in the old days carried not only a 'play-club' (meaning a driver), a 'grassed driver' (meaning a brassey) and a 'driving cleek' (equivalent to a modern No 1 iron) but also a 'driving putter'—a club for playing low-flying shots along the fairway. See BRASSEY ; CLEEK ; DRIVING PUTTER.

## DRIVE THE GREEN
Although this phrase means to reach the putting green in one shot from the tee, it usually connotes a shot that reaches the green at a hole where the par is more than three.

## DRIVES WITH 'FEATHERY', LONGEST
See FEATHERY ; MESSIEUX, SAMUEL.

## DRIVES WITH 'GUTTY', LONGEST
Many long drives with the old gutta-percha ball have been recorded. Possibly the longest on record was a drive by Edward Blackwell, a renowned long hitter, in 1892 from the 18th tee on the Old Course at St Andrews to the steps of the R. and A. clubhouse—a distance of 366 yards. It was done under summer conditions with a helping wind. In 1893, on frozen ground, 'Freddie' Tait drove a 'gutty' 341 yards at the 14th on the Old Course. The carry was measured at 245 yards. On another occasion he was said to have played a shot with a carry of 280 yards. In 1900 at the Balmacewan Club, a New Zealand golfer named Andrew Todd is said to have driven a 'gutty' 428 yards. See GUTTY.

## DRIVING PUTTER
In modern golf, a putter is used on or near the green with the object of getting the ball into the hole. In the old days, however, there was also a flat-faced club called a 'driving putter', used for hitting a very low ball against the wind. As the Rev. J. Gordon McPherson rather rudely put it in his *Golf and Golfers—Past and Present* (1891): "Third-class players use with advantage a driving putter with a wind in their teeth." That this club was used by good players, however, is shown in a poem called "Golfiana" (1833), in which George Fullarton Carnegie describes the famous John Whyte-Melville of Mount Melville:
There to the left, I see Mount Melville stand
Erect, his driving putter in his hand;
It is a club he cannot leave behind,
So well it works the ball against the wind.
Even as early as 1889 (according to W. T. Linskill's *Golf)* the driving putter was not much in use.

## DRIVING RANGES
Since the end of the Second World War, golf driving ranges have sprung up all over the country, catering for those who want to practise without the trouble of collecting the balls or who wish to have basic instruction from a professional or have some fault attended to. Some centres have not only a large driving range, but par-3 pitching and putting courses, and practice greens ; some also have restaurant and bar facilities.

Driving ranges have been operating in the United States and other countries for many years ; in Japan they have almost become a way of life, with hundreds of would-be golfers hitting hundreds of balls by day and (floodlit) by night.

Apart from outdoor driving ranges, there are a number of indoor golf schools in London and other cities, including at least one founded as long ago as 1908.

## DUB
See DUFFER.

## DUCK HOOK
An Americanism, which has crossed the Atlantic, meaning a hooked shot that flies, normally fairly low, sharply

to the left of the intended line. Also called 'Snap Hook'.

## DUDLEY, Edward ('Ed') (b 1901)

Ryder Cup team, 1929, 1933, 1937; manager U.S. team, 1949. President U.S. Professional Golfers' Association, 1945-48.

## DUDOK van HEEL, J. F.

One of Holland's best-known amateurs. Dutch Amateur Champion, 1952, 1953, 1955; runner-up, 1959, 1964, 1971.

## DUFFER

An unkind term, of long standing, to describe an indifferent golfer. More or less synonymous with 'rabbit'. Americans favour the term 'dub' or 'happy hacker'. The verb 'to duff' means to make any indifferent stroke, particularly to cause the ball to roll feebly along the ground. 'Muff' has a similar meaning. See RABBIT.

## DUNCAN, Anthony Arthur (b 1914)

Runner-up, British Amateur Championship, 1939. Welsh Amateur Champion, 1938, 1948, 1952, 1954. Army Champion, 1937, 1938, 1948, 1952, 1954, 1956. Won Worplesdon Mixed Foursomes, with Miss Jacqueline Gordon, 1946, 1947. Colonel Duncan was non-playing captain of the British Walker Cup team, 1953.

## DUNCAN, George (1883-1964)

Son of the village policeman at Methlick, Aberdeenshire. British Open Champion, 1920; runner-up, 1922. Irish Open Champion, 1927. French Open Champion, 1913, 1927. Belgian Open Champion, 1912. British Professional Match Play Champion, 1913. Ryder Cup team, 1927, 1929 (captain), 1931.

The title of Duncan's book of reminiscences, *Golf at the Gallop* (1951), was an apt one, for no professional ever played his shots—even the putts —faster. In his heyday he played in

a number of challenge matches with Charles H. Mayo as his partner. Also author of *Present Day Golf* (1921).

## DUNK, William ('Bill') (b 1940)

Australian Professional Champion, 1962, 1966, 1971. New Zealand Open Champion, 1972.

## DUNLAP, George T.

U.S. Amateur Champion, 1933. Walker Cup team, 1932, 1934, 1936.

## DUNLOP MASTERS TOURNAMENT

This popular tournament, restricted to winners of recent professional events and other invited players, was founded immediately after the Second World War in 1946. It is a four-rounds stroke-play competition and has always produced a worthy winner.

Bobby Locke has won the event twice (1946, 1954) and so have Harry Bradshaw (1953, 1955), Harry Weetman (1952, 1958), D. J. Rees (1950, 1962), Christy O'Connor (1956, 1959), Bernard Hunt (1963, 1965), Peter Thomson (1961, 1968), and Cobie Legrange (1964, 1969). In winning in 1967, at Royal St George's, Sandwich, Tony Jacklin had a spectacular hole-in-one at the 16th in the last round— a feat seen by millions of spectators 'live' on television.

## DUNN, Willie (1870-1952)

Born Musselburgh. Known as 'Young Willie' to distinguish him from his father, member of the famous Musselburgh golfing family. Emigrated to America and, in 1894, won the first unofficial American Open Championship, beating another Scot, Willie Campbell, in the final by two holes. Runner-up in the first official championship next year, which was decided by stroke play and continues to be so.

Willie Dunn experimented with steel shafts about the turn of the century and also with a type of peg tee instead of the pinch of sand that was then universally used.

See PEG TEES; STEEL SHAFTS.

## DURBAN COUNTRY CLUB

Durban, Natal, South Africa. Founded 1922. Length 6,500 yards. S. A. Golf Union rating, 72. The course has reminded many visitors of British seaside links, particularly the holes among the sandhills. Housed S. A. Open Championship, 1928, 1939, 1950, 1956, 1963, 1969; S. A. Amateur Championship, 1928, 1933, 1939, 1950, 1956, 1963; S. A. Ladies' Championship, 1956, 1967.

## DUTRA, Olin (b 1901)

U.S. Open Champion, 1934. U.S. P.G.A. Champion, 1932. Ryder Cup team, 1933, 1935. His brother, Mortie Dutra, was also a professional golfer. See BROTHER GOLFERS.

## DYKES, John Morton (b 1905)

Scottish Amateur Champion, 1951. Walker Cup team, 1936.

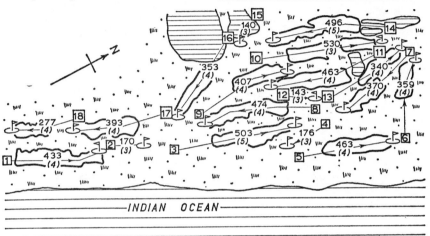

DURBAN COUNTRY CLUB

## EAGLE

A term, of American derivation, for a score two under par for the hole ; associated with the term 'birdie' (one under par) and 'albatross' (three under par) ; also called 'double eagle'. See ALBATROSS ; BIRDIE.

## EARLIEST ENGLISH REFERENCES TO GOLF

The earliest printed reference by name to the game of golf in England, as far as is known, occurs in a song from the play *Westminster Drollery* (1671), by Thomas Shadwell, the dramatist who succeeded Dryden as Poet Laureate (1642-1692). The lines run:

And instead of Court revels, we merrily play
At Trap, at Rules, and at Barley-break run;
At Goff, and at Football, and when we have done
These innocent sports, we'll laugh and lie down,
And to each pretty lass we will give a green gown.

An earlier, but very mysterious and unauthenticated, reference is said to be in a letter written by Henry VIII's first wife, Catherine of Aragon, to Cardinal Wolsey on 13th August 1513, in which she states that all the King's "subjects be very glad, I thank God, to be busy with the golf, for they take it for pastime, my heart is very glad to it".

See EARLIEST SCOTTISH REFERENCES TO GOLF.

## EARLIEST SCOTTISH REFERENCES TO GOLF

The earliest known printed reference to the game is contained in an Act of the Scottish Parliament dated March 1457, in which it was "decreeted and ordained that wapinschawingis be halden by the Lordis and Baronis spirituale and temporale, four times in the zeir, and that the Fute-ball and Golf be utterly cryit doune, and not usit." A 'wapinschaw'—it was spelt in a variety of ways—was (Chambers's Dictionary) "a periodical gathering of the people within an area for the purpose of seeing that each man was armed in accordance with his rank and ready to take the field when required".

In subsequent Acts golf was similarly 'cried down'. In May 1471 it was decreed "that the Fute-ball and Golfe be abusit in tyme cuming", and in May 1491 it was ordained that "in no place of the realm there be usit Fute-ball, Golfe or uther sik unprofitabill sportis."

See EARLIEST ENGLISH REFERENCES TO GOLF ; ROYAL GOLFERS.

## ECKERSLEY, Carline (b 1954)

English Girls' Champion, 1971.

## ECLECTIC COMPETITION

Competitors play two or more rounds of stroke play and count the best score returned at each hole in any of the rounds. These competitions can take place over any agreed time and any number of rounds, although there is often a limit of two in any one week. The winner is the player who has the best eclectic score at the end of the competition, after adjustment for handicap.

## ECLIPSE

A controversial ball of the 1880s and 1890s, made from a mixture of gutta-percha, vulcanised indiarubber and cork. According to an advertisement in *Golfing* (published by W. and

R. Chambers in 1887), "they are almost indestructible, no club or iron will hack them; they fly beautifully, and retain their perfectly round shape; they can be driven farther than the gutta-percha ball, and are quite true on the putting green". Horace Hutchinson played with the Eclipse ball in winning his two British Amateur Championships, 1886, 1887. From its softness, it was nicknamed 'putty' to rhyme with 'gutty'. See BALL, MAKES OF.

## EDEN TOURNAMENT

The Eden Course at St Andrews was started in the early summer of 1914, but work on it had to be postponed until after the war. It was ready, however, for the first Eden Tournament in 1919. This is a match-play event on handicap, the winner now receiving a Silver Cup presented to the R. and A. by the Duke of York (later King George VI) when he was Captain in 1930. Up to 1925 the final was decided over 18 holes, but subsequently over 36 holes.

## EDINBURGH GOLFERS, HONOURABLE COMPANY OF

Although golf had been played at Leith—and golfers fined for playing there on the sabbath—for hundreds of years, the golfers who played over the links had no written evidence of existence until 1744. In that year the Honourable Company of Edinburgh Golfers—also called 'The Gentlemen Golfers of Edinburgh', the 'Leith Society' and other names—was founded when "several Gentlemen of Honour, Skilfull in the ancient and healthfull exercise of Golf" petitioned the magistrates of Edinburgh to provide a silver club for annual competition. It was to be an open championship for "as many Noblemen or Gentlemen or other Golfers, from any part of Great Britain or Ireland" as should send their names in. The winner was to be 'the Captain of the Golf'. A code of Rules, dated 1744, was drawn up for the benefit of strangers.

The competition was a failure as an open meeting, only 12 local men entering, the winner being John Rattray, an Edinburgh surgeon. As players from outside continued to fail to try their skill, the previous 'Captains of Golf' in 1764 petitioned the Edinburgh magistrates for authority to "admit such Noblemen and Gentlemen as they approve to be Members of the Company of Golfers" and to restrict the silver club competition to them. Thus they became a club and play for the trophy a club competition.

Until 1768 the company had no clubhouse, but used to meet at a tavern called Luckie Clephan's. In 1768 a 'Golf House' was built on the south-west corner of the Leith links and the company's business and social meetings were held there until 1831, when the old links ceased to be suitable for golf.

After a homeless interval of five years, the company settled at Musselburgh in 1836, but did not build a clubhouse there until 1865. They had to share the old Musselburgh links with the Edinburgh Burgess and Bruntsfield Links Societies and, suffering from overcrowding, moved in 1891 to Muirfield, on the East Lothian coast, where the present magnificent course was created.

With the Prestwick Club and the R. and A., the Honourable Company subscribed for the Open Championship Cup in 1872, after 'Young Tommy' Morris had won the original challenge belt outright, and their course at Musselburgh was one of three played on in rotation. In 1892 their new course at Muirfield became available and has continued to be used ever since.

The reason why the Honourable Company was superseded as the leading and most fashionable club by the R. and A. is clear: while the Edinburgh golfers were having their course troubles, the St Andrews links continued to improve and, once their clubhouse was built in 1854, the R. and A. achieved stability and continuity.

See BRITISH OPEN CHAMPIONSHIP; BRUNTSFIELD; MUIRFIELD; ROYAL BURGESS GOLFING SOCIETY OF EDINBURGH; RULES, FIRST CODE OF.

## EGAN, H. Chandler (b 1878)

U.S. Amateur Champion, 1904, 1905; runner-up, 1909.

## EGYPT (UNITED ARAB REPUBLIC), GOLF IN

Under President Nasser, golf, which the British brought to Egypt in the nineteenth century, remained a popular game, and British golfers still play there. Cairo's famous Gezira Sporting Club, founded in 1882, has over 5,000 members, and there are also big memberships at the almost equally famous Alexandria Sporting Club, the Heliopolis Sporting Club, the Maadi Sporting Club and the New Sports Club at Smouha City, Alexandria. The Egyptian Golf Federation has offices in the Gezira Club.

The Egyptian Amateur Championship dates from 1908 and the Open Championship from 1921. In the early days the Open was usually won by British amateurs resident in the country, but since the Second World War winners (apart from Bobby Locke in 1954 and Bernard Hunt in 1956) have been Egyptian professionals.

In the days before the Gezira Club was founded, a Scottish clergyman, the Rev. J. T. Tait, of Aberlady, East Lothian, on a visit to Cairo, climbed to the top of the Great Pyramid of Gizeh. He happened to have a golf ball in his pocket and, using his umbrella as a club, drove off. The ball was never seen again—but this could claim to be the first golf shot struck in Egypt. See LAIDLAY, JOHN E.

## EIGHTEEN HOLES, WHY?

The round was fixed at 18 holes quite fortuitously. Both St Andrews and Prestwick originally had 12 holes, and players went round either once, twice or three times during the day.

The first Open Championships were decided over 36 holes—three rounds —of the Prestwick links.

At Prestwick the 12th hole brought you back to the starting place, but at St Andrews the 11th hole finished at the far end of the course, so golfers originally had to play back again to the same greens and same holes in the greens (apart from the 11th and 18th), in the reverse direction, making a normal round of 22 holes. In 1764, however, the first four holes were converted into two and, as the same thing happened on the way in, the round became 18 holes. It was not until 1832, however, that a member, the Chief of Clanranald, proposed the cutting of two holes on the greens.

The old links at Leith, Edinburgh, had only five holes. Their length was 414, 461, 426, 495 and 435 yards respectively, and, to make a round, you played the five holes three times— which must have been quite a feat in the days of 'featheries'.

Blackheath, the oldest English club, followed Leith and also had five holes. When Leith added two more holes, Blackheath followed suit, the length of their seven holes being 170, 335, 540, 500, 230 and 410 yards; players did either two or three circuits. When the London Scottish Club was founded on Wimbledon Common in 1865, they copied Leith and Blackheath and had seven holes; when the course was enlarged, for a time there were not 18, but 19 holes!

Other courses had a variety of numbers of holes. The old Musselburgh links had five and, later, eight holes; Bruntsfield had six; Royal Aberdeen 15; and Montrose no fewer than 25!

## EISENHOWER TROPHY

See WORLD CUP (FORMERLY EISENHOWER TROPHY).

## ELLISON, T. Froes

Winner of the first two English Amateur Championships, 1925, 1926. He was a well-known Hoylake golfer.

## ELYSIAN FIELDS

The somewhat narrow area of safety on the Old Course, St Andrews, between the 14th tee and Hell Bunker, bounded on the left by the Beardies and the Benty Bunker, and on the right by the Eden Course.

## EMERY, Mrs Graham

Welsh Ladies' Champion, 1930, 1931, 1933 (as Miss M. J. Jeffreys), 1937 (as Mrs Emery); runner-up, 1932, 1934, 1938.

## ENGLISH AMATEUR CHAMPIONSHIP

This championship was founded in 1925—the most junior of the four British National Amateur Championships—largely through the efforts of the Royal Liverpool Club, the first meeting being held on its course at Hoylake. The chief conditions are that entrants must be British subjects either born in England, the Channel Islands or the Isle of Man, or the son of parents, one of whom was born there; must not have played for Scotland, Ireland, Wales or any other country or competed in their Close Championships; and must have a handicap of three or better.

The winner of the first two Championships was T. Froes Ellison, and nearly all England's best amateurs have won the English at least once.

## ENGLISH GIRLS' CHAMPIONSHIP

Its full name is the English Girls' Amateur Close Championship, and it is open to all girls with English nationality under 19 on the final day of the championship. It is run by the English Ladies' Golf Association and began in 1964.

## ENGLISH GOLF UNION

The E.G.U. was founded in 1924—the youngest of the four National Unions—and has under its wing 35 county unions and some 1,125 clubs spread throughout the country. Its chief objects are:
1. To further the interests of amateur golf in England.
2. To assist in maintaining a uniform system of handicapping.
3. To arrange the English Championships and any other matches and competitions.
4. To co-operate with the R. and A. through the medium of the Council of National Golf Unions.
5. To co-operate with other National Golf Unions as necessary.

See COUNCIL OF NATIONAL GOLF UNIONS.

## ENGLISH OPEN AMATEUR STROKE PLAY CHAMPIONSHIP

This championship began in 1947 as the English Golf Union International Brabazon Trophy, donated by Lord Brabazon of Tara, pioneer aviator and great sportsman. It is a 72-holes scratch stroke play event, spread over three days. By the time it changed its name in 1957, it had already become virtually the Amateur Stroke Play Championship, among the winners in the first ten years being Charles Stowe (1948, 1953), R. J. White (1950, 1951), Philip Scrutton (1952, 1954, 1955).

Since becoming the official championship, the winners have included Douglas Sewell (1957, 1959), Ronnie Shade (1961, 1963, 1967), Michael Bonallack (1964, 1968, 1969, 1971), Peter Townsend (1966).

## ENGLISH SEASIDE COURSES, FIRST

Although golf was played on Blackheath at least as early as the mideighteenth century, there was no seaside golf with a properly constituted club until the formation of the North Devon (later Royal North Devon) Club at Westward Ho! in 1864 and the Liverpool (later Royal Liverpool) Club at Hoylake and the Alnmouth Club, Northumberland, in 1869.

## ESPINOSA, Al (b 1905)

Runner-up, U.S. Open Championship, 1929, after a tie with Bobby

Jones. Runner-up, U.S.P.G.A. Championship, 1928. Mexican Open Champion, 1944-7, the first four years of the event. Ryder Cup team, 1929, 1931.

## ESPIRITO SANTO TROPHY

See WORLD WOMEN'S AMATEUR TEAM CHAMPIONSHIP.

## ETIQUETTE

The etiquette of golf is as old as the game itself. Horace Hutchinson, in the old Badminton Library volume on *Golf* (1890), put the matter nicely when he wrote: "The laws of etiquette prescribe for us a certain line of conduct not only to our partner in a foursome, and to our antagonist in a single, but also to our other neighbours on the golf links."

The etiquette of the game now comprises Section I of the Rules of Golf:

### Courtesy on the Course
*Consideration for Other Players*

In the interest of all, players should play without delay.

No player should play until the players in front are out of range.

Players searching for a ball should signal the players behind them to pass as soon as it becomes apparent that the ball will not easily be found: they should not search for five minutes before doing so. They should not continue play until the players following them have passed and are out of range.

When the play of a hole has been completed, players should immediately leave the putting green.

*Behaviour During Play*

No one should move, talk or stand close to or directly behind the ball or the hole when a player is addressing the ball or making a stroke.

The player who has the honour should be allowed to play before his opponent or fellow-competitor tees his ball.

### Priority on the Course

In the absence of special rules, two-ball matches should have precedence of and be entitled to pass any three- or four-ball match.

A single player has no standing and should give way to a match of any kind.

Any match playing a whole round is entitled to pass a match playing a shorter round.

If a match fails to keep its place on the course and loses more than one clear hole on the players in front, it should allow the match following to pass.

### Care of the Course
*Holes in Bunkers*

Before leaving a bunker, a player should carefully fill up and smooth over all holes and footprints made by him.

*Restore Divots and Ball-marks*

Through the green, a player should ensure that any turf cut or displaced by him is replaced at once and pressed down, and that any damage to the putting green made by the ball or the player is carefully repaired.

*Damage to Greens—Flagsticks, Bags, etc.*

Players should ensure that, when putting down bags, or the flagstick, no damage is done to the putting green, and that neither they nor their caddies damage the hole by standing close to it, in handling the flagstick or in removing the ball from the hole. The flagstick should be properly replaced in the hole before the players leave the putting green.

*Golf Carts*

Local Notices regulating the movement of golf carts should be strictly observed.

*Damage Through Practice Swings*

In taking practice swings, players should avoid causing damage to the course, particularly the tees, by removing divots.

## EUROPEAN GOLF ASSOCIATION

The Association Européenne de Golf was founded in 1937 at a representative meeting held in Luxembourg.

Membership is open to any European National Amateur Association or Union representing the golf clubs of its country. It concerns itself solely with international golfing matters, such as championship dates, matches between countries and so on.

## EUROPEAN OPEN CHAMPIONSHIP

It is hoped by the sponsors that this new tournament will in time rank with the British and American Opens, the Masters and the U.S.P.G.A. Championship, to form a 'Big Five'. It was inaugurated in October, 1978, at the Walton Heath Club and attracted a good entry with an international flavour. The first prize of £18,000 went to Bobby Wadkins, the younger brother of Danny, after a sudden death play-off with Bernard Gallacher and Gil Morgan.

## EVANS, Albert David (b 1911)

Welsh Amateur Champion, 1949, 1961. Has done a great deal as player and administrator for Welsh golf.

## EVANS, Charles ('Chick') (b 1890)

American. U.S. Open Champion, 1916; runner-up, 1914. U.S. Amateur Champion, 1916, 1920; runner-up, 1912, 1922, 1927. He was the first man to win both titles in the same year. French Amateur Champion, 1911. Walker Cup team, 1922, 1924, 1928. In 1962 'Chick' Evans played in his 50th consecutive U.S. Amateur Championship; he also played in several British Amateurs.

As a golfer he was famous for carrying only seven clubs, although sometimes he took out as many as four putters, because his putting was apt to be erratic. His total of 286 in the 1916 U.S. Open was a record that was not beaten until 1936.

## EVERARD, Mary (b 1942)

Runner-up, British Ladies' Championship, 1967. Runner-up, English Ladies' Championship, 1964. British Women's Open Stroke Play Champion, 1970; runner-up, 1971. Curtis Cup team, 1970, 1972 1974.

## EWING, R. Cecil (1910-73)

Runner-up, British Amateur Championship, 1938. Irish Open Amateur Champion, 1948, 1951; runner-up, 1950, 1954. Irish Amateur Close Champion, 1948, 1958; runner-up, 1946. West of Ireland Champion, 1930, 1932, 1935, 1939, 1941, 1942, 1943, 1945, 1949, 1950; runner-up, 1928, 1934, 1937, 1944 1947, 1948, 1956, 1958. Walker Cup team, 1936, 1938, 1947, 1949, 1951, 1955.

## EXTRA HOLES, GREATEST NUMBER OF

The record number of extra holes played in a leading British match play tournament is 12. In the third round of the British Professional Match Play Championship at Walton Heath in 1952, Fred Daly defeated Alan Poulton at the 30th hole. Daly went on to win the event.

In the second round of the American Amateur Championship at Merion, Pennsylvania, in 1930, Maurice McCarthy beat George Von Elm at the 28th—the 10th extra.

## EYLES, Richard D.

Walker Cup team, 1975.

## FACE

That part of the club-head with which one strikes the ball. "The club shall have only one face designed for striking the ball, except that a putter may have two faces if the loft of both faces is substantially the same" (Rule 2-2d).

The word 'face', in another meaning, connotes the slope of a bunker or hillock facing towards the player.

## FADE, CONTROLLED

A stroke made deliberately so that the ball in flight bends slightly from left to right. Adopted by a number of players—including Ben Hogan—as being safer than the shot with controlled draw from right to left played by many top-class golfers. An uncontrolled fade is a slice. See SLICE.

## FAIRLIE IRONS

A type of club invented in the 1890s by Frank A. Fairlie, son of Colonel J. O. Fairlie—both well-known amateur golfers. The principle of the Fairlie iron was that the goose-neck brought the face of the club slightly in front of the line of the shaft, the main object being to make socketing or shanking the ball more difficult. They were quite popular up to the 1920s. See GOOSE-NECKED PUTTER; SOCKETING.

## FAIRWAY

According to Chambers's Dictionary, "the smooth turf between tee and putting green, distinguished from the uncut rough and from hazards". The Rules of Golf do not acknowledge the existence of fairway, but include it in the term 'through the green'— "the whole area of the course except the teeing ground and putting green of the hole being played and all hazards on the course". Thus 'fairway' is not distinguished from 'rough' —which is similarly not acknowledged in the rules.

In the old days, the term 'fair green' had a similar meaning to 'through the green'; it is mentioned in the earliest code of Rules (1744), clause IV. See ROUGH; RULES, EARLIEST CODE OF.

## FALKLAND ISLANDS, GOLF IN THE

The Stanley Club (9 holes) at Port Stanley, Falkland Islands, is the most southerly course in the world. The group of islands, in the South Atlantic, lies some 300 miles east of the Straits of Magellan.

## FALLON, John (b 1913)

Runner-up, British Open Championship to Peter Thomson, 1955, and also runner-up to him in the British Professional Match Play Championship, 1954. Ryder Cup team, 1955, 1963 (non-playing captain).

## FARNIE, Henry B.

See GOLF BOOKS, EARLIEST.

## FARQUHAR, John (b 1947)

American Walker Cup team, 1971.

## FARRELL, John (b 1901)

Of Irish ancestry. U.S. Open Champion, 1928, beating Bobby Jones by one stroke in the 36 holes play-off. Runner-up, British Open Championship, 1929. Runner-up, U.S.P.G.A. Championship, 1929. Ryder Cup team, 1927, 1929, 1931.

## FALDO, Nick (b 1957)

A most promising young player. English Amateur Champion, 1975. Played for England in World Cup, 1977. Turned professional, 1976. Ryder Cup team, 1977.

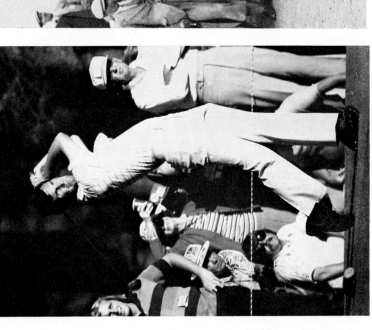

(*left*) GOLF WIDOW. This term, connoting the non-golfing wife of a golfer, goes back at least to the 1890s when this drawing by Harry Furniss appeared in the Badminton Library volume on golf. (*centre*) GREEN, HUBERT. One of the younger school of American professionals, he won the U.S. Open in 1977 and played in the Ryder Cup team. He is here seen playing in the 1976 Masters, which he won. (*right*) HAGEN, WALTER C. The great American professional playing at St Andrews in the 1920s

(*above left*) HEATHCOAT-AMORY, LADY. Still better remembered as Miss Joyce Wethered, Lady Heathcoat-Amory may be regarded as the greatest lady golfer of all time. (*above right*) HOGAN, BENJAMIN WILLIAM, "Bantam Ben", as he was called, has won almost all the leading tournaments in the world

JACKLIN, ANTHONY. Tony Jacklin is seen here turning to his playing partner, Christy O'Connor, after holing his tee shot at the 16th in the 1967 Dunlop Masters at Royal St George's, Sandwich

## FAT

To hit a ball 'fat' means to make a stroke, normally with an iron club, that hits the ground behind the ball, causing too much turf (or sand in a bunker) to be taken and the ball to fail to travel as far as was hoped.

## FAULK, Mary Lena (b 1930)

U.S. Ladies' Champion, 1953. Curtis Cup team, 1954. Now a professional.

## FAULKNER, Max (b 1916)

British Open Champion, 1951. Spanish Open Champion, 1952, 1953, 1957. British Professional Match Play Champion, 1953. British Senior Professional Champion, 1968 (losing to Chandler Harper in the World Senior Championship), 1970. Won Dunlop Masters, 1951. Ryder Cup team, 1947, 1949, 1951, 1953, 1957. Author of *The Faulkner Method* (1952); *Play Championship Golf All Your Life* (1972). Is famous for the elegance and brightness of his golf clothes.

## FEATHERY

Balls made with a leather case stuffed tight with feathers were usually called 'featheries' in the same way that the gutta-percha balls that superseded them were called 'gutties'. The 'feathery' has a very long history, being used by the Romans *(Pila Pluma Facta)* in their game called Paganica and later in fourteenth-century England for playing Cambuca. Essentially the same sort of ball went on being used for golf until the coming of gutta-percha about 1848. It was in the make of ball that these games differed from such games as Jeu de Mail and Pell Mell, where the ball was made from wood.

A good description of the arduous method of making featheries is given in what may be regarded as the first golf instruction book, *The Golfer's Manual* (1857), by 'A Keen Hand' (H. B. Farnie):

Feather balls were constructed with great trouble to the maker, and a cor-

**F**

responding expense to the players . . . They were formed by stuffing boiled soft feathers in quantities that would seem to many apocryphal, by means of a kind of awl, into a stout leather case, sewed into the similitude of a sphere; a little opening being left for the insertion of feathers. This hole was then stitched up; the case hammered round and painted; and the ball was ready for use.

The amount of feathers needed for one ball was supposed to be the quantity that would fit into a 'lum hat'—the tall hat worn in the mid-nineteenth century.

The manufacture of featheries—with the pressure of the awl on the chest and the constant inhalation of particles of feather-dust—threw a great strain on the workman, often leading to asthma and other bronchial ailments. The price, too, was inevitably high, the best-quality balls costing as much as 5s. each—a considerable sum in the eighteenth and early nineteenth centuries. This naturally compared unfavourably with the new gutties, which were soon being sold for as little as 12s. a dozen.

See CAMBUCA; CHOLE; CROSSE; GOURLAY; GUTTY; JEU DE MAIL; PAGANICA; PELL MELL; ROBERTSON, ALLAN.

## FEEL OF A CLUB

This expression denotes the feeling that a club gives when one handles it or, more particularly, when one plays a shot with it. It was more often heard in the days of hickory shafts, when clubs seemed to have far more originality and 'feeling' than they have in these days of matched sets with steel or aluminium shafts.

## FELLOW-COMPETITOR

See COMPETITOR.

## FERGUSON, Bob (1844-1915)

Born Musselburgh. One of the four players to win the British Open Championship three times running (1880, 1881, 1882). In 1883 tied with

Willie Fernie at Musselburgh, after doing each of the last three holes in three; lost the play-off by one stroke after taking four at the last hole to Fernie's two. His skill at approaching with a putter caused the club so used to be called 'the Musselburgh iron'— a hundred years before American golfers invented the 'Texas wedge'! See BRITISH OPEN CHAMPION MORE THAN ONCE; TEXAS WEDGE.

## FERGUSSON, S. Mure (b 1854)

Runner-up, British Amateur Championship, 1894, 1898.

## FERNIE, Willie (1857-1924)

Born St Andrews. Open Champion, 1883, at Musselburgh, after tie with Bob Ferguson, to whom he had been runner-up in 1882. He won after taking a 10 at one hole, finishing the last hole of the play-off with a two against Ferguson's four. Professional at Troon, 1887-1924. See FERGUSON, BOB.

## FERRIER, James (b 1915)

Australian. Runner-up British Amateur Championship, 1936. Australian Open Champion, 1938, 1939; runner-up, 1931, 1933, 1935, 1948. Australian Amateur Champion, 1935, 1936, 1938, 1939. Won *Golf Illustrated* Gold Vase, 1936. In 1940 went to America and turned professional. U.S.P.G.A. Champion, 1947; runner-up, 1960. Canadian Open Champion, 1950, 1951.

## FIDDIAN, Eric Westwood (b 1910)

Runner-up, British Amateur Championship, 1932. English Amateur Champion, 1932; runner-up, 1935. Runner-up, Irish Open Amateur Championship, 1933; in the 36 holes final against Jack M'Lean he holed in one at the 7th in the first round and the 14th in the second round. British Boys' Amateur Champion, 1927. Walker Cup team, 1932, 1934.

## 'FIERY'

'Fiery' (John Carey) was caddie to Willie Park, Jun, for many years. J. H. Taylor has left an impression of him in *Golf: My Life's Work* (1943): "His lean, rather emaciated face, without a sign of hair upon it, was the colour of deep-red mahogany, tanned by a lifetime spent in the open air, and its gravity showed that he derived from it great and almost ennobling contentment." In *Golfing Reminiscences* (1925), William Reid tells how 'Fiery', caddying for Park in a match, was seen returning to the clubhouse alone. Asked what had happened, 'Fiery' said: "'A' wanted him to play his iron, and he wud tak' his cleek, and we've faun oot." In another match a tee shot struck the flagstick and lay on the rim of the hole. "A bad thing for the caddie," said a spectator. "No' for Park's caddie," said 'Fiery'.

## FIJI, GOLF IN

There are already eight clubs in the Fiji Islands in the South Pacific and now an ambitious project is coming into being at Pacific Harbour; Robert Trent Jones has designed the course and Peter Oosterhuis is attached as tournament professional.

## FINLAND, GOLF IN

As it is in Norway and Sweden, golf in Finland is limited to the summer and early autumn months. The chief clubs are in the south of the country—the Helsingin Golfklubi, near Helsinki, the capital, and the Aulangon Golfklubi, Hameenlinna, about 60 miles to the north. The Helsinki Club, which dates back to 1932, has 18 holes, while the Aulangon Club, which was founded only in 1959, has 9 holes. There is a Finnish Golf Union, operating from Helsinki.

## FINSTERWALD, Dow (b 1929)

U.S.P.G.A. Champion, 1958, the first time it was decided by stroke play; runner-up, 1957. Runner-up, U.S. Masters, 1962. Tied Canadian Open Championship, 1956, with Doug Sanders, but lost play-off. Ryder Cup team, 1957, 1959, 1963.

## FISCHER, John William ('Johnny') (b 1912)

U.S. Amateur Champion, 1936, defeating British Jack M'Lean in the final at the 37th hole. Walker Cup team, 1934, 1936, 1938.

## FISHER, Mrs Elizabeth Price

British. British Ladies' Champion, 1959; runner-up, 1954, 1958. Runner-up, English Ladies' Championship, 1953, 1955—both times, and in the 1954 British Ladies', to Miss Frances Stephens (Mrs Roy Smith). Danish Ladies' Champion, 1952. Runner-up, German Ladies' Championship, 1957. Curtis Cup team, 1950, 1952, 1954, 1956, 1958, 1960.

## FLAT SWING

A swing in which the club is taken back nearer the horizontal than the vertical is called flat; one that is nearer the vertical than the horizontal is called upright. A swing in which the backswing is kept short is more apt to be flat than a long swing.

## FLECK, Jack (b 1922)

American. U.S. Open Champion, 1955, after tie and play-off with Ben Hogan.

## FLEISCHER, Bruce (b 1949)

U.S. Amateur Champion, 1968. He was the youngest winner after Robert Gardner and Jack Nicklaus. Brazilian Open Champion, 1971. Walker Cup team, 1969. World Cup team, 1968. Turned professional, 1970.

## FLENNIKEN, Mrs W. W. (b 1943)

Born Carol Sorenson. British Ladies' Champion, 1964. Curtis Cup team, 1964, 1966.

## FLOYD, Raymond ('Ray') (b 1943)

U.S.P.G.A. Champion, 1969. U.S. Masters, 1976. Ryder Cup team, 1969, 1975, 1977.

## FLUFF

Synonymous with 'duff' or the more old-fashioned 'foozle', it just means any thoroughly bad shot. Used either as noun or verb. See DUFFER ; FOOZLE.

## FOLLOW-THROUGH

The movement of the hands and arms after the ball has been hit. Although the follow-through cannot, of course, influence the flight of the ball, it can often provide evidence for the goodness or badness of the shot, for a good follow-through will more often follow a good stroke than a bad one. See BACK-SWING.

## FOOZLE

According to Chambers's Dictionary, "a bungled stroke at golf"; according to the Badminton Library volume on *Golf* (1890), "a bad, bungling stroke". Also used as a verb. A word not so often heard as it was in the old days when *Punch* was apt to make jokes about 'Colonel Foozle' and other indifferent golfers. See DUFFER ; FLUFF.

## FORD, Doug (b 1922)

U.S.P.G.A. Champion, 1955. Won U.S. Masters, 1957; runner-up, 1958, to Arnold Palmer. Canadian Open Champion, 1959, 1963. Ryder Cup team, 1955, 1957, 1959, 1961. Author of *Start Golf Young* (1955); *The Wedge Book* (1964).

## FORE!

A warning cry to players (or bystanders) in front that they are in danger of being hit by a ball. The Oxford Dictionary gives the derivation as "probably for Before"—which was a shortened form of "Beware before!" This form of warning goes back to the earliest days of golf. It is doubtful whether the Dutch word *voor*, meaning 'before', has any connection with golf or even the Dutch game of Kolven. See KOLVEN.

## FORECADDIE

"One employed by the Committee to indicate to players the position of balls on the course, and is an outside agency" (Rules of Golf Definition).

The code of rules issued in January 1956 was the last in which it was stated (Rule 37-2) that "the player may not employ anyone to act as forecaddie, under penalty of disqualification". In the 1968 code it was stated (Rule 37-2) that "the player may have only one caddie," but "may send his own caddie forward to mark the position of any ball".

## FORGAN, Robert

Founder of the St Andrews club-making firm bearing his name. A nephew of the great Hugh Philp, he was also his assistant from 1852 until his uncle's death in 1856. He was one of the first to use the American wood, hickory, for club shafts; it became the standard material until the introduction of steel shafts.

Robert Forgan was succeeded by his son, Thomas, who introduced several innovations, including an ebony putter and, possibly, the 'Bulger' driver. Among the apprentices to the firm were Jamie Anderson, British Open Champion three times running, and Willie Auchterlonie, who was working for the firm when he won the Championship in 1893.

See ANDERSON, JAMIE; AUCHTER-LONIE, WILLIE; BULGER; PHILP, HUGH; WOODS USED IN CLUBMAK-ING.

## FORMBY

Freshfield, Lancashire. Founded 1884. Links with towering sandhills, but also many trees and not immediately adjacent to the sea. Length: 6,862 yards. S.S.S. 73. Housed Amateur Championship, 1957, 1967; Ladies' Championship, 1930; English Amateur Championship, 1934, 1959; English Ladies' Championship, 1958; Boys' Amateur Championship, 1928, 1952, 1964; Girls' Championship, 1950, 1965; E.G.U. Brabazon Trophy, 1951; first Senior Open Amateur Championship, 1969.

## FORMOSA, GOLF IN

See TAIWAN, GOLF IN.

## FORWARD PRESS

The slight movement of the body, usually made deliberately, but sometimes almost involuntarily, in a forward direction immediately before the backward movement of the club in the back-swing.

Although the movement is usually regarded as being one with the hands and hips, the well-known American teacher, Joe Novak, says that it is "a slight forward bend of the right knee with the weight moving to the left side even more".

The 'forward press' was taught more in the old days than it is now because, as Joe Novak says, "it opposes the present-day theory of teaching the one-piece swing."

## FOSTER, Rodney (b 1941)

Runner-up, English Amateur Championship, 1964. Tied English Open Amateur Stroke Play Championship (with Michael Bonallack), 1969, 1970. Walker Cup team, 1965, 1967, 1969, 1971. Played in winning World Cup (formerly Eisenhower Trophy) team, 1964.

## FOULIS, James (b 1868)

A Scotsman who emigrated to U.S. Winner of the second U.S. Open Championship in 1896 at the Shinnecock Hills Club, Long Island, New York. Foulis was professional at the Chicago Club, Wheaton, Illinois. His score of 78 and 74, total 152, was no fewer than 21 strokes better than the winning score of the previous year. The runner-up was young Horace Rawlins, winner of the first championship; his score was 79, 76 (155), 18 shots better than his first winning total.

## FOUR-BALL

See MATCHES, TYPES OF.

## FOURSOME

See MATCHES, TYPES OF.

## FOWLER, Herbert (b 1856)

British. Well-known golf architect. Among his creations were Walton

Heath (Surrey), Berkshire (near Ascot, Berkshire) and Saunton (Devon).

## FOWNES, William C. (b 1883)

U.S. Amateur Champion, 1910. Captain of first American Walker Cup team, 1922, and also of the informal Anglo-American match in 1921. Member of the team in 1924. President U.S. Golf Association, 1925, 1926.

## FRANCE, GOLF IN

France, like India, can claim to have a golf club older than any in England apart from Blackheath, for the Golf Club de Pau in the Basses-Pyrenees was founded as long ago as 1856. Other French clubs, if not quite so venerable, have been established a long time, for the game was given a fillip by the victory of Biarritz-born Arnaud Massy in the British Open Championship at Hoylake in 1907 and in several continental championships. There are now 100 clubs spread over most of the country, including several fine courses in the Paris neighbourhood (Chantilly, La Boulie, St Cloud, the new Saint-Nom-La-Breteche, etc.), half a dozen on the Riviera, and the spectacular Chamonix Club up in the Alps 3,600 feet above sea level.

Apart from Arnaud Massy, France has bred many fine golfers such as Jean Gassiat, Pierre Maneuvrier, André Vagliano, Jacques Leglise, Henri de Lamaze, Marcel Dallemagne, Jean Garaialde and, particularly among the ladies, Mme René Lacoste (Mlle Thion de la Chaume), Mme Patrick Segard, Mme Jean Garaialde (Mlle O. Semelaigne), Mlle Brigitte Varangot, Mme Rubin (Mlle Claudine Cros) and Mme Jaime de Prado.

The French Amateur Open Championship dates from 1904, the Open Championship from 1906 (the winner in the first two years being Arnaud Massy), the Ladies' Close Championship from 1908, the Ladies' Open Championship from 1909, the Native Professional Championship from 1911 (the first winner being Arnaud Massy) and the Native Amateur Championship from 1923.

Golf affairs are managed by the Federation Francaise de Golf and the French Professional Golfers' Association. See PAU CLUB.

## FRASER, Mrs Alexa Stirling (b 1898)

Born Atlanta, Georgia, Bobby Jones's home-town, and a lifelong friend of Bobby. U.S. Ladies' Champion, 1916, 1919, 1920—three times running including the gap for the war years 1917, 1918; runner-up, 1921, 1923, 1925. Canadian Ladies' Champion, 1920, 1934; runner-up, 1922.

## FREARSON, Mrs Diane (b 1943)

Born Diane Robb. Runner-up, British Ladies' Championship, 1961. British Girls' Champion, 1961. Curtis Cup team, 1962, 1972.

## FREEZE

To 'freeze' on a shot (usually a short putt), or to suffer from 'a freeze', denotes the state of mind that prevents a player from taking the club-head back to begin the stroke. This disease has several other names —the twitch, the jitters, the yips, and so on—but they all mean that the player has got himself into a psychological situation that forces him to make a hurried jab at the ball or go on waggling the club indefinitely or otherwise fail to complete a stroke that should be a perfectly easy one. See TWITCH, PUTTING.

## FRESH AIR SHOT

See AIR SHOT.

## FRONT NINE

An American term for the first nine holes of a course, the second nine being the Back Nine. Also called Out and Home.

## FRY, Sidney H. (1869-1960)

Runner-up, British Amateur Championship, 1902. Runner-up, Irish Open Amateur Championship, 1900, 1907. British Amateur Billiards Champion, 1893, 1896, 1900, 1916, 1919, 1920, 1921, 1924.

## 'FRYING-PAN', THE

A name given by Allan Robertson (1815-58) to a favourite iron club that seems to have been a sort of niblick, with which he made many famous recoveries in his matches. His other favourites were called 'Sir David Baird', 'The Doctor', 'Sir Robert Peel' and 'Thraw-cruik'. See ROBERTSON, ALLAN.

## FURGOL, Ed (b 1917)

American. U.S. Open Champion, 1954. With Jack Fleck (1955), Lee Trevino (1968) and Orville Moody (1969), one of the 'unknown' winners of the title. Furgol overcame a childhood injury that left him with a bent left arm, shorter than his right. Ryder Cup team, 1957. His brother, Marty Furgol, played in the Ryder Cup team, 1955. See BROTHER GOLFERS.

*One-Upmanship* (1952).

Although J. B. Priestley, in reviewing *Gamesmanship*, described it as "solemn drollery", the 'ploys' or stratagems, described by Stephen Potter (a keen golfer and member of the R. and A.), are often used on a golf course either consciously or unconsciously. Golf lends itself to psychological warfare.

## GAN ISLAND, GOLF ON
See MALDIVE ISLANDS, GOLF IN THE.

## GANTON
Near Scarborough, Yorkshire. Founded 1891. A heathland course with many of the features of a links. The only non-seaside course to house the Amateur Championship, 1964. Ryder Cup match, 1949. Both Harry Vardon and Ted Ray were professionals here for some years.

## GABRIELSEN, James R. (b 1948)
American Walker Cup team, 1971.

## GALLACHER, Bernard (b 1949)
Scottish Professional Champion, 1971, 1973, 1974, 1977. Spanish Open Champion, 1977. Dunlop Masters, 1974, 1975. Tied British Youths' Championship, 1967, but lost play-off to Peter Benka. Ryder Cup team, 1969 —at 20 years, 5 months the youngest to be chosen—1971, 1973, 1975, 1977.

## GALLARDO, Angel (b 1946)
Spanish Open Champion, 1970. Portuguese Open Champion, 1967. Mexican Open Champion, 1971. Italian Open, 1977.

## GAME, ONE'S
Most golfers have what they call their 'game', a degree of excellence that they feel they should reach when playing normally to their handicap. Often, however, what a golfer calls his 'game' bears little resemblance to what it is in reality.

## GAMESMANSHIP
A term invented by Stephen Potter (1900-69), in his book, *The Theory and Practice of Gamesmanship* (1947). Its sub-title, "How to Win Games without Actually Cheating", explains the object of the exercise. The subject was further elaborated in his later studies, *Lifemanship* (1950) and

## GARAIALDE, Jean (b 1935)
French Open Champion, 1969 (after tie with Roberto De Vicenzo) ; runner-up, 1970. French Native Professional Champion, 1957, 1958, 1963, 1966, 1967, 1968, 1970, 1971. German Open Champion, 1969, 1970, 1971, 1972, 1973, 1974, 1975. Spanish Open Champion, 1969. Runner-up, Swiss Open Championship, 1970.

## GARDNER, Robert A. (b 1890)
American. U.S. Amateur Champion, 1909 (at 19 and five months the youngest winner), 1915 ; runner-up, 1916, 1921. Runner-up in British Amateur Championship, 1920, being beaten by Cyril Tolley at the 37th at Muirfield in the final. Walker Cup team, 1922, 1923, 1924, 1926, captain in the last three years. See YOUNGEST AMATEUR CHAMPIONS.

## GARDNER, Robert W. (b 1921)
Runner-up, U.S. Amateur Championship, 1960. Walker Cup team, 1961, 1963. In winning World Cup (formerly Eisenhower Trophy) team, 1960.

## GARNER, John Robert (b 1947)

British P.G.A. Champion, 1972, beating Neil Coles in the final. Runner-up, Italian Open Championship, 1969. Ryder Cup team, 1971.

## GARON, Mrs Percy (b 1904)

Born Marjorie Parkinson. Runner-up in the British Girls' Championship, 1921. English Ladies' Champion, 1935. Runner-up, British Ladies' Championship, 1926. Belgian Ladies' Open Champion, 1934. Runner-up, French Ladies' Open Championship, 1928. German Ladies' Open Champion, 1931, 1933.

## GARRIDO, Antonio (b 1945)

Spanish Open Champion, 1972, after tie with Valentine Barrios.

## GARVEY, Philomena (b 1927)

British Ladies' Champion, 1957; runner-up, 1946, 1953, 1960. Irish Ladies' Champion, 1946, 1947, 1948, 1950, 1951, 1953, 1955, 1957, 1958, 1959, 1960, 1962, 1963, 1970. Won Worplesdon Mixed Foursomes, with Philip Scrutton, 1955. Curtis Cup team, 1948, 1950, 1952, 1954, 1956, 1960.

## GASSIAT, Jean (b 1883)

French Open Champion, 1912. French Native Professional Champion, 1912, 1919, 1927, 1929. Invented the once-popular big-headed wooden putter that bears his name.

## GATE MONEY, FIRST

The first time gate money was charged at a British Open Championship was in 1926, at Royal Lytham and St Anne's, when Bobby Jones was the winner. As a result the prize money was increased the following year to what was then the highest total of £275.

In 1926, too, there was gate money for the first time for the British Amateur Championship, at Muirfield. For the British Ladies' Championship gate money was charged in 1931 at the Portmarnock Club.

The first time that gate money was charged for any golf contest in Britain was on the occasion of an Anglo-Scottish challenge match in 1892 between Douglas Rolland and Jack White at the now-defunct Chesterfield Park Club, Cambridge.

In America spectators were charged admission fees for the first time at the 1922 Open Championship at the Skokie Country Club, Glencoe, Illinois, won by Gene Sarazen.

## GAVIN, Mrs W. A.

A British golfer who was runner-up three times in the U.S. Ladies' Championship, 1915, 1919, 1922. Canadian Ladies' Open Champion, 1922; runner-up, 1923. Belgian Ladies' Open Champion, 1924. Runner-up, French Ladies' Open Championship, 1922. Swiss Ladies' Open Champion, 1924.

## GEE, Hon. Mrs Adrian

Born Joan Hives. English Ladies' Champion, 1950.

## GEIBERGER, Allen L. ('Al') (b 1938)

U.S.P.G.A. Champion, 1966. Runner-up, U.S. Junior Amateur Championship, 1954. Ryder Cup team, 1967.

## 'GENERAL, THE'

See LLOYD, JOE.

## GERMANY, GOLF IN

Before the First World War, golf was much encouraged by the Kaiser, who always admired British sport; he even provided royal land for the development of the game. Golf naturally suffered a set-back during the war years (there were no Open Championships between 1913-25), but it recovered between the wars, in spite of the Hitler regime, and since the end of the Second World War there has been another boom. In 1939 there were some 50 clubs, now there are over 80; all in West Germany, of course. Several more are planned.

The senior German clubs in age

are the Golf und Land Club, Berlin-Wannsee (1895), the Wiesbadener Club, Wiesbaden (1895) and the Homburger Club, Bad Homburg (1899) —the spa made fashionable by King Edward VII. Percy Alliss was professional at Berlin-Wannsee for some years, being German Open Champion many times. Two of Hamburg's six clubs date back to the early years of the twentieth century.

The German Open Championship was established in 1911, being won by Harry Vardon at the Baden-Baden Club. After 1912 came a gap until 1926, after which the championship continued until 1939, the winner in the last three years being Henry Cotton. The event was resumed in 1951 and has always had worthy winners. The German Amateur Close Championship ran from 1907-27 apart from the war years, and was again held in 1938, for the last time, being succeeded by an Amateur Open Championship. The German Ladies' Open Championship began in 1927 and, apart from the years 1940-50, has continued ever since. Both the German men and lady golfers have held their own in their championships, from the days of Frau Sellschopp in the 1920s and her son, Eric, in the 1950s to Fraulein Monika Moller and Fraulein Marian Petersen today. Golf affairs are looked after by the German Golf Association.

## GHANA, GOLF IN

Since Ghana became an Independent Republic in 1960 golf has declined somewhat. The first President, Dr Nkrumah, preferred tennis to golf. There are clubs at Achimota, Kumasi, Takoradi and Obuasi ; previously there were others at Accra, the capital, and Sekondi. There is a Ghana Golf Association.

There has been a Ghana Championship (until 1960 Gold Coast Championship) since 1929, always won by a British golfer until S. Appiah became champion in 1963. Other Ghanaian golfers won in 1970 and 1971.

## GHEZZI, Victor ('Vic') (b 1914)

Tied for U.S. Open Championship, 1946, with Lloyd Mangrum and Byron Nelson, but lost play-off to Mangrum. U.S.P.G.A. Champion, 1941. Tied for Argentine Open Championship, 1946 (also with Lloyd Mangrum), but lost play-off.

## GIBRALTAR, GOLF IN

The 9-holes Campamento Club, to all intents and purposes the Gibraltar club, unfortunately stands on Spanish soil. At the time of writing the only way to get there is to take the ferry to Tangier and another one back to Spain. The Campamento Club was founded in 1891 by Army and Naval officers stationed on the Rock.

## GILES, Marvin ('Vinny') (b 1943)

U.S. Amateur Champion, 1972. Runner-up, 1967, 1968, 1969. Walker Cup team, 1969, 1971. Member of U.S. team in World Cup (formerly Eisenhower Trophy), 1968, 1970.

## 'GIMME'

An Americanism for 'give me', indicating a putt so short that even the hardest-hearted opponent would not fail to concede it. To 'give' a putt is to concede it, the ball being regarded as holed with the next stroke.

## GLADYS

A jocular term for a drive that is scooped up in the air, the ball falling feebly only a short distance down the fairway.

## GLENEAGLES

Auchterarder, Perthshire. Founded 1925. Fine moorland turf, with many holes running down valleys and set in superb mountain scenery. Length (King's Course): 6,577 yards. S.S.S. 72. Housed Ladies' Championship, 1933, 1957 and Curtis Cup match, 1936. Also Scottish Ladies' Championship, 1937, 1948. Also Queen's Course (6,055 yards: S.S.S. 69).

## GLENNIE, George

Scottish. A great Victorian golfer

both at St Andrews, where he was Captain of the R. and A. in 1884, and Blackheath, of which he was honorary secretary for many years, until his death in 1886, and Captain in 1862, 1863.

When what was really the first inter-club foursomes tournament was arranged at St Andrews in 1857, 11 clubs taking part, the winners were George Glennie and Captain J. C. Stewart, representing Blackheath. George Glennie's score of 88 in the R. and A. autumn meeting of 1855 remained unbeaten until Horace Hutchinson returned an 87 in the autumn meeting in 1884.

In 1882 the George Glennie Medal, presented to the R. and A. by the Royal Blackheath Club, was instituted, being held by the player with the lowest aggregate score at the spring and autumn meetings.

See INTER-CLUB FOURSOMES, FIRST ; STEWART, JOHN CAMPBELL.

## GLOVES WORN BY GOLFERS

A fashion started before the Second World War among good golfers of wearing a left-hand glove of thin leather. After the war the fashion spread and now there are probably more golfers, of all classes, wearing a glove than not.

There is nothing new in the wearing of a glove or gloves. Lord Wellwood, in the Badminton Library volume on *Golf* (1890), in discussing the correct way to grip the club, wrote: "If you examine gloves that have been worn by a good player, you will find that the left-hand glove shows more signs of wear and tear than the right-hand glove, across the palm and between the fore-finger and thumb."

About the time of the First World War many golfers wore ordinary leather, chamois-leather or cotton gloves, and were more apt to wear both gloves than merely the left-hand one. About 1905 or 1906, however, there were special left-hand gloves on the market with no backs or fingers, but with strengthened palms, costing 9d. or 1s. each. Many famous golfers,

of course, from the time of Vardon, Taylor and Braid, never wore a glove of any sort.

## GLUTTING, Charlotte (b 1910)

American. Like her contemporary, Miss Maureen Orcutt, a fine golfer unlucky not to have won a national title. Curtis Cup team, 1934, 1936, 1938.

## GOALBY, Robert ('Bob') (b 1931)

Runner-up (with Doug Sanders) U.S. Open Championship, 1961. Runner-up, U.S.P.G.A. Championship, 1962. Won U.S. Masters, 1968 ; he should have tied with Roberto De Vicenzo, but the latter had a mistake on his score-card, causing him to be credited with one more stroke than he actually took. Ryder Cup team, 1963.

## GOBBLE

An archaic term for a putt that goes into the hole at such speed that, if it had missed, it would have gone a long way past. The hole 'gobbles up' the ball. See STEAL.

## GOBERT, André (b 1890)

French Native Amateur Champion, 1927. Runner-up, French Open Amateur Championship, 1925.

## 'GOLDEN BEAR, THE'

See NICKLAUS, JACK WILLIAM.

## GOLDEN EAGLE

See ALBATROSS.

## GOLDSCHMID-BEVIONE, Signora Isa

Italian Ladies' Open Champion, 1952, 1957, 1958, 1960, 1961, 1963, 1964, 1967, 1968, 1969 ; runner-up, 1956, 1965. Wife of the well-known Italian amateur, Franco Bevione.

## GOLF BALL, EVOLUTION OF

See BALL, MAKES OF ; FEATHERY ; GUTTY ; HASKELL BALL.

## GOLF BALL, VELOCITY OF

In the 1890s Professor Peter Guthrie Tait, father of the famous amateur golfer, 'Freddie' Tait, carried out many experiments into the flight of golf balls, often using his son as a model. They worked out that the initial velocity of a good drive (with a gutty ball) was between 215 and 240 feet a second, although in a letter to his brother in 1898 'Freddie' wrote: "As far as I can remember, he got the initial velocity at one time nearly up to 400 feet a second; his theory is underspin." Nowadays we call it 'backspin', and Professor Tait's theory was that the force of gravity pulling the ball downwards is partly neutralised by the underspin or backspin.

Commenting on this in *The Search for the Perfect Swing* (1968), an account of the Golf Society of Great Britain Scientific Study, Alastair Cochran and John Stobbs write:

The story goes that on more than one occasion the Professor calculated that a golf ball could not be hit more than x yards through the air—only to have his own son, Freddie, sending one ten yards further the following morning. . . . There had to be an explanation; and thus the Professor came in the end to perceive the significance of backspin in producing lift in a shot and thereby making the ball carry further through the air than had seemed mathematically possible without it.

The findings of this scientific study agree with Professor Tait's that a good drive goes off the clubface at about 200 feet a second, "which is 136 miles per hour and which would require a clubhead speed of about 100 miles per hour".

SEE HITTING THE BALL: STATISTICS.

## GOLF BALL SALES

It is reckoned that about 12,000,000 new golf balls are sold in Britain every year. In the United States the figure is put at 120,000,000.

## GOLF BALLS, BRAMBLE AND DIMPLE MARKINGS

All the earlier rubber-cored balls were made with bramble, or convex, markings, and it was only after the First World War that almost every make of ball went over to dimple, or concave, markings.

As early as 1906, however, the Spalding White Dimple ball was on the market. The 'dimple' marking, it was claimed, "causes a certain amount of suction when passing over a closely-cut or rolled green, naturally therefore allowing a harder stroke to be played, and the harder a ball is struck the less chance there is of deflection. The sharp cutting of the 'dimpling' gives less resistance to the atmosphere and consequently the golfer gets a longer carry."

The new 'dimpled' balls cost 30s. a dozen in 1906 as against 24s. a dozen charged for other balls, except the 'Spalding Bob', which lived up to its name by costing only a shilling each.

There were other concave markings besides the conventional dimples, such as stars and crescents as well as the square markings rather like the old 'gutty' balls. See BALL, MAKES OF; DIMPLES IN A GOLF BALL.

## GOLF BOOK, FIRST AMERICAN

Under the title of *Golf in America: A Practical Manual*, the first golf book appeared in America in 1895, only seven years after the first club —the St Andrews Club of Yonkers, New York—had been formed and less than a year after the formation of the United States Golf Association.

The author was James P. Lee and his preface began: "A new game has lately been added to the list of our outdoor sports." Readers will, of course, find the contents of the book amusingly elementary—including such passages as: "There is no racing or any effort to accomplish a hole in less time than your opponent."

It contained the rules, the etiquette and a glossary of golf terms, and mentioned the leading British clubs as well as listing the first 19 American clubs and the first nine Canadian clubs.

## GOLF BOOKS, EARLIEST

The first book solely devoted to golf and how to play the game was *The Golfer's Manual*, published in 1857 under the pen-name of 'A Keen Hand'. The author, a Scottish golfer named Henry B. Farnie, amusingly divided players into two classes according to their build and style—Golfers Agile and Golfers Non-Agile. His book appeared only nine years after the advent of the gutta-percha ball had revolutionised the game.

Some years were to elapse before the real stream of golf books began. Among the earliest of these were Robert Clark's *Golf: A Royal and Ancient Game* (1875): Sir Walter G. Simpson's *The Art of Golf* (1887); *Golfing* (1887) by Robert Chambers and others; James Balfour's *Reminiscences of Golf on St Andrews Links* (1887); and W. T. Linskill's *Golf* (1889) in the "All England" series.

The first comprehensive book on the subject was the Badminton Library volume on *Golf* (1890), edited by Horace Hutchinson. The first American book was *Golf in America: A Practical Manual* (1895), by James P. Lee.

## GOLF BOOKS FOR REFERENCE

The following are among the most useful annual or constantly revised reference books: *Rules of Golf*, as approved by the Royal and Ancient Golf Club of St Andrews and the United States Golf Association (revised edition every four years, available free in a booklet from the Royal Insurance Co. Ltd, Liverpool); *Golf Rules Illustrated*, arranged by the R. and A., 75p.; *The Golfer's Handbook*, edited by Percy Huggins (published from 94, Hope Street, Glasgow C.2, £3); *Golf Gazetteer* (Harmsworth Press, Stratton Street, London W.1, 50p.); *The Encyclopedia of Golf*, a record of major and minor American championships, compiled by Nevin H. Gibson (A. S. Barnes and Co. Inc., 1958, and revised periodically).

Among the books that are particularly interesting to students of the game are: *Golf: A Royal and Ancient Game*, by Robert Clark (1875, revised edition 1899); *The Art of Golf*, by Sir W. G. Simpson (1887); *Golf* (Badminton Library, 1890)) *Chronicles of Blackheath Golfers*, by W. E. Hughes (1897); *The Spirit of the Links*, by Henry Leach (1907); *The Life of Tom Morris*, by W. W. Tulloch (1908); *The Royal and Ancient Game of Golf*, edited by Harold Hilton and Garden Smith (1912); *Scotland's Gift—Golf*, by Charles Blair Macdonald (1928); *A History of Golf*, by Robert Browning (1955); *The Story of the R. and A.*, by J. B. Salmond (1956); *The Story of Golf*, by Tom Scott (1972).

See GOLF BOOK, FIRST AMERICAN; GOLF BOOKS, EARLIEST.

## GOLF CLUB, RECOGNISED

The R. and A. definition is that a recognised golf club is one which has regularly appointed office-bearers. The English Golf Union's ruling is that, for the purposes of competitive golf, a recognised club is one affiliated to the English Golf Union through its County Union or, if there is no County Union, direct to the English Golf Union as an associate member.

## GOLF CLUB SECRETARIES, ASSOCIATION OF

This association was founded in 1933 "with the main object of bringing into closer relationship the Secretaries of Golf Clubs throughout the country, so that individual members might benefit from the experiences of others, and the difficulties and problems which arise in Golf Club administration might be discussed and their solution made available to all". There is an employment bureau, a benevolent fund, various matches and meetings and a journal, *Golf Course and Club House Management*, published bi-monthly and sent free to all members.

## GOLF DEVELOPMENT COUNCIL

This association was formed in 1965 with the object of co-ordinating the efforts of all bodies concerned with the development of golf. Its chief aims are to stimulate the provision of facilities, improve the standard of coaching and to co-operate with both local authorities and national and regional Sports Councils.

The founder members of the Council were: The R. and A., the English, Scottish and Welsh Golf Unions, the Ulster branch of the Golf Union of Ireland, the Ladies' Golf Union, the P.G.A., the Golf Foundation, the National Association of Public Golf Courses, the Artisan Golfers' Association.

## GOLF FOUNDATION

The Golf Foundation Ltd was founded to encourage young people to take up the game. Its scheme of professional class instruction is available to every type of school throughout the British Isles; by 1971 24,000 children were being taught in 1,287 schools. The Secretary's address is City Wall House, 84-90, Chiswell Street, London EC1Y 4TN (638-9063).

## "GOLF ILLUSTRATED" GOLD VASE

This famous 36-holes invitation amateur stroke play competition was inaugurated by the weekly golf paper, *Golf Illustrated,* in 1909. The first venue was the Mid-Surrey Club (not yet Royal Mid-Surrey), Richmond, and the winner was Captain Cecil K. Hutchison with a score of 140; next year, at Sunningdale, Berkshire, the winner was Abe Mitchell, who won again in 1913 shortly before turning professional.

Almost every famous amateur has won the Gold Vase, including Harold Hilton (1914), Bernard Darwin (1919), Cyril Tolley (1923, 1928), Roger Wethered (1927), Bobby Jones (1930), R. D. Chapman (1948), R. J. White

(1949), Joe Carr (1951), John Langley (1952, 1953), David Blair (1955, 1956), Guy Wolstenholme (1957), Michael Lunt (1958), Michael Bonallack (1961, 1967, 1968, 1969, 1971), Clive Clark (1965), Peter Townsend (1966).

## GOLF LIBRARY, BIGGEST

The world's biggest and most comprehensive library of golf books is owned by Colonel R. Otto Probst and housed in the Golf Library, 334, North Hill Street, South Bend, Indiana.

## GOLF-LIKE GAMES, OLD

See CAMBUCA; CHOLE; CROSSE; JEU DE MAIL; KOLVEN; PAGANICA; PELL MELL; RUSSIA, GOLF IN; TAKOURA.

## GOLF MUSEUMS

The United States Golf Association has established a Golf Museum at its headquarters, Golf House, Far Hills, New Jersey 07931. Golfing items of all kinds are housed there as well as a large library of golf literature. Laurie Auchterlonie, honorary professional to the R. and A., has created an interesting museum at Pilmour Links, St Andrews.

## GOLF, ORIGIN OF WORD

It is generally accepted that golf derives from the Scottish word 'gouf' meaning (Chambers's Dictionary) "to strike, cuff"; as a noun it meant a blow. The word does, however, have affinities with other languages. Skeat's famous *Etymological Dictionary* says that golf, as a game, was mentioned in 1457 and "the name is from that of a Dutch game played with club and ball". It then compares the Dutch *kolf,* "a club used to strike balls with"; Low German *kulf,* "hockey-stick"; Icelandic *kolfr,* "clapper of a bell", *kylfa,* "a club"; Danish *kolbe,* "butt-end of a weapon", *kolv,* "bolt, shaft, arrow"; Swedish *kolf,* "butt-end"; German *kolbe,* "club, mace, knob".

There was also an Old High German word *cholbo,* meaning a club, so that *golf, kolf* and *chole* might all have had a similar derivation indicating a game played with a club. The Oxford Dictionary reminds us, however, that *"kolf* was never used to denote the game as well as the implement, though the game was and is called *kolven* (the infinitive of the derived verb). Additional difficulty is caused by the absence of any Scottish form with the initials *c* or *k"*.

There is also a Greek word, *kolaphos,* meaning a cuff or box on the ear—but it is not thought that this has any connection with the word golf. Nor, in spite of Skeat, is there much affinity between Kolven and Golf.

See CHOLE ; EARLIEST SCOTTISH REFERENCES TO GOLF ; KOLVEN.

## GOLF PAPERS, WORLD'S

The following are the chief golf papers published throughout the world:

### Britain
*Golf Illustrated*. Weekly. General.
*Golf International*. Weekly. General.
*Golf Monthly*. Monthly. General.
*Golf World*. Monthly. General.
Also the following available only by direct subscription:
*English Golf Union Fixtures*. Monthly. The E.G.U.'s calendar of all golfing events.
*Golf Course and Club House Management*. Bi-monthly. The journal of the Association of Golf Club Secretaries.
*Professional Golfers' Association Magazine*. Bi-monthly. For British golf professionals.

### United States
*Golf*. Monthly. General.
*Golf Digest*. Monthly. General.
*Golf World*. Weekly. General.
Also the following available only by direct subscription.
*Professional Golfer*. Monthly. For American golf professionals.
*The Golf Journal*. Eight times a year. The official journal of the U.S.G.A.

### Australia
*Australian Golf*. Monthly. Mainly about Australian golf.
### France
*Golf Europeen*. Monthly. Mainly about French tennis and golf.
### Germany
*Golf*. Monthly. German and continental golf.
### Holland
*Dutch Golf*. Monthly. Dutch and Continental Golf.
### Italy
*Golf*. Monthly. Italian and continental golf.
### Japan
Japan has no fewer than six papers: *Asahi Golf ; Golf ; Golf Digest ; Golf Magazine ; Golf Monthly ; Golf World*.
### New Zealand
*New Zealand Golf*. Monthly. Mainly New Zealand golfing matters.
### South Africa
*South African Golf*. Monthly. South African golf.
### Sweden
*Svensk Golf*. Monthly. The official journal of the Swedish Golf Association ; mainly Scandinavian golf.

## GOLF, PRONUNCIATION OF WORD

Chambers's Dictionary gives the pronunciation as *golf*, but adds "Scot *gowf* ; by some Englishmen *gof"*.

## GOLF SOCIETY OF GREAT BRITAIN

This Society was founded in 1955 mainly through the efforts of the late Sir Aynsley Bridgland. Its chief objects are " promoting golfing goodwill both nationally and internationally and providing funds to further the interests of the game in all its aspects". The society has helped to provide hospitality to Commonwealth and foreign visitors and has contributed handsomely towards the expenses of international matches. It has also carried out extensive research into the science of the golf swing and has published its findings in an interesting book called *The Search for the Perfect Swing,* by Alastair Cochran and John Stobbs (Heinemann, 1968, 63s.).

For payment of an annual subscription, members of the society have the privilege of playing, without payment of green fees, at some 20 leading clubs in England, Scotland and Wales.

Spring and summer meetings are held annually at one of the participating clubs and there is a society championship in the autumn. Members receive a quarterly bulletin dealing with the affairs of the society and golf matters in general.

## GOLF STICKS

A synonymous term for golf clubs, no longer in use, but heard commonly enough in the old days. Although usually employed only by the uninitiated, one of the earliest golf books, *The Golfer's Manual* (1857), says that clubmakers "always aim at turning out good 'sticks' ".

## GOLF WIDOW

This term, used to describe the non-golfing wife of a golfer, dates back at least to the 1890s. In the old Badminton Library volume on *Golf* (1890) is a drawing by Harry Furniss, the *Punch* artist, with the caption "A Golf Widow", showing a charming lady sitting gazing out of a window presumably towards the golf course that her husband has found so attractive. At the turn of the century, too, *Punch* printed a poem ('after Elizabeth Barrett Browning') called "The Golf Widows", beginning:

Do you hear the widows weeping, O my brothers,
Wedded but a few brief years?

Today there are such people as golf widowers.

## GONZALES, Mario (b 1923)

Son of a Brazilian professional. Leading amateur in the 1948 British Open Championship at Muirfield, nine strokes behind the winner, Henry Cotton. Turned professional, 1949. Brazilian Open Champion, 1946, 1948, 1949, 1950, 1951, 1953, 1955, 1969; runner-up, 1959, 1961. Brazilian Amateur Champion, 1939, 1940, 1941, 1943, 1945, 1946, 1947, 1948, 1949. Argentine Open Champion, 1940. Argentine Amateur Champion, 1940, 1944, 1946. Spanish Open Champion, 1947.

## GOODMAN, John G. ('Johnny') (b 1909)

U.S. Open Champion, 1933, the fifth amateur winner. U.S. Amateur Champion, 1937; runner-up, 1932. Walker Cup team, 1934, 1936, 1938.

## GOOSE-NECKED PUTTER

A putter made with a curve in the neck that brings the line of the shaft nearer to the centre of the head; a type of putter quite common in the days before centre-shafts were made legal. Also called 'wry-necked'. The modern 'Ping Putter' is a goose-necked type. See PING PUTTER.

## GORDON, Jacqueline (1920–72)

British. Runner-up, British Ladies' Championship, 1947, being beaten in the final by 'Babe' Zaharias. Runner-up, English Ladies' Championship, 1952. Runner-up, German Ladies' Championship, 1956. Won Worplesdon Mixed Foursomes, with A. A. Duncan, 1946, 1947; with Geoffrey Knipe, 1953.

## GOURLAY

The Gourlay family of Edinburgh were famous makers of featheries, so much so that the name Gourlay was used to indicate balls of the highest quality from the late eighteenth to the mid-nineteenth century. Early golf history contains many references to Gourlay balls, including one in verse by Dr William Graham called "In Praise of Gutta-Percha", which ran:

Though Gouf be of our games most rare,
Yet truth to speak, the tear and wear
O' balls was felt to be severe
And source of great vexation;
When Gourlay's balls cost half-a-croun,
And Allan's no' a farthing doun. . . .

Actually the best 'Gourlays' cost as much as 5s. and so did those made by 'Allan'—the great St Andrews golfer, Allan Robertson. Although the gutta-percha ball soon ousted the feathery, Gourlay received a medal for making featheries as late as 1851.

In a Minute of the Bruntsfield Club, dated 29th July 1820, we find: "Mr Douglas proposed that the prize balls in future should be 'Gourlay' balls instead of those given at present."

See FEATHERY; GUTTY; McEWAN FAMILY; ROBERTSON, ALLAN.

## GOURLAY, Mary P. ('Molly') (b 1898)

English Ladies' Champion, 1926, 1929; runner-up, 1931. French Ladies' Open Champion, 1923, 1928, 1929. Swedish Ladies' Open Champion, 1932, 1936, 1939. Won Worplesdon Mixed Foursomes, with Major C. O. Hezlet, 1929, 1930; with T. A. Torrance, 1934. Curtis Cup team, 1932, 1934. Veteran Ladies' Champion, 1962.

## GRAFTON MORRISH TROPHY

A match-play competition begun in 1962 by the Public Schools Old Boys' Golf Association. Venue, Hunstanton Club, Norfolk, with Brancaster in the early stages. Decided by teams of six, playing three foursomes.

The other tournament for public school old boys, the Halford Hewitt, is restricted to 64 schools; the Grafton Morrish finals are played by 32 schools which have reached Hunstanton after qualifying from all over Britain, thus giving a chance to schools not represented in the older tournament. See HALFORD HEWITT CHALLENGE CUP.

## GRAHAM, David (b 1947)

Runner-up, Australian Open Championship, 1972, after tie with Peter Thomson. French Open Champion, 1970. Runner-up, Dunlop Masters, 1970. Runner-up, India Open Championship, 1971. World Match-play Tournament, 1976.

## GRAHAM, John (b 1877)

One of the greatest British amateur golfers never to win the championship, although he was leading amateur in the Open Championship several times between 1904 and 1914. He was a little younger than his famous fellow-members at the Royal Liverpool Club, John Ball and Harold Hilton, and was killed in the First World War.

## GRAHAM, Lou (b 1938)

U.S. Open Champion, 1975; runner-up, 1977. Ryder Cup team, 1973, 1975, 1977.

## GRAND SLAM

The term 'Grand Slam' was used in golf to describe Bobby Jones's unique four victories in 1930, when he won the British and American Open and Amateur Championships. It was also called the 'Impregnable Quadrilateral'.

The modern use of 'Grand Slam' covers the four major professional events—the United States and British Open Championships, the United States Professional Golfers' Association Championship and the Masters tournament at the Augusta National Club, Georgia. No player has pulled off this 'Grand Slam' in one year, although Ben Hogan, Jack Nicklaus and Gary Player have won all four titles in different years.

## GRAPPASONNI, Ugo (b 1922)

Italian Open Champion, 1950, 1954. Italian Native Professional Champion, 1941, 1954, 1955, 1957. Dutch Open Champion, 1954. French Open Champion, 1949. Swiss Open Champion, 1948, 1952.

## GRASSED DRIVER

A term, already becoming obsolete by the 1890s, for a driver with the face slightly sloping backwards, intended to get the ball up more quickly than with an ordinary driver. Very similar to a brassey, but without the brass plate. See BRASSEY.

## GRAY, A. Downing (b 1937)

Runner-up, U.S. Amateur Cham-

JONES, ROBERT TYRE. The immortal Bobby Jones is seen here driving from the first tee at St Andrews, while looking on are Robert Harris (with club), Willie Auchterlonie and Norman Boase (in plus-fours)

(*above left*) JEU DE MAIL. An ancient golf-like game played mainly in southern France. This picture of an eighteenth-century player is taken from a book called *Nouvelles Regles de Jeu de Mail* (1717). (*above right*) KOLVEN. This etching by Rembrandt, dated 1654, shows the interior of an inn with a Kolven player in the court outside

(*left*) LOCKE, ARTHUR D'ARCY ("BOBBY"). South Africa's most famous golfer before Gary Player came on the scene. He is seen here holding the British Open Championship Cup. (*below left*) MORRIS, TOM (SENIOR). Born and bred in St Andrews, he played in every British Open Championship from the first in 1860 to 1896—and won the title four times. (*below right*) MORRIS, TOM (JUNIOR). "Young Tommy" Morris, the son of "Old Tom", is seen here wearing the British Open Championship Challenge Belt, which became his property after he had won it three times running

pionship, 1962. Walker Cup team, 1963, 1965, 1967.

## 'GREAT EXCAVATOR, THE'
See GUILFORD, JESSE P.

## GREECE, GOLF IN
There are only two clubs in Greece. The Glyfada Club, at Glyfada, near Athens, was founded in 1963 and has a membership of over 600. The other club, the Hellenic, is also near Athens. See CORFU, GOLF IN.

## GREEN, Charles Wilson (b 1932)
Scottish Amateur Champion, 1970; runner-up, 1971. Runner-up, Scottish Open Amateur Stroke Play Championship, 1967. Walker Cup team, 1963, 1969, 1971.

## GREEN
In the old days, the word green connoted the whole area of the course, similar to the phrase 'through the green' that is still used in the Rules of Golf. The first code of rules (1744) refers to "the fair green". Now the word is restricted to mean the surface prepared for putting.

## GREEN, Hubert (b 1946)
U.S. Open Champion, 1977. Ryder Cup team, 1977.

## GREEN, THROUGH THE
"The whole area of the course except (a) Teeing ground and putting green of the hole being played (b) All hazards on the course" (Rules of Golf Definition).
This wider use of the word 'green' survives in 'Green Committee' and 'Greenkeeper'. In the old days golfers spoke of 'playing on the green' of such-and-such a club rather than 'playing on the course'.
See COURSE; FAIRWAY; GREEN; HAZARD.

## GREENHALGH, Julia (b 1943)
English Ladies' Champion, 1966.

G

Runner-up, British Girls' Championship, 1959. Curtis Cup team, 1964, 1966, 1970.

## 'GREENIE'
An American method of adding to the gambling in a match, the 'greenie' being won by the player whose tee shot at a short hole is on the green and nearest to the hole. See 'NASSAU'; 'SYNDICATE'.

## GREENSOME
A type of four-ball match, not recognised in the Rules of Golf, in which all four players drive and then the two sides select the ball with which they wish to continue playing the hole. Normally, of course, the longer drive would be chosen, so long as it is in a suitable place; if one partner has a particularly good tee shot, the other partner need not drive if he so wishes. Also called 'Canadian Foursome' or 'Selective Scotch Ball'. See MATCHES, TYPES OF.

## GREGSON, Malcolm (b 1943)
British Assistant Professionals' Champion, 1964. Ryder Cup team, 1967. World (formerly Canada) Cup team, 1967.

## GRENADA, GOLF IN
The Grenada Club is at St George's, the capital of this West Indian island. It was founded in 1923 and has a 9-holes course.

## GRIP
This has three meanings—(a) the way in which the player grasps the club; (b) the part of the shaft of the club, covered with leather, rubber or other material, by which the club is grasped; (c) the actual material.

## GRIP, TYPES OF
There are three main ways of gripping the club (interpreted here for right-handed golfers):
1. The overlapping grip (often called the Vardon grip), in which the little finger of the right hand overlaps the index finger of the left hand, and does not touch the grip of the club at all.

2. The interlocking grip, in which the little finger of the right hand interlocks with the index finger of the left hand, and again is not in contact with the grip of the club.

3. The two-handed grip, in which both hands lie separately on the shaft and are not joined in any way.

There are slight variations in these three basic grips, including that of the Irish professional, Harry Bradshaw, who has the three last fingers of his right hand overlapping the left hand. There are also some players who grip the club with the left hand below the right; this grip is more commonly used in putting, particularly by golfers who have lost confidence when using the orthodox grip with the right hand below the left. Also for putting many golfers use the reverse overlapping grip, with the index finger of the left hand overlapping the little finger of the right hand; Walter Hagen used this putting grip.

The most popular grip—the overlapping—was used by the famous Scottish amateurs, Leslie Balfour-Melville and John Laidlay, and others, before Vardon's time, but he certainly popularised it. The two-handed (cricketer's) grip was used almost universally up to the 1890s and continued to be used by such players as Cyril Tolley and Dai Rees. The interlocking grip was used by the Whitcombe brothers, Francis Ouimet and Gene Sarazen, among others, and is to be found quite often among modern professionals, including Jack Nicklaus and Bernard Gallacher. See LEFT HAND BELOW RIGHT.

## GROOVED SWING

An Americanism, to describe a good swing that is so much in a metaphorical groove that the player can go on repeating it with every stroke.

## GROUND SCORE

See BOGEY.

## GROUND THE CLUB

To place the clubhead on the sur-face of the ground behind the ball, preparatory to making a stroke. See RULES OF GOLF, Rules 17, 27, 33.

## GUILFORD, Jesse P. (b 1894)

U.S. Amateur Champion, 1921. Walker Cup team, 1922, 1924, 1926. For his terrific hitting he was nicknamed the 'Boston Siege Gun' and the 'Great Excavator'.

## GULDAHL, Ralph (b 1912)

U.S. Open Champion, 1937, 1938; runner-up, 1933. Won U.S. Masters, 1939; runner-up, 1937, 1938. Runner-up, Canadian Open Championship, 1939. Ryder Cup team, 1937.

## GULLANE

Gullane, East Lothian. Founded 1859. Typical linksland. Length (No 1 Course): 6,461 yards. S.S.S. 71. Housed Ladies' Championship, 1897, 1947, 1970. Boys' Amateur Championship, 1965. Also Scottish Ladies' and Professional Championships. Also Nos 2 and 3 Courses (6,021 yards, S.S.S. 69; and 5,079 yards, S.S.S. 64).

## GUNDERSON, JoAnne

See CARNER, MRS D. R.

## GUNN, Watts (b 1904)

Runner-up, U.S. Amateur Championship, 1925, losing in the final to Bobby Jones, his friend and mentor. Walker Cup team, 1926, 1928.

## GUTERMANN, Dr Peter (b 1933)

Swiss Open Amateur Champion, 1957, 1964, 1965; runner-up, 1953, 1966. Swiss National Amateur Champion, 1953, 1957, 1963, 1965, 1969, 1970; runner-up, 1954, 1964, 1971. Represented Switzerland in World Cup (formerly Eisenhower Trophy) and other international events.

## GUTTY

The golf ball made of gutta-percha, a rubber-like substance obtained chiefly from the latex of certain Malaysian trees. The gutty replaced the ball made from a leather cover stuffed with feathers about 1848 and was in turn replaced about 1902 with the rubber-cored ball. The pioneer was a Rev. Robert Adams Paterson, who made some balls out of gutta-percha used as packing round a marble statue sent to him from India. His 'Paterson's Patent' was not a success, but the possibilities of the material were soon widely realised—and the 'feathery' was doomed.

In the 1880s and 1890s there were dozens of different makes of gutty, British and American; C. B. Macdonald, who did much to popularise golf in America, said in *Scotland's Gift—Golf* (1928) that he had a list of 166 makes.

The first gutty balls flew badly when new, but improved after the surface became marked with blows of the club. Realising this, makers hammered them with a chisel, but before long they were made in moulds that gave them a regular pattern of criss-crossing lines.

See BALL, MAKES OF; FEATHERY; HASKELL BALL; GOURLAY.

## GUYANA, GOLF IN

The only club in the South American country of Guyana is the Mackenzie Club, at Mackenzie, founded in 1956. When the country was called British Guiana there was also the Georgetown Club, founded in 1923, just outside the capital city.

## HAAS, Fred (b 1916)

One of the few American golfers to play in both Walker Cup (1938) and Ryder Cup (1953) teams. Turned professional, 1945. U.S. Senior Professional Champion, 1960, defeating D. J. Rees in the World Senior Championship. See WALKER AND RYDER CUPS, PLAYED IN BOTH.

## HAGEN, Walter Charles (1892-1969)

The greatest figure in American and international professional golf immediately before the First World War and through the 1920s. U.S. Open Champion, 1914, 1919; runner-up, 1921. U.S.P.G.A. Champion, 1921, 1924, 1925, 1926, 1927. British Open Champion, 1922, 1924, 1928, 1929. Canadian Open Champion, 1931; runner-up, 1928. French Open Champion, 1920. Belgian Open Champion, 1924. Played in the 1921 and 1926 matches between British and American professionals that led to the Ryder Cup series and captained the American Ryder Cup team, 1927, 1929, 1931, 1933, 1935; non-playing captain, 1937. Played in a number of famous challenge matches, in one losing to Archie Compston by 18 and 17 and in another beating Bobby Jones by 11 and 10.

Hagen did much to raise the status of professional golfers and many stories are told of his showmanship and flamboyance. At one tournament where professionals were not allowed to use the clubhouse, he put on his golf clothes in a Rolls Royce parked just outside the door. He once said: "I never wanted to be a millionaire— just to live like one"; 'Chick' Evans, the great American amateur, once said: "Hagen's in golf to live—not to make a living"; and 'The Haig', as he was called, summed up his philosophy thus: "You're here only for a short time. Don't hurry; don't worry—and be sure to smell the flowers along the way."

Hagen could be said to have invented the pullover or cardigan for playing golf in; before he made them popular—in colours either matching or contrasting with his plus-four stockings—golfers had always worn a coat of some kind, often old and disreputable. He also popularised the black-and-white golf shoes that are still fashionable. He was the first golfer to employ a manager—Robert E. Harlow. In 1937-8 he went round the world with the trick-shot expert, Joe Kirkwood, giving exhibitions—a tour that did much to spread the golf idea. Author of *The Walter Hagen Story* (1957).

## 'HAIG, THE'

See HAGEN, WALTER CHARLES.

## HALF

"A hole is halved if each side holes out in the same number of strokes" (Rules of Golf). A game is halved when each side has either halved every hole or won the same number of holes (in match play) or taken the same number of strokes (if calculated by stroke play). In all cases, allowance having been made for handicapping. See RULES OF GOLF, Rules 6, 12.

## HALF ONE

In the old days, to give 'half one' in handicap meant to give a stroke every other hole; to give 'a third' meant to give a stroke every third hole. Nowadays, when handicaps are more official, the better player normally gives three-quarters of the difference in handicap to the weaker player. See HANDICAP ALLOWANCE FOR MATCH PLAY.

## HALFORD HEWITT CHALLENGE CUP

This famous competition for public school old boys was inaugurated in 1924 by a very keen Carthusian named Halford Hewitt—known to everybody as 'Hal'. It is the world's largest tournament, 640 players being the usual number, in teams of 10 a side from 64 public schools in England and Scotland. It is played by foursomes matches.

In the first year of its inception, the cup was played for, round by round, on different courses, but in 1925 the present system was fixed, all matches being played over three days at the Royal Cinque Ports Club, Deal, of which 'Hal' was a member of long standing. Later, as more schools entered teams, it had to be spread over four days and Royal St George's, Sandwich, was brought in to accommodate part of the first round.

Innumerable stories are told about strange happenings at the Halford Hewitt, including one about a school that found itself a man short on the first tee. The only handy camp-follower was aged 80, but he was quickly found some clubs and suitable clothes and sent out to play. The fact that defeat was heavy made no difference to the spirit of the gesture. See GRAFTON MORRISH TOURNAMENT.

## HALF SHOT

In the old days golfers played a 'half shot' with an iron, meaning that they played it with only about half the maximum strength. They also spoke of a 'three quarter shot or stroke' or even a 'quarter stroke', according to this quotation:

Alike correct whatever may befall,
Swipe, Iron, Putter, Quarter-stroke and all.

With modern graded irons golfers seldom need to play such things as a half shot.

## HALIBURTON, Thomas Bruce (1915-1975)

Runner-up, Scottish Professional Championship, 1938. Runner-up, Spanish Open Championship, 1952. Runner-up, British Professional Match Play Championship, 1957. Ryder Cup team, 1961, 1963. Played for Scotland in World (formerly Canada) Cup, 1954. Author of *Rabbit into Tiger* (1963).

## HAMILTON, Edward D. (b 1910)

Scottish Amateur Champion, 1936, 1938.

## HAMILTON, Robert ('Bob') (b 1919)

U.S.P.G.A. Champion, 1944, beating Byron Nelson in the final. Ryder Cup team, 1949.

## HAMLIN, Shelly (b 1949)

Runner-up, U.S. Ladies' Championship, 1969. Curtis Cup team, 1968, 1970.

## HANDICAP ALLOWANCE FOR MATCH PLAY

In singles, three-quarters of the difference between the handicaps is given; in foursomes, three-eighths. Half-strokes or over are counted as one, smaller fractions are disregarded. See HALF ONE; LAMB, HENRY; PURVES, W. LAIDLAW.

## HANSON, Beverly (b 1926)

U.S. Ladies' Champion, 1950. Curtis Cup team, 1950. Turned professional, 1951.

## HARBERT, M. R. ('Chick') (b 1915)

U.S.P.G.A. Champion, 1954; runner-up, 1947, 1952. Ryder Cup team, 1949, 1955 (captain).

## HARMON, Claude (b 1921)

Won U.S. Masters, 1948, by a record margin of five strokes that was equalled only by Ben Hogan in 1954.

## HARPER, Chandler (b 1914)

U.S.P.G.A. Champion, 1950. U.S. Senior Professional Champion, 1968, defeating Max Faulkner in World Senior Championship. Ryder Cup team, 1955.

## HARRIMAN, Herbert M. (b 1871)

U.S. Amateur Champion, 1899—the second native-born American to gain the title. In the final he beat the holder, Findley S. Douglas, by 3 and 2.

## HARRIS, John D. (b 1912)

Famous golf course architect and head of firm of Harris, Thomson, Wolveridge and Associates—the Thomson being Peter Thomson. Designer of many courses in Britain, the Continent, the West Indies and the South Pacific.

## HARRIS, Labron E. (b 1941)

U.S. Amateur Champion, 1962. Walker Cup team, 1963. World Cup (formerly Eisenhower Trophy) team, 1962.

## HARRIS, Mrs Marley (b 1928)

As Mrs Spearman, British Ladies' Champion, 1961, 1962. English Ladies' Champion, 1964. Runner-up, Worplesdon Mixed Foursomes, with J. C. E. Atkins, 1953; with Alan Thirwell, 1964, Curtis Cup team, 1962, 1964.

## HARRIS, Robert (b 1882)

British Amateur Champion, 1925; runner-up, 1913, 1923. Won *Golf Illustrated* Gold Vase, 1911, 1912. Captain, Walker Cup team in first two years, 1922 and 1923, and again in 1926. Author of *Sixty Years of Golf* (1953).

## HARRISON, E. J. ('Dutch') (b 1910)

American. Canadian Open Champion, 1949. Ryder Cup team, 1947, 1949.

## HARRY VARDON TROPHY

Both the British and the American Professional Golfers' Associations have an annual Harry Vardon Trophy for the association members who have the best average scores in all the major tournaments of the year. These tournaments are designated by the association committees respectively. Both the British and American awards date from 1937, the year of Vardon's death, the American one being a successor to the Harry A. Rodix Trophy, instituted in 1934.

The British award takes the form of a statuette of Vardon, and the American version is a large bronze-coloured plaque.

## HASKELL BALL

The rubber-cored ball superseded the solid 'gutty' ball from 1901 onwards. Its invention by Coburn Haskell, of Cleveland, Ohio, was quite fortuitous. One day in 1898 he visited a golfing friend, Bertram Wirk, President of the Goodrich Rubber Co., at his factory at Akron, Ohio. Between them they saw the possibilities of a golf ball wound with rubber yarn in the same way that the baseball was wound with wool yarn. They wound some balls by hand, covering them with gutta-percha (later balata), and made some experiments with them. They saw that the rubber would have to be wound under tension and went on experimenting for the next three years until they had a marketable proposition.

The first triumph of the new ball was in the U.S. Amateur Championship in the autumn of 1901, when it was used by the victor, Walter J. Travis, at Atlantic City. Out of the 124 entrants, only 20 used the Haskell, but Travis was one of them. In the 1902 British Open Championship next spring, Sandy Herd won with the new ball, although Vardon—the runner-up—and many other great players stuck to the gutty. This, however, was really the end of the gutty and the rubber-cored ball had come to stay.

As soon as it was realised that the Haskell would supersede the gutty, the inventors were involved in law-suits to try to protect the patent. In England the case went as far as the House of Lords before a decision was made that the rubber-cored ball was not patentable. Needless to say, there were soon dozens of types of ball on the market. See BALL, MAKES OF; FEATHERY; GUTTY.

## HASTINGS, Mrs J. L. (b 1934)

Born Dorothea Sommerville. Scottish Ladies' Champion, 1958; runner-up, 1960. Curtis Cup team reserve, 1958.

## HAVERS, Arthur Gladstone (b 1898)

British Open Champion, 1923. Ryder Cup team, 1927, 1931, 1933. In 1923, during a tour of America, defeated Bobby Jones by 2 and 1 in a 36-holes challenge match and Gene Sarazen by 5 and 4 in a 72-holes match.

## HAWAIIAN ISLANDS, GOLF IN THE

Golf has been played in Hawaii since the American annexation in 1898. There are several courses, including the Oahu Country Club (called after the island on which Honolulu, the capital, is situated), the Moanalua Club, Honolulu, and the Kukuiolono Park Club, on the island of Kauai, some 60 miles from Oahu. SEE PUNG, MRS JACQUELINE.

## HAWTREY, Beryl (Mrs F. Cautley)

Runner-up in first English Ladies' Championship, 1912; runner-up, British Ladies' Championship, 1924.

## HAYES, Dale (b 1952)

South African Amateur Stroke Play Champion, 1967, 1970. Scottish Open Amateur Stroke Play Champion, 1970. German Open Amateur Champion, 1969. Spanish Open Champion, 1971. French Open Champion, 1978. Italian Open Champion, 1978.

## HAZARDS

The Rules of Golf definition is:

Any bunker or water hazard. Bare patches, scrapes, roads, tracks and paths are not hazards.

(a) A 'bunker' is any area of bare ground, often a depression, which is usually covered with sand. Grass-covered ground bordering or within a bunker is *not* part of the hazard.

(b) A 'water hazard' is any sea, lake, pond, river, ditch, surface drainage ditch or other open water course (regardless of whether or not it contains water), and anything of a similar nature. All ground or water within the margin of a water hazard, whether or not it be covered with any growing substance, is part of the water hazard. The margin of a water hazard is deemed to extend vertically upwards.

(c) A 'lateral water hazard' is a water hazard or that part of a water hazard running approximately parallel to the line of play and so situated that it is not possible or is deemed by the Committee to be impracticable to drop a ball behind the water hazard and keep the spot at which the ball last crossed the hazard margin between the player and the hole. The committee may declare any water hazard or any part of a water hazard to be a lateral water hazard.

(d) It is the duty of the Committee in charge of a course to define accurately the extent of the hazards and water hazards when there is any doubt. That part of a hazard to be played as a lateral water hazard should be distinctively marked. Stakes and lines defining the margins of hazards are not in the hazards.

Hazards were recognised in the first code of rules (1744) and by 1891 were elaborated to include "any bunker of whatever nature: water, sand, loose earth, molehills, paths, roads or railways, whins, bushes, rushes, rabbit scrapes, fences, ditches, or anything which is not the ordinary green of the course, except sand blown onto the grass by wind, or sprinkled on grass for the preservation of the links, or snow or ice, or

bare patches on the course". See
BUNKER ; RULES, FIRST CODE OF.

## HEAD-UP

Raising the head and taking the
eyes off the ball before the stroke is
completed, normally resulting in a
poor stroke. This fault can occur with
any sort of shot, even a putt.

## HEAFNER, Clayton (1920-60)

Runner-up, U.S. Open Championship, 1949, 1951. Ryder Cup team,
1949, 1951.

## HEATHCOAT-AMORY, Lady (b 1901)

Born Joyce Wethered. British
Ladies' Champion, 1922, 1924, 1925,
1929 ; runner-up, 1921. English Ladies'
Champion, 1920, 1921, 1922, 1923,
1924. Runner-up, French Ladies' Open
Championship, 1921. Won Worplesdon Mixed Foursomes, with Roger
Wethered, 1922 ; with Cyril Tolley,
1923, 1927 ; with J. S. F. Morrison,
1928 ; with the Hon. Michael Scott,
1931 ; with Raymond Oppenheimer,
1932 ; with Bernard Darwin, 1933 ;
with the Hon. Thomas Coke, 1936 ;
runner-up, with Roger Wethered,
1921. Curtis Cup team, 1932.

Comparisons in such matters are, of
course, impossible, but Lady Heathcoat-Amory may well be regarded as
the greatest lady golfer of all time.
It was claimed that, in her heyday,
she could have played No 4 or 5 in
the British Walker Cup team. Any
claim for Lady Heathcoat-Amory in
no way belittles the magnificent 'Babe'
Zaharias, whose golf, too, was remarkable—indeed she was said to
have beaten, without strokes, all the
members of an American Walker Cup
team when in her prime. The two
great ladies met during Lady Heathcoat-Amory's 1935 American tour
and played two exhibition four-ball
matches with male professional partners. The fact that Lady Heathcoat-
Amory's rounds were 77 and 78 and
'Babe's' 81 and 88 means nothing because 'Babe' was then virtually a be-
ginner.

"In my time", Henry Cotton has
said, "no golfer has stood out so far
ahead of his or her contemporaries
as Lady Heathcoat-Amory...I do
not think a golf ball has ever been
hit, except perhaps by Harry Vardon,
with such a straight flight by any
other person. This feature alone
made Lady Heathcoat-Amory's game
unique to watch." Bobby Jones once
said gallantly of her, after a round
they played together at St Andrews:
"I have not played golf with anyone,
man or woman, amateur or professional, who made me feel so utterly
outclassed." See ZAHARIAS, 'BABE'.

## HEBERT, Jay (b 1923)

U.S.P.G.A. Champion, 1960. Ryder
Cup team, 1959, 1961. Brother of
Lionel Hebert.

## HEBERT, Lionel (b 1920)

U.S.P.G.A. Champion, 1957, the
last time it was decided by match
play. Ryder Cup team, 1957. Brother
of Jay Hebert. See BROTHER GOLFERS.

## HECHER, Genevieve

U.S. Ladies' Champion, 1901, 1902.

## HELME, Eleanor E. (1887-1967)

Won the first of the Worplesdon
Mixed Foursomes, with T. A. Torrance, 1921, beating Joyce and Roger
Wethered in the final. Well-known for
many years as a writer on women's
golf. "With reporter's pad and pencil
in her hands", Miss Enid Wilson has
written, "a camera slung over one
shoulder and a pair of binoculars over
the other, she tramped tirelessly after
the contestants in all the major championships from 1910 to the end of the
season in 1939." Author of *After the
Ball* (1931), one of the most interesting accounts of the early days of
ladies' golf in Britain.

## HENNING, Harold (b 1933)

South African Open Champion,
1957, 1962. Runner-up, French Open
Championship, 1958. German Open
Champion, 1965. Italian Open Cham-

pion, 1967. Swiss Open Champion, 1960, 1964, 1965. Played for South Africa in World (formerly Canada) Cup, with Gary Player, 1957, 1958, 1959, 1961, 1965, 1966, 1967, 1970. See BROTHER GOLFERS.

## HERD, Alexander ('Sandy') (1868-1944)

Born St Andrews. British Open Champion, 1902; runner-up, 1892, 1895, 1910, 1920. British Professional Match Play Champion, 1906, 1926; runner-up, 1909.

The year 1902 was the first in which the new American Haskell rubber-cored ball became available. The championship was at Hoylake and Sandy Herd played his first practice round with John Ball, the great local amateur who had won the Open in 1890. Ball was using a Haskell brilliantly and at the 15th hole gave Sandy one to try. "That was the end of the gutty ball for me," he wrote in his autobiography, *My Golfing Life* (1923). "The first drive I made with the Haskell was longer than any drive I had ever made with the gutty." He managed to buy four Haskells from the Hoylake professional, Jack Morris, nephew of 'Old Tom' Morris of St Andrews, and eventually won the championship—although by only one stroke from Harry Vardon, who was using a gutty.

He was professional at several clubs, including Huddersfield, Coombe Hill and (for many of his later years) Moor Park. As a golfer he was famous for his 'waggles' while addressing the ball; the reason he gave was: "All the time the club waggles in my hand, I am getting my wrists supple and shifting my feet inch by inch till I know everything is right for the shot." See HERD, FRED.

## HERD, Fred (b 1874)

U.S. Open Champion, 1898, winning, like Tony Jacklin in 1970, with a clear lead of seven strokes. He was a brother of 'Sandy' Herd, British Open Champion in 1902. Born in St Andrews, he crossed the Atlantic and

spent many years as professional at the Washington Park Club, Chicago, before returning to Britain. His brothers James and John were also professionals in Chicago. See BROTHER GOLFERS.

## HERRESHOFF, Fred (b 1878)

American. Runner-up, U.S. Amateur Championship, 1904 (to H. Chandler Egan), 1911 (to Harold Hilton, who was also British Amateur Champion that year).

## HERRON, S. Davidson (b 1892)

U.S. Amateur Champion, 1919, defeating Bobby Jones, then aged 17, in the final. Walker Cup team, 1923.

## HETHERINGTON, Mrs G. W.

See HOLMES, MRS JEAN.

## HEZLET, Charles (1891-1965)

Runner-up, British Amateur Championship, 1913. Irish Open Amateur Champion, 1926, 1929; runner-up, 1923, 1925. Irish Native Amateur Champion, 1920. Walker Cup team, 1924, 1926, 1928.

As a golfer, Major Hezlet was always famous for the extreme width of his straddle, called by his friends 'the Cape to Cairo'. His three sisters, May, Florence and Violet, were all good golfers. See BROTHER AND SISTER GOLFERS.

## HEZLET, May (b 1882)

First entered for British Ladies' Championship at the age of 13. Won 1899, 1902, 1907; runner-up, 1904. Irish Ladies' Champion, 1899, 1904, 1905, 1906, 1908; runner-up, 1898. Her sister, Florence, was runner-up in the Ladies' Championship, 1907, 1909, and in the Irish Championship, 1905. 1906, 1908, 1912, 1920. Her other sister, Violet, was runner-up in the Ladies' Championship, 1911, and in the Irish Ladies' Championship, 1900, 1909. The Hezlet sisters and another Irish lady golfer, Rhona Adair, were all members at Royal Portrush. May Hezlet became Mrs Adrian Ross, Florence, Mrs Cramsie and Violet.

Mrs J. M. Hulton. See ADAIR, RHONA ; BROTHER AND SISTER GOLFERS.

## HICKORY

The wood from which many shafts were made in the days before the advent of steel shafts, made legal in 1929. Hickory, however, was not the only wood used. See WOODS USED IN CLUBMAKING.

### HICKS, Betty (Mrs Newell)

U.S. Ladies' Champion, 1941. Turned professional, 1941. Author of *Golf Manual for Teachers*, in collaboration with Miss Griffin, Professor of Physical Education, University of North Carolina.

### HICKS, Helen (Mrs W. Harb) (b 1911)

U.S. Ladies' Champion, 1931, defeating Mrs Glenna Collett Vare in the final and preventing her from winning the title four times running ; runner-up, 1933. Curtis Cup team, 1932. Nicknamed 'Hard-Hitting Helen'.

## HIGHEST COURSES IN EUROPE

See ITALY, GOLF IN.

## HIGHEST COURSES IN THE COMMONWEALTH

See INDIA, GOLF IN ; KENYA, GOLF IN.

## HIGHEST COURSES IN THE WORLD

See BOLIVIA, GOLF IN.

### HILL, Cynthia (b 1950)

Runner-up, U.S. Ladies' Championship, 1970, 1972.

### HILL, David ('Dave') (b 1937)

Runner-up (to Tony Jacklin), U.S. Open Championship, 1970. Ryder Cup team, 1969. Like Tommy Bolt, he is inclined to be outspoken and during the 1970 U.S. Open was fined by the U.S.P.G.A. for criticising the Hazeltine course, near Minneapolis, where the event was held.

### HILL, George Alec (b 1909)

Runner-up, Danish Open Amateur Championship, 1948. Walker Cup team, 1936 ; non-playing captain, 1955. Captain, R. and A., 1964.

### HILTON, Harold Horsfall (1869-1942)

British Open Champion, 1892 (the first year that the British Open was decided over 72 holes) and 1897— the only amateur, apart from John Ball and Bobby Jones, to win the title. British Amateur Champion, 1900, 1901, 1911, 1913 ; runner-up, 1891, 1892, 1896. U.S. Amateur Champion, 1911. Irish Open Amateur Champion, 1897, 1900, 1901, 1902.

He learned his golf as a boy at the Royal Liverpool Club, Hoylake, where at one time his handicap was plus 10. He was only 5ft 7in in height, but was powerfully built. Bernard Darwin has left a splendid word picture of him in *Golfing By-Paths* (1946):

The first sight of him hitting a ball did not convey a notion of accuracy, but rather of a wholehearted flinging himself at the ball. His address to the ball was, to be sure, very careful and precise; he placed his feet and faced his club to the line with great exactness. These preliminaries over, he seemed to throw care to the winds, and one had a wild and whirling vision of a little man jumping on his toes and throwing himself and his club after the ball with almost frantic abandon. Yet this was the most deceptive possible appearance, for though he certainly hit for all he was worth, he had a gift of balance such as is given to few. His cap might fall off the back of his head, he might twist his shoulders round in producing the hook which he used so skilfully, but he was always firmly poised, the master of himself and of the ball.

The one man who consistently got the better of him—and that only in match play—was Lieutenant 'Freddie' Tait, the great Scottish amateur who

was killed in the Boer War in 1900.
Harold Hilton wrote a great deal on the subject of golf. He edited *Golf Illustrated* for some years and was the first editor of *Golf Monthly*. Among his books was *My Golfing Reminiscences* (1907).

## HISTORY OF GOLF

The main entries dealing with the history of the game are: EARLIEST SCOTTISH REFERENCES TO GOLF; EIGHTEEN HOLES, WHY; OLDEST GOLF CLUBS; ROYAL AND ANCIENT GOLF CLUB OF ST ANDREWS; ROYAL BLACK-HEATH CLUB; ROYAL GOLFERS; UNITED STATES, EARLY REFERENCES TO GOLF IN THE; UNITED STATES, GOLF IN THE.

For information on other historical aspects, the following are relevant: AMATEUR INTERNATIONAL, FIRST; BALFOUR, EARL; BALL, MAKES OF; BALL, SIZE OF; BELT, BRITISH OPEN CHAMPIONSHIP; BOGEY; BRITISH AMATEUR CHAMPIONSHIP; BRITISH LADIES' CHAMPIONSHIP; BRITISH OPEN CHAMPIONSHIP; BUNKER; CADDIE-CAR; CADDIES, PAYMENT FOR; COURSE; EARLIEST ENGLISH REFER-ENCES TO GOLF; EDINBURGH GOLFERS, HONOURABLE COMPANY OF; ENGLISH SEASIDE COURSES, FIRST; FEATHERY; GATE MONEY, FIRST; GOLF BOOK, FIRST AMERICAN; GOLF BOOKS, EARLIEST; GOLF-LIKE GAMES, OLD; GOLF, ORIGIN OF THE WORD; GOUR-LAY; GUTTY; HASKELL BALL; HOLE; HOLE-IN-ONE, EARLIEST RECORDED; INTER-CLUB FOURSOMES, FIRST; LADIES' CLUBS, OLDEST; LADY GOLFER, FIRST; LEITH LINKS; MAN-CHESTER CLUB, OLD; MOLESEY HURST, GOLF AT; MUSSELBURGH; PAU CLUB; PRIZE MONEY, BRITISH OPEN CHAM-PIONSHIP; PRIZE MONEY, UNITED STATES OPEN CHAMPIONSHIP; PRO-FESSIONAL INTERNATIONAL, FIRST; PUBLIC HOUSES AS CLUBHOUSES; ROYAL BURGESS SOCIETY OF EDIN-BURGH; ROYAL CLUB, OLDEST; RULES, FIRST CODE OF; ST ANDREWS GOLF CLUB OF YONKERS; SCHENECTADY PUTTER; SCORE-CARDS, FIRST; SMOL-LETT ON GOLF; STEEL SHAFTS; STROKE

PLAY, FIRST RECORDS OF; STYMIE; SWILCAN BURN; TEE, ORIGIN OF WORD; UNIFORMS WORN BY GOLFERS; UNITED STATES AMATEUR CHAMPION-SHIP; UNITED STATES LADIES' CHAM-PIONSHIP; UNITED STATES OPEN CHAMPIONSHIP.

## HITCHCOCK, James (b 1930)

Tied British Assistant Professional Championship with David Thomas, 1955, but lost play-off. Won Dunlop Masters, 1960. Ryder Cup team, 1965.

## 'HITTEE-BALL-SAY-DAMN'

An expression used—for obvious reasons—to describe the game of golf by caddie boys at Royal Hong Kong Club in less sophisticated days.

## HITTING THE BALL: STATISTICS

What exactly happens when a play-er hits the ball? The Golf Society of Great Britain carried out a scien-tific study for six years and published its findings in 1968 in *The Search for the Perfect Swing* (Heinemann, 63s.), under the authorship of Alastair Cochran and John Stobbs. Among the interesting conclusions are:

During the downswing, a good golfer can generate up to four horse-power. This is a surprisingly high power; and must need at least thirty pounds of muscles, working flat-out, to produce it. . . .

During a full drive, the face of the driver is in contact with the ball for only half a thousandth of a second (half a millisecond). . . .

From the moment it first touches the ball until the moment the ball springs clear of it, the face of the club in a full drive travels forward only three-quarters of an inch. . . .

The force applied to the ball by the clubhead during impact in a full drive rises to a *peak* of about 2,000 pounds —nearly a ton. The *average* force applied at all stages during the half millisecond contact, that is to say dur-ing the compression and springing away again of the ball, is around

1,400 pounds. The time, distance and force involved are very much the same for either the British size of ball or the American size. . . .

During the downswing, the top-class golfer may accelerate his clubhead about one hundred times as fast as the fastest sports car can accelerate: from rest at the top of the backswing, to 100 miles per hour at impact, all in as little as one-fifth of a second. . . .

Travelling at 100 miles per hour, a driver head of the usual weight, seven ounces, sends a top-class ball away at about 135 miles per hour. If the head could be swung at 200 miles per hour, it would send the ball away almost twice as fast, at 250 miles per hour. . . .

Outstandingly long drivers get their length simply by being able to swing the clubhead faster than the majority. For instance, to carry 280 yards before the ball hits the ground, a player has to send the ball off at 175 miles per hour. To do this he would have to swing:

a 6-ounce clubhead at 134 m.p.h.;
a 7-ounce clubhead at 130 m.p.h.;
an 8-ounce clubhead at 127 m.p.h. . . .

A warm ball is more lively than a cold one. A drive which carries 200 yards through the air with the ball at 70°F (21°C) would carry only 185 yards if the ball were at freezing point. See GOLF BALL, VELOCITY OF.

## 'HOCKEY AT THE HALT'

A name given jocularly to golf by non-golfers when the game was becoming popular in the 1890s. See 'SCOTCH CROQUET'.

## HODSON, Bert (b 1905)

Welsh Professional Champion, 1927, 1929. Ryder Cup team, 1931.

## HOGAN, Benjamin William ('Ben') (b 1912)

Born just ten years after Bobby Jones and 20 years after Walter Hagen, and, like them, one of golf's 'greats'. Like Hagen, he began as a caddie and became a professional at 17. U.S. Open Champion, 1948, 1950, 1951, 1953. British Open Champion,

1953—one of the few to hold both titles in the same year. Won U.S. Masters, 1951, 1953. U.S.P.G.A. Champion, 1946, 1948. Apart from these major championships he has won practically every other event on the American professional circuit. Ryder Cup team, 1947, 1949 (non-playing captain), 1951, 1967 (non playing captain). World (formerly Canada) Cup team, 1956.

In February 1949 Ben Hogan was involved in a near-fatal accident when driving back from a tournament to his home in Fort Worth, Texas. It looked as though his golf career might have been finished, but by September he was well enough to come to England as non-playing captain of the American Ryder Cup team. By the middle of December he played his first full round, and in January 1950 he played in the Los Angeles Open, losing to Sam Snead after a play-off. Three months later he finished fourth in the Masters at Augusta, and in June won the U.S. Open at the Merion Club after defeating Lloyd Mangrum and George Fazio in a play-off. He finished, as may be imagined, a very tired man, but showed his remarkable resilience by winning the Open again in 1951.

A film about his life, *Follow the Sun*, was made in 1951, Glenn Ford playing the lead. Author of *Power Golf* (1949) and *The Modern Fundamentals of Golf* (1957). See also *My Partner, Ben Hogan* (1954), by fellow Texan, Jimmy Demaret.

## HOLDERNESS, Sir Ernest (1890-1968)

British Amateur Champion, 1922, 1924. Won Oxford and Cambridge Golfing Society's President's Putter in its first four years, 1920-23, and again in 1929; runner-up, 1925, 1930. Walker Cup team, 1923, 1926, 1930.

## HOLE

The 'hole' is officially "4¼ inches in diameter and at least 4 inches deep. If a lining be used, it shall be sunk at least 1 inch below the putting green surface unless the nature of the soil makes it impractical to do so ; its outer diameter shall not exceed 4¼ inches" (Rules of Golf Definition).

This was the size when the first mention was made of it in the 1891 code of rules. In golf's early days the size of the hole was left to the greenkeeper ; the bottom of the hole was filled with sand and players took a pinch out before teeing up and driving off "within a club's length of the hole" (1744 code) or "not nearer the hole than two club lengths, nor further distant from it than four" (1775 code).

See UNITED STATES, GOLF IN THE.

## HOLE HIGH
See PIN HIGH.

## HOLE-IN-ONE
Striking the ball from the teeing ground into the hole in one stroke. Often called an 'ace'. The odds against doing a hole-in-one are reckoned to be about 2,000 to one.

## HOLE-IN-ONE, EARLIEST RECORDED
The earliest recorded hole-in-one was accomplished by 'Young Tommy' Morris in winning his first Open Championship at Prestwick in 1868. He holed out at the 8th hole, 145 yards, of the original 12-holes course. It enabled him to do the first round in 50 strokes, the others being done in 55 and 52 for a total of 157. In the 1878 Open, also at Prestwick, Jamie Anderson, the winner, had an ace at the last hole but one, 132 yards.

## HOLE-IN-ONE, LONGEST
According to the *Golfer's Handbook*, the longest hole-in-one was accomplished at the Miracle Hill Club, Omaha, in October 1965 by a 21-year-old American student named Bob Mitera. He claims to have holed his drive at the 10th, measuring 444 yards. The hole slopes downhill and there was a strong following wind.

The longest authenticated hole-in-one in Britain is 380 yards. This was done in 1961 by David Hulley at the 5th at Tankersley Park, High Green, near Sheffield, Yorkshire.

## HOLES-IN-ONE, GREATEST NUMBER OF
The golfer who claims to have done the most holes-in-one in his career is Art Wall—37. He had his first in 1936 at the age of 12 and his last in 1968.

The British record—30—is held by Charles T. Chevalier, professional at Heaton Moor, near Stockport, Lancashire, until he retired in 1969. He has kept a complete list of place, time and length of hole.

Curiously enough, Harry Vardon and Walter Hagen holed-in-one only once during their long and distinguished careers.

## HOLLAND, GOLF IN
Holland and Scotland can claim to be the original homes of golf—or at least in the case of Kolven, of a game of rather tenuous associations with golf ; the game shown by Dutch artists as being played either on the ice or in enclosed spaces bears little resemblance to golf.

The modern game of golf grew rapidly in Holland between the First and Second World Wars, and now there are 18 clubs. Near Amsterdam is the Amsterdamsche Club ; near The Hague the Haagsche Golf and Country Club ; at Zandvoort the Kennemer Country Club ; at Arnhem the Rosendaelsche Club (founded in 1896) ; and other good courses are at Hilversum, Eindhoven and the Utrechtsche Club at Huis ter Heide. The Dutch Golf Union looks after the game in Holland.

The Dutch Open Championship dates from 1919 and the Open Amateur and Ladies' Championships from 1921. Holland's most successful amateur golfer has been J. F. Dudok van Heel, champion in 1952, 1953, 1955 and runner-up in 1959, 1964, 1968 ; among professionals are Gerard

de Wit and the rising star, Martin Roesink, famous for his big hitting.
See KOLVEN.

## HOLLINS, Marion (b 1890)

U.S. Ladies' Champion, 1921, beating Alexa Stirling in the final and preventing her from winning the title four times running; runner-up, 1913. Non-playing captain of the first U.S. Curtis Cup team, 1932.

## 'HOLLYWOOD HANDICAP'

An Americanism for a handicap that is too low, but makes you sound like a star player.

## HOLM, Mrs Andrew (1907-71)

British. Born Helen Gray. British Ladies' Champion, 1934, 1938. Scottish Ladies' Champion, 1930, 1932, 1937, 1948, 1950; runner-up, 1933, 1938, 1949, 1956, 1957. Curtis Cup team, 1936, 1938, 1948.

## HOLMES, Mrs Jean (b 1923)

Born Jean McClure. British Ladies' Champion, 1946 (as Mrs G. W. Hetherington, while on her honeymoon). Runner-up, English Ladies' Championship, 1966.

## HOMER, Trevor (b 1944)

British Amateur Champion, 1972, 1974. World Cup (formerly Eisenhower Trophy) team, 1972. Walker Cup team, 1973.

## HONG KONG, GOLF IN

Golf has been played for a long time in Hong Kong, for Royal Hong Kong dates back to 1889. It comprises four courses—the Old, New and Eden (echoes of St Andrews) at Fanling and the Deep Water Bay course, about 6 miles from the centre of Hong Kong. The club has a membership of over 3,000, most of whom are, of course, non-resident.

There is also the Shek-O Country Club, about 14 miles from the city, created since the Second World War. Before the war there was a flourishing club at Kowloon.

The Hong Kong Amateur Championship has been held since 1931 and the Open Championship since 1959, among the winners of the latter being Peter Thomson and Kel Nagle.
See CHINA, GOLF IN ; HITTEE-BALL-SAY-DAMN.

## HONOUR

"The side which is entitled to play first from the teeing ground is said to have the 'honour'" (Rules of Golf Definition). On the first tee the option of taking the honour is decided by lot (i.e. tossing for it) unless there has been a draw for a competition in which case the player whose name is higher on the draw takes the honour. The term first appeared in the R. and A. Rules of 1888.

## HONOURABLE COMPANY OF EDINBURGH GOLFERS

See EDINBURGH GOLFERS, HONOURABLE COMPANY OF.

## HOODING THE CLUB

A type of shot in which the loft of the club is lessened by addressing the ball nearer the right foot and shutting the club face by advancing the hands so that they are slightly in front of the ball. Also called shutting the face.

## HOODS

See WOODEN CLUBS, COVERS FOR.

## HORNE, Reginald W. ('Reg') (b 1908)

Born London. Runner-up (with Frank Stranahan), British Open Championship, 1957. British Professional Match Play Champion, 1945. British Senior Professional Champion, 1960. His brother, Cyril, has been for many years professional at the Singapore Island Country Club.

## HORTON, Tommy (b 1941)

Born in Jersey, like a number of famous golfers. British Professional Match Play Champion, 1970. South African Open Champion, 1970—breaking a five-year run of victories by

Gary Player. Runner-up, Portuguese Open Championship, 1972. Ryder Cup team, 1975, 1977. Captain, 1978. Dunlop Masters, 1978.

## HOWARD, Mrs Ann (b 1935)

Born Ann Phillips. British Girls' Champion, 1952. Danish Ladies' Champion, 1955. Curtis Cup team, 1956, 1968.

## HOWELL, Henry Rupert (b 1899)

Welsh Amateur Champion, 1920, 1922, 1923, 1924, 1929, 1930, 1931, 1932.

## HOYLAKE

See ROYAL LIVERPOOL CLUB.

## HOYT, Beatrix (b 1880)

U.S. Ladies' Champion in the second, third and fourth years of the event, 1896, 1897, 1898—the first time at the age of 16, making her the youngest holder of the title. In 1900 she retired from tournament golf, a gesture similar to that of Lady Margaret Scott after winning the first three British Ladies' Championships, 1893, 1894, 1895.

In 1896 she became the first winner of the permanent trophy donated by Robert Cox, of Edinburgh; in 1895 a silver pitcher was won by Mrs Charles Brown, the first champion.

## HUGGETT, Brian G. C. (b 1936)

Runner-up (with Christy O'Connor), British Open Championship, 1965. Dutch Open Champion, 1962. German Open Champion, 1963; runner-up, 1972. Portuguese Open Champion, 1974. Won Dunlop Masters, 1970. Ryder Cup team, 1963, 1967, 1969, 1971, 1973, 1975. Played for Wales in World (formerly Canada) Cup, 1963, 1965, 1969. Author of *Better Golf* (1964).

## HUKE, Beverly (b 1950)

Runner-up, British Ladies' Championship, 1971. Curtis Cup team, 1972.

## HUMPHREYS, Warren (b 1952)

English Amateur Champion, 1971. Runner-up, British Youths' Championship, 1971. Runner-up, Portuguese Open Amateur Championship, 1971. Walker Cup team, 1971. Turned professional, autumn, 1971. See SUNNINGDALE OPEN FOURSOMES.

## HUNGARY, GOLF IN

It is sad to think that no golf is now played in Hungary, a country which had an Amateur Open Championship going back to 1920 and a Ladies' Open Championship back to 1922. Before the Second World War, the Magyar Club, Budapest, had a good 18-holes course, and there were others at Balatonfured (Lake Balaton), Lillafured and the Radvany Castle Hotel Golf Club.

Hungary had an outstanding lady golfer in Frau Erzsebet (Elizabeth) von Szlavy, many times winner of the Hungarian and Austrian Ladies' Championships.

The fact that the game has survived in Czechoslovakia, in spite of the troubles, and is showing signs of revival in Romania, might mean that golf will again return to Hungary some day. See ROMANIA, GOLF IN.

## HUNSTANTON

Hunstanton, Norfolk. Founded 1891. Traditional links, divided from the sea by dunes. Length: 6,723 yards. S.S.S. 72. Housed Ladies' Championship, 1914, 1928, 1946, 1958; English Amateur Championship, 1931, 1951, 1960; English Ladies' Championship, 1922, 1956, 1968; English Open Amateur Stroke Play Championship, 1966.

## HUNT, Bernard John (b 1930)

French Open Champion, 1967. Belgian Open Champion, 1957. German Open Champion, 1961. Egyptian Open Champion, 1956. Runner-up, British Professional Match Play Championship, 1958. Ryder Cup team, 1953, 1957, 1959, 1961, 1963, 1965, 1967, 1969; non-playing captain, 1973. Played for England in World (formerly Canada) Cup, 1958, 1959, 1960, 1962, 1968.

He is the son of a professional golfer and his brother Geoffrey also played in the 1963 Ryder Cup team. See BROTHER GOLFERS.

## HUNTER, Charles (1836-1921)

Born Prestwick, Ayrshire. An apprentice under Tom Morris at Prestwick, he succeeded him as professional to the club in 1864, when 'Old Tom' went to St Andrews; previously he had been professional at Blackheath for three years.

He played in the Open Championship for the first four years, 1860-63, but thereafter contented himself with acting as starter at the Open and other tournaments at Prestwick until his death.

## HUNTER, William Irvine ('Willie') (b 1892)

British Amateur Champion, 1921. First amateur in British Open Championship, 1920. He was a post-office clerk in Kent until he turned professional in 1925 and went to America, where he won a number of tournaments, particularly on the west coast.

## HURD, Mrs Dorothy Campbell (1883-1946)

Under her maiden name of Dorothy Campbell, the first golfer to win both the British Ladies' (1909, 1911) and the U.S. Ladies' Championships (1909, 1910, 1924). Runner-up, British Championship, 1908, and (under her married name of Mrs J. V. Hurd) in the U.S. Championship, 1920. She was also Canadian Ladies' Open Champion, 1910, 1911, 1912, and Scottish Ladies' Champion, 1905, 1906, 1908; runner-up, 1907, 1909.

## HUTCHINGS, Charles (b 1849)

British Amateur Champion, 1902, at what was then the record age of 53, until the Hon. Michael Scott won in 1933 at the age of 54. Hutchings and the other finalist, Sidney Fry, both used the new Haskell ball in the

1902 championship. He was one of the great Hoylake golfers.

## HUTCHINSON, Horace (1859-1932)

Born Horatio Gordon Hutchinson. British Amateur Champion, 1886, 1887; runner-up, 1885, 1903. He learned his golf at the Westward Ho! Club, North Devon, and at the age of 16 won the Scratch Medal, which carried with it the captaincy of the club! He played in the first Oxford and Cambridge match at Wimbledon in 1878, was Captain of the R. and A. in 1908 and wrote prolifically about golf in books and magazines for many years. Among the books he wrote or edited were: *Fifty Years of Golf* (1919); *Hints on the Game of Golf* (1886); *Famous Golf Links* (1891); *Book of Golf and Golfers* (1899); The Badminton Library volume on *Golf* (1890); *The Golfing Pilgrim* (1898) and a novel called *Bert Edward, The Golf Caddie* (1903).

## HUTCHISON, Cecil K. (b 1882)

Runner-up, British Amateur Championship, 1909. Won *Golf Illustrated* Gold Vase, 1909. Well-known golf-course architect. Among the courses with which he was associated were Gleneagles (with James Braid), Turnberry and West Sussex (Pulborough).

## HUTCHISON, Jock (1884-1977)

Born St Andrews. British Open Champion, 1921, after a tie with Roger Wethered. U.S.P.G.A. Championship, 1920; runner-up, 1916. Runner-up, U.S. Open Championship, 1920, with Harry Vardon, Leo Diegel and Jack Burke. Settled in America as a young man.

## HYNDMAN, William (b 1916)

American. Runner-up, U.S. Amateur Championship, 1955. Runner-up, British Amateur Championship, 1959, 1969, 1970; the oldest finalist since the Hon. Michael Scott won the 1933 title. Walker Cup team, 1957, 1959, 1961, 1969, 1971. World Cup (formerly Eisenhower Trophy) team, 1958, 1960,

## IBIZA, GOLF IN

The first course on this small Balearic island, Golf de Roca Llisa, is under construction. See MAJORCA, GOLF IN ; MENORCA, GOLF IN.

## ICELAND, GOLF IN

The presence of British and American troops in Iceland during the Second World War helped to popularise the game. Clubs are increasing and where there were three in 1963, there are five now. The oldest is the Golfklubbur Reykjavikur, founded in 1934, and in 1964 a new club— the Ness Country Club—was opened near Reykjavik. The Icelandic Golf Association and the Golf Union of Iceland both operate from the capital.

## 'IMPREGNABLE QUADRI-
## LATERAL'

See GRAND SLAM.

## IN CONTENTION

A modern Americanism indicating that the player 'in contention' has a good chance of winning the tournament in which he is playing.

## INDIA, GOLF IN

The oldest golf clubs outside Scotland and England—and indeed older than any extant English club except Royal Blackheath—are Royal Calcutta (1829) and Royal Bombay (1842) ; both had close ties with Black-

H

heath, although originally they owed their foundation to Scottish merchants —particularly those in the Dundee jute industry—exiled in India.

In view of this, it is not surprising that the India Amateur Championship is the oldest national championship outside the British Isles. In 1892 the Calcutta Club wrote to all clubs in India, Burma, Ceylon and the Straits Settlements, proposing an "Amateur Championship of India and the East" and the first tournament was held in December of that year. The championship has been held at Royal Calcutta ever since, among the winners being the famous Indian golfers, I. S. and A. S. Malik, and R. K. Pitamber, who played for Oxford University from 1951-54.

The India Ladies' Championship dates from 1932 (dominated since the Second World War by Mrs G. W. Ribbins and Mrs Duncan Smith) and the Open Championship only from 1963, the first (and third) winner being Peter Thomson of Australia.

In spite of the fact that Britons are not so numerous in India as they used to be, golf flourishes, and there are 80 clubs, of various degrees of goodness and prosperity. At Gulmarg, in Kashmir, is the highest course in the Commonwealth, 8,500 feet up in the Himalayas. See PAKISTAN, GOLF IN.

## INDONESIA, GOLF IN

Golf is flourishing in the Republic of Indonesia, particularly in the main islands of Java and Sumatra. The game began when the islands were under Dutch control, and Java had three clubs—at Batavia (now Djakarta, the capital of Indonesia), Surabaya and Semarang. There was naturally a setback when the Japanese overran Indonesia in the Second World War, but the game was resumed after liberation and has grown remarkably since independence from Holland was achieved in 1949.

Java now has five clubs—the Djakarta Club, the Yani Club, Surabaya (which as the Surabaya Club was founded in 1898), the Subang Club, the Bandung Club (dating back to 1917) and the Tjandi Club. Sumatra also has five clubs—the Palembang Club (founded in 1933), the Medan Club, the Lirik Club and two clubs belonging to the Goodyear Co. In the Indonesian part of the island of Borneo there is a club at Balikpapan, founded in 1955.

## INSIDE THE LEATHER

An American expression indicating that a short putt is given by an opponent because the distance between the player's ball and the hole is not longer than the leather (or rubber, of course) grip on the putter. In even more friendly matches putts are conceded if they can be measured by the whole length of the putter. See CONCEDE.

## INTER-CLUB FOURSOMES, FIRST

The Prestwick Club, which instituted the first Open Championships, also ran the first inter-club competition in 1857. Seven other clubs—St Andrews, Perth, Musselburgh, Blackheath, Carnoustie, North Berwick and Leven—were invited to enter teams of four players. All accepted and, in addition, the Honourable Company of Edinburgh Golfers, the Royal Burgess Society, Bruntsfield, Montrose and Dirleton Castle asked to be allowed to enter.

In the event, the teams were reduced to one foursome partnership each; the Honourable Company and Carnoustie failed to raise teams, and the other eleven clubs fought it out at St Andrews. The winners were George Glennie and Lieutenant John C. Stewart, representing Blackheath.

Next year the foursome tournament was changed to an individual event on much the same lines as the present Amateur Championship, the first winner being Robert Chambers, later the famous publisher.

See GLENNIE, GEORGE; STEWART, JOHN CAMPBELL.

## IN-TO-OUT

A term used to indicate either a swing or a stroke in which the club is taken back inside the line of flight and finishes with the club-face travelling slightly to the right of the line of flight before straightening out again. This action causes the ball to fly from right to left of the line of flight—i.e. with draw on the ball. Bobby Locke was the greatest exponent of the in-to-out shot. See OPEN-TO-SHUT; OUT-TO-IN; SHUT-TO-OPEN; SQUARE.

## IRAN, GOLF IN

The oldest club in Iran is the Fields Golf Club, near Abadan in the Persian Gulf oil area. It is a private club owned by the National Iranian Oil Company and kindred concerns. It was established as long ago as 1924. A new course, designed by Peter Alliss and Dave Thomas, is under construction near Teheran.

## IRAQ, GOLF IN

The British are said to have brought the game to Baghdad in the 1890s, but the Baghdad Club (formerly called Royal Baghdad) does not claim to go back further than 1925. There are two other clubs—at Basrah and Kirkuk, in the oil areas. As in other desert areas, the Iraq greens are 'browns'.

## IRELAND, GOLFING UNION OF

Founded in 1891, it is the oldest of the four National Unions. It embraces 217 clubs and its chief objects are:

1. To secure the federation of the various clubs.

2. To arrange Irish amateur and professional championships and other competitions and matches.

3. To secure a uniform system of handicapping.

4. To promote the game in general and advise the affiliated clubs in all matters appertaining to golf.

## IRISH AMATEUR CLOSE CHAMPIONSHIP

Ireland was very quick off the mark

in organising its championships—
Open Amateur in 1892, Close Amateur
in 1893, Ladies' in 1894 and South of
Ireland in 1895. Like the other National Amateur Championships, the
Irish Amateur Close Championship is
open to those of Irish birth or one of
whose parents is Irish. For the purposes of golf, Ireland is regarded as
being one country, golfers from Eire
and Ulster having equal rights, and
courses in the north and south being
equally used. No one who has played
for England, Scotland or Wales, or in
their Close Championships, is eligible.

One man—John Burke—dominated
the Close Championship to an extraordinary extent in the 1930s and
1940s, winning the title eight times
between 1930 and 1947, including four
times in a row (1930-33). At much
the same time he won the South of
Ireland Championship 11 times. The
only man to approach this record is
Joe Carr, who was Close Champion
six times between 1954 and 1967.

## IRON CLUBS

Clubs whose heads are made from
steel (or other metal) as opposed to
wood. Nowadays there are complete
sets of irons, numbered from one to
10 (with pitching and sand wedges as
well), but in the old days wooden
clubs usually out-numbered iron ones.

According to H. B. Farnie, who
wrote *The Golfer's Manual* (under
the pseudonym of 'A Keen Hand') in
1857, there were only three iron clubs
—the driving iron, the bunker iron
and the 'cleek or click'. In time,
however, there were many more, including such strange weapons as 'rut
irons', for getting the ball out of
wheel tracks; 'lofting irons' and the
'mashie iron' that Bobby Jones used
to make the famous stroke that won
him the Open Championship in 1926
and a commemorative plaque at
Royal Lytham and St Anne's.

See 'CARRICK IRON'; 'CARRUTHERS
CLEEK'; FAIRLIE IRONS; JIGGER;
NAMES OF IRONS, EQUIVALENT;
'PARK'S PATENT LOFTER'; PRESIDENT;
SAMMY.

## IRVIN, Ann Lesley (b 1943)

British Ladies' champion, 1973;
runner-up, 1969. English Ladies'
Champion, 1967. Runner-up, British
Girls' Championship, 1960. Won first
British Women's Open Stroke Play
Championship, 1969. Curtis Cup team,
1962, 1968, 1970, 1976.

## IRWIN, Hale (b 1945)

U.S. Open, 1974. World Match Play
tournament, 1974, 1975. Ryder Cup
team, 1975, 1977.

## ISLE OF MAN, GOLF IN THE

There are seven clubs in the Island,
the oldest being the Ramsey Club
(1890) and the Castletown Club (1892).
The capital, Douglas, has two separate clubs, both playing over the
Douglas Municipal Course. The
other clubs are the Peel Country Club,
the Rowany Club, Port Erin, and the
Howstrake Club. There is an Isle of
Man Golf Union.

## ISLE OF WIGHT, GOLF IN THE

The island has seven courses, but
only two are 18 holes—the Shanklin
and Sandown Club and the Fresh-
water Bay Club. Even the venerable
Royal Isle of Wight Club, St Helens,
dating back to 1882, but now vanished, had only 9 holes. The other
clubs are the Cowes Club, the Newport Club (1896); the Osborne Club,
East Cowes; the Ryde Club and the
Ventnor Club (1892). What they lack
in length they make up for in pleasant-
ness for holiday golf. The Isle of
Wight Ladies' Championship dates
from 1923 and the Amateur Championship from 1924. There is an Isle
of Wight Golf Union.

## ISRAEL, GOLF IN

The Caesarea Golf and Country
Club was opened, with exhibition matches and other ceremonies, in 1961,
since when it has attracted a big membership, both local and overseas. It
has 18 holes and a length of 6,413
yards. There is a luxury hotel nearby
in the Gleneagles tradition.

# ITALY, GOLF IN

The first recorded golf shots played in Italy occurred in 1738 when David Wemyss, later Lord Elcho, found the exiled Prince Charles Edward, the 'Young Pretender', and his brother Henry knocking a golf ball about in the Borghese Gardens, Rome. In the '45 Lord Elcho was to command the Prince's Life Guards; his descendant, a nineteenth-century Lord Elcho, was first president of the London Scottish Golf Club, Wimbledon.

Many years were to elapse before the game was to be firmly established in Italy; indeed, of the 50 clubs throughout the country, no fewer than 20 were founded after the Second World War, including those at Genoa, Bologna, Padova and the now famous Circolo Golf Olgiata, Rome, venue of the 1964 World Cup (formerly Eisenhower Trophy) and the 1968 World (formerly Canada) Cup. Many of Italy's championships have been held at the delightful Villa D'Este Club, Como, and the equally delightful Country Club at San Remo, on the Italian Riviera. Many new courses are under construction.

Several Italian courses are among the highest in Europe—Sestriere, near Turin, being over 6,500 feet above sea level and the Carezza Club, at Carezza al Lago in the Dolomites, being 5,500 feet.

The Open Amateur, established in 1905, is easily the oldest of the Italian championships, the winner in the first two years being the Hon. Denys Scott, who beat his brother, Osmund, in the 1906 final. The Italian Open Championship dates from 1925, the Native Amateur Championship from 1930, the Ladies' Championship from 1931 and the Native Professional Championship from 1935. Golf affairs are controlled by the Federazione Italiana Golf.

## JACK, Robert Reid (b 1924)

British Amateur Champion, 1957. Scottish Amateur Champion, 1955. Walker Cup team, 1957, 1959. Played for Great Britain in Eisenhower Trophy (World Cup), 1958.

## JACKLIN, Anthony ('Tony') (b 1944)

British Open Champion, 1969—the first British winner since Max Faulkner's victory in 1951. U.S. Open Champion, 1970—the first British winner since Ted Ray in 1920. Broke the par of the Hazeltine course, Chaska, near Minneapolis, in each round—71, 70, 70, 70—and won by seven strokes. As Ben Hogan did in 1953, Jacklin held the lead all the way. Assistant Professionals' Champion, 1965. Won Dunlop Masters, 1967. British P.G.A. Champion, 1972. Runner-up, Swiss Open Championship, 1972. Ryder Cup team, 1967, 1969, 1971. Played for England in World (formerly Canada) Cup team, 1966, 1970. In winning the Greater Jacksonville Open, 1968, became the first British golfer to win an American tournament for many years. Author of *Golf With Tony Jacklin* (1969); *Jacklin: The Champion's Own Story* (1970). See DUNLOP MASTERS TOURNAMENT.

## JACKSON, Bridget (b 1936)

Runner-up, British Ladies' Championship, 1964. English Ladies' Champion, 1956; runner-up, 1958. Canadian Ladies' Open Champion, 1967. British Girls' Champion, 1954. German Ladies' Open Champion, 1956. Curtis Cup team, 1958, 1964, 1968.

## JACKSON, Mrs H. Arnold

U.S. Ladies' Champion (as Miss Katherine Harley), 1908 and (as Mrs Jackson), 1914.

## JACOBS, John Robert Maurice (b 1925)

Dutch Open Champion, 1957. Runner-up, Italian Open Championship, 1954, after tie with Ugo Grappasonni. South African Professional Champion, 1957. Ryder Cup team, 1955. One of the best known teaching professionals in Britain. Tournament Director, P.G.A., 1971-72.

## JACOBS, Tommy (b 1935)

Tied U.S. Masters Championship, 1966, with Jack Nicklaus and Gay Brewer, but lost play-off. Ryder Cup team, 1965.

## JACQUET-ENGEL, Mme F. (b 1930)

Born Arlette Jacquet. Belgian Ladies' Champion, 1954, 1956, 1957, 1959, 1960, 1962; runner-up, 1949. Runner-up, Belgian Ladies' Open Championship, 1951. Italian Ladies' Open Champion, 1955, 1962. Swiss Ladies' Open Champion, 1957. Runner-up, Scandinavian Ladies' Open Championship, 1959. Runner-up, British Girls' Championship, 1949.

## JAECKEL, Barry (b 1949)

American. French Open Champion, 1972.

## JAMAICA, GOLF IN

The game is long established in Jamaica, the largest of the West Indian Islands; indeed the Manchester Club, Mandeville, claims to have been founded in 1868, which would make it one of the world's oldest clubs. The Liguanea Club, Kingston, dates from 1908. The capital has another club,

Constant Springs, and other clubs include the Caymanas Country Club, Spanish Town, the Montego Bay Country Club, the Malvern Club, and the Westmoreland Country Club, Savanna-la-Mar.

## JAMES, Louis N. (b 1882)

U.S. Amateur Champion, 1902. At 19 years and 10 months, he was the youngest winner of the title until Robert Gardner, a few months younger, won in 1909. See YOUNGEST AMATEUR CHAMPIONS.

## JAMES, Mark (b 1953)

English Amateur Champion, 1974. Runner-up, Amateur Championship, 1975. Turned professional, 1975. Ryder Cup team, 1977; Walker Cup team, 1975.

## JAMESON, Betty (b 1918)

U.S. Ladies' Champion, 1939, 1940. U.S. Women's Open Champion, 1947; runner-up, 1946, 1952.

## JAMIESON, Andrew (b 1905)

Scottish Amateur Champion, 1927; runner-up, 1931. Walker Cup team, 1926.

## JAMIESON, Jim (b 1943)

Runner-up, U.S. P.G.A. Championship, 1972. World (formerly Canada) Cup team, 1972.

## JANUARY, Don (b 1929)

U.S.P.G.A. Champion, 1967; runner-up, 1961. Ryder Cup team, 1965.

## JAPAN, GOLF IN

Japan has seen the most extraordinary golf boom. At the end of the Second World War there were fewer than 30 clubs; now there are over 400. It is reckoned that some 5 million Japanese either play golf or at least use the driving ranges that have sprung up all over the country.

Golf is an expensive game in Japan. At the 300 Club, Yokohama (so called because the membership is restricted to 300), the entrance fee is £2,000 and at many clubs the annual subscription is around £250.

An ambitious new project is the creation of a course modelled on the Old Course, St Andrews, called the New St Andrews Club and designed by Jack Nicklaus and his partner, Desmond Muirhead. The sponsor, a Japanese businessman, Zenya Hamada, presented St Andrews with £50,000 'for the good of the town and golf', with a promise of further sums.

Golf began in Japan in 1903 when 4 holes were opened, through the efforts of a Scot named Arthur Groome, on the summit of Mount Rokko, near Kobe. The Kobe Club soon had 18 holes. Other courses followed at Yokohama and around Tokyo. Most of the early members were British and other foreigners, but now the great majority are Japanese. The first winners of the Japan Amateur Championship, founded in 1907 and played at either Kobe or Yokohama, were exclusively British or American, but since the Second World War they have been exclusively Japanese. The Japan Open Championship dates from 1927 and the Professional Championship from 1931. Golfing affairs are looked after by the Japan Golf Association.

The 1957 World (formerly Canada) Cup was held at the Kasumigaseki Country Club, near Tokyo, and the fact that it was won by the Japanese pair, Torakichi Nakamura and Koichi Ono, beating Sam Snead and Jimmy Demaret into second place, gave great impetus to Japanese golf.

## JAVA, GOLF IN

See INDONESIA, GOLF IN.

## JENKINS, J. L. C. (b 1883)

British Amateur Champion, 1914. Leading amateur, British Open Championship, 1914. Played in the match against America at Hoylake, 1921, that led to the Walker Cup series.

## JERSEY GOLFERS

The island of Jersey has always been a breeding ground of professional golfers, among them being the Vardons, Ted Ray, the Gaudins, the

Boomers, the Renoufs, the Becks, Charles Chevalier and, in more recent times, such young golfers as Tommy Horton, Terry Le Brocq and Carol Le Feuvre, English Girls' Champion, 1969, 1970. See CHANNEL ISLANDS, GOLF IN THE.

## JEU DE MAIL

An ancient Southern French game, whose origins have never been firmly established, but might be derived from the Roman game of Paganica. It was played with a supple wooden mallet *(mail)* and a wooden ball, which could be driven considerable distances across country. The object was to play the ball along the prescribed course (about half a mile) towards a marker, the winner being the player taking the fewest strokes. More modern versions of the game were Chole and Crosse.

A form of Jeu de Mail was still played at Montpellier, in southern France, at the beginning of the twentieth century; there are photographs of a game in operation in *The Royal and Ancient Game of Golf*, edited by Harold Hilton and Garden Smith (1912).

A good description of Jeu de Mail is given in a little book by A. Robb, *Historical Gossip About Golf and Golfers* (1863): "It is exactly like our golf, but played under different circumstances...The club is made in the shape of a hammer. The handle is rather longer than that of a golf club, of the same size and thickness, and having a good deal of spring in it." One end of the club, he says, is nearly flat, "like the flat end of a hammer, with which the ball is usually hit, while the other is more sloped, so as to give a facility for striking the ball when it gets into a position of difficulty. Both ends are strongly bound with iron, which is necessary to give weight to the club as well as prevent the wood from breaking. The ball is solid and round, made of the root of the box tree, about 2 inches in diameter."

See CAMBUCA; CHOLE; CROSSE; PAGANICA; PELL MELL; TAKOURA.

## JIGGER

A thin-faced iron club, usually little longer in the shaft than a putter, used by old-time golfers for run-up shots to the green. Normally it had roughly the same loft as a modern No 6 iron, but could vary in accordance with personal preference. Some modern club manufacturers still make jigger-type clubs under various names.

## JITTERS

See FREEZE.

## JOHNSTON, Harrison R. (b 1896)

U.S. Amateur Champion, 1929. Walker Cup team, 1923, 1924, 1928, 1930.

## JONES, Ernest (1887-1966)

British. In spite of losing a leg in the First World War, he was a professional in England until 1943, when he went to America and opened a famous indoor golf school in New York. His favourite way of impressing on pupils the essence of the golf swing was to demonstrate with a penknife attached to a piece of string. His tenets were set out in a book called *The Golf Swing* (1920).

## JONES, Robert Trent

Leading American golf-course architect, responsible for many new and renovated courses all over the world, including two of Spain's spectacular new ones in the Costa del Sol— Sotogrande and Nueva Andalucia— and the fine Dorado Beach Club, Puerto Rico. Among his newer American courses is the Hazeltine National, near Minneapolis, where Tony Jacklin won the 1970 U.S. Open Championship.

## JONES, Robert Tyre ('Bobby') (1902-72)

One of the world's best-loved and greatest golfers of all time, his record was unsurpassed. U.S. Open Champion, 1923, 1926, 1929, 1930; tied, 1925, 1928, but lost play-off; runner-up, 1922, 1924. British Open Champion, 1926, 1927, 1930. U.S. Amateur Champion, 1924, 1925, 1927, 1928, 1930; runner-up, 1919, 1926. British Amateur Champion, 1930. Played in the 1921 match against Great Britain that led to the Walker Cup series; played in the American team, 1922, 1924, 1926, 1928, 1930; captain, 1928, 1930. He won all his singles matches.

Played in his first U.S. Amateur Championship at the age of 14 in 1916, in which year he won the Georgia State Amateur Championship and in the following year the Southern Amateur Championship. He paid his first visit to Britain in 1921 and played in the Amateur Championship at Hoylake, got through three rounds, but, as he himself put it later, in the fourth round "a genial, sandy-haired gentleman, Allan Graham, fairly beat me to death with a queer brass putter". His first experience of the Old Course at St Andrews, where the Open was held, was not auspicious, for at the 11th hole in the third round, having taken 46 to the turn, he teed his ball up and drove it far out into the river Eden. Later he came to love the Old Course above all others. After winning his second Open at St Andrews in 1927, he said: "I had rather win a championship at St Andrews than anything else that could happen to me."

In the previous year he won the Open at Royal Lytham and St Anne's, in the course of which he played a wonder shot from a bunker to the green at the 17th in the last round that is marked by a bronze plaque; this shot, with a carry of some 175 yards, played with what was called a mashie-iron, enabled him to beat his playing partner, Al Watrous, into second place. This was the year in which regional qualifying rounds were played, Bobby—or Bob, as he is now called—producing at Sunningdale, Berkshire, one of the greatest rounds

of his life—a 66 in which he had 33 putts and 33 other shots.

In 1930, his *annus mirabilis,* he brought off what was called the Grand Slam or Impregnable Quadrilateral, winning the American and British Open and Amateur Championships, a feat that is never likely to be repeated. He was still only 28, but he had already decided that the strain was too great, so gave up competitive golf. The only occasion he was tempted to play big-time golf again was in the opening year, 1934, of the Augusta National Invitation meeting, the great event that later became known simply as The Masters. The Augusta National Club, at Augusta, Georgia, was the brain-child of Bobby and his friend, Clifford Roberts.

He served in the Second World War as a Lieutenant-Colonel in the U.S. Army, but after the war he was stricken by a disease that confined him to a wheel chair. All the same, he came over to Britain in 1958 and received the Freedom of St Andrews. As a mark of the esteem in which he was held, the 10th hole on the Old course has been named 'The Bobby Jones Hole'.

Author (with O. B. Keeler) of *Down the Fairway* (1927), *Golf is My Game* (1961), *Bobby Jones on Golf* (1968). See also *The Bobby Jones Story,* by O. B. Keeler and Grantland Rice.

See CALAMITY JANE; MASTERS TOURNAMENT; OLD MAN PAR; ST ANDREWS, NAMES OF HOLES AND BUNKERS AT.

## JUNGLE
See TIGER COUNTRY.

## JURADO, José (1899-1971)
Argentinian. Runner-up, British Open Championship, 1931, one stroke behind Tommy Armour. Argentine Open Champion, 1920, 1924, 1925, 1927, 1928, 1929, 1931.

## KEISER, Herman (b 1915)
Won U.S. Masters, 1946. Ryder Cup team, 1947.

## KEMPSHALL BALL
The Kempshall Arlington and the Kempshall Flyer were invented early in the twentieth century by an American named Eleazor Kempshall as a rival to the Haskell. The chief difference was that the Kempshall was built up with rubber tape while the Haskell had rubber thread. See GOLF BALLS, MAKES OF; HASKELL BALL.

## KENYA, GOLF IN
Golf has continued to flourish since Kenya became an independent republic in 1964, and there are 30 clubs. The senior club in age is Royal Nairobi, founded in 1906, and most of the others were born between the First and Second World Wars. Nairobi, the capital, has another fine course, that of the Muthaiga Club; there are two by the sea at Mombasa—the Mombasa and Nyali Clubs; and other 18-holes courses are the Karen Country Club, near Nairobi, the Kitale Club, the Nakuru Club, the Sigona Club, Kikuyu, and the Limuru Country Club, founded just after the Second World War at 7,000 feet above sea level.

The Kenya Open Amateur Championship was established in 1946 and continued to be played for throughout the change in regime. A new Kenya Open Championship began in 1967, the first winner being Guy Wolstenholme and the runner-up Peter Thomson. The Kenya Golf Union has offices in Nairobi.

## KIDD, Tom
Born St Andrews, where he became a caddie. British Open Champion, 1873—with the very high score of 179 for 36 holes, the highest in the history of the championship before it went over to 72 holes. The weather was not to blame, for it was known to have been a perfect day for golf, and Kidd's "style all through was easy and graceful".

## KIELTY, Dorothy (b 1926)
Runner-up, U.S. Ladies' Championship, 1949. Curtis Cup team, 1948, 1950.

## KING, Samuel Leonard ('Sam') (b 1911)
Assistant Professionals' Champion, 1933; runner-up, 1932. British Senior Professional Champion, 1961, 1962, losing on both occasions to Paul Runyan in the World Senior Championship. Ryder Cup Team, 1937, 1947, 1949.

## KIRBY, Dorothy (b 1919)
U.S. Ladies' Champion, 1951; runner-up, 1939, 1947. Curtis Cup team, 1948, 1952, 1954.

## KIRKALDY, Andrew (1860-1934)
Born near St Andrews. Tied with Willie Park, Jun, for British Open Championship, 1889, but lost play-off; runner-up, 1879, 1891 (to brother Hugh), 1893. Appointed Honorary Professional to the R. and A. 1910, in succession to Tom Morris, who died in 1908.

At the age of 18 he enlisted in the Black Watch and fought at the battle of Tel-el-Kebir in Egypt in 1882. He was professional to the Winchester Club (where J. H. Taylor was also the professional later on) for a short time, but spent most of his career as a playing professional at St Andrews. 'Andra', as he was called, played in many famous challenge matches (sometimes partnered by his brother Hugh). He was one of the great characters of golf, and many stories (some probably apocryphal) are told about the things he did and said. One concerned the spelling of his name; if anybody spelled it Kirkcaldy he used to say: "I'm a man, no' the linoleum toon!" Author of *Fifty Years of Golf* (1921). See BROTHER GOLFERS.

## KIRKALDY, Hugh (1865-94)

Born St Andrews, younger brother of Andrew Kirkaldy. British Open Champion, 1891; joint runner-up (with John Ball and Sandy Herd) 1892. Hugh Kirkaldy was the last British Open Champion to win over only 36 holes, the championship being increased to four rounds in 1892. A wooden putter that belonged to him is the club that has given its name to the famous competition of the Oxford and Cambridge Golfing Society, the President's Putter.

## KIRKWOOD, Joseph H. ('Joe') (1899-1970)

Australian Open Champion, 1920. New Zealand Open Champion, 1920. Canadian Open Champion, 1933. Joe Kirkwood settled in America and became famous as a trick-shot specialist, giving scores of exhibitions. In 1937-8 he toured the world with Walter Hagen, playing in many countries. Played for America in the 1926 match that led to the Ryder Cup series.

## KIROUAC, Mrs Martha (b 1949)

Born Martha Wilkinson. U.S. Ladies' Champion, 1970. Curtis Cup team, 1972.

## KITE, Thomas O. (b 1947)

Runner-up U.S. Amateur Championship, 1970. Walker Cup team, 1969, 1971. Runner-up, U.S. Amateur, 1970.

## KNOCK-OUT COMPETITION

Another term for match play, in which players are drawn against each other, the last two left playing the final. Can be either singles, foursomes or four-balls. See MATCH PLAY.

## KNOWLES, Robert W. (b 1915)

French Open Amateur Champion, 1951, beating Henri de Lamaze in the final. American Walker Cup team, 1951.

## KNUDSON, George (b 1937)

Canadian P.G.A. Champion, 1964, 1968; tied 1962, but lost play-off. Played for Canada in World (formerly Canada) Cup, 1966 (individual winner), 1967, 1968 (team winner with Al Balding), 1969.

## KOCSIS, Charles R. (b 1917)

Runner-up, U.S. Amateur Championship, 1956. Walker Cup team, 1938, 1949, 1957.

## KOLBE

The German word for club. See GOLF, ORIGIN OF WORD.

## KOLF

The Dutch word for club. See GOLF, ORIGIN OF WORD.

## KOLVEN

There has for long been a theory (or heresy) that golf originated in Holland, the chief evidence being those old Dutch paintings of men playing with club and ball, sometimes on the ice. The earliest of these paintings, however, a scene by Hendrick Avercamp, was painted about 1625, while golf had been played in Scotland 200 years earlier.

The Dutch game of Kolven, which is still played in Friesland and North Holland, bears little resemblance to golf. According to the golf historian, Robert Browning,

it is not a field game at all, but is played in a covered space on a wooden floor or on kolf-courts such as are found attached to some inns. It is played with a club that does certainly resemble a clumsy golf club, but the balls are large and heavy—about the size of a cricket ball and a couple of pounds in weight. The object of the game is to strike two posts set up from 40 to 80 feet apart at opposite ends of the court, and the whole art of the game consists in controlling the heavy ball on the hard smooth surface of the court, or of the ice, which of course makes an excellent substitute.

The side which succeeds in striking the post in the fewest strokes wins the game.

The Dutch took Kolven to America with them in the seventeenth century. In a court record of 1657 at Fort Orange (now Albany, New York), several men were charged with playing *Kolven op het ijs* (Kolven on the ice) on a day of public prayer, and three years later the magistrates similarly forbade the playing of Kolven in the streets, "which causes great damage to the windows of houses and also exposes people to the danger of being injured". This was clearly not a game remotely like golf.

See PELL MELL ; UNITED STATES, GOLF IN THE.

## KOREA, GOLF IN

The game was introduced to Korea in 1919, when a 9-holes course was opened in Hyochang Park in Seoul,

the capital. In 1924 a course of 16 holes was constructed on the north-eastern outskirts of the city and, finally, in 1931 the present Seoul Country Club was opened with an 18-holes course of 6,500 yards. This suffered severe damage by the Japanese in the Second World War and in the Korean War, but it was reconstructed and is now a course of 6,800 yards, one of the best in the Orient. Altogether there are 10 courses in Korea, including one in Pusan, the second largest city.

A Korean professional, Hahn Chang Sang, won the 1972 Japanese Open Championship. See MOODY, ORVILLE.

## KROLL, Ted (b 1919)

Runner-up, U.S.P.G.A. Championship, 1956. Runner-up U.S. Open, 1960. Canadian Open Champion, 1962. Ryder Cup team, 1953, 1955, 1957.

## KUWAIT, GOLF IN

The Persian Gulf State of Kuwait has an 18-holes course at the Ahmadi Club. See BAHRAIN, GOLF IN ; TRUCIAL STATES, GOLF IN.

## KYLE, Alexander T. (b 1907)

British Amateur Champion, 1939. Runner-up, Irish Amateur Championship, 1946. Walker Cup team, 1938, 1947, 1951.

## LACEY, Arthur J. (b 1904)

British. Belgian Open Champion, 1931, 1932. French Open Champion, 1932. Ryder Cup team, 1933, 1937, non-playing captain, 1951. Now lives in America with his brother, Charles, also a professional golfer. See BROTHER GOLFERS.

## LACOSTE, Catherine (Mme Jaime De Prado) (b 1945)

Daughter of M. and Mme René Lacoste (*see below*). U.S. Ladies' Champion, 1969. U.S. Women's Open Champion, 1967. British Ladies' Champion, 1969. French Ladies' Open Champion, 1967, 1969, 1970 ; runner-up, 1965. French Ladies' Close Champion, 1968, 1969 ; runner-up, 1966. Spanish Ladies' Champion, 1972.

## LACOSTE, Mme René (b 1908)

Born Simone Thion de la Chaume. British Ladies' Champion, 1927. French Ladies' Open Champion, 1926, 1927, 1930, 1935, 1938, 1939 ; runner-up, 1925. French Ladies' Close Champion, 1925, 1926, 1927, 1928, 1929, 1930, 1936, 1937, 1938 ; runner-up, 1939. British Girls' Champion, 1924. Won Worplesdon Mixed Foursomes, with Roger Wethered, 1926 ; runner-up, 1927. Mme Lacoste married the famous French lawn tennis player, René Lacoste.

## LADIES' CLUBS, OLDEST

The earliest recorded ladies' golf club is the St Andrews Ladies' Club, founded in 1867. Referring to this club, the *St Andrews Gazette* in its issue of 31st August 1872 stated: "Its remarkable success has led to the introduction and culture of golf as a female recreation in England and elsewhere ... Of course, the wielding of the club assumes a mild form under the sway of the gentler sex and has never as yet extended beyond the simple stroke of the putting green."

In *Our Lady of the Green* (1899) Miss Issette Pearson, one of the pioneers of ladies' golf, says that in 1886 the St Andrews Ladies' Club had 500 members, "but it is doubtful if any club but a putter was used". She adds that the Westward Ho! Ladies' Club was instituted in 1868 and that "the next two clubs are Musselburgh Ladies' and the London Scottish Ladies', both instituted in 1872". These were followed by Carnoustie (1873), Troon (1882), Bath (1883), Hayling (1884) and Cupar and Great Yarmouth (1885).

By then the ladies had progressed beyond the putting green and the first British Ladies' Championship was played in 1893 on the 9-holes ladies' course of the Lytham and St Anne's Club, Lancashire.

See BRITISH LADIES' CHAMPIONSHIP ; PEARSON, ISSETTE ; SCOTT, LADY MARGARET.

## LADIES' GOLF UNION

Ladies' golf in Britain really began seriously in 1893 with the formation of the Ladies' Golf Union, soon followed by the first British Ladies' Championship. The prime movers were the lady members of the Royal Wimbledon Club, particularly Miss Issette Pearson, who received much help and encouragement from a male member of the club, Dr W. Laidlaw Purves. Miss Pearson (later Mrs T. H. Miller) became the first honorary secretary of the Union and served it in various capacities until it was firmly established.

The primary objects of the Union were set out as follows:
1. To promote the interests of the game of golf.
2. To obtain a uniformity of rules of the game by establishing a representative legislative authority.
3. To establish a uniform system of handicapping.
4. To act as a tribunal and court of reference on points of uncertainty.
5. To arrange the Annual Championship Competition and to obtain the funds necessary for that purpose.

These five objects have remained the basis of L.G.U. activities to the present day, with the addition of the arranging of international matches. The efficiency of the first committee is shown by the fact that the union was formed on 19th April 1893, and the first championship held on 13th-16th June.

In addition to the L.G.U., there are: English Ladies' Golf Association, Irish Ladies' Golf Union, Scottish Ladies' Golf Association and Welsh Ladies' Golf Union. See BRITISH LADIES' CHAMPIONSHIP.

## LADY ASTOR TROPHY
See COMMONWEALTH TOURNAMENT (LADIES).

## LADY GOLFER, FIRST
The first lady golfer, of whom there is any record, was Mary, Queen of Scots, daughter of James V of Scotland. A few days after the murder in 1567 of her second husband, Lord Darnley (father of James I of England and VI of Scotland), she caused a scandal by being seen "playing golf and pall-mall in the fields beside Seton". This is all we know of her as a golfer, but her father and son were both golfers. See PELL MELL ; ROYAL GOLFERS.

## LAG UP
A term, probably originating in America, used in describing the execution of a long putt, in such phrases as: "He lagged up a 40-foot putt from the far end of the green."

## LAIDLAY, John E. (b 1860)
British Amateur Champion, 1889, 1891 ; runner-up, 1888, 1890, 1893. Runner-up, British Open Championship, 1893, only two shots behind Willie Auchterlonie. He is said to have been the first man to play golf in Egypt and laid out a 9-holes course at Mena House, near the Pyramids of Gizeh, just outside Cairo. See EGYPT, GOLF IN.

## LAMB, Henry A. (1845-93)
Runner-up, British Amateur Championship, 1886. Founder, with Dr W. Laidlaw Purves and other golfers from Wimbledon, of the course on the Kent coast that was to become the Royal St George's Club, Sandwich. He was also said to have been the inventor of the wooden club with a convex face called a 'bulger' and, with Dr Laidlaw Purves, the method of handicapping in match play by giving three-quarters of the difference in handicap. He was secretary of the Royal Wimbledon Club for some years until his death in 1893. See BULGER ; PURVES, W. LAIDLAW.

## LAMB, Willie (b 1902)
Left Scotland and became professional in Canada, 1924. Canadian Professional Champion, 1928, 1929, 1930, 1933, 1935.

## LANGLEY, John D. A. (b 1918)
English Amateur Champion, 1950 ; runner-up, 1936. British Boys' Amateur Champion, 1935. Won *Golf Illustrated* Gold Vase, 1952, 1953. Walker Cup team, 1936, 1951, 1953.

## LANGRIDGE, Mrs Susan (b 1943)
Born Susan Armitage. Scottish Girls' Open Stroke Play Champion, 1962. Curtis Cup team, 1964, 1966.

## LAPLAND, GOLF IN
The world's most northerly golf course is Bjorkliden in Lapland. It is situated well inside the Arctic Circle, near the border between Sweden and Norway. The terrain is gorse-covered

moorland; there are mat teeing grounds; the tiny 'greens' are of gravel, not turf; the caddies are Lapps, dressed in their traditional clothes; the clubhouse is the only hotel in the neighbourhood. Needless to say, golf is strictly seasonal at Bjorkliden.

## LASSEN, E. A. (b 1883)
British Amateur Champion, 1908; runner-up, 1911.

## LATERAL WATER HAZARD
See HAZARDS; RULES OF GOLF, Rule 33-3.

## LAWRENCE, Joan B. (b 1930)
Scottish Ladies' Champion, 1962, 1963, 1964; runner-up, 1965. Fife County Ladies' Champion every year except one between 1957 and 1969. Curtis Cup team, 1964.

## LAWRIE, Charles D. (b 1923)
Non-playing captain, Walker Cup team, 1961, 1963.

## LEATHER MASHIE
A facetious term indicating that a player or caddie has used his shoe—the 'leather mashie'—to improve the lie of his ball. It goes back to the days when over-zealous caddies were sometimes suspected of such practice.

## LEBANON, GOLF IN
On the outskirts of Beirut, the capital, is the Golf Club of Lebanon. It has a 9-holes course, with a two-round length of 6,738 yards. Another 9-holes course is that of the Ras el Lados Club, Tripoli. The recent troubles have had a bad effect on golf.

## LE BLAN, Manette (b 1908)
French. British Ladies' Champion, 1928. Runner-up, French Ladies' Close Championship, 1926. She married a brother of Mlle Simone Thion de la Chaume (Mme René Lacoste).

## LEES, Arthur (b 1908)
Irish Open Champion, 1939. Runner-up, Czechoslovak Open Championship, 1935, 1937. Runner-up, German Open Championship, 1938. Won Dunlop Masters (after tie with Norman Von Nida), 1947. British Senior Professional Champion, 1959. Ryder Cup team, 1947, 1949, 1951, 1955.

## LE FEUVRE, Carol (b 1952)
British Girls' Champion, 1970. English Girls' Champion, 1969, 1970; runner-up, 1968. Dutch International Ladies' Champion, 1972. See JERSEY GOLFERS.

## LEFT HAND BELOW RIGHT
A number of players have played golf—and good golf too—with the left hand held below the right on the shaft. They include the coloured South African professional, Susunker Sewgolum, who won the Dutch Open Championship in 1959, 1960, 1964, and Joseph Charles, Belgian Open Amateur Champion, 1949; this remarkable golfer, who did not take up golf until he was 43, got through three rounds of the British Amateur Championship in 1947 and won the Luxembourg Open Amateur Championship, 1950, 1952.

Several golfers have found that this grip helps to cure putting problems; well-known 'wrong way round' putters include Orville Moody, 1969 American Open Champion, and Peter Alliss, the British Ryder Cup player.

When they first pick up a golf club, children often hold the club this way, and it is interesting to find H. S. C. Everard writing in the Badminton Library volume on *Golf* (1890) about young Tom Morris that: "At the age of ten or twelve Tom began to knock balls about and, curiously enough, began to drive with his left hand below the right—a mode of play adopted by only two players in the writer's experience." It is also interesting to note what Ed Dudley said in his foreword to Ben Hogan's *Power Golf* (1949): "Watching Ben Hogan now it is hard to believe that such a smooth golfing machine started left-handed, shifted over to play from the right side, but cross-handed, and then tried both the conventional right-handed interlocking and overlapping grips, before he finally settled upon an adaptation of the overlapping grip which he uses today."

## LEFT-HANDED GOLFERS

Considering how many famous cricketers have played left-handed, it is surprising how few famous golfers have done so. Easily the best-known left-handed professional has been Bob Charles of New Zealand, winner of the British Open Championship in 1963 and many other events. The best-known amateur has been P. B. ('Laddie') Lucas, member of the British Walker Cup team, 1936, 1947, 1949. A distinguished Australian left-hander is Len Nettlefold, Australian Amateur Champion, 1926, 1928. Harry Vardon could play almost equally well left-handed.

A young amateur who plays left-handed is Peter Dawson, of Ganton, Yorkshire, winner of the Carris Trophy (1968) and runner-up in the 1969 English Amateur Championship. One of the few lady left-handers is Miss Kathryn Phillips, English Girls' Champion, 1968. An old-time left-hander was 'Old Walkinshaw', whose name is perpetuated in the bunker on the Old Course, St Andrews, called 'Walkinshaw's Grave'.

## LEGLISE, Jacques (b 1906)

French Open Amateur Champion, 1937; runner-up, 1939, 1947. French Amateur Native Champion, 1937; runner-up, 1935, 1938, 1949. Belgian Open Amateur Champion, 1948. Life Vice-President, European Golf Association. President, French Golf Federation.

## LEGRANGE, Cobie (b 1942)

Born South Africa. Won British Dunlop Masters tournament, 1964, 1969. Tied French Open Championship (with Roberto De Vicenzo), 1964, but lost play-off; runner-up, 1965.

## LEITCH, Cecilia (Cecil) (1891-1977)

British Ladies' Champion, 1914, 1920, 1921, 1926; runner-up, 1922, 1925, both times to Joyce Wethered, whom she had defeated in the 1921 final. English Ladies' Champion, 1914, 1919; runner-up, 1920, to Miss Wethered. Canadian Ladies' Open Champion, 1921, winning the final against Miss M. M'Bride by the margin of 17 and 15. French Ladies' Open Champion, 1912, 1914, 1920, 1921 (defeating Miss Wethered in the final), 1924; runner-up, 1926.

Her sister, Edith (Mrs Guedalla), won the English Ladies' Championship in 1927; another sister, May (Mrs Millar), was also a good golfer.

Of Miss Leitch as a golfer, Miss Enid Wilson has written: "Miss Leitch was the first of the Amazons. Her swing was graceful, but more powerful than had hitherto been seen in women's events. In particular her crisp shots with the iron clubs set a new standard for her sex." In 1910, receiving nine strokes a round, she defeated Harold Hilton in a 72-holes match at Walton Heath and Sunningdale by 2 and 1.

See HEATHCOAT-AMORY, LADY; HILTON, HAROLD; SISTER GOLFERS.

## LEITH LINKS

The links at Leith, on the Firth of Forth, were the first—and for many years only—playground of the golfers of Edinburgh. Charles I was playing there in 1642 when news reached him of the rebellion in Ireland, causing him to abandon his game. His younger son, James, Duke of York, played —and won—the first international foursome there, partnered by a shoemaker named Patersone against two English noblemen. By the end of the seventeenth century golf at Leith was the favourite amusement of the Edinburgh aristocracy and the accounts of Sir John Foulis of Ravelstoun—to take one example—include an entry of 14th February 1672: "Spent at Leith at Golfe . . . £2 0. 0."

There was no club, as we know it

today, at Leith until 1768 when the Honourable Company of Edinburgh Golfers built a 'Golf House' on a corner of the links. The Edinburgh Burgess Society also played at Leith until the course became unsuitable. This was in the early 1830s, and Edinburgh's many golfers had to find fresh playgrounds.

See EDINBURGH GOLFERS, HONOURABLE COMPANY OF; ROYAL BURGESS GOLFING SOCIETY OF EDINBURGH; SMOLLETT ON GOLF.

## LEMA, Anthony David ('Tony') (1934-66)

British Open Champion, 1964, playing amazing golf at St Andrews in a high wind on his first visit to Britain and after only one practice round. Runner-up, U.S. Masters, 1963. Mexican Open Champion, 1961, 1962. Ryder Cup team, 1963, 1965. Nicknamed 'Champagne Tony', he was killed in an air crash in 1966.

## LENCZYK, Grace (Mrs Cronin) (b 1928)

American. U.S. Ladies' Champion, 1948. Canadian Ladies' Champion, 1947, 1948. Curtis Cup team, 1948, 1950.

## LEONARD, Stan (b 1915)

Canadian P.G.A. Champion, 1940, 1941, 1950, 1951, 1954, 1957, 1959, 1961. Individual winner, World (formerly Canada) Cup, 1959.

## LESOTHO, GOLF IN

There is a 9-holes course at Maseru, the capital of what was formerly the enclave of Basutoland within the Republic of South Africa.

## LESSER, Pat (Mrs Harbottle) (b 1933)

U.S. Ladies' Champion, 1955. Curtis Cup team, 1956.

## LIBYA, GOLF IN

During the Second World War, those who fought up and down the Western Desert may have thought that the green and flower-strewn Jebel Akhdar had certain golfing possibilities. And in 1949 the Benghazi Club was founded, with 9 holes and a full-round length of some 5,500 yards. There is another club at Tripoli. Now that Libya has severed its close association with Britain, the game is still officially encouraged.

## LIE

The situation of the ball on the ground after a stroke has been played. A 'lie' may be of several kinds—good, bad, indifferent, uphill, downhill, hanging, tight (i.e. nestling into the ground) and various adjectives from 'perfect' to 'impossible'. Also used as a verb in 'lying well', etc.

The term 'lie' is also used to describe the inclination of the clubhead when it is resting on the ground behind the ball.

One of the fundamental rules is that a player shall not improve the lie of his ball (Rules of Golf, Rule 17-1).

## LIKE-AS-WE-LIE

An old term, not so often used nowadays, indicating that the opposing sides have played the same number of strokes at a hole.

## LIKE, PLAYING THE

A player (or side) playing a stroke that makes his score for the hole the same as that of his opponent is said to be 'playing the like'. See ODD, PLAYING THE.

## LINDRICK

Near Sheffield, Yorkshire. Founded 1891. Length: 6,525 yards. S.S.S. 71. Fashioned on sandy heathland soil akin to seaside conditions. Housed Ryder Cup match, 1957; Curtis Cup match, 1960.

## LINE

The correct direction that the ball should travel towards the green or hole. It may not necessarily be the straightest direction—in the case of a dog-leg hole, for instance, the correct line for one golfer might be different from that of another either stronger or weaker player. There is a correct line for every shot in golf, from the longest drive to the shortest putt. See Dog-Leg.

## LINKS

A word, used both in the singular and the plural, indicating a stretch of flat or gently undulating land along the seashore, covered with short grass ; derivation probably from the Old English 'hlinc', a ridge of land. To merit the term 'links', a golf course should strictly be a seaside one on true links turf, but 'golf links' is sometimes given a wider application to include any area where golf is played. Apart from Blackheath, London, where golf may have been played in the early seventeenth century, all original golf courses were true links.

## LINSKILL, W. T. (1855-1929)

Founder and for many years honorary secretary of the Cambridge University Golf Club and chief instigator of the first Oxford and Cambridge match in 1878. Author of *Golf* in the All-England Series (1889).

## LIP

The extreme edge of the hole ; a ball that finishes there without dropping is said to 'lip the hole'. A similar word is 'rim'.

## LISTER, John (b 1947)

Runner-up, New Zealand Open Championship, 1969.

## LITTLE ASTON

Streetly, Sutton Coldfield, Staffordshire. Founded 1908. Mature parkland. Length: 6,693 yards. S.S.S. 72. Housed English Amateur Championship, 1927, 1948. English Open Amateur Stroke Play Championship, 1970.

## LITTLE, W. Lawson (1910-68)

The only man to win the American and British Amateur Championships in the same year twice running—

I

1934 and 1935. In the 1934 British final he defeated James Wallace by 14 and 13, but in 1935 won against Dr William Tweddell by only one hole. U.S. Open Champion, 1940, after tie with Gene Sarazen. Canadian Open Champion, 1936. Walker Cup team, 1934. Turned professional, 1936.

Of him as a golfer Bernard Darwin wrote: "Lawson was intimidating. Not very tall, but enormously broad and enormously strong, capable of a daunting pugnacity of expression, he was as a bull in the long game, and yet no dove could be gentler near the hole." In 1934 he carried no fewer than 23 clubs in his bag.

## LITTLER, Gene A. (b 1930)

U.S. Open Champion, 1961. U.S. Amateur Champion, 1953. Tied U.S. Masters, 1970, with Billy Casper, but lost play-off. Runner-up, Piccadilly World Match Play Tournament, 1969. Turned professional, 1954. Played in both Walker Cup team (1953) and Ryder Cup team (1961, 1963, 1965, 1967, 1969, 1971). See WALKER AND RYDER CUPS, PLAYED IN BOTH.

## LLOYD, Joe

The third U.S. Open Champion (1897) was an Englishman from Hoylake, who was professional at the Essex Country Club, near Boston, Massachusetts, in the summer and at the Pau Club, in the Pyrenees, in the winter. The runner-up was the famous Willie Anderson, who was to win the title four times, including the hat-trick in 1903, 1904, 1905.

Lloyd—he was nicknamed 'The General'—laid out the nine holes of the first course at Cannes for the Grand Duke Michael of Russia ; later, however, a better site was found at La Napoule. See PAU CLUB ; ROYAL GOLFERS.

## LOCAL KNOWLEDGE

The useful knowledge acquired by a golfer based on the experience he has gained of the best way to play a particular hole or a particular course.

## LOCKE, Arthur D'Arcy ('Bobby') (b 1917)

British Open Champion—first from the Commonwealth—1949, 1950, 1952, 1957; runner-up, 1946, 1954. Leading amateur in British Open, 1936, 1937. South African Open Champion, 1935, 1937, 1938, 1939, 1940, 1946, 1950, 1951. South African Amateur Champion, 1935, 1937. South African Professional Champion, 1938, 1939, 1940, 1946, 1950, 1951. Canadian Open Champion, 1947. Egyptian Open Champion, 1954. French Open Champion, 1952, 1953. German Open Champion, 1954. Irish Open Champion, 1938. Mexican Open Champion, 1952. Swiss Open Champion, 1954. Winner of many tournaments in America. Turned professional, 1938. Author of *Bobby Locke on Golf* (1953).

## LOCKHART, Robert

A Scot from Dunfermline and, with his schoolfriend, John Reid, one of the founders of golf in the United States. He was a linen-merchant and had learnt to play golf at Musselburgh. In 1887, on a visit to Scotland, he bought some clubs and balls from Old Tom Morris's shop in St Andrews and took them back to Yonkers-on-Hudson, New York, where he lived. In that year he was arrested for hitting a ball about in Central Park, but, not discouraged, interested various American friends in the game and became one of the founders in 1888 of the St Andrews Golf Club of Yonkers, the pioneer American club. See REID, JOHN ; ST ANDREWS GOLF CLUB OF YONKERS ; UNITED STATES, GOLF IN THE.

## LOFT

Used as a verb, to loft the ball merely means to hit it well up into the air, particularly over an obstacle. Used as a noun, it means the backward slope of the face of a club, each club having a certain degree of loft unless they are absolutely flat in the face as may be the case with a put-ter; a driver and a No 1 iron always have at least a small degree of loft.

## LOFTER

Also called a lofting iron or lofting cleek, it corresponded in the old days to the modern No 5 or 6 iron. By the 1890s it had already superseded the wooden baffy for playing approach shots. Willie Park, Jun, invented a club called 'Park's Patent Lofter'. See 'PARK'S PATENT LOFTER'.

## LONDON SCOTTISH CLUB

See WIMBLEDON COMMON, GOLF ON.

## LONGEST CHAMPIONSHIP FINAL MATCHES

The longest final matches in leading match play championships were:

British Amateur. 39th: Gordon Clark against Michael Lunt, Ganton, 1964.

U.S. Amateur. 39th: Sam Urzetta against Frank Stranahan, Minneapolis Country Club, 1950.

British Ladies'. 38th: Moira Paterson against Frances Stephens, Troon, 1952.

U.S. Ladies'. 41st: Mrs JoAnne Carner against Mrs J. D. Streit, Pittsburg, 1966.

U.S.P.G.A. 38th: Gene Sarazen against Walter Hagen, Pelham, New York, 1923 ; Paul Runyan against Craig Wood, Buffalo, New York, 1934 ; Vic Ghezzi against Byron Nelson, Denver, Colorado, 1941.

## LONGEST HOLES

According to the *Golfer's Handbook*, the world's longest hole is the 17th—745 yards—at the Black Mountain Club, North Carolina. The longest hole on a British Championship course is the 6th at Troon, Ayrshire—580 yards, and the longest American one the 17th at Baltusrol, Springfield, New Jersey—623 yards.

## LONGEST OPEN CHAMPIONSHIP COURSES

For the 1968 British Open Championship the Carnoustie course, Angus, was stretched to a record 7,252 yards. Gary Player won with a score of 289, and the fact that nobody broke the strict par of 288 is not surprising when one realises that holes of 475, 473 and 468 yards were assessed as par fours and that one of the three short holes measured 243 yards. Gary Player called it "the toughest course in the world", and Byron Nelson, who was there as a spectator, said that it was the toughest course any professionals have ever had to play in any country in the world.

The longest U.S. Open Championship course is the Hazeltine National, near Minneapolis, scene of the 1970 event—7,151 yards, par 72.

## LONGHURST, Henry Carpenter (1909-1978)

German Open Amateur Champion, 1936. Runner-up, French Open Amateur Championship, 1936. Runner-up, Swiss Open Amateur Championship, 1928. One of Britain's best-known golf writers and television commentators. Golf correspondent of the *Sunday Times* since 1947. Author of many books on golf and other subjects. M.P. Acton Division of Middlesex, 1943-45.

## LOOP

The term given to a swing in which the clubhead doesn't follow the orthodox up-and-down line, but executes a loop either outside or inside the line. With a good player—and there are two outstanding examples of players with a loop in their swings, James Bruen, the Irish amateur, and Gay Brewer, the American professional—the clubhead is brought back to the correct plane before the ball is struck, but in the case of an indifferent player the odds are against this happening.

## LOOP, THE

On the Old Course at St Andrews, the 'loop' is the name given to the 8th, 9th, 10th and 11th holes at the far end of the course. The 8th and 11th are the only two short holes and the 9th and 10th are comparatively

short par four holes, so that good players have been able to get a run of four threes round the loop. In his third round of 68, when winning the 1964 Open Championship, Tony Lema not only had threes at all the loop holes, but a three at the 7th as well. In setting up a record 72 in 1894, 'Freddie' Tait had threes at the 8th-12th holes inclusive.

## LOOSE IMPEDIMENTS

"The term 'loose impediments' denotes natural objects not fixed or growing and not adhering to the ball, and includes stones not solidly embedded, leaves, twigs, branches and the like, dung, worms and insects and casts or heaps made by them. Snow and ice are either casual water or loose impediments, at the option of the player" (Rules of Golf Definition).

In the R. and A. code for 1857, under which the first Open Championships were played, clause IV stated that "all loose impediments within twelve inches of the ball may be removed on or off the course, when the ball lies on grass".

See OBSTRUCTIONS ; RULES OF GOLF, Rules 18, 27, 28, 35.

## 'LORD BYRON'

See NELSON, BYRON.

## LOW, John Laing (1869-1929)

Runner-up, British Amateur Championship, 1901. He captained the Oxford and Cambridge team that toured America in 1903, helping to popularise the game there ; on his return he made the prophetic remark, looking to the day when American golfers would be invading the British courses: "Already I hear the hooting of their steamers in the Mersey." He was in 1897 a founder—and for 20 years captain or secretary—of the Oxford and Cambridge Golfing Society.

He was a great golf legislator and was for many years chairman of the R. and A. Rules of Golf Committee. He was a pioneer of matched sets of clubs, suggesting in *Concerning Golf* (1903) that golfers should get a favourite iron copied exactly by other clubs with varying degrees of loft. His one blind spot was the Haskell ball, which ousted the old 'gutty' in 1902, claiming that the rubber-cored ball spoilt the game. Besides *Concerning Golf*, he wrote *The Royal and Ancient Game of Golf* (1912).

See OXFORD AND CAMBRIDGE GOLFING SOCIETY ; SET.

## LOWEST ROUNDS IN OPEN CHAMPIONSHIPS

The lowest rounds—65—in the British Open Championship have been played by the following golfers: Henry Cotton (Royal St George's, 1934), Eric Brown (Royal Lytham and St Anne's, 1958), Leopoldo Ruiz (Royal Lytham and St Anne's, 1958), Peter Butler (Muirfield, 1966), Christy O'Connor (Royal Lytham and St Anne's 1969), Neil Coles (St Andrews, 1970).

The lowest round—63—in the U.S. Open Championship was played by Johnny Miller (Oakmont Country Club, Pittsburgh, Pa., 1973).

## LOWEST WINNING SCORES IN OPEN CHAMPIONSHIPS

In the British Open Championship the lowest winning score was Arnold Palmer's 276 (71, 69, 67, 69) at Troon, 1962. Next best were Bob Charles's 277 (68, 72, 66, 71) and Phil Rodgers's 277 (67, 68, 73, 69) at Royal Lytham and St Anne's, 1963—Charles winning the play-off.

In the U.S. Open Championship the lowest winning scores were Jack Nicklaus's 275 (71, 67, 72, 65) at Baltusrol, Springfield, New Jersey, 1967, and Lee Trevino's 275 (69, 68, 69, 69) at Oak Hill, Rochester, New York, 1968.

## LU LIANG HUAN (b 1936)

Runner-up, to Lee Trevino, British Open Championship, 1971. With his nickname of 'Mr Lu', endeared himself to the spectators. French Open Champion, 1971. Winner, with Hsieh Min-Nam, World (formerly Canada) Cup, 1972. See TAIWAN, GOLF IN.

## LUCAS, Percy Belgrave ('Laddie') (b 1915)

British Boys' Amateur Champion, 1933. Played for Cambridge against Oxford, 1935, 1936, 1937 (captain). Won President's Putter, Oxford and Cambridge Golfing Society, 1949 ; runner-up, 1947, 1950, 1953. Walker Cup team, 1936, 1947, 1949 (captain). One of Britain's best left-handed golfers. M.P. Brentford and Chiswick, 1950-59.

## LUCIFER GOLFING SOCIETY

This famous society was founded in 1921 by a small group of keen golfers, mainly London business men, with the object of serving the interests of golf and golfers and creating and cementing golfing friendships. As golf matches were to be one of its chief functions, the original choice of name was the Match Society, but as one was already in existence, the name Lucifer—an old name for a friction match—was adopted. Membership is restricted to 100.

The society's best-known function is the promotion of the Lucifer Society Empire meeting, a gathering of overseas golfers which began in 1926 ; players have come to England from the dominions and colonies and from such minor but equally keen places as the Ascension Islands, Fiji, Mauritius and the Falkland Islands.

Winners of the Empire Trophy (which has Lucifer on top wearing cap and plus-fours and carrying a club over his shoulder) have come from India, South and East Africa, Burma, Ceylon and Australia, but the best-known was a young man of 19 when he won in 1936—Bobby Locke. See LOCKE, ARTHUR D'ARCY.

## 'LUCY LOCKIT'

See SOCKETING.

## LUNT, Michael (b 1935)

Runner-up, English Amateur Championship, 1962. Won *Golf Illustrated* Gold Vase, 1958. Walker Cup team,

1959, 1961, 1963, 1965. Son of Stanley Lunt.

## LUNT, Stanley (b 1900)

English Amateur Champion, 1934. President English Golf Union, 1960.

## LUXEMBOURG, GOLF IN

Golf has been played at the Golf Club Grand-Ducal de Luxembourg since 1936. It has a good length course of 18 holes. The amateur record of 71 is held by Hans Sachs, who one would like to think was a meistersinger as well as a golfer! The Luxembourg International Amateur Championship was held from 1938-57, with an interruption in the war years; the Ladies' Open Championship in 1938, 1939.

## LYLE, Sandy (b 1958)

British Youths' Champion, 1977. English Open Amateur Stroke Play Champion, 1975, 1977. Walker Cup team, 1977.

## LYON, George S. (b 1878)

Canadian. Canadian Amateur Champion, 1898, 1900, 1903, 1905, 1906, 1907, 1912, 1914; runner-up, 1904, 1910. Runner-up, U.S. Amateur Championship, 1906.

## MacCANN, Mrs P. G. (b 1922)

Born Catherine Smye. British Ladies' Champion, 1951. Irish Ladies' Champion, 1949, 1961; runner-up, 1947, 1952, 1957, 1960. Curtis Cup team, 1952 (reserve).

## M'CREADY, Samuel Maxwell ('Max') (b 1918)

British Amateur Champion, 1949. Walker Cup team, 1949, 1951,

## McDERMOTT, John J. (b 1891)

The first American-born golfer to win the U.S. Open Championship, becoming champion in 1911 (after a tie with Mike Brady and George Simpson) and successfully defending his title in 1912; runner-up, 1910, with the Smith brothers, Alex and Macdonald, losing to Alex in the play-off.

## MACDONALD, Charles Blair (1856-1932)

Born Niagara Falls, New York. At the age of 16 entered the University of St Andrews and began a lifelong interest in golf. In 1895 he became the first U.S. Amateur Champion, defeating a young man called Charles E. Sands in the 36 holes final by 12 and 11. There were 32 entrants. His son-in-law, H. J. Whigham, won the Amateur Championship in 1896, 1897.

Macdonald laid out the Chicago Club's course at Wheaton and also —in 1909—his most famous golf course architectural achievement, the National Links on Long Island, where he reproduced, as far as was possible, various classic British holes such as the 3rd, 11th and 17th at St Andrews, the 'Cardinal' and 'Alps' at Prestwick, the 'Redan' at North Berwick, the 'Sahara' at Royal St George's, Sandwich, and the 5th and 9th at the Royal West Norfolk Club, Brancaster.

He was well-known as a golf legislator and was an original member, in 1894, of the Amateur Golf Association of the United States, which became the American Golf Association and finally the United States Golf Association; he and Laurence Curtis were appointed "a special committee to interpret the rules of golf" and they worked in conjunction with the R. and A. for many years.

In 1913 Macdonald offered to put up a cup to be played for by teams of four amateurs from any country— an idea which led after the First World War to the Walker Cup series, the first match being played appropriately at Macdonald's National Links in 1922. Author of *Scotland's Gift: Golf* (1928), one of the most interesting books on early American golf.

## MACDONALD, Scott (b 1944)

Runner-up, English Open Amateur Stroke Play Championship, 1970, 1971. Scottish Amateur Stroke Play Champion, 1969. Walker Cup team, 1971.

## McEVOY, Peter (b 1953)

British Amateur Champion, 1977, 1978. English Amateur Champion, 1977. Walker Cup team, 1977.

## McEWAN FAMILY

A great clubmaking family of the 18th and 19th centuries. James McEwan set up business at Leith about 1770 and was succeeded by his son Peter (1781-1836), who married a daughter of Douglas Gourlay, the 'feathery' ball-maker; his grandson Douglas (1809-1886); and great-grandson Peter (1834-1895). One of this Peter's sons, Douglas, carried on the business, while three other sons opened a branch at Freshfield, Lancashire. Douglas's son, Peter, also a clubmaker, died in St Andrews in 1971.

Of the first Douglas McEwan it was said (by W. Dalrymple, a contemporary authority on golf): "He was without doubt one of the very best clubmakers who ever lived and his clubs were models of symmetry and shape. Undoubtedly McEwan clubs show that the much-praised elegance which is associated with Philp clubs is not missing in these McEwan clubs, and viewed impartially there is little to choose between the clubs of these two makers, with possibly a preference to McEwan in the matter of putters."

The McEwans used to bring clubs for sale over to St Andrews from Edinburgh until in 1827 the society announced that "the salary or allowance of two guineas now payable annually to the Leith clubmaker for attending at the General Meeting should be discontinued"—and Hugh Philp was given a free hand.

See GOURLAY ; PHILP, HUGH.

## MACFARLANE, Willie (1890-1961)

Scottish. U.S. Open Champion, 1925, after tie with Bobby Jones. They both went round in 75 in the first 18-holes play-off and then Macfarlane's 72 beat Jones's 73.

## MACFIE, Allan Fullarton (1859-1943)

Winner, 1885, of the Open Amateur meeting held at the Royal Liverpool Club, Hoylake, that was later recognised as being the first British Amateur Championship. In the final he beat Horace Hutchinson, winner of the championship in 1886 and 1887, by which time the event had been officially established.

## MACGREGOR, George (b 1944)

British Walker Cup team, 1971.

## McHALE, James B. (b 1916)

American Walker Cup team, 1949, 1951.

## McINTIRE, Barbara (b 1935)

American. U.S. Ladies' Champion, 1959, 1964. British Ladies' Champion, 1960. Tied U.S. Women's Open Championship, 1956, but lost play-off with Mrs K. Cornelius. Curtis Cup team, 1958, 1960, 1962, 1964, 1966, 1972.

## McKENNA, Mary (b 1949)

Irish Ladies' Champion, 1969, 1972 ; runner-up, 1968. Curtis Cup team, 1970, 1972, 1974, 1976.

## MACKENZIE, Dr C. Alister (1890-1934)

Scottish. Well-known golf-course architect, both in Britain and America. His courses include the Augusta National, Georgia (with Bobby Jones), Cypress Point (California), Alwoodley (Yorkshire). Author of *Golf Course Architecture* (1920).

## M'LEAN, Jack (1911-59)

Scottish. Scottish Amateur Champion, 1932, 1933, 1934; runner-up, 1935. Irish Open Amateur Champion, 1932, 1933 ; runner-up, 1935. Runner-up, U.S. Amateur Championship, 1936, after being the victim of a dead stymie on the 34th green against Johnny Fischer. Walker Cup team, 1934, 1936. Turned professional, 1936. See STYMIES, FAMOUS.

## McLEOD, Fred (b 1882)

U.S. Open Champion, 1908, after tie with Willie Smith; runner-up, 1921. Runner-up, U.S.P.G.A. Championship, 1919. McLeod, who was born in Scotland, was professional at the Midlothian Club when he won the U.S. Open ; he then went to the Columbia Country Club, where he stayed for over 50 years until he retired in 1968. He came over to England to play in the 1926 Open at Royal Lytham and St Anne's, finishing seventh. Afterwards he took part in the informal Anglo-American match at Wentworth, which developed into the Ryder Cup series, beginning in 1927.

## McNAMARA, Tom (1885-1939)

Three times runner-up in the U.S. Open Championship—1909, 1912, 1915.

## McRUVIE, Eric (b 1909)

Irish Open Amateur Champion, 1931. British Boys' Amateur Champion, 1926. Walker Cup team, 1932, 1934.

## MADEIRA, GOLF IN

The Club de Golf do Santo da Serra, 2,300 feet up, but within easy reach of Funchal, has been established since 1937. It has 9 holes and a length of 2,622 yards. Henry Cotton has designed a new full-length course called Campo de Golf Lagoa, about six miles from Funchal.

## MAHAFFEY, John (b 1948)

American. U.S.P.G.A. Champion, 1978, after three-way tie with Tom Watson and Jerry Pate. Also tied U.S. Open in 1975, but lost play-off with Lou Graham.

## MAJORCA, GOLF IN

Golfers are catered for in Majorca, in the Spanish Balearic Islands, just as they are in Spain. There are two new 18-holes courses, at Son Severa and Costa de los Pinos, and two 9-holes courses—the Son Vida Club, about three miles from Palma, the capital, and the Punta Rotja Club, about 45 miles away.

## MALAWI, GOLF IN

There are five flourishing clubs in what was formerly the territory of Nyasaland until independence under Dr Banda in 1963. At Zomba, the capital, is the Zomba Gymkhana Club, where various other sports are also played. Other clubs are at Blantyre, Lilongwe, Limbe and Mlanje.

## MALAYSIA, GOLF IN

The Federation of Malaysia comprises 13 states—and golf is played in seven of them. By far the senior clubs in age are the Perak Club, at Taiping in Perak State, which claims to go back to 1888, and Royal Selangor, in the capital of Selangor State, Kuala Lumpur, which claims 1893 as its date of birth.

The Perak Club's course has 9 holes, but the newer Perak Turf Club, at Ipoh, the state capital, has a full-length 18-holes course. Royal Selangor has two 18-holes courses (the Old and the New—like St Andrews), with a par-3 9-holes course. The Malayan Amateur Championship was held at Royal Selangor from 1894-1962 and since 1963 it has housed the Open Championship of Malaysia.

In the state of Johore, near the capital, Johore-Bahru, is the Royal Johore International Club, owned by the Sultan. It has 18 holes, and, although a private club, visitors are welcomed.

In Malacca, capital of the state of that name, is the Ayer Keroh Club, with an 18-holes course of nearly 7,000 yards. The Penang Turf Club, in the state of Penang, also has an 18-holes course. So has the Miri Club, in the state of Sarawak (governed until recent years by the Brooke family), while the Kinabalu Club, in Kota Kinabalu, in the state of Sabah, has one of 9 holes.

In the 1969 World (formerly Canada) Cup at Singapore, Malaysia, represented by two amateurs, finished on 598—a better score than the Irish team's and many others.

## MALDIVE ISLANDS, GOLF IN THE

The Maldive Islands are a chain of coral atolls in the Indian Ocean, some 400 miles south-east of Ceylon. On one of the chief inhabited islands—Gan —is the Gan Island Club, founded in 1962. The course measures 4,900 yards and there are 18 holes. Many of the players belong to the R.A.F. station there. See CHRISTMAS ISLAND, GOLF ON.

## MALTA, GOLF IN

There is only one club in Malta—
the Royal Malta Club, at The Marsa.
It is a sporting course of 5,100 yards,
founded before the Second World
War.

## MANCHESTER CLUB, OLD

The Old Manchester Club claims
foundation in 1818, which could make
it the second oldest in England after
Royal Blackheath. Some Manchester
golfers began playing over Kersal
Moor about 1814 and formed a club
four years later. They had to leave
Kersal Moor in 1882 and, after a
homeless interval of nine years, settled
at Broughton Park in 1891. Again
they had to move in 1904, to a course
at Vine Street, where they stayed until Salford Council took over the land
in 1960. The ancient club is kept in
being by holding two annual meetings
at other Manchester area clubs, and
it still has its three historic trophies—
the Bannerman Gold Medal (1837),
the Atherton Silver Medal (1842) and
the Shaw Medal (1843).

## MANERO, Tony (b 1911)

American. U.S. Open Champion,
1936, his total of 282 being a record
up to that time. Ryder Cup team,
1937.

## MANGRUM, Lloyd (1914-1973)

U.S. Open Champion, 1946, after
a play-off with Byron Nelson and Vic
Ghezzi; runner-up, 1950, after a tie
with Ben Hogan and George Fazio,
Hogan winning the play-off. Runner-
up U.S. Masters, 1940. Argentine
Open Champion, 1946. Ryder Cup
team, 1947, 1949, 1951, 1953 (captain).

## MAPONITE

An indiarubber-like substance from
which experimental balls were made
in the 1890s. Being very hard they
were apt to damage the faces of
wooden clubs and were never a com-
mercial success.

## MARKER

"A scorer in stroke play who is appointed by the Committee to record
a competitor's score. He may be a fellow-competitor. He is not a referee.
A marker should not lift the ball or
mark its position and, unless he is a
fellow-competitor, should not attend
the flagstick or stand at the hole or
mark its position" (Rules of Golf
Definition). See RULES OF GOLF, Rule
38.

## MARKS, Geoffrey (b 1938)

Walker Cup team, 1969, 1971.
World Cup (formerly Eisenhower
Trophy) team, 1970.

## MARR, Dave (b 1934)

U.S.P.G.A. Champion, 1965. Joint
runner-up, with Jack Nicklaus, U.S.
Masters, 1964. Ryder Cup team, 1965.

## MARSH, Dr David M. (b 1934)

English Amateur Champion, 1964,
1970. Selected for 1959 Walker Cup
team, but did not play in the match;
1971 team; captain, 1973.

## MARSH, Graham (b 1947)

Australian. German Open Cham-
pion, 1972. Swiss Open Champion,
1970, 1972. Runner-up, Dutch Open
Championship, 1971. India Open
Champion, 1971, 1973. World Match
Play Championship, 1977.

## MARSTON, Maxwell R. ('Max') (b 1892)

U.S. Amateur Champion, 1923;
runner-up, 1933. Walker Cup team,
1922, 1923, 1924, 1934.

## MARTIN, Bob (b 1848)

Born St Andrews. British Open
Champion, 1876, 1885; runner-up,
1875, 1887. In 1876 he tied with
David Strath, but after an argument
about an alleged breach of the rules,
Strath refused to take part in the play-
off and the title was awarded to
Martin.

## MARTIN SMITH, Eric (1909-51)

British Amateur Champion, 1931, the last time it was held at Westward Ho! Among the entrants that year was Douglas Fairbanks, Senior. Eric Martin Smith was M.P. for Grantham at the time of his death.

## MARY, QUEEN OF SCOTS

See LADY GOLFER, FIRST; ROYAL GOLFERS.

## MASHIE

The old-fashioned term for the club now called a No 5 iron. According to the Oxford and Chambers's Dictionaries, possibly derived from the French *massue,* a club. Exactly how and when it became applied to a club between a mid-iron and a niblick is obscure. Writing in the Badminton Library volume on *Golf* (1890), Horace Hutchinson says: "The mashie may be said to be a hybrid growth. But a few years back it was almost unknown. Now its use is universal." Bernard Darwin wrote: "I'm pretty sure there was no such hybrid as the mashie in 1885, and by 1890 it had become essential."

The first master of the mashie was J. H. Taylor, and this is what he said in his book, *Golf: My Life's Work* (1943), about the naming of his favourite club:

I have often been asked the derivation of the name mashie. I have read many answers, but all, I think, are wrong. I am old enough to remember that in the year of its appearance, 1888, the term 'masher' was applied to those ultra-smart young fellows who, with monocle in eye, and arrayed in clothes of the latest fashionable style and cut, were, we were told, the idol of every lady . . . the new-fashioned club was considered to be a violent departure from the orthodox, a dude among clubs, so what better name could be given it than the mashie, a parody on the popular conception of smartness.

Robert Browning, in *A History of Golf* (1955), suggests that mashie—like spoon, cleek and bunker—is a name familiar to Scottish domesticity: "The mashie does not specially resemble the utensil employed to mash potatoes; it took the name from its effect upon the ball when entrusted to unskilful hands."

## MASSENGALE, Don (b 1943)

Runner-up, U.S.P.G.A. Championship, 1967. Canadian Open Champion, 1966.

## MASSY, Arnaud (1877-1958)

British Open Champion, 1907—the first foreigner and the only Frenchman to win the title; tied with Harry Vardon, 1911, but lost play-off. French Open Champion, 1906, 1907, 1911, 1925. French Native Professional Champion, 1911, 1913, 1914, 1925, 1926. Belgian Open Champion, 1910. Spanish Open Champion, 1911, 1927, 1928. Massy, of French and Basque descent, was 'discovered' at Biarritz by Sir Everard Hambro, who arranged for him to have a course of lessons at North Berwick under Ben Sayers.

The 1907 Open was at Hoylake, and when his daughter was born shortly afterwards he christened her Hoylake (in the same way that James Braid called his son Muirfield). According to Bernard Darwin, Massy "had a fine swashbuckling air and a cheerful, chuckling way with him that were most engaging. His account of his career as a bomb-thrower at Verdun, where he was wounded, was as picturesque as his description of his matches against rich Spanish visitors at Nivelle." For many years he was professional at the La Boulie Club, near Paris, and was also at one time private professional to the Pasha of Marrakesh, Morocco, the famous T'hami El Glaoui. See TAKOURA.

## MASTERS TOURNAMENT

This famous 'championship of champions' is held annually at the Augusta National Club, Augusta, Georgia. The club was the brainchild

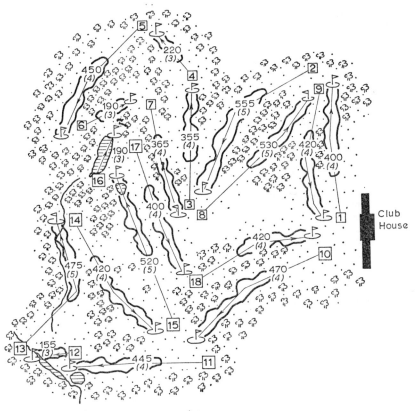

AUGUSTA

of Bobby Jones and his friend Clifford Roberts, conceived shortly after Bobby's 'Grand Slam' year of 1930. The terrain—a former famous horticultural nursery, covering some 365 acres—was ideal for golf, containing many trees and shrubs and even a convenient brook or burn. Out of this promising material, Bobby Jones and the noted golf-course architect, Dr Alister Mackenzie, created a course that was as beautiful to the eye of the golfer as it was challenging to his skill.

Work on the course began in 1931 —Bobby hitting hundreds of shots to pinpoint the best positions of teeing grounds, greens and hazards— and only three years later the first Augusta National Invitation meeting was held. Entry was by invitation and restricted to current and past winners of major tournaments, with the result that it soon became known simply as The Masters, a name Bobby Jones considered too presumptuous.

The first winner was Horton Smith, whose steady rounds of 70, 72, 70, 72 gave him a total of 284, one stroke better than the 285 of Craig Wood. Bobby Jones himself played and so did Walter Hagen, both returning respectable scores of 294.

Almost all the great American professionals have earned the right to wear the winner's green jacket, including Arnold Palmer and Jack Nicklaus with a record four victories and Jimmy Demaret and Sam Snead with three each. The only non-American winner has been Gary

Player (1961), although Argentinian Roberto De Vicenzo might have won in 1968 but for an error in his score-card.

The following are the winners of the Masters with their scores:

1934 Horton Smith: 284
1935 Gene Sarazen: 282
1936 Horton Smith: 285
1937 Byron Nelson: 283
1938 Henry Picard: 285
1939 Ralph Guldahl: 279
1940 Jimmy Demaret: 280
1941 Craig Wood: 280
1942 Byron Nelson: 280
1946 Herman Keiser: 282
1947 Jimmy Demaret: 281
1948 Claude Harmon: 279
1949 Sam Snead: 283
1950 Jimmy Demaret: 282
1951 Ben Hogan: 280
1952 Sam Snead: 286
1953 Ben Hogan: 274
1954 Sam Snead: 289
1955 Cary Middlecoff: 279
1956 Jackie Burke: 289
1957 Doug Ford: 283
1958 Arnold Palmer: 284
1959 Art Wall: 284
1960 Arnold Palmer: 282
1961 Gary Player: 280
1962 Arnold Palmer: 280
1963 Jack Nicklaus: 286
1964 Arnold Palmer: 276
1965 Jack Nicklaus: 271
1966 Jack Nicklaus: 288
1967 Gay Brewer: 280
1968 Bob Goalby: 277
1969 George Archer: 281
1970 Billy Casper: 279
1971 Charles Coody: 279
1972 Jack Nicklaus: 286
1973 Tommy Aaron: 283
1974 Gary Player: 278
1975 Jack Nicklaus: 271
1976 Ray Floyd: 271
1977 Tom Watson: 276
1978 Gary Player: 277

## MATCH

Any game of golf, but normally a game decided by match play. The term can also mean the players engaged in the game—i.e. "Our match went through the match in front."

## MATCHES, TYPES OF

According to the Rules of Golf (Definition 28) recognised matches are:

*Single:* A match in which one plays against another. Also called a Twosome.

*Threesome:* A match in which one plays against two, and each side plays one ball.

*Foursome:* A match in which two play against two, and each side plays one ball.

*Three-Ball:* A match in which three play against one another, each playing his own ball.

*Best-Ball:* A match in which one plays against the better ball of two or the best ball of three players.

*Four-Ball:* A match in which two play their better ball against the better ball of two other players.

See GREENSOME ; SCOTCH FOURSOME.

## MATCH PLAY

The form of golf in which the winner is the player (or in the case of a foursome, the players) who has won more holes than there are holes left to play or, if the game goes to the full 18 holes, wins the last hole. In other words, match play is reckoned by holes, stroke (or medal) play by strokes. Also called 'Knock Out'.

Match play, which the famous old professional, Andrew Kirkaldy, called "the verra life o' gowf", was the original form of the game.

See STROKE PLAY ; TERMS USED IN RECKONING.

## MAURITIUS, GOLF ON

The island of Mauritius, in the Indian Ocean, can claim the distinction of having an older club than any in England apart from Royal Black-heath. The Mauritius Naval and Military Gymkhana Club was founded in 1844, only 30 years after the island had been conceded to Britain by France by the Treaty of Paris after the Napoleonic Wars. The course has 18 holes and a length of 5,237 yards; until the Second World War it had 9 holes and until 1964 only 12. The other Mauritius club is the 9-holes Brabant Hotel Golf Links, opened as recently as 1965.

## MAXWELL, Robert (b 1876)

British Amateur Champion, 1903, 1909. First amateur in British Open Championship, 1902, 1903. On the first day of his first Amateur Championship, 1897, he beat both the two great Hoylake golfers, John Ball and Harold Hilton.

See ROYAL AND ANCIENT GOLF CLUB OF ST ANDREWS.

## MAXWELL, W. J. ('Billy') (b 1929)

U.S. Amateur Champion, 1951. Mexican Open Champion, 1956. Mexican Open Amateur Champion, 1953; runner-up, 1951. Ryder Cup team, 1963. Became a professional, 1954.

## MAYER, Dick (b 1924)

U.S. Open Champion, 1957, after tie with Cary Middlecoff, the holder. Ryder Cup team, 1957. Became a professional, 1949.

## MAYO, Charles Henry (b 1884)

Like Abe Mitchell, one of the best golfers never to win the British Open Championship. Runner-up to Sandy Herd in the British Professional Match Play Championship, 1906. He was a close friend of George Duncan, with whom he played in a number of challenge foursomes. He was professional at various clubs in England until he went to the United States in 1919. See DUNCAN, GEORGE.

## MEDAL PLAY

See STROKE PLAY.

## MEHLHORN, William ('Wild Bill') (b 1894)

Runner-up, U.S.P.G.A. Championship, 1925. Played in the two Anglo-American matches (1921, 1926) and in first Ryder Cup team, 1927.

## MELNYK, Steve (b 1948)

U.S. Amateur Champion, 1969. British Amateur Champion, 1971.

Leading amateur, British Open Championship, 1970. Walker Cup team, 1969, 1971. Turned professional 1971.

## MELVILLE, Janet (b 1958)

British Women's Open Champion, 1978.

## MENORCA, GOLF IN

This Balearic Island's first course—the San Clemente Golf and Country Club—was opened in 1973. Another—the Son Parc Club—is in preparation.

## MERRY

In golf merry means too strong, in such phrases as "That putt was a bit merry"—when the ball has run a couple of yards past the hole. See STEAMY.

## MESSIEUX, Samuel (1793-1859)

A Swiss who came to Dundee about 1815, where he taught French and became a friend of the poet, Thomas Hood. He moved to St Andrews, taught at the university and at Madras College, and developed into a fine golfer. He won the R. and A. Gold Medal, 1825, 1827 and the Silver Cross, 1840. His most remarkable feat, however, was driving a ball (a 'feathery' in those days) from the 14th tee into Hell Bunker—a distance reckoned to be about 380 yards. It was said to have been a slightly frosty day with a gentle wind behind him. At the same hole 'Freddie' Tait was said to have driven a gutty ball a distance of 341 yards. Messieux died in 1859 and a fine portrait of him in a red coat hangs in the R. and A. clubhouse.

See BLACKWELL BROTHERS; DRIVES WITH 'GUTTY', LONGEST; TAIT, FREDERICK GUTHRIE.

## MEXICO, GOLF IN

The game has really become popular in Mexico only since the Second World War. Apart from a 9-holes course at the seaside resort of Acapulco, clubs are in the neighbourhood of Mexico City. They include the Churubusco Country Club, the Club de Golf Bellavista, the Club de Golf Campestre de la Ciudad de Mexico, the Club de Golf Chapultepec, the Club de Golf la Hacienda and the Club de Golf de Mexico.

The Mexican Open Championship was established in 1944, the winner for the first years being the American professional Al Espinosa. Other famous golfers who have won it include Roberto De Vicenzo, Bobby Locke, Tony Lema and the Canadian Al Balding. The Mexican Amateur Championship dates from 1948, the first winner being Frank Stranahan. The World (formerly Canada) Cup was held in Mexico City in 1958, when it was won for Ireland by Christy O'Connor and Harry Bradshaw—in spite of the high altitude that made Bradshaw's nose bleed.

Added interest has been given to the game in Mexico by the Americas Cup inaugurated in 1952. This competition, between amateur teams from the United States, Mexico and Canada, is held biennially in each country in turn.

Golf affairs are looked after by the Association Mexicana de Golf.

## MICKLEM, Gerald Hugh (b 1911)

English Amateur Champion, 1947, 1953. Won Oxford and Cambridge Golfing Society's President's Putter, 1953; runner-up, 1948, 1956, 1957. Walker Cup team, 1947, 1949, 1953, 1955; non-playing captain, 1957, 1959. Captain R. and A., 1968. Chairman, R. and A. Rules of Golf Committee, 1960-63. Chairman, R. and A. Selection Committee, 1959-63. President, English Golf Union, 1965-6. Has done a great deal to encourage young golfers in Britain.

## MIDDLECOFF, Cary (b 1921)

Worked as a dental surgeon before turning professional in 1947. U.S. Open Champion, 1949, 1956; tied 1957, but lost play-off with Dick Mayer. Won U.S. Masters, 1955, winning by a record margin of seven strokes from Ben Hogan; runner-up, 1959. Ryder Cup team, 1953, 1955,

1959. Author of *Golf Doctor* (1952); *Advanced Golf* (1958).

## MIGUEL, Sebastian (b 1931) and Angel (b 1930)

These Spanish brothers have been well known on the European golfing scene for some years. Sebastian has been Spanish Open Champion, 1954, 1960, 1967; Portuguese Open Champion, 1954, 1956, 1959. Angel has been Spanish Open Champion, 1961, 1964; French Open Champion, 1956; Mexican Open Champion, 1959; Portuguese Open Champion, 1964.

## MILLENSTED, Dudley J. (b 1942)

Runner-up, English Amateur Championship, 1966. Tied English Open Amateur Stroke Play Championship (with Clive Clark and Michael Burgess), 1965. Walker Cup team, 1967. Turned professional, 1967.

## MILLER, Allen L. (b 1948)

American Walker Cup team, 1969, 1971. World Cup (formerly Eisenhower Trophy) team, 1970.

## MILLER, Johnny (b 1947)

U.S. Open Champion, 1973. British Open Champion, 1976. His last round of 63 is the lowest ever scored in the championship. Ryder Cup team, 1975.

## MILLWARD, Ernest B. (b 1923)

English Amateur Champion, 1952. Walker Cup team, 1955.

## MILTON, Mrs John C. (b 1923)

Born Moira Paterson. British Ladies' Champion, 1952. Runner-up, Scottish Ladies' Championship, 1951. Runner-up, French Ladies' Open Championship, 1949. Curtis Cup team, 1952.

## MINIKAHDA

Minneapolis, Minnesota. Founded 1898, on the west side of Lake Calhoun—Minikahda being Chippewa for 'by the side of water'—the largest of Minneapolis's many lakes. Length: 6,550 yards. Par 71. The original course was laid out by William Watson, who became the club's first professional. Housed U.S. Open Championship, 1916 (won by amateur 'Chick' Evans—the first time the event was held west of Chicago); U.S. Amateur Championship, 1927 (Bobby Jones beating 'Chick' in the final). Also Walker Cup match, 1957.

## MINORCA, GOLF IN
See MENORCA, GOLF IN.

## 'MISS 'EM QUICK'
See SMITH, WILLIE AND ALEX.

## 'MISS HIGGINS'
In the early days of ladies' golf, voluminous skirts often made it difficult for their wearers to see the ball on the ground, particularly in a wind. "So", writes Miss Eleanor Helme in *After the Ball* (1931), "Miss Higgins of the U.S.A. earned immortal fame and the undying gratitude of her generation by inventing a piece of

elastic which could be slipped from the waist (yes, we did have waists even if we had no ankles) downwards, so as to hold the irrepressible skirt in place." This piece of elastic became known as a 'Miss Higgins'.

## MISS THE GLOBE
See AIR SHOT.

## MITCHELL, Abe (1887-1947)
Runner-up, British Amateur Championship, 1912, being beaten by John Ball at Westward Ho! at the 38th hole. Turned professional, 1913, and became with George Duncan and Ted Ray the immediate successors to the triumvirate of Vardon, Taylor and Braid. British Professional Match Play Champion, 1919, 1920, 1929. Ryder Cup team, 1929, 1931, 1933.

Mitchell was often called the greatest golfer who never won the British Open Championship; in 1920 he led the field by six strokes after two rounds, but on the final day was over-

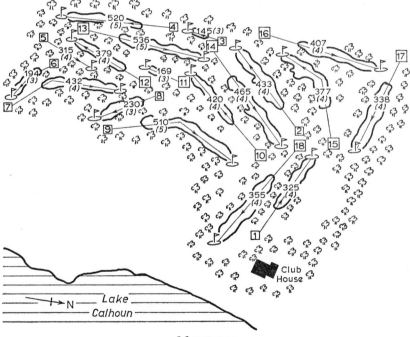

MINIKAHDA

hauled by George Duncan, who made up a deficit of 13 strokes. With Duncan he made three tours of the United States, 1921, 1922, 1924. Author of *Essentials of Golf* (1927); *Length on the Links* (1936).

## MIXED FOURSOME

A foursome in which a lady golfer is teamed with a man golfer. Also facetiously called a 'gruesome' or 'quarrelsome'. See MATCHES, TYPES OF.

## MOFFITT, Ralph L. (b 1932)

Runner-up, Dunlop Masters, 1962, 1963 (after tie with Bernard Hunt), 1964. Runner-up, British Professional Match Play Championship, 1961. Ryder Cup team, 1961.

## MOLESEY HURST, GOLF AT

There is not much doubt that Blackheath was the oldest place where golf was played in the London area, but there is evidence of some sort of course at Molesey Hurst, near Kingston-on-Thames, Surrey, in the mid-eighteenth century. A certain Dr Carlyle, of Inveresk, near Edinburgh, describes in his *Autobiography* how David Garrick, the actor, gave a dinner at his house at Hampton, Middlesex, in 1758 to a number of Scottish friends, asking them to bring their golf clubs with them. According to Dr Carlyle only three of them —"John Home and myself and Parson Black from Aberdeen"—were golfers, but soon after their arrival, they "crossed the river to the golfing ground, which was very good". After dinner Dr Carlyle amused the others by pitching a ball into the mouth of an archway between the upper and lower garden of Garrick's house, so that it rolled through the opening and down the slope into the river. Garrick, he said, "begged the club of me by which such a feat had been performed".

Dr Carlyle was apparently a very keen golfer and won the Musselburgh medal in 1775. A putter belonging to John Home is in the possession of the Royal Blackheath Club.

Unfortunately, there is no other record of golf at Molesey in the old days, although there was a Molesey Hurst Club up to the end of the First World War.

## MONTAGUE, John M. (d 1972)

An American known as the 'rake and shovel golfer', who was alleged to be able to drive 300 yards with a baseball bat, scoop his ball out of bunkers with a shovel and putt unerringly with a rake. The trouble was that nobody had seen him doing it!

## MONTGOMERY, Clementine Purvis Russell

Runner-up, British Ladies' Championship, 1932. Scottish Ladies' Champion, 1924; runner-up, 1936.

## MONTROSE, MARQUESS OF (1612-50)

James Graham, the great Marquess of Montrose, was a keen golfer from his earliest days, as his father had been before him. His father's accounts show sums expended on "six bowstrings" and "one dozen golf balls" and his own accounts include payments for "sax new clubs and dressing some auld ones, and for balls" and "to the boy who carried my Lord's clubbes to the field". He was playing golf with his brother-in-law on the day before his marriage to "sweet Mistress Magdalene Carnegie", and nine days afterwards there is a payment for "ane going to St Andrews for clubs and balls to my Lord". The fact that he played golf at St Andrews (where he was at the University), Montrose and Leith shows that the game was established on the links there in the early seventeenth century. The latter part of his life was taken up more in fighting than in golf, until his execution in Edinburgh in 1650.

## MONTSERRAT, GOLF IN

Montserrat forms part of the Leeward Islands, in the West Indies. Its golf club is the Belham River Valley

(*above left*) OUIMET, FRANCIS DE SALES. He is seen here playing himself in as Captain of the R. and A. on the first tee in front of the clubhouse. (*above right*) PALMER, ARNOLD. The most popular of living American golfers is seen here looking at the plaque erected to mark a wonder shot played by Bobby Jones in winning the 1926 Open at Royal Lytham

PAU CLUB. This was the Ladies' Course (only putting!) at the Pau Club, in the Pyrenees, in the days of the crinoline

(*above left*) PLAYER, GARY. The only South African to have won all four major professional tournaments of the world. (*above right*) PRESIDENTS AS GOLFERS, UNITED STATES. General Dwight D. Eisenhower was easily the keenest golfing president. Here he is sharing a joke with Arnold Palmer, with whom he played many games

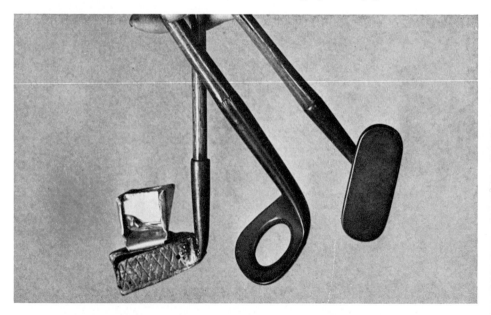

REJECTED CLUBS. In the centre is the now vanished club called a "President", mainly intended for getting the ball out of water. The other clubs have also been banned by the R. and A.—a putter with an adjustable head and one fixed with a reflex view-finder

Club, with a 9-holes course, length 3,222 yards. See St Vincent, Golf in.

## MOODY, Orville (b 1934)

U.S. Open Champion, 1969. Served in the U.S. Army for 14 years, during which time he won the Korean Open Championship three times. Left the army, as a sergeant, 1968. See Korea, Golf in.

## MOORTOWN

Leeds, Yorkshire. Founded 1908. Fine moorland lay-out. Length: 6,604 yards. S.S.S. 72. Housed English Amateur Championship, 1938, 1962; English Ladies' Championship, 1955; English Open Amateur Stroke Play Championship, 1957, 1969. British Boys' Amateur Championship, 1934, 1958, 1966.

## MOREY, Dale (b 1931)

Runner-up, U.S. Amateur Championship, 1953. Walker Cup team, 1955, 1965.

## MORGAN, John Llewellyn (b 1918)

Welsh Amateur Champion, 1950, 1951; runner-up, 1952. Walker Cup team, 1951, 1953, 1955. Was a professional for four years.

## MORGAN, Wanda (b 1910)

British Ladies' Champion, 1935; runner-up, 1931. English Ladies' Champion, 1931, 1936, 1937. Won Worplesdon Foursomes, with E. F. Storey, 1948; runner-up, with K. A. Morrice, 1938. Curtis Cup team, 1932, 1934, 1936.

## MOROCCO, GOLF IN

Visitors to Morocco may play golf at the Royal Country Club de Tangier, founded in 1904; at the Royal Golf Club de Mohammedia; at the Royal Golf Club de Agadir; the Royal Golf Club, Rabat; and at the remarkable course at Marrakesh, in the Atlas Mountains, where Winston Churchill stayed several times during the Second World War. Before the war he had played golf there with the

K

famous Pasha of Marrakesh, T'hami el Glaoui.

The Pasha, born in 1879, was a passionate golfer (he even wore plusfours) and built the course on desert land, water being piped at great cost from the Atlas Mountains, each green and fairway being surrounded by cypress, olive and eucalyptus trees and flowering shrubs. The Pasha died in 1956, and, although his family was dispossessed or exiled, the golf course is still well maintained.

Several more courses are planned for Morocco, including one designed by Robert Trent Jones. See Massy, Arnaud; Takoura.

## MORRIS, Jack (1847-1929)

Born St Andrews, died Hoylake. He was a nephew of 'Old Tom' Morris and a cousin of 'Young Tommy' Morris. Professional to the Royal Liverpool Club, Hoylake, for 60 years, from 1869 to 1929, a record for length of service to one club.

## MORRIS, Tom (Junior) (1851-75)

Born and died at St Andrews. 'Young Tommy', 'Old Tom's' son, was a phenomenal golfer. By winning the Open Championship three times running, 1868, 1869, 1870, he won the original Championship Belt outright and when, after the lapse of a year, the Championship Cup was instituted in 1872, he won the title for the fourth time. He would no doubt have won it again but for his early death. Partnered by his father, he was playing a match at North Berwick in September 1875 against Willie Park and Mungo Park when a telegram arrived saying that his wife was dangerously ill. The Morrises started off in a yacht, but had barely cleared the harbour when another telegram brought the news that young Mrs Morris and her newborn baby were dead. Tommy never recovered from this tragedy and died on Christmas Day 1875.

One can judge his skill by the fact that his score of 149, when winning the Open Belt in 1870, was never equalled while the championship continued to be decided over 36 holes until the year 1892. He was a dashing type of golfer, hitting the ball so furiously that the Scotch bonnet he wore often flew off and waggling the club so fiercely that he sometimes broke the shaft. Old Tom, in comparing his master, Allan Robertson, and his son, Tommy, once said: "I could cope wi' Allan masel', but never wi' Tommy."

His memorial in St Andrews Cathedral churchyard says: "He thrice in succession won the Championship Belt and held it without rivalry and yet without envy, his many amiable qualities being no less acknowledged than his golfing achievements."

See BRITISH OPEN CHAMPION MORE THAN ONCE.

## MORRIS, Tom (Senior) (1821-1908)

Born and died at St Andrews. After Allan Robertson, to whom he was apprenticed in 1839, the greatest of the old-time professional golfers. He played in every Open Championship from its inception in 1860 to 1896 and won the title, 1861, 1862, 1864, 1867. At the age of 30 he left Allan Robertson to become greenkeeper at Prestwick, but returned to St Andrews in 1865, being greenkeeper to the R. and A. until he retired in 1904, holding an honorary position until his death.

'Old Tom', as he was always called to distinguish him from his brilliant son, 'Young Tommy', took part in many famous challenge matches— one against Willie Park, Sen., being so acrimonious that it nearly led to a law-suit! Tom Morris's bearded face is famous in pictures wherever golf is played, and his name is remembered at St Andrews by the 18th hole— the Tom Morris hole—on the Old Course. A fine portrait of him hangs in the clubhouse of the R. and A.

His other son, J. O. F. Morris, was also a good golfer and his nephew, Jack Morris, was professional at the Royal Liverpool Club, Hoylake, for many years.

See BRITISH OPEN CHAMPION MORE THAN ONCE ; ROBERTSON, ALLAN.

## MORRISON, John S. F. (1892-1961)

British. Belgian Open Amateur Champion, 1929. Won Worplesdon Mixed Foursomes, with Lady Heathcoat-Amory, 1928. Golf-course architect whose work included the new Prince's Sandwich (with Sir Guy Campbell) and Wentworth (with Colt and Alison).

## 'MR LU'

See LU LIANG HUAN.

## MUFF

See DUFFER.

## MUIRFIELD

Gullane, East Lothian. Home of the Honourable Company of Edinburgh Golfers, who moved there from Musselburgh in 1891. The best type of linksland on the edge of the Firth of Forth ; said to have 180 bunkers. Length: 6,806 yards. S.S.S. 73. Housed Open Championship, 1892, 1896, 1901, 1906, 1912, 1929, 1935, 1948, 1959, 1966, 1972. Amateur Championship, 1897, 1903, 1909, 1920, 1926, 1932, 1954. Walker Cup match, 1959, and Curtis Cup match, 1952 ; Scottish Amateur and Open Amateur Stroke Play Championships. See EDINBURGH GOLFERS, HONOURABLE COMPANY OF.

## MULLIGAN

A light-hearted American convention, by which a player who has had a bad drive at the first hole is allowed a free second chance by his opponent. Normally, the good player would grant a Mulligan to his less good opponent, who would be more likely to miss his drive. I don't know whether there was a Mr Mulligan—but a Miss Mulligan (later Mrs Inglis) won the first Irish Ladies' Championship in 1894. Mrs Inglis was for some years honorary secretary of the Irish L.G.U. Another theory is that Mulligan is a contraction of 'Have it again!'

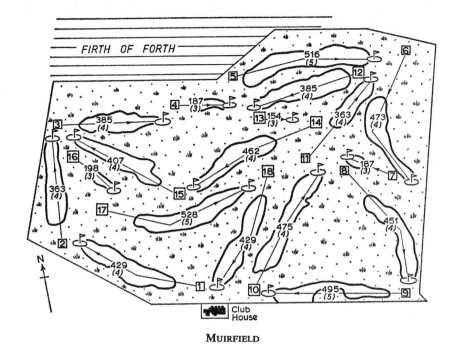

MUIRFIELD

## MUNICIPAL COURSES
See NATIONAL ASSOCIATION OF PUBLIC GOLF COURSES.

## MUNN, Lionel (b 1887)
Runner-up, British Amateur Championship, 1937. Irish Amateur Champion, 1909, 1910, 1911. Irish Native Amateur Champion, 1908, 1911, 1913, 1914; runner-up, 1910. Belgian Open Amateur Champion, 1931, 1932.

## MURPHY, Robert J. (b 1941)
U.S. Amateur Champion, 1965. Runner-up (with Arnold Palmer), U.S.P.G.A. Championship, 1970. Walker Cup team, 1967.

## MURRAY, Alex (b 1910)
Scottish. Emigrated to New Zealand and won New Zealand Open Championship, 1935, 1948, 1952. New Zealand Professional Champion, 1935, 1939, 1947, 1948.

## MURRAY, Mae (Mrs H. B. Jones) (b 1926)
Runner up, U.S. Ladies' Championship, 1950. Curtis Cup team, 1952.

## MURRAY, Stuart (b 1933)
Scottish Amateur Champion, 1962; runner-up, 1961. Walker Cup team, 1963. Turned professional, 1963.

## MURRAY, William Alexander (b 1886)
Won *Golf Illustrated* Gold Vase, 1922, 1931. Walker Cup team, 1923, 1924. His younger brother, John James, was also a well-known Scottish amateur.

## MUSSELBURGH
The links of Leith and Musselburgh were the early golfing grounds of Edinburgh golfers. The original Musselburgh (later Royal Musselburgh) Club, in the modern sense of the word, dates from 1774 when a

cup for competition was presented to 'the Musselburgh golfers' by Thomas Macmillan, who was the first winner.

A Musselburgh golfer, Willie Park, Sen, was the first Open Champion in 1860 (he won four times altogether) and when the Championship Belt was won outright by young Tommy Morris, Musselburgh joined with Prestwick and St Andrews in providing the Championship Cup that has been played for ever since.

At one time the historic links was shared by the Bruntsfield Links Society, when golf became impossible on their original ground in the centre of Edinburgh; by the Edinburgh Burgess Society and (from 1836 to 1891) by the Honourable Company of Edinburgh Golfers. The links eventually became a racecourse. The modern Royal Musselburgh Club has its course at Prestongrange House, Prestonpans. See BRUNTSFIELD; EDINBURGH GOLFERS, HONOURABLE COMPANY OF; MUSSELBURGH IRON; ROYAL BURGESS GOLFING SOCIETY OF EDINBURGH.

## MUSSELBURGH IRON

The use of the putter in approaching from off the green—a type of shot made famous by Bob Ferguson, of Musselburgh, thrice British Open Champion. See TEXAS WEDGE.

## NAGLE, Kelvin D. G. ('Kel')
## (b 1920)

Australian. British Open Champion in the centenary year, 1960, beating Arnold Palmer by one stroke; runner-up, to Arnold Palmer, 1962. Tied U.S. Open Championship, 1965, but lost play-off to Gary Player. Canadian Open Champion, 1964. Australian Open Champion, 1959. Australian Professional Champion, 1949, 1954, 1958, 1959, 1965, 1968. New Zealand Open Champion, 1957, 1958, 1962, 1964, 1967, 1968, 1969. New Zealand Professional Champion, 1957, 1958, 1960, 1970. French Open Champion, 1961. British Senior Professional Champion, 1971, beating Julius Boros in World Senior Championship. Won World (formerly Canada) Cup, with Peter Thomson, 1954, 1959; runners-up, 1961.

## NAMES OF IRONS, EQUIVALENT

The equivalent names of old-fashioned iron clubs and the modern numbered set are approximately as follows:

Driving Iron: No 1 iron.
Cleek: No 2 iron.
Driving Mashie: No 3 iron.
Mid-Iron: No 4 iron.
Mashie: No 5 iron.
Spade Mashie: No 6 iron.
Mashie Niblick: No 7 iron.
Niblick: Nos 8-10 irons.

There were variations in names, including 'mashie iron' (No 4 iron) and 'lofting iron' (No 6 iron). There were also clubs like 'jiggers', which have no modern equivalent. See IRON CLUBS; JIGGER; SAMMY.

## NAMES OF WOODEN CLUBS

As there were more variations of wooden clubs in the old days, it is impossible to give the exact equivalent to the modern numbered set. The driver is the No 1 wood, the brassey the No 2 and the spoon the No 3, but there were also long-spoons, middle-spoons, short-spoons, baffys (baffing spoons) or even brassey-niblicks. See BAFFY; PLAY CLUB; SPOON.

## NAP

A term to describe the surface of a green as it influences the roll of the ball, the degree of influence depending on how the actual blades of grass lie, grow or are affected by cutting. On a 'nappy' green one putts either with the nap (or grain), against the nap or across the nap, the ball naturally travelling further with the nap than against or across it. The ideal green (and this is true of those at many British seaside clubs) has no nap, the grass standing straight up.

## 'NASSAU'

An American match refinement in which the winner of each nine holes gains a point, and another point goes to the 18 holes winner—the point being worth a dollar or whatever is being played for. See 'GREENIE'; 'SYNDICATE'.

## NATIONAL ASSOCIATION OF PUBLIC GOLF COURSES

This association was founded in the 1920s largely through the efforts of J. H. Taylor and F. G. Hawtree, Taylor being the first Chairman of Committee. Its objects are to co-ordinate the clubs established on public courses and their course management authorities in the furtherance of the interests of the game; to promote an annual National Public Courses Championship and other tournaments; and to afford direct representation of public course interests in the National Union. See UNITED STATES PUBLIC LINKS CHAMPIONSHIP.

## NATIONAL GOLF CLUBS' ADVISORY ASSOCIATION

Founded in 1922 with the object of protecting the interests of British golf clubs in general, by giving legal advice and, if necessary, financial assistance, in cases taken to the law courts for a decision on points of law involving the interests of golf clubs.

## NATIONAL LINKS, UNITED STATES

See MACDONALD, CHARLES BLAIR.

## NEGRO GOLFERS

Among America's well-known black golfers are Charlie Sifford, George Johnson, Chuck Thorpe, Pete Brown and Lee Elder. The best known South African 'coloured' golfer is Susunker Sewgolum.

## NELSON, Byron (b 1912)

U.S. Open Champion, 1939, after tie with Craig Wood and Densmore Shute. Tied for title, 1946, with Lloyd Mangrum and Vic Ghezzi, but lost play-off to Mangrum. Won U.S. Masters, 1937, 1942; runner-up, 1941, 1947. U.S.P.G.A. Champion, 1940, 1945; runner-up, 1939, 1941, 1944. French Open Champion, 1955. Ryder Cup team, 1937, 1947; non-playing captain, 1965.

'Lord Byron', one of the world's greatest golfers, played on the complete American professional circuit for only two years, 1944, 1945, winning over $100,000. In 1944 he won 13 out of 23 tournaments and in 1945 17 out of 31, being runner-up in seven more. He played in only one British Open—in 1937, before he had reached his peak—finishing in fifth place at Carnoustie. In 1946 he retired from regular competition.

Byron Nelson always claims that his greatest shot was in the second play-off with Craig Wood after a tie in the 1939 U.S. Open at the Philadelphia Country Club. After three holes Nelson had gained a one-stroke lead and then at the par-4 460 yards 4th, after Wood was safely on in two, Nelson holed a No 1 iron shot for an eagle two. This put him three shots ahead and he held his lead to finish in 70 against 73. Author of *Winning Golf* (1947).

## NEPAL, GOLF IN

Visitors to Nepal don't usually expect to find a golf course in such a mountainous country, high up in the Himalayas. However, the Royal Nepal Club at Katmandu, the capital, was founded in 1962, with a 9-holes course; it has 130 members of 14 nationalities. The game is encouraged by the Maharaja of Nepal and his family. There is also a 9-holes course at Dharan.

## NETTLEFOLD, Leonard ('Len') (b 1905)

Australian Amateur Champion, 1926, 1928. Tasmanian Amateur Champion seven times. Runner-up, Swiss Open Amateur Championship, 1927. One of the world's few first-class left-handers. See LEFT-HANDED GOLFERS.

## NEVER UP, NEVER IN

A famous cliché, meaning that if the ball fails to reach the hole it cannot possibly go in. But Bobby Jones, for one, distrusted this theory and quoted his early teacher, Stewart Maiden: "When the ball dies at the hole, there are four doors; the ball can go in at the front, or the back, or at either side, wherever it touches the rim. But a ball that comes up to the hole with speed on it must hit the front door fairly in the middle." Bobby said that he always tried to gauge a putt, except the very short holing-out ones, "to reach the hole with a dying ball".

## NEVILE, Elinor C.
Runner-up, British Ladies' Championship, 1898, 1900, 1902.

## NEWELL, Betty Hicks
See HICKS, BETTY (MRS NEWELL).

## NEW GUINEA, GOLF IN
See PAPUA AND NEW GUINEA, GOLF IN.

## 'NEWS OF THE WORLD' TOURNAMENT
See BRITISH PROFESSIONAL MATCH PLAY CHAMPIONSHIP.

## NEWTON, Jack (b 1950)
Australian. Dutch Open Champion, 1972. Runner-up to Tom Watson, Open Championship, 1975. British P.G.A. Match Play Champion, 1974.

## NEW ZEALAND, GOLF IN
Golf is flourishing in New Zealand, and there are more than 330 clubs. The oldest is the Otago Club (where there was always a strong Scottish influence), founded in 1871, followed by the Christchurch Club, 1873. The Hutt Club, near Wellington, dates from 1892, the Auckland and Wanganui Clubs from 1894, the Wellington and Manawatu Clubs from 1895 and the Napier Club from 1896. Golfing matters are looked after by the New Zealand Golf Association, the Ladies' Golf Union and the Professional Golfers' Association of New Zealand.

The New Zealand Open Championship dates from 1907, but the Amateur and Ladies' Championships, starting in 1893, are older than their Australian counterparts. The Professional Championship dates from 1920. There is a professional tournament circuit—in 1971-72 for prizes worth £35,500—lasting from the end of November to mid-January.

The best known modern New Zealand golfer is Bob Charles, winner of the 1963 British Open Championship and many other tournaments.

## NIBLICK
There is no certain derivation of this word, although Robert Browning in *A History of Golf* (1955) suggests that it might be a corruption of 'neb laigh'—"i.e. a broken nose, and refers to the short face of the club, originally designed for playing out of ruts". 'Laigh' also means 'low' in Scottish dialect.

The shape of the club has changed considerably through the years. In *Golfing*, published by W. and R. Chambers (1887), we read:

> The niblick, or track iron, is of very important service when the ball lies in a narrow cart-rut, horseshoe or other print in sand, thick and stiff whins, or in any round deep hollow not altogether beyond the player's reach. The head, which is of iron, is very small and heavy, about one-half the size of that of the sand-iron, and is shaped into a hollow, with the iron sloping slightly backward. This peculiarity of shape enables the player to raise his ball out of difficulties from which no other club could extricate it.

This old-type niblick was also called a rut iron. When such features as cart-tracks, however, began to be found less often on golf courses, the shape of the niblick changed until it fitted the description given in Chambers's Dictionary: "A golf club with a heavy head with wide face, used for lofting." The modern niblick corresponds to the No 10 iron, differing from the sand wedge or blaster in that its sole has a sharp edge instead of a flanged one.

Some old-time golfers also used a wooden niblick for getting a ball out of a hollow or rut. It had a short, broad head and was well laid back.

See BLASTER ; PRESIDENT ; RUT IRON ; SAND IRON ; WEDGE.

## NICHOLS, Bobby (b 1936)
U.S.P.G.A. Champion, 1964, with record score of 271. Runner-up, U.S. Masters, 1967. Ryder Cup team, 1967.

## NICKLAUS, Jack William (b 1940)

U.S. Amateur Champion, 1959, at 19 the second youngest winner, 1961. Turned professional, 1961. U.S. Open Champion, 1962 (after tie with Arnold Palmer), 1967, 1972; tied with Lee Trevino, 1971, but lost play-off. British Open Champion, 1966, 1970 (after tie with Doug Sanders); runner-up, 1964, 1967, 1968, 1972. Won U.S. Masters, 1963, 1965, 1966, 1972; runner-up, 1971. U.S.P.G.A. Champion, 1963, 1971. Australian Open Champion, 1964, 1968, 1971, 1978. Won Piccadilly World Match Play Tournament, 1970. Walker Cup team, 1959, 1961. Ryder Cup team, 1969, 1971, 1973, 1975, 1977. In winning U.S. team in World (formerly Canada) Cup team, with Arnold Palmer, 1963, 1964, 1966, 1967.

With Arnold Palmer and Gary Player, Jack Nicklaus has formed what has often been called the modern 'Big Three' of the golf world. Known familiarly as 'The Golden Bear'. Author of *My 55 Ways to Lower Your Golf Score* (1967); *Take a Tip from me* (1968); *The Greatest Game of All* (1969).

See WALKER AND RYDER CUPS, PLAYED IN BOTH.

## NIGERIA, GOLF IN

Golf, like everything else in the country, was disrupted by the civil war—a sad fact because the game was firmly established at Sapele and Zaria (both before the First World War), Port Harcourt, Lagos, Benin City, Kaduna, Kano, Ibadan, Enugu, Abeokuta and elsewhere. All the same, golf is now flourishing again and the Nigerian Open Championship has continued to be held at the Lagos Club.

## NINE

A term meaning half an 18-hole course—i.e. the first 9 and the second 9. All courses, except 9-holes ones, are so divided, each half being roughly the same length and normally having a similar number of short holes. On a 9-holes course, the first nine would constitute the round of 9 holes played, the second round often being varied by the use of different teeing grounds. See FRONT NINE.

## NINETEENTH

If an 18-holes match ends up all-square, and a decision has to be reached, it continues at the first hole again, which automatically becomes the 19th; the match may end there or go on to the second (or 20th) and so on.

## NINETEENTH HOLE

A colloquialism for the club bar; having played 18 holes one naturally goes to the 19th.

## NORTH AND SOUTH CHAMPIONSHIPS

Since their inauguration, these tournaments, always held at the Pinehurst Club, North Carolina, have ranked among America's best. The Amateur section dates from 1901, the year that Pinehurst was founded; the Open section from 1903 until it was discontinued in 1952; and the Women's section from 1950. Almost all America's leading golfers have won the North and South. See PINEHURST.

## NORTHERLY COURSE, WORLD'S MOST

See LAPLAND, GOLF IN.

## NORTHUMBERLAND

High Gosforth Park, Newcastle-upon-Tyne. Founded 1898. Fine moorland turf. Length: 6,498 yards. S.S.S. 71. Housed English Amateur Championship, 1929; E.G.U. Brabazon Trophy (later English Open Amateur Stroke Play Championship), 1955; first British Women's Open Stroke Play Championship, 1969.

## NORWAY, GOLF IN

Considering that the golf season is limited to a period from the middle of April to the middle or end of November, the game is very popular.

This is shown by the fact that four new clubs—Trondheim, Stavanger Borregaard and the Vestfold Club, Stokke—have been established since the end of the Second World War. The two older Norwegian clubs—Oslo and Bergen—are both pre-war. Two more courses are being made.

The Norwegian Open Amateur Championship was held over the Oslo course from 1937-55, being dominated in the early years by the brothers N. and O. Heyerdahl—namesakes of Thor Heyerdahl of *Kon-Tiki* fame.

After 1955 it was incorporated in the Scandinavian Open Amateur Championship. Golf in Norway is managed by the Norges Golfforbund.

## NOTTS

Hollinwell, near Nottingham. Founded 1887. Sandy heathland. Length: 6,931 yards. S.S.S. 72. Housed English Amateur Championship, 1935, 1964 ; English Ladies' Championship, 1913 ; English Open Amateur Stroke Play Championship, 1959 ; Girls' Championship, 1959.

## OAKLAND HILLS

The Oakland Hills Country Club, Birmingham, Michigan. Founded 1918, with Walter Hagen as the first professional. Designed by Donald J. Ross; modernised, 1951, by Robert Trent Jones. Length: 6,910 yards (Par 70). Housed U.S. Open Championship, 1924, 1937, 1951, 1961; U.S. P.G.A. Championship, 1972; U.S. Ladies' Championship, 1968.

## OBSERVER

'An "observer" is appointed by the Committee to assist a referee to decide questions of fact and to report to him any breach of a Rule or Local Rule. An observer should not attend the flagstick, stand at or mark the position of the hole, or lift the ball or mark its position' (Rules of Golf Definition). See REFEREE.

## OBSTRUCTIONS

Anything artifical, whether erected, placed or left on the course, except:
(a) Objects defining out of bounds, such as walls, fences, stakes and railings.
(b) Artificial surfaces and sides of roads and paths.
(c) In water hazards, artificially surfaced banks or beds, including bridge supports when part of such a bank. Bridges and bridge supports which are not part of such a bank are obstructions.

(d) Any construction declared by the Committee to be an integral part of the course.
[Rules of Golf Definition.]
In a hazard a player would be allowed to lift a cigarette-packet, a newspaper or a brick (being obstructions), but not a dead rat or mouse (not being artificial and therefore being loose impediments).
See LOOSE IMPEDIMENTS ; RULES OF GOLF, Rule 31.

## O'CONNOR, Christy (b 1925)

Runner-up (with Brian Huggett), British Open Championship, 1965. Irish Native Professional Champion, 1958, 1960, 1961, 1962, 1963, 1965, 1966, 1971. British Professional Match Play Champion, 1957. Ryder Cup team, 1955, 1957, 1959, 1961, 1963, 1965, 1967, 1969, 1971. With Harry Bradshaw won World (formerly Canada) Cup, 1958.

## ODD, PLAYING THE

Playing one more stroke than one's opponent. With his next stroke he will then be 'playing the like', when both players will have played the same number of strokes. If you have played two more strokes than your opponent, with his next stroke he will be playing 'one off two'; if three more, 'one off three' and so on. See LIKE, PLAYING THE.

## OLANDER, Clarence (b 1909)

South African Open Champion, 1936. South African Amateur Champion, 1932, 1934, 1936; runner-up, 1937.

## OLDEST AMATEUR CHAMPIONS

The oldest winner of the British Amateur Championship was the Hon. Michael Scott, who was 54 when he won at Hoylake in 1933. He was a year older than Charles Hutchings was when he won the title, 1902. The oldest winner of the U.S. Amateur Championship was Jack Westland, who was 47 when he won at Seattle, Washington, 1952.

## OLDEST GOLF CLUBS

It is difficult to assess the age of a golf club because, before the foundation of a club with duly elected officers and a meeting place, there was often just a 'society' or 'company' of kindred spirits playing golf over a links or heath. The following, however, are the oldest clubs (up to 1900), of which we have written evidence:

*England* Tradition gives Royal Blackheath a foundation date of 1608, but the earliest concrete evidence is a list of 55 "subscribers of the Goff Club for 1787" and a Silver Club bearing the date 1766.

*Scotland* In 1744 the Honourable Company of Edinburgh Golfers—also called 'The Gentlemen Golfers of Edinburgh' and the 'Leith Society'—organised an open competition and drew up a code of Rules for the benefit of strangers playing in it.

*India* Many Scots were engaged in trade in India, and the oldest clubs outside Scotland and England are Royal Calcutta (1829) and Royal Bombay (1842).

*Mauritius* The Mauritius Naval and Military Gymkhana Club claims origin in 1844.

*France* The Golf Club de Pau, in the Basses Pyrenees, was founded by British visitors in 1856.

*New Zealand* The Otago Club dates from 1871.

*Canada* Only one year separates Royal Montreal (1873) and Royal Quebec (1874).

*Ireland* Although the Curragh Club, Kildare (once Royal Curragh) could claim to have had some soldier golfers from the garrison playing over a few holes near the camp round about 1856, the oldest club in Ireland is Royal Belfast, founded in 1881.

*Sri Lanka (Ceylon)* Royal Colombo was founded in 1882.

*Wales* The Borth and Ynyslas Club, Cardiganshire, dates from 1885.

*South Africa* Royal Cape dates from 1885.

*Belgium* Royal Antwerp dates from 1888.

*United States* Golf began officially in November 1888, when John Reid invited four friends to dinner at his house in Yonkers, New York, and founded the St Andrews Club of Yonkers.

*Hong Kong* Royal Hong Kong was founded in 1889.

*Australia* Although golf of a sort was played at Adelaide as early as 1780, the three official oldest Australian clubs are Royal Melbourne (1891), Royal Adelaide (1892) and Royal Sydney (1893).

*Germany* The two oldest clubs are Berlin-Wannsee and Wiesbaden, both founded in 1895.

*Holland* The Rosendaelsche Club, Arnhem, was founded in 1896.

## OLDEST OPEN CHAMPIONS

The oldest winner of the British Open Championship was Roberto De Vicenzo, of Argentina, who was 44 when he won at Hoylake, 1967. He was nearly two months older than Harry Vardon was at the time of his sixth and last victory, 1914.

The oldest winner of the U.S. Open Championship was Ted Ray, the British golfer, who was 43 when he won at the Inverness Club, Toledo, Ohio, 1920. Julius Boros was one month younger when he won at the Country Club, Brookline, Massachusetts, 1963. Boros was the oldest winner, at 48, of the U.S.P.G.A. Championship, 1968.

## 'OLD MAN PAR'

Bobby Jones used to say that, in a match, he never played his opponent, but 'Old Man Par'—i.e. he ignored what his opponent was doing and concentrated on playing to the par of the course. Of a round played in 1913, at the age of 11, against a friend, Perry Adair, after watching Harry Vardon, Bobby wrote in *Down the Fairway* (1927): "I suppose that is the first round I ever played against the invisible opponent whose tangible form is the card and pencil; the toughest opponent of them all—Old Man Par."

## 'OLD PAWKY'

The nickname given by Willie Park, Jun, to his favourite putter, which helped him to win his reputation as the greatest putter of his day. It now hangs in the clubhouse of the Woking Club, Surrey, and round the shaft is a silver band containing Park's own words: "It holed mony a guid putt." See PARK, WILLIE (JUN).

## OLIVER, Edward ('Porky') (1917-1961)

Runner-up, U.S. Open Championship, 1952. Runner-up, U.S. Masters, 1953. Runner-up, U.S.P.G.A. Championship, 1946. Ryder Cup team, 1947, 1951, 1953.

## OLYMPIC

The Olympic Country Club, San Francisco, California. It claims to be the oldest athletic club in the world, having been founded in 1860. The Lake Course, designed by Sam Whiting, was taken over by the Olympic Club in 1922. Length: 6,727 yards

(Par 70). Housed U.S. Open Championship, 1955 (when Jack Fleck beat Ben Hogan in a play-off), 1966 (when Billy Casper beat Arnold Palmer in a play-off); U.S. Amateur Championship, 1958. Also Ocean Course (5,904 yards: Par 69).

## ONE-ARMED CHAMPIONSHIP

This championship was inaugurated in 1933, in that year being decided by two rounds of stroke play. In 1934 it went over to match play (after two qualifying medal rounds) and has remained so except in 1948, 1949, when it was decided by four rounds of stroke play. The moving spirit in the championship and the Society of One-Armed Golfers was G. A. Wilde. The main condition is that competitors must play with one hand only and must not make use of any artificial appliance.

## ONE-ARMED PLAYERS' INTERNATIONAL

A match has been played every year since 1934, except during the Second World War, between teams of one-armed amateurs of England

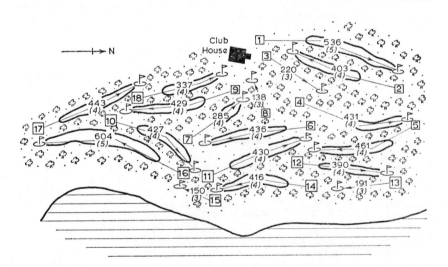

OLYMPIC, SAN FRANCISCO

and Scotland. Winners receive the
cup presented by the late Brigadier
A. C. Critchley. See CRITCHLEY, MRS
DIANA.

## 'ONE-BALL TWOSOME'
See SCOTCH FOURSOME.

## OOSTERHUIS, Peter A.
### (b 1948)
Runner-up, British P.G.A. Championship, 1972. Runner-up, Dunlop
Masters, 1972. French Open Champion, 1973, 1974. Italian Open Champion 1974. British Youths' Champion,
1966. Walker Cup team, 1967. Ryder
Cup team, 1971, 1973, 1975, 1977.
Played in World Cup (formerly Eisenhower Trophy), 1968. World (formerly
Canada) Cup team, 1971. Attached as
tournament professional and con-
sultant, Pacific Harbour Club, Fiji. See
WALKER AND RYDER CUPS, PLAYED IN
BOTH.

## OPEN STANCE
See STANCE.

## OPEN-TO-SHUT
A stroke in which the wrists are
allowed to turn to the right on the
backswing and then, on the downswing, turn back again just before
impact. Sometimes called the 'scissors
action'. See SHUT-TO-OPEN.

## OPEN UP THE HOLE
One is said to have opened up the
hole when one has played the ball so
that no obstacle lies between it and
the green or hole.

## OPPENHEIMER, Raymond H.
### (b 1905)
British. Won Worplesdon Mixed
Foursomes, with Miss Joyce Wether-
ed, 1932. Non-playing captain, Walker
Cup team, 1951.

## OPPONENT'S BALL LEGALLY,
### PLAYING
For a period of four years—1852-
56—the R. and A. Rules allowed a
player to play his opponent's ball
legally under certain circumstances.
Rule 14 ran thus:

When the ball lies in a hole or in any
place that the player considers is not
playable, he shall, with the consent of
his adversary, lift the ball, drop it
in the hazard, and lose a stroke.
Should the adversary say, however,
that he thinks the ball playable in
two strokes, then he (the adversary)
plays the ball; if he makes the ball
playable in two strokes, the two strokes
count as if the player had played the
ball; the player then plays the ball as
if he himself had played it out; but if
the adversary does not get the ball
out at the two strokes, then, as stated
above, it is lifted and dropped, a stroke
being lost.

As may be imagined, a rule so at
variance with the fundamental principle of a player playing his ball without interference from his opponent
proved a failure; it was eliminated in
the code of 1857, under which the
first Open Championships were played.

## ORCUTT, Maureen
One of America's best lady golfers
unlucky enough not to win the Ladies'
Championship;        runner-up,      1927.
Canadian Ladies' Open Champion,
1930, 1931. First winner (1962) of the
U.S. Senior Women's Amateur Cham-
pionship;     runner-up,     1963.   Curtis
Cup team, 1932, 1934, 1936, 1938.

## ORR SISTERS
The final of the British Ladies'
Championship in 1897, at Gullane,
was fought between two sisters, Miss
E. C. Orr, the winner, and her eldest
sister, the runner-up. On only one
other occasion have two sisters appeared in the final—in 1907, at Newcastle, Co. Down, when Miss May
Hezlet defeated Miss Florence Hezlet.
The Orr sisters—there were three—
came from North Berwick. See SISTER
GOLFERS.

## ORTOGO SINGER

The invention of the Haskell rubber-cored ball was followed by many variations and refinements, some very odd. One was the Ortogo Singer. This was a ball in whose centre was a hollow globe with a small ball inside, which, the inventors claimed, would make it drop into the hole should it touch the edge. Singer was the name of the inventor, and, according to J. H. Taylor, "it was aptly named, for on its way to the hole with a short putt it made a rattle like dry peas in a pod and had a disconcerting effect when one watched to see if gravitation was to be defied or not." See BALL, MAKES OF ; HASKELL BALL.

## O'SULLIVAN, Dr William M. (b 1911)

Irish Open Amateur Champion, 1949 ; runner-up, 1936, 1953. Runner-up, Irish Amateur Close Championship, 1940.

## OTAGO

Balmacewan, Dunedin, New Zealand. Founded 1871—the oldest club in the Southern Hemisphere. Length: 6,383 yards. S.S.S. 70. Recently a new clubhouse has been built and some of the holes re-designed. Housed first New Zealand Amateur Championship, 1893, and subsequently 1895, 1900, 1904, 1908, 1913, 1928, 1948, 1953 ; New Zealand Open Championship, 1908, 1913, 1928, 1938, 1949, 1953 ; first New Zealand Ladies' Open Championship, 1893, and subsequently 1895, 1898, 1902, 1908, 1914, 1926, 1936, 1964 ; New Zealand Professional Championship, 1928, 1938, 1948, 1953.

## OUIMET, Francis de Sales (1893-1967)

As an unknown amateur, U.S. Open Champion, 1913, after a tie with Harry Vardon and Ted Ray. U.S. Amateur Champion, 1914, 1931 ; runner-up, 1920. French Open Amateur Champion, 1914. Played in the first Anglo-American match, 1921, that led to the Walker Cup series and played in every Walker Cup match,

either as player or as non-playing captain, from 1922 to 1949. Captain R. and A., 1951, the first non-British golfer to be so honoured. As a member of the committee of the U.S. Golf Association for many years, and in other capacities, did much for golf in America and internationally.

Of Francis Ouimet, Bernard Darwin has truly said: "No more popular golfer has ever come out of America." And of his victory in the 1913 Open at The Country Club, Brookline, when Darwin was his marker in the play-off, he wrote: "It was one of the most momentous of all rounds, because, in a sense, it founded the American Golfing Empire." Author of *A Game of Golf* (1933).

## OUT OF BOUNDS

"Ground on which play is prohibited. When out of bounds is fixed by stakes or a fence, the out of bounds line is determined by the nearest inside points of the stakes or fence posts at ground level: the line is deemed to extend vertically upwards. When out of bounds is fixed by a line on the ground, the line itself is out of bounds. A ball is out of bounds when all of it lies out of bounds" (Rules of Golf Definition).

The Rules of Golf did not recognise 'out of bounds' until the code of 1899, although a local St Andrews rule stated that: " A ball in the enclosure (between the road and dyke holes) called the Station-Master's Garden shall be a lost ball." Even a ball on the railway line at St Andrews had to be played where it lay.

See RULES OF GOLF, Rule 29 ; STATION-MASTER'S GARDEN.

## OUT-TO-IN

The opposite of In-to-Out. A term used to indicate either a swing or a stroke in which the club is taken back outside the line of flight and finishes with the club-face travelling slightly to the left of the line of flight before straightening out again. Such action causes the ball to fly from left to right of the line of flight—i.e. with fade on the ball. In the hands of an expert golfer this action constitutes a controlled fade; in those of an inexperienced golfer it may become an uncontrolled slice. See IN-TO-OUT; OPEN-TO-SHUT; SHUT-TO-OPEN; SQUARE.

## OUTSIDE AGENCY

"Any agency not part of the match or, in stroke play, not part of a competitor's side, and includes a referee, a marker, an observer, or a fore-caddie employed by the Committee" (Rules of Golf Definition). See FORE-CADDIE; MARKER; OBSERVER; REFEREE; RULES OF GOLF, Rules 26, 27.

## OVER-40 FINGER

A simple putting technique, attributed to Gene Sarazen, in which the index finger of the right hand is placed down the back of, not round, the shaft. It is supposed to help older golfers who may be losing their putting touch.

## OVERSPIN

See TOPSPIN.

## OWEN, Simon (b 1950)

New Zealander. Runner-up to Nicklaus, 1978 British Open. German Open, 1974. Won New Zealand Open 1976. Runner-up World Match Play Championship, 1978.

## OXFORD AND CAMBRIDGE GOLFING SOCIETY

The idea of this famous golfing society—it is usually just referred to as 'The Society'—dates from 1897 when R. H. de Montmorency, captain of the Oxford University team, invited a team of old university men to come and play a match on the now-vanished Hinksey course. A dinner followed at the Gridiron Club and, in replying to the toast of 'The Visitors', John Low, the famous Cambridge golfer, suggested forming a peripatetic society of university golfers on the lines of the Free Foresters in cricket and the Harlequins in rugby. Another great sportsman, Arthur Croome, who was there, agreed to act as temporary secretary, and the society came into official being on 23rd March 1898. The first President was Horace Hutchinson, the first Captain John Low, the first Secretary Arthur Croome and the first Treasurer R. H. de Montmorency.

The first match took place on 23rd June 1898 against St George's, Sandwich, and in the team was a youngster just down from Cambridge called Bernard Darwin. Most of the society's activities consisted in matches and tours (and still does), but it is best known for its annual match-play competition, the President's Putter, played at Rye in January.

The actual Putter, to which the ball used by the winner in the final is attached by a silver band and chain, once belonged to Hugh Kirkaldy, the 1891 Open Champion, and was given to the society by John Low.

A tour made in the United States by a society team in 1903 may be said to have paved the way for the Walker Cup series. The team sailed, appropriately, in a ship called the *Mayflower*, and packed ten matches and a couple of stroke competitions into 33 days. Writing of this tour, Charles B. Macdonald, one of the pioneers of American golf, said: "The fine spirit of their game enlightened the golfing community of America and did much to bring the various warring factions in the States together, inspiring them in some measure to live up to the traditional golf of Scotland."

## OXFORD AND CAMBRIDGE MATCH

Both the Oxford and the Cambridge Golf Clubs were founded in 1875 and the University Match dates from 1878. According to Horace Hutchinson, who played for Oxford in the first three matches, W. T. Linskill was the chief instigator of the event, as he was of the game in general at Cambridge.

From 1878-93, the match was played at Wimbledon, and, in Bernard Darwin's words, "we caught an excruciatingly early train from Cambridge to King's Cross, whence we drove in a brake and a very imposing manner down to Wimbledon. We played our one round of the rather moderate golf provided by Wimbledon Common, with nobody paying any great attention to our proceedings, and so home again by coach and train to Cambridge."

Including 1977, 88 matches have been played, Cambridge winning 50, Oxford 33 and 5 being halved. See OXFORD AND CAMBRIDGE GOLFING SOCIETY.

## OXLEY, Dinah (b 1948)

British Ladies' Champion, 1970. English Ladies' Champion, 1970; runner-up, 1968. Runner-up British Stroke Play Championship, 1969. British Girls' Champion, 1963; runner-up, 1966. English Girls' Champion, 1965, runner-up 1966. Curtis Cup team 1968, 1970, 1972, 1976. Now Mrs James Henson.

ROBERTSON, ALLAN. This photograph shows some of the old-time St Andrews professionals and caddies. The man bending down is the great Allan Robertson. Behind him are "Old Tom" Morris (then quite young) and Willie Park (Sen.), and about to hole out is Willie Dunn. On the extreme left is James Wilson, the clubmaker

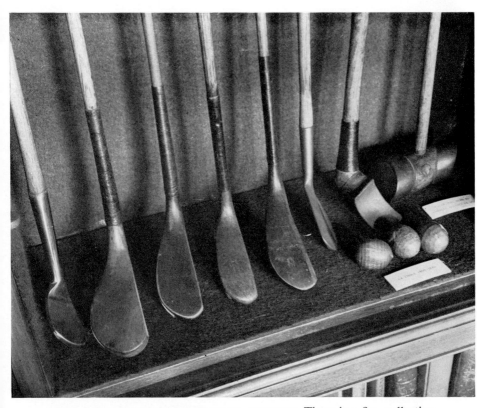

ROYAL AND ANCIENT GOLF CLUB OF ST. ANDREWS. There is a fine collection of old clubs in the R. and A. clubhouse. On the right are clubs used in the old French games of Chole and Jeu de Mail

ROYAL AND ANCIENT GOLF CLUB OF ST ANDREWS. This is a painting of the R. and A. in the 1890s, showing many of the better-known members. In the centre is Arthur Balfour, with "Old Tom" Morris bending to tee up his ball

## PACIFIC MASTERS

This tournament, hailed as being the richest in the world, outside America, has prize money of £123,000, the winner getting £26,500. It was held in 1972 at the Sobu Country Club, Injai, near Tokyo, and was won by Gay Brewer.

## PADGHAM, Alfred H. (1906-64)

British Open Champion, 1936; runner-up, 1935. Irish Open Champion, 1932. Dutch Open Champion, 1938. German Open Champion, 1934. British Professional Match Play Champion, 1931, 1935; runner-up, 1940. Ryder Cup team, 1933, 1935, 1937. Captain P.G.A., 1936. In the 1936 season Alf Padgham won nearly every tournament he entered. Author of *The Par Golf Swing* (1936).

## PAGANICA

This Roman word, derived from *paganus* (rustic or belonging to the country), meant a leather ball stuffed with feathers; it was struck with a crooked stick in a game about which unfortunately nothing is known. The interesting connection, however, is that early golf balls (until the advent of the gutty ball about 1848) were also made with a leather cover stuffed tight with feathers. See CAMBUCA; CHOLE; CROSSE; FEATHERY; GUTTY; TAKOURA.

L

## PAGE, Mrs Julius A.

U.S. Ladies' Champion, 1937; runner-up, 1938. Curtis Cup team, 1938, 1948.

## PAKISTAN, GOLF IN

Since Partition in 1947, golf has not flourished in Pakistan to quite the same extent as it has in India. Nevertheless, there are 14 clubs in West Pakistan and eight in East Pakistan, now known as Bangladesh. Leading clubs are at Abbotabad, Karachi, Lahore, Peshawar and Rawalpindi. There are no championships of Pakistan. The Pakistan Golf Union has offices in Lahore. See INDIA, GOLF IN.

## PALL MALL

See PELL MELL.

## PALMER, Arnold (b 1929)

With Jack Nicklaus and Gary Player, one of the so-called modern 'Big Three' of golf. U.S. Amateur Champion, 1954. Turned professional 1954. U.S. Open Champion, 1960; tied with Jack Nicklaus, 1962, but lost play-off; tied with Billy Casper, 1966, but lost play-off; runner-up, 1967. British Open Champion, 1961, 1962; runner-up, 1960. Won U.S. Masters, 1958, 1960, 1962, 1964; runner-up (with Charles Coe), 1961. Runner-up, U.S.P.G.A. Championship, 1964 (with Jack Nicklaus), 1968 (with Bob Charles), 1970 (with Bob Murphy). Canadian Open Champion, 1955. Australian Open Champion, 1966. Ryder Cup team, 1961, 1963 (captain), 1965, 1967, 1971, 1973. Represented U.S. in World Cup, 1960, 1962, 1963, 1964, 1965, 1966, 1967.

Arnold Palmer's dynamic personality has made him one of the world's most popular sporting figures and his fans—nicknamed 'Arnie's Army'—follow him even when he is playing badly in preference to a less exciting golfer who may be playing much better. In the same way that Bobby Jones had a plaque placed on the spot at the 17th at Royal Lytham and St Anne's where he played a championship-winning shot in 1926, Palmer has had one set up at the 16th at Royal Birkdale to mark what he called his 'clincher' in winning his first Open Championship in 1961.

Author of *Portrait of a Professional Golfer* (1964); *My Game and Yours* (1965); and the subject of *Arnold Palmer; The Man and the Legend*, by Mark McCormack (1967).

## PALMER, Johnny (b 1919)
Runner-up, U.S.P.G.A. Championship, 1949. Canadian Open, 1952. Mexican Open Champion, 1954. Ryder Cup team, 1949.

## PANAMA CANAL ZONE, GOLF IN THE
The Fort Davis Club, in the Canal Zone, was founded in 1939. It has 18 holes and measures 6,575 yards.

## PANDEMONIUM
The name—shortened to 'Pandy'—given to a famous bunker on the old Musselburgh links, near Edinburgh, once shared by the Musselburgh Club, the Bruntsfield Links Society, the Edinburgh Burgess Society and the Honourable Company of Edinburgh Golfers. See MUSSELBURGH.

## PANTON, John (b 1916)
British Professional Match Play Champion, 1956; runner-up, 1968. British Senior Professional Champion, 1967 (defeating Sam Snead in World Senior Championship), 1969; joint runner-up, 1971. Scottish Professional Champion, 1948, 1949, 1950, 1951, 1954, 1955, 1959, 1966 (tied with Eric Brown). Ryder Cup team, 1951, 1953, 1961. Represented Scotland in World (formerly Canada) Cup, 1955-66 inclusive.

## PAPUA AND NEW GUINEA, GOLF IN
Golf has been played—often under rather difficult conditions—in the Territory of Papua and New Guinea, brought there from Australia that has been the administrating authority for many years. Papua comprises the south-eastern part of the island of New Guinea. There is an 18-holes course at the chief centre of Lae and several other clubs.

## PAR
"The score in which a first-class player should play a hole in summer conditions" (*The Standard Scratch Score and Handicapping Scheme*, prepared by the Council of National Golf Unions). Par for each hole is fixed as follows:

Holes of 250 yards and under:
Par 3.
Holes between 251 and 475 yards:
Par 4.
Holes of 476 yards and over:
Par 5.

"The total of the par figures for each hole of a course will not necessarily coincide with the Standard Scratch Score, although in many cases it will."

The term par has replaced bogey. See BOGEY; STANDARD SCRATCH SCORE.

## PAR COMPETITION
See BOGEY (OR PAR) COMPETITION.

## PARK, Doris
See PORTER, MRS AYLMER.

## PARK, Willie (Junior) (1864-1925)
Born Musselburgh, son of Willie Park, Sen. British Open Champion, 1887, 1889 (after tie with Andrew Kirkaldy). Runner-up to Harry Vardon, 1898. Like his father, he played many famous money matches, including one which he won against Andrew Kirkaldy in 1889, another which he lost against Harry Vardon in 1899 and a third he won against J. H. Taylor in 1907.

He was undoubtedly one of the greatest players of the late nineteenth and early twentieth centuries. He was a deadly putter and used to say that "the man who can putt is a match for anyone." His favourite putter, 'Old Pawky', was almost as famous as Bobby Jones's 'Calamity Jane'. He was a keen student of the game and invented several types of club, including 'Park's Patent Lofter', a light iron with a concave face, which imparted a lot of backspin. In many of his matches and championships, Park had the services of a famous Musselburgh caddie, John Carey, nicknamed 'Fiery'.

He was a pioneer of golf-course construction and during his last 25 years he designed many courses (sometimes with Jack White) in Britain, America, Canada and on the Continent; indeed, in the end he worked himself to death.

As an architect, wrote Sir Guy Campbell (himself a golf-course designer of note) in a chapter on "Links and Courses" in *A History of Golf in Britain* (1952), Park "set the standard by which the famous architects who followed—Colt, Abercromby, Fowler, Croome, Mackenzie, Hutchison and Simpson—developed his methods and amplified his art". Among the courses he designed were the Old Course at Sunningdale, Huntercombe, West Hill and Worplesdon. Author of *The Game of Golf* (1896); *The Art of Putting* (1920).

See 'FIERY'; 'OLD PAWKY'; 'PARK'S PATENT LOFTER'.

## PARK, Willie (Senior)

The Park family was for many years associated with Musselburgh, the course of the ancient Musselburgh club and of the Honourable Company of Edinburgh Golfers before the move to Muirfield. Willie Park, Sen, was the first winner of the British Open Championship in 1860 and was champion again in 1863, 1866, 1875. His brother, Mungo Park, was champion in 1874; another brother, David, was also a good player.

For 20 years Willie Park had a standing challenge to play any other golfer for a stake of £100 and he played many famous matches against 'Old Tom' Morris of St Andrews.

See MUSSELBURGH; PARK, WILLIE (JUNIOR).

## 'PARK'S PATENT LOFTER'

This was a club invented by Willie Park, Jun, British Open Champion, 1887, 1889. It was described thus by H. S. C. Everard in the Badminton Library volume on *Golf* (1890): "Without being either a lofting-iron or a mashie, it partakes of the nature and characteristics of both; its shape brings the upper part of the blade, which is very concave, nearer to the ball and so, while less turf is taken, a very considerable backspin is put upon the ball, which is sent very high in the air and falls almost without any roll." See PARK, WILLIE (JUNIOR).

## PARKS, Sam (b 1909)

American. U.S. Open Champion, 1935. Ryder Cup team, 1935.

## PARTNER

"A player associated with another player on the same side. In a threesome, foursome or four-ball where the context so admits, the word 'player' shall be held to include his partner" (Rules of Golf Definition).

There is an old golf saying that "one should always assume that one's partner is doing his best—until one has direct evidence to the contrary".

See RULES OF GOLF, Rules 37, 40, 41.

## PASCOE, Amy Bennet ('Polly')

British Ladies' Champion, 1896. One of the pioneers of ladies' golf.

## PATE, Jerry (b 1954)

U.S. Amateur Champion, 1974. U.S. Open Champion, 1976. Canadian Open, 1976. Walker Cup team, 1975.

## PATTON, William Joseph ('Billy Joe') (b 1922)

Runner-up as amateur to Ben Hogan and Sam Snead in 1954 U.S. Masters—having had a hole-in-one at the 6th in the final round. Walker Cup team, 1955, 1957, 1959, 1963, 1965, 1969 (non-playing captain).

World Cup (formerly Eisenhower Trophy) team, 1958, 1962.

## PAU CLUB

The Golf Club de Pau, at Billere in the Basses-Pyrenees, is one of the oldest in the world, having been founded in 1856 by the Duke of Hamilton and other British golfers who wintered in this part of France; it is older than any English club with the exception of Blackheath. There is a tradition that golf was first played along the banks of the river Gave at Pau in 1814 by Scottish officers billeted there during the Peninsular War, after Wellington's defeat of Marshal Soult at nearby Orthez. See FRANCE, GOLF IN ; LLOYD, JOE.

## PEARSON, Dorothy M. W. (b 1908)

Runner-up, British Ladies' Championship, 1927. English Ladies' Champion, 1933 ; runner-up, 1928. Runner-up British Girls' Championship, 1924.

## PEARSON, Issette (Mrs T. H. Miller)

Runner-up to Lady Margaret Scott in the first two British Ladies' Championships, 1893, 1894. One of the pioneers of British ladies' golf and first honorary secretary of the Ladies' Golf Union, she was closely associated with the game until her retirement in 1921. In 1911 she married T. H. Miller, who presented the shield played for in the Ladies' Home Internationals.

## PEEL, Mrs R. T.

See DRAPER, MRS MARJORIE LILIAN.

## PEG TEES

Until the late 1920s, golfers teed up their balls, preparatory to driving, on a pinch of sand ; originally the sand was taken out of the actual hole on the green and later from a wooden or metal box provided for the purpose. Various claims have been made for the invention of the now universal wooden (or plastic) tee, but the most likely is that of an American doctor named Lowell, who made a number of small wooden tees for himself and his friends in the 1920s. The use of sand gradually died out in the 1930s. See DUNN, WILLIE.

## PELL MELL

Or Pall Mall ; from the Latin *pila malleus*— ball (and) mallet. A somewhat golf-like game played with a wooden mallet and wooden ball, differing from the French Chole, Crosse or Jeu de Mail in that, instead of being played across country, it was played in a restricted place bordered with palisades. In the sixteenth century it spread from France to Scotland and thence in Stuart times to England. Mary, Queen of Scots is recorded as having played golf and pell mell in "the fields beside Seton".

Pepys, in his diary, records a conversation in which "the Keeper of the Pall Mall" describes how "powdered cockle-shells" are spread over the surface "to keep it fast ; which, however, in dry weather turns to dust and deads the ball". Another entry says: "Thence to St James's, where the Duke of York was playing in the Pall Mall ; and so he called me to him most part of the time that he played, which was an hour." The Duke was also a keen golfer. The famous London street preserves the name of the game.

See CHOLE ; CROSSE ; JEU DE MAIL ; KOLVEN ; LADY GOLFER, FIRST ; ROYAL GOLFERS.

## PENALTY STROKE

"One added to the score of a side under certain Rules. It does not affect the order of play" (Rules of Golf Definition). See RULES OF GOLF, Rules 5, 10.

## PENNINK, J. J. Frank (b 1913)

English Amateur Champion, 1937, 1938. Walker Cup team, 1938. President, English Golf Union, 1967. Well-known golf course architect. Author of *Golf*, in Homes of Sport series (1952).

## PERKINS, T. Philip (b 1904)

British Amateur Champion, 1928. English Amateur Champion, 1927; runner-up, 1928. Runner-up U.S. Amateur Championship, 1928, being beaten in the final by Bobby Jones, the holder. This was the first—and only—time that the Amateur Champions of the two countries had met in a final. Walker Cup team, 1928. Went to America in 1932 and turned professional, in that year being runner-up, U.S. Open Championship.

## PEROWNE, Arthur (b 1930)

British. Swedish Open Amateur Champion, 1947. English Open Amateur Stroke Play Champion, 1958. Walker Cup team, 1949, 1953, 1959.

## PERRY, Alfred (1904-74)

British Open Champion, 1935. Runner-up, British Professional Match Play Championship, 1932. Ryder Cup team, 1933, 1935, 1937.

## PERSIA, GOLF IN

See IRAN, GOLF IN.

## PERSIMMON

An American wood used for many years in the manufacture of club heads. See WOODS USED IN CLUB-MAKING.

## PERU, GOLF IN

The leading club is the Lima Club, at Mira Flores, Lima, founded in 1923. It has a full-length 18-holes course. Other clubs include the Granja Azul Club, Santa Clara, and several in the Lima neighbourhood.

## PETER GARNER BOWL

See BRITISH BOYS' AMATEUR CHAMPIONSHIP.

## PHILIPPINES, GOLF IN THE

Having recovered from the difficulties engendered by the Second World War, golf has boomed in the Philippine Islands. The game began in a modest way after the spread of American influence following the Spanish-American war of 1898-1901, and the Manila Club, near the capital, was founded in 1909; the Manila Municipal Club is in Luneta Park. The Filipinos have now taken to golf in a big way and there are more than 50 clubs of various sorts. The best known is Wack Wack (named after the noise made by the local crows), where the Philippines Open Championship was held from 1962 until it went to the San Pedro Club in 1968.

The first two winners were Filipinos, Celestino Tugot and Ben Arda, and in 1966 the title went to a Filipino amateur, Luis Silverio. Their chief rivals have been professionals from Taiwan (Formosa). Golfing affairs are managed by the Philippines Golf Association, operating from Manila.

## PHILLIPS, Kathryn (Mrs John Lumb) (b 1952)

English Girls' Champion, 1968; runner-up, 1969. Curtis Cup team, 1970, 1972. She is a left-hander.

## PHILP, Hugh (1782-1856)

Born St Andrews. A joiner by trade, at first he made and repaired clubs as a sideline, but soon became the Chippendale or Stradivarius of clubmakers. Genuine Philp putters, with long, narrow heads, have become the rarest of collector's items and forgeries are common.

In 1819 Philp was appointed official clubmaker to the Society of St Andrews Golfers. For the heads of his clubs he used thorn, apple or pear, and ash for the shafts. Between 1845 and 1852 he had a brilliant assistant, James Wilson; he left to set up business on his own and Philp then employed a nephew, Robert Forgan, who succeeded him and made the firm of Forgan a worldwide one.

Of Philp, H. Thomas Peter in his *Reminiscences of Golf and Golfers* (1891) wrote: "The only clubmaker was Hugh Philp. It is questionable if any other—whether before or since his time—has shaped and set a club better than he did. Hugh was a dry-haired man; rather gruff to strangers, but quite the reverse to those who knew him, with a fund of dry, caustic humour, but withal a kind heart." He was always a keen but indifferent golfer.

See FORGAN, ROBERT; WILSON, JAMES; WOODS USED IN CLUBMAKING.

## PHOTOGRAPHIC FINISH

The ideal posed finish to a shot, so called because it is the natural one for a golfer to strike when having a photograph taken. Henry Cotton was the great exponent of the natural photographic finish to all shots. Many modern stars, including Arnold Palmer, never seem to mind how they look when they have finished so long as the shot was a good one.

## PICARD, Henry (b 1906)

Won U.S. Masters, 1938. U.S.P.G.A. Champion, 1939. Ryder Cup team, 1935, 1937.

## PICCADILLY WORLD MATCH PLAY TOURNAMENT

This popular match-play event— now run by Colgate—was inaugurated in 1964. It is by invitation, and eight of the world's current leading professionals take part in 36-holes matches, spread over three days, over the West Course ('Burma Road') at Wentworth Surrey. The winner receives £5,750 and the runner-up £3,450.

Until 1969, when Bob Charles was the victor, the winner had been either Arnold Palmer (1964, 1967) or Gary Player (1965, 1966, 1968).

One of the most remarkable matches was in the semi-final in 1965 between Gary Player and the late Tony Lema. After 18 holes Lema was six up, after 19 holes seven up, and after 27 holes still five up. Yet as Player said, "I really felt in my heart that I was going to beat Lema", and he stood on the 36th tee only one down. He won it with a birdie four—and then won the match at the 37th hole.

## 'PICCOLO' GRIP

This is a term used, if not invented, by Henry Cotton to describe the very loose grip, particularly with the last two fingers of the left hand, adopted by some players—with the result that at the top of their backswing such players look as though they were playing a piccolo, not gripping a golf club. Although this is regarded as a fault, a number of old-time golfers— in particular, Harold Hilton—showed pronounced 'piccolo' grips in photographs, but they tightened their grip on the way down.

## PICKARD, Mrs Anthony (b 1937)

Born Margaret Nichol. English Ladies' Champion, 1960; runner-up, 1957, 1967. Curtis Cup team, 1968, 1970.

## PICK-UP HOLE

One in which the player has a good chance of picking up a birdie.

## PICKWORTH, H. O. ('Ossie') (1920-1969)

Australian Open Champion, 1946, 1947, 1948 (after tie with Jim Ferrier), 1954. Australian Professional Champion, 1947, 1953, 1955; runner-up, 1951. Irish Open Champion, 1950.

## PIN

Another name for the flagstick on the putting green.

## PINEHURST

Pinehurst, North Carolina. There are five 18-holes courses, the championship course (No 2) having been founded in 1901 to the design of Donald J. Ross. Various changes have been made through the years and the present length of the No 2 course is 7,051 yards (Par 73). Housed U.S. Amateur Championship, 1962; U.S.P.G.A. Championship, 1936. Also Ryder Cup match, 1951. The North and South Amateur Championships are held annually at Pinehurst.

## PING PUTTER

A modern type of goose-necked putter so made that when the ball is struck a sharp 'ping' is heard. See GOOSE-NECKED PUTTER.

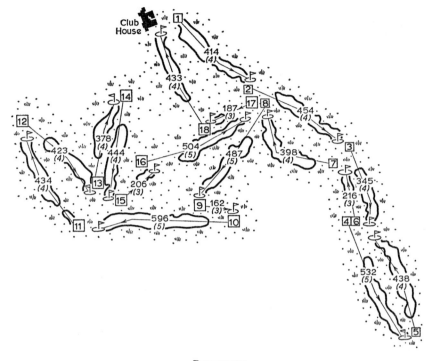

PINEHURST

## PIN HIGH
A ball is said to be 'pin high' or 'hole high' when it has been played as far as the hole and any distance to either side of the hole.

## PIRIE, Alexander K. ('Sandy') (b 1942)
Runner-up, Scottish Amateur Championship, 1972, 1974. Walker Cup team, 1967.

## PITCH
A stroke to the putting green in which the ball is struck so that it lands near the hole, with very little run or even none at all. The opposite of a pitch-and-run or run-up shot. See CHIP ; RUN-UP SHOT.

## PITCH MARK
See BALL MARK.

## PLACING
See PREFERRED LIES.

## PLATTS, Lionel (b 1934)
Portuguese Open Champion, 1971. Assistant Professionals' Champion, 1961. Ryder Cup team, 1965.

## PLAY CLUB
An old term for a club used for driving or playing from a good lie on the fairway, equivalent to the modern driver or brassey. The word was in common use up to the early 1890s. See BRASSEY ; DRIVER.

## PLAYER, Gary (b 1935)
With Bobby Locke, South Africa's greatest golfer and a member, with Arnold Palmer and Jack Nicklaus, of the modern 'Big Three'. Became a professional in 1952. British Open Champion, 1959, 1968, 1974. U.S.

Open Champion, 1965; runner-up 1958. Won U.S. Masters, 1961, 1974, 1978. U.S.P.G.A. Champion, 1962, 1972, South African Open Champion, 1956, 1960, 1965, 1966, 1967, 1968, 1969, 1972; runner-up, 1971. Australian Open Champion, 1958, 1962, 1963, 1965, 1969, 1970, 1974. Represented South Africa nine times in World (formerly Canada) Cup, winning (with Harold Henning) in 1965 and being runner-up (with Bobby Locke) in 1956. Won Piccadilly World Match Play Tournament, 1965, 1966, 1968, 1971. Author of *Grand Slam Golf* (1966); *Positive Golf* (1967); *Gary Player's Golf Secrets* (1964).

## PLAYING THE LIKE
See LIKE, PLAYING THE.

## PLAYING THE ODD
See ODD, PLAYING THE.

## PLAY-OFF
In the event of a tie, a stroke-play competition is usually decided by a play-off; this may be over 36, 18, 9 or any other number of holes fixed by the committee. If a play-off is impractical for any reason, a result may be decided by 'sudden death'—the first player of those involved in the tie to have a better score than the other or others being the winner. In a match-play competition, if the players finish the round all square, the issue is decided either by another round or 'sudden death'.

## PLAY SHORT
To play short is to strike the ball so that it does not reach the hole or, in a long stroke, deliberately playing short of the green to avoid possible trouble.

## PLAY THROUGH
According to the etiquette of golf, "if a match fail to keep its place on the course and lose more than one clear hole on the players in front, it should allow the match following to pass." The slower players 'call' or

'wave' or 'let' the others through and the quicker players 'play' or 'go' through.

## PLUGGED BALL
A ball that digs a small hole for itself on landing and does not move out of it. Unless there is a local rule allowing you to lift a plugged ball, it must be played as it lies except as provided for in the Rules of Golf (Rules 23, 32 and 35). Also called a 'sucker'.

## PLUMPTON, Diana
See SABINE, MRS N.

## PLUS
A handicap of less than scratch, the player concerned being said to play off plus one, plus two, or whatever his official handicap may be. A first-rate professional might be rated at plus four when he is opposed to amateurs at his club, but the lowest handicap for an amateur today is plus two. In the old days, however, some players were rated plus eight or more; at one time Harold Hilton was plus ten at Hoylake.

## PNEUMATIC BALLS
In the early years of this century, some pneumatic balls were on the market in Britain and America. Alex Smith won the 1905 U.S. Open Championship using one. They travelled a long way, but tended to burst when being struck or even in the pocket.

## 'POINTS' SYSTEM OF THREE-BALL SCORING
Instead of playing two separate matches, three players may use the 'points' system of scoring. They play off handicap and six points are available for each hole. If A wins from both B and C, he scores four points; if B wins from C, he scores two points, while C has no points. If, however, B and C halve the hole, they score one point each. If A and B halve the hole they score three points each, while C has no points. If A, B and C all halve the hole, they score two points each.

If after, say three holes, A has eight points, B six points and C four points, to make feats of memory easier, you can reduce A to four points, B two points and C no points —the total, after subtraction, always making six points.

## POLAND, GOLF IN

Unfortunately, golf in Poland has failed to survive the Second World War and the subsequent Russian occupation. Before the war there were clubs at Warsaw, the capital, and at Katowice, the mining town in Upper Silesia. Unlike Romania, there are no signs of a golf revival in Poland. See ROMANIA, GOLF IN.

## PORTER, Mrs Aylmer

Born Doris Park, of a famous Scottish family. Runner-up, British Ladies' Championship, 1937. Scottish Ladies' Champion, 1936; runner-up, 1929, 1930, 1931. Curtis Cup team, 1932. See PARK, WILLIE (SENIOR AND JUNIOR).

## PORTER, Mrs Mark A. (b 1923)

U.S. Ladies' Champion, 1949. Curtis Cup team, 1950.

## PORTER, Ruth (b 1939)

English Ladies' Champion, 1959, 1961, 1965. British Girls' Champion, 1956; runner-up, 1957. Curtis Cup team, 1960, 1962, 1964.

## PORTMARNOCK

Portmarnock, Co. Dublin, Eire. Founded 1894. Set among the sand-dunes, its length makes it very challenging. Length: 7,093 yards. S.S.S. 73. Housed Amateur Championship, 1949; Ladies' Championship, 1931; Canada (now World) Cup, 1960.

## PORTUGAL, GOLF IN

There are ten clubs in Portugal, including five fine new ones in the Algarve, two designed by Henry Cotton (Penina and Vale do Lobo) and another (Vilamoura) designed by Frank Pennink. Three more are also planned in the Algarve, one by Cotton,

one by Pennink and another by Robert Trent Jones. Other clubs are the Lisbon Sports Club, the Estoril Club, the Oporto Club, the Club de Golf de Miramar and the Club de Golf de Vidago.

The Portuguese Open Championship has been held since 1953, the Open Amateur Championship since 1930, the National Amateur Championship since 1934, the Ladies' Open Amateur Championship since 1931, the Ladies' National Championship since 1950.

## PORTUGUESE EAST AFRICA, GOLF IN

The game has been played here almost as long as it has in Portugal, for the Beira Club was founded in 1907. It has 18 holes and a length of 6,490 yards. Only one year its junior is the Club de Polana at Lourenço Marques, which also has 18 holes, with a length of 6,495 yards—just 5 yards longer!

## PORTUGUESE WEST AFRICA, GOLF IN

See ANGOLA, GOLF IN.

## POSE, Martin (b 1911)

Argentinian. Argentine Open Champion, 1933, 1939. French Open Champion, 1939. In the 1939 Open at St Andrews, this "truly great golfer", as Bernard Darwin called him, reached the 17th needing two fours for a round of 72, which would have given him a chance for the title. Owing to his lack of English, he incurred a penalty stroke for grounding his club on the grass verge of the wall beyond the green (a hazard) and eventually ran up an eight, leaving him five strokes behind the winner, Dick Burton.

## POVALL, John K. (b 1938)

Runner-up, British Amateur Championship, 1962. Welsh Amateur Champion, 1962, 1967; runner-up, 1963, 1968, 1970. Welsh Close Champion, 1961; runner-up, 1967. Walker Cup reserve, 1963.

## PRACTICE SWING
Any swing made, for the purpose of loosening up or otherwise, without the intention of striking the ball. Practice swings are perfectly legal at all times—but too many are time-wasting and a nuisance to other players. See RULES OF GOLF, Rule 8, Note 1.

## PREFERRED LIES
Also called 'winter rules' or 'placing'. On many inland courses, but seldom on seaside courses where the turf is better, the lie of a ball on the fairway may be improved in winter conditions under a local rule. The object is twofold—to prevent wet fairways from being carved up and to give the player a better chance to play a satisfactory shot. Normally the local rule lays down that the ball may be lifted, cleaned, dropped and then rolled into a decent lie with the clubhead, as near to the original spot as possible. A pathway cut through rough is not regarded as fairway for the purposes of preferred lies and a ball thereon must be played as it lies.

See RULES OF GOLF for when a ball may be legally moved.

## PRENTICE, James A. W.
### (b 1885)
Born Edinburgh. South African Open Champion, 1913. South African Amateur Champion, 1908, 1909, 1911, 1913 ; runner-up, 1907, 1910.

## PRESIDENT
This long-out-of-date club was a niblick with a small rounded head, through the face of which was a hole about an inch and a quarter in diameter. The "celebrated professional" quoted by W. T. Linskill in his book, *Golf* (1889), was probably right in maintaining "that in using this club it was next to impossible to avoid striking the ball twice, the penalty for which is losing the hole". The derivation of the name is unknown. It was mainly intended for playing out of water and was also called the Water, or Ring, Mashie. See NIBLICK ; RUT IRON.

## PRESIDENTS AS GOLFERS, UNITED STATES
The late President Dwight D. Eisenhower was the keenest golfer among United States Presidents. During his term of office he gave the Eisenhower Trophy, now called the World Cup, for international amateur team championships. He had a house adjoining the Augusta National Club course, Georgia.

President John F. Kennedy was also fond of the game and so were Presi-

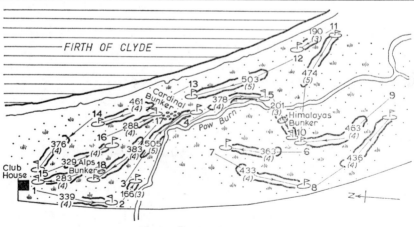

PRESTWICK

dent Nixon and Gerald Ford. See WORLD CUP (FORMERLY EISENHOWER TROPHY).

## PRESIDENT'S PUTTER

See OXFORD AND CAMBRIDGE GOLFING SOCIETY.

## PRESS

To strive to hit the ball with unnecessary force—and often with disastrous results. See FORWARD PRESS.

## PRESTWICK

Prestwick, Ayrshire. Founded 1851. Historic, old-fashioned links. Length: 6,598 yards. S.S.S. 72. Housed the first 12 Open Championships, founded by the club, from 1860-1872 ; subsequently, 1875, 1881, 1884, 1887, 1890, 1893, 1898, 1903, 1908, 1914, 1925. Housed Amateur Championship, 1888, 1893, 1899, 1905, 1911, 1922, 1928, 1934, 1952. Ceased to be the venue of Open and Amateur Championships because of the difficulty of crowd control.

## PRETTY

A term, now seldom heard, for the fairway. There is no official derivation, but might it not have some analogy with filling a glass 'up to the pretty', meaning (Oxford Dictionary) up to the "fluted or cut part of wine glass or tumbler"—the 'pretty' in golf being the cut part of the course?

## PREUSS, Phyllis ('Tish') (b 1939)

Runner-up, U.S. Ladies' Championship, 1961. Curtis Cup team, 1962, 1964, 1966, 1968, 1970.

## PRICE FISHER, Mrs Elizabeth

See FISHER, MRS ELIZABETH PRICE.

## PRINCE'S

Sandwich, Kent. Founded 1907 ; redesigned after destruction in Second World War. Length (Championship Course): 6,843 yards. S.S.S. 73. Traditional linksland. Housed Open Championship, 1932; Ladies' Championship, 1922, 1964 ; English Ladies' Championship, 1953. Also Curtis Cup match, 1956. Also 9-holes Red Course (6,440 yards : S.S.S. 72).

## PRIZE MONEY, BRITISH OPEN CHAMPIONSHIP

The winner of the first British Open Championship in 1860 at Prestwick, Willie Park, Sen, won nothing except the honour and glory and the right to hold the Challenge Belt for a year. The other competitors received nothing at all.

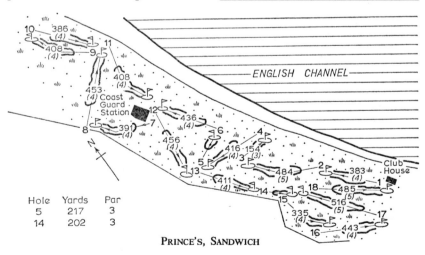

| Hole | Yards | Par |
|------|-------|-----|
| 5 | 217 | 3 |
| 14 | 202 | 3 |

PRINCE'S, SANDWICH

PRIZE MONEY, UNITED STATES OPEN CHAMPIONSHIP 172

In 1863 Willie Park again won the belt, but now the runner-up, Tom Morris, received £5; the third best, David Park, £3; and the next, Andrew Strath, £2. In 1864 the winner, Tom Morris, won £6 as well as the belt; the next best returns winning £5, £3 and £1. In 1868 the prizes were increased to £6, £4 and £2.

In 1872, after Tom Morris, Jun, had won the belt outright by his three victories, 1868, 1869, 1870, and the championship had lapsed for a year, a new Challenge Cup was provided and the prize money increased slightly. 'Young Tommy' Morris, who won for the fourth time running, received £8, while the next best received £5, £4, £3, £2 and £1. By 1886 the champion was getting a gold medal, valued at £10 as well as £8, the next best getting £5, £3 and four prizes of £1.

In 1893 for the first time an entrance fee of 10s. was charged and the prize money fixed at £100, of which the winner, Willie Auchterlonie, received £30 and a gold medal. By 1910 the total had risen to £125, of which the winner received £50. Ten years later the total was £225, and in 1927, as a result of gate money being charged the year before, prize money was £275.

After this the total rose steadily. In 1931 the total was £500 (winner £100); in 1946 £1,000 (winner £150); in 1949 £1,500 (winner £300); in 1954 £3,500 (winner £750); in 1955 £3,750 (winner £1,000); in 1959 £5,000 (winner £1,000); in 1960—the Open Centenary year— £7,000 (winner £1,250); in 1961 £8,500 (winner £1,400).

For the 1968 Open at Carnoustie, the total was £20,000, the winner— Gary Player—getting £3,000, the runner-up £2,000 and the third £1,475. For the 1969 Open at Royal Lytham and St Anne's, the total was raised to £30,000, the winner—Tony Jacklin— getting £4,250, the runner-up £3,000, the third £2,250. In 1970 the total was £40,000, with £5,250 for the winner, and in 1979 the total will be £155,000, with £15,000 for the winner.

## PRIZE MONEY, UNITED STATES OPEN CHAMPIONSHIP

The prize money for the first U.S. Open Championship in 1895 was $335. The winner, Horace Rawlins, received $150 and the runner-up, Willie Dunn, $100.

This sum remained constant for the next three years and in 1899 rose to $650, although the winner still received only $150. It actually went down, from $970 to $900, between 1906 and 1916, when it went up to $1,200—the runner-up, Jock Hutchison, collecting the first prize of $500 because the winner was an amateur, 'Chick' Evans.

After the 1914-18 war the total rose to $1,745 and stayed at that figure until 1926, when it rose to $2,145, although the first prize remained all the time at $500. In spite of the great depression, the total rose again in 1929 to $5,000, with the runner-up getting $1,000 because the winner in that year and 1930 was amateur Bobby Jones. That figure remained at $5,000 until 1938, when it was increased to $8,000.

When the championship was resumed after the 1939-45 war, the total was still $8,000, but went on rising steadily until in 1962 Jack Nicklaus won $17,500, out of a total of $81,600.

For the 1969 championship, at the Champions Club, Houston, Texas, the prize money was increased by $10,000 from the 1968 figure to a total of $200,000. Prizes for the first three places were $30,000, $15,000 and $10,000, so that the surprise winner, Orville Moody, was richer by about £12,500. In 1973 the winner received £14,000.

## PROFESSIONAL, DEFINITION OF

A professional golfer is defined as follows by the R. and A.:

1. *Professionalism.* Receiving payment or compensation for serving as:

a. A professional golfer.

b. A teaching or playing assistant to a professional golfer.

2. *Professional intent.* Taking any action which clearly indicates the in-

tention of becoming a professional golfer.

3. *Instruction*. Receiving payment or compensation for giving instruction in playing golf, either orally, in writing, by pictures or by other demonstrations, to either individuals or groups. Exception: teachers of physical training or other subjects whose duties include instruction in games to pupils of a recognised educational establishment.

See AMATEUR STATUS, RULES OF.

## PROFESSIONAL GOLFERS' ASSOCIATION (P.G.A.)

The P.G.A., which dates from 1901, grew out of the London and Counties Professional Golfers' Association, formed to protect the interest of club professionals who felt that their livelihood was being threatened by certain clubs announcing that they were prepared to let the sales of the professional's shop and other perquisites to the highest bidder. J. H. Taylor was the first chairman of the London association and James Braid the first captain, and one of their first activities was to hold a tournament at the now-vanished Tooting Bec Club—the winner being the chairman.

The idea received a good deal of support and soon Midland, Northern, Scottish, Welsh and Irish committees were formed and the title widened to the Professional Golfers' Association.

Its objects are to promote interest in the game; to protect and advance the mutual and trade interests of its members; to hold meetings and tournaments periodically for the encouragement of the younger members; to institute a benevolent fund for the relief of deserving members; to act as an agency for assisting any professional golfer or clubmaker to obtain employment; and to effect any other objects of a like nature as may be determined from time to time by the association.

Women golfers may apply for election to the ladies' section of the association.

## PROFESSIONAL GOLFERS' ASSOCIATION CLOSE CHAMPIONSHIP

Instituted 1955. Although lacking the cachet of the U.S.P.G.A. Championship (which ranks as one of the 'Big Four' of professional golf), the British equivalent has usually produced a worthy winner. Ken Bousfield won the first championship and other winners have included Peter Alliss (1957, 1962, 1965), Harry Bradshaw (1958), D. J. Rees (1959), Peter Butler (1963), Brian Huggett (1967), Peter Townsend (1968). It has been held on a variety of courses and has had several sponsors, the present one being the Viyella Company.

## PROFESSIONAL GOLFERS' ASSOCIATION OF AMERICA

The American P.G.A. was founded in 1916, 15 years after its British counterpart. The foundations, however, had been laid as early as 1907, mainly through the efforts of Robert White, who had come from Scotland in 1894 and had been professional at several American clubs. White became the first president of the association and Herbert Strong the first secretary. The basic aims were to foster interest in the game and to maintain a high standard of professional ethics. A keen supporter of the scheme was Mr Rodman Wanamaker, who gave the cup for the P.G.A. Championship.

By the time that White retired in 1920, there were about 100 members, but in the next ten years numbers had increased to over 2,000, and the total membership is around 7,000. From its first modest offices in New York it has grown to a powerful concern with headquarters in the premises of the association's own golf club at Palm Beach, Florida.

The association has had its troubles, particularly in 1968, when a disagreement between its committee and the tournament players, which had been brewing for a couple of years, came to a head. The tournament players felt that they did not have a strong enough representation on the executive committee and, consequently, not enough voice in the running of the association in general. Matters got as far as a break-away organisation being formed under the name of American Professional Golfers Inc, which proceeded to make independent arrangements for tournaments and other activities; its committee included such famous names as Frank Beard, Billy Casper, Gardner Dickinson, Doug Ford, Don January, Jack Nicklaus and Dan Sikes. Fortunately, the differences were resolved in December 1968 with the formation of a tournament players division within the P.G.A. framework.

One of the first actions of the association, when it was formed in 1916, was to organise an annual national U.S.P.G.A. Championship; it is now recognised as one of the most important events in the golfing calendar. It began as a match-play tournament, but went over to four rounds of stroke play in 1958. Only one foreigner (apart from Anglo-Americans) has won the title—Gary Player (1962, 1972). The following are the winners and runners-up in match play, with the venues and scores:

| Year | Winner | Runner-up | Venue | By |
|------|--------|-----------|-------|-----|
| 1916 | Jim Barnes | Jock Hutchison | Siwanoy, N.Y. | 1 hole |
| 1917-18 | No Championships | | | |
| 1919 | Jim Barnes | Fred McLeod | Engineers', N.Y. | 6 and 5 |
| 1920 | Jock Hutchison | Douglas Edgar | Flossmoor, Ill. | 1 hole |
| 1921 | Walter Hagen | Jim Barnes | Inwood, N.Y. | 3 and 2 |
| 1922 | Gene Sarazen | Emmet French | Oakmont, Pa. | 4 and 3 |
| 1923 | Gene Sarazen | Walter Hagen | Pelham, N.Y. | 38th |
| 1924 | Walter Hagen | Jim Barnes | French Lick Springs, Ind. | 2 holes |
| 1925 | Walter Hagen | Bill Mehlhorn | Olympia Fields, Ill. | 6 and 5 |
| 1926 | Walter Hagen | Leo Diegel | Salisbury, N.Y. | 5 and 3 |
| 1927 | Walter Hagen | Joe Turnesa | Cedar Crest, Tex. | 1 hole |
| 1928 | Leo Diegel | Al Espinosa | Five Farms, Mich. | 6 and 5 |
| 1929 | Leo Diegel | Johnny Farrell | Hillcrest, Cal. | 6 and 4 |
| 1930 | Tommy Armour | Gene Sarazen | Fresh Meadow, N.Y. | 1 hole |
| 1931 | Tom Creavy | Densmore Shute | Wannamoisett, R.I. | 2 and 1 |
| 1932 | Olin Dutra | Frank Walsh | Keller, Minn. | 4 and 3 |
| 1933 | Gene Sarazen | Bill Goggin | Blue Mound, Wis. | 5 and 4 |
| 1934 | Paul Runyan | Craig Wood | Park Club, N.Y. | 38th |
| 1935 | Johnny Revolta | Tommy Armour | Twin Hills, Okla. | 5 and 4 |
| 1936 | Densmore Shute | Jimmy Thompson | Pinehurst, N.C. | 3 and 2 |
| 1937 | Densmore Shute | Harold McSpaden | Pittsburg, Pa. | 37th |
| 1938 | Paul Runyan | Sam Snead | Shawnee, Pa, | 8 and 7 |
| 1939 | Henry Picard | Byron Nelson | Pomonok, N.Y. | 37th |
| 1940 | Byron Nelson | Sam Snead | Hershey, Pa. | 1 hole |
| 1941 | Vic Ghezzi | Byron Nelson | Cherry Hills, Colo. | 38th |
| 1942 | Sam Snead | Jim Turnesa | Seaview, N.J. | 2 and 1 |
| 1943 | No championship | | | |
| 1944 | Bob Hamilton | Byron Nelson | Manito, Wash. | 1 hole |
| 1945 | Byron Nelson | Sam Byrd | Moraine, Ohio | 4 and 3 |
| 1946 | Ben Hogan | Ed Oliver | Portland, Ore. | 6 and 4 |
| 1947 | Jim Ferrier | Chick Harbert | Plum Hollow, Mich. | 2 and 1 |
| 1948 | Ben Hogan | Mike Turnesa | Norwood Hills, Mo. | 7 and 6 |
| 1949 | Sam Snead | Johnny Palmer | Hermitage, Va. | 3 and 2 |
| 1950 | Chandler Harper | Henry Williams | Scioto, Ohio | 4 and 3 |
| 1951 | Sam Snead | Walter Burkemo | Oakmont, Pa. | 7 and 6 |
| 1952 | Jim Turnesa | Chick Harbert | Big Springs, Ky. | 1 hole |
| 1953 | Walter Burkemo | Felice Torsa | Birmingham, Mich. | 2 and 1 |

| Year | Winner | Runner-up | Venue | By |
|------|--------|-----------|-------|-----|
| 1954 | Chick Harbert | Walter Burkemo | Keller, Minn. | 4 and 3 |
| 1955 | Doug Ford | Cary Middlecoff | Meadowbrook, Mich. | |
| | | | | 4 and 3 |
| 1956 | Jack Burke | Ted Kroll | Blue Hills, Mass. | 3 and 2 |
| 1957 | Lionel Hebert | Dow Finsterwald | Miami Valley, Ohio | 2 and 1 |

Here are the winners in stroke play:

| Year | Winner | Venue | Score |
|------|--------|-------|-------|
| 1958 | Dow Finsterwald | Llanerch, Pa. | 278 |
| 1959 | Bob Rosburg | St. Louis Park, Minn. | 277 |
| 1960 | Jay Hebert | Firestone, Ohio | 281 |
| 1961 | Jerry Barber | Olympia Fields, Ill. | 277 |
| 1962 | Gary Player | Aronimink, Pa. | 278 |
| 1963 | Jack Nicklaus | Dallas, Tex. | 279 |
| 1964 | Bobby Nichols | Columbus, Ohio | 271 |
| 1965 | Dave Marr | Ligonier, Penn. | 280 |
| 1966 | Al Geiberger | Firestone, Ohio | 280 |
| 1967 | Don January | Denver, Colo. | 281 |
| 1968 | Julius Boros | San Antonio, Tex. | 281 |
| 1969 | Ray Floyd | Dayton, Ohio | 276 |
| 1970 | Dave Stockton | Tulsa, Okla. | 279 |
| 1971 | Jack Nicklaus | Palm Beach, Fla. | 281 |
| 1972 | Gary Player | Birmingham, Mich. | 281 |
| 1973 | Jack Nicklaus | Cleveland, Ohio | 277 |
| 1974 | Lee Trevino | Clemmons, N. Carolina | 276 |
| 1975 | Jack Nicklaus | Akron, Ohio | 276 |
| 1976 | Dave Stockton | Congressional, Washington | 281 |
| 1977 | Lanny Wadkins | Pebble Beach, Cal. | 281 |
| 1978 | John Mahaffey | Oakmont, Pittsburgh | 276 |

## PROFESSIONAL GOLFERS' CO-OPERATIVE ASSOCIATION

The P.G.C.A. was founded in 1920 when a number of professionals felt that there should be some sort of wholesale centre for supplying everything needed in their shops. One of the moving spirits was John Henry Turner, for many years professional at Frilford Heath, Berkshire, and he became the first chairman.

The professionals raised £9,000, which was enough in those days to start the association in a warehouse in Farringdon Street, London E.C.4, and soon a branch was opened in Manchester. In 1929 the headquarters were removed to larger premises in George Street, Marylebone, where they stayed until moving to their present building near Putney Bridge.

From here the association serves the needs of professionals all over the world.

## PROFESSIONAL INTERNATIONAL, FIRST

The first Professional International, between England and Scotland, took place at Prestwick in 1903, a year after its amateur counterpart. Matches were over 18 holes singles and foursomes. Scotland won the first three internationals, but then England gained control and won every time from 1906 until the series were discontinued after 1938.

## PROFESSIONAL SIDE OF THE HOLE

If the hole is cut on a slope, the side from which the slope goes towards the hole is called the 'professional side' and the side from which the slope goes away from the hole, the 'amateur side'. The reasoning is that the professional is more likely to allow correctly for the slope of the green and putt so that the ball, in slowing up, may have a chance to drop in or finish near the hole; if the ball is already falling away it would, of course, have no chance to drop in and every roll would take it further away. The 'amateur side' is also called the 'sucker's side'.

## PUBLIC COURSES

See NATIONAL ASSOCIATION OF PUBLIC GOLF COURSES.

## PUBLIC HOUSES AS CLUBHOUSES

In the days before clubhouses, golfers usually forgathered at a public house convenient to the course. The St Andrews golfers first met at 'Glass's Inn', later the 'Black Bull'; the Old Golf Tavern at Bruntsfield— an inn has stood on the site since 1456—was since the eighteenth century a meeting place for Edinburgh golfers; the clubhouseless golfers at Musselburgh repaired to the tavern called 'Mrs Forman's'—a name also given to the 3rd hole on the old links; until their 'Golf House' was built in 1768, the Honourable Company of Edinburgh Golfers met at an inn called 'Luckie Clephan's' at Leith; the late eighteenth and early nineteenth century Blackheath golfers met at the 'Green Man' (originally called the 'Bowling Green' and mentioned in Evelyn's diary); Prestwick members met at the 'Red Lion' before their first clubhouse was built in 1867; a room at the Royal Hotel, owned by John Ball's family, was the first Hoylake clubhouse; the earliest golfers at the Richmond Club, Sudbrook Park, changed at the 'Fox and Duck' until their fine clubhouse was ready.

## PUERTO RICO, GOLF IN

There are ten clubs in the American West Indian island of Puerto Rico, which measures some 100 by 35 miles in area. Among them is the fine Dorado Beach course, designed by Robert Trent Jones, where the 1961 World (formerly Canada) Cup tournament was held. In the 1969 event in Singapore, Puerto Rico, represented by Juan ('Chi Chi') and Jesus Rodriguez, professionals at Dorado Beach, finished higher than Ireland, Denmark, India and several other countries.

## PULL

"To strike to the left" (Chambers's Dictionary). Used either as a noun or a verb. A pull is a shot that is pulled by the action of the club to the left of the line of flight. A pull differs from a shot played with draw in that it goes direct to the left while a ball with correctly played draw starts to the right of the line and finishes down the middle or even slightly to the left of the line.

See DRAW, PLAYING WITH; DUCK HOOK; PUSH; SLICE.

## PUNG, Mrs Jacqueline

A colourful personality from the Moanalua Club, Honolulu, she was the first golfer from Hawaii to win the U.S. Ladies' Championship, 1952. She later turned professional and tied for the U.S. Women's Open Championship, 1953, losing to Betsy Rawls in the play-off. She seemed certain to have won the 1957 Women's Open, when it was discovered that, although her score-card total was correct, a four had been marked at one hole instead of a 5. She and her playing partner, Betty Jameson, were both disqualified and the title went to Betsy Rawls.

## PURVES, Dr W. Laidlaw

A Scottish golfer who, with a fellow Scot, Henry Lamb, and other Wimbledon members, founded the course that became the Royal St George's Club, Sandwich, in the late 1880s. He also gave valuable support to Miss Issette Pearson and other members of the Wimbledon Ladies'

Club in arranging a meeting in 1893 that led to the formation of the Ladies' Golf Union. He was the first captain of Royal St George's and was also closely connected with the founding of the Littlestone Club, Kent, in 1888. See LAMB, HENRY; PEARSON, ISSETTE.

## PUSH

The opposite of pull; i.e. a ball pushed by the action of the club to the right of the line of flight. It differs from a controlled fade in that the ball travels direct to the right of the line while a ball with controlled fade starts to the left of the line and finishes either down the middle or slightly to the right of the line. See FADE, CONTROLLED; PULL.

## PUTT

According to Chambers's Dictionary, a putt is "a delicate stroke such as is made with a putter on, or sometimes near, a putting green, with the object of rolling the ball, if possible, into the hole". A "putter" is either "one who putts or can putt" or "a short stiff golf club with upright striking-face, used in putting". There is, of course, also a verb 'to putt'.

Chambers's and other dictionaries give the derivation as from 'put'—the pronunciation being different, however, 'putt' having a short 'u', to rhyme with 'but'. See DRIVING PUTTER.

## PUTTING GREEN

The 'putting green'—usually shortened to 'green'—is "all ground of the hole being played which is specially prepared for putting or otherwise defined as such by the Committee" (Rules of Golf Definition). "A ball is considered to be on the putting green when any part of it touches the surface specially prepared for putting" (R. and A. Rules of Golf Committee Decision No 68/42/364). See RULES OF GOLF, Rule 35 and various other rules.

## 'PUTTY'

See ECLIPSE.

M

## QUAIL HIGH

A shot that is deliberately played low—as high as the flight of a quail. In *Power Golf* (1949), Ben Hogan says that in Texas, where he comes from, the wind blows all the time and the good Texan golfers learn shots that keep the ball down. "Quail high is the way we describe them in Texas. Keep the ball quail high and you will find yourself scoring better than the player who has plenty of power but is up in the clouds on every shot."

A ball that only just rises above the ground is facetiously called 'mouse high'.

## QUICK, Smiley Lyman (b 1907)

Runner-up, U.S. Amateur Championship, 1946. Walker Cup team, 1947. Turned professional, 1948. U.S. Public Links Champion, 1946. He was nicknamed 'Smiley' because of his infectious grin and adopted it as his first name.

## QUITTING

Quitting on a shot really means what it says—failing to hit firmly through the ball, the result nearly always being a bad stroke.

## RABBIT

An uncomplimentary name for an indifferent golfer; the opposite of tiger. It has been said that golfing rabbits are so called because of their timid natures and habit of dashing about the course rather aimlessly, but no derivation is watertight. See TIGER.

## R. AND A.

See ROYAL AND ANCIENT GOLF CLUB OF ST ANDREWS.

## RAP

A player who hits the ball firmly on the putting green, with a short backswing and a short follow-through, is said to 'rap' it or 'give it a rap'.

## RATCLIFFE, Noel (b 1946)

Australian. Won Belgian Open Championship, 1978.

## RAWLINS, Horace (b 1876)

Winner of the first U.S. Open Championship, 1895. He was born in England and had been in America only about nine months as assistant professional at the Newport Club, Rhode Island, where the championship was held. He scored 91 and 82 for a total of 173, beating Willie Dunn by two strokes. He was only 19 and remains the youngest U.S. Champion. In 1896 he was runner-up to James Foulis. See DUNN, WILLIE; FOULIS, JAMES; YOUNGEST OPEN CHAMPIONS.

## RAWLS, Elizabeth Earle ('Betsy') (b 1928)

U.S. Women's Open Champion, 1951, 1953, 1957; runner-up, 1950 (as amateur), 1961. Turned professional, 1951.

## RAY, Edward ('Ted') (1877-1945)

Born Jersey. British Open Champion, 1912; runner-up, 1913, 1925. U.S. Open Champion, 1920; runner-up, with Harry Vardon, to Francis Ouimet, 1913. Runner-up, British Professional Match Play Championship, 1911, 1912. Captain, Ryder Cup team, 1927.

Ted Ray was renowned for his forthright manner, his big hitting and for the pipe that was almost permanently clenched between his teeth. There is a story of a pupil, asking him how he could hit the ball farther, receiving the reply: "Hit it — side harder, mate."

He was a great iron player and once said. "The golfer who has not a friendly feeling for his irons is no gentleman." One of his favourite clubs was a 'Snieler' niblick, used for a variety of shots of various lengths; its origin is obscure.

## RECORD SCORE

An official record score can be made only in a stroke competition, with the holes and tees in their proper medal positions.

## REDDAN, Mrs Val (b 1916)

Irish. Born Clarrie Tiernan. Runner-up, British Ladies' Championship, 1949. Irish Ladies' Champion, 1936; runner-up, 1946, 1948. Runner-up, Canadian Ladies' Championship, 1938. Curtis Cup team, 1938, 1948.

## REES, David James ('Dai') (b 1913)

Son of a Welsh golf professional. Runner-up, British Open Championship, 1953 (with Peter Thomson and Frank Stranahan), 1954 (with Bobby Locke and Syd Scott), 1961. Irish

Open Champion, 1948. Belgian Open
Champion, 1954; runner-up, 1937,
1938, 1957. Runner-up, German Open
Championship, 1954. Swiss Open
Champion, 1956, 1959, 1963; runner-
up, 1961. British Professional Match
Play Champion, 1936, 1938, 1949,
1950; runner-up, 1953, 1967. British
Senior Professional Champion, 1966,
losing to Fred Haas in the World
Senior Championship; runner-up,
1964, 1965, 1969. Won Dunlop
Masters, 1950, 1962. Ryder Cup team,
1937, 1947, 1949, 1951, 1953, 1955
(captain), 1957 (captain), 1959 (captain), 1961 (captain), 1967 (non-playing captain). Represented Wales in
World (formerly Canada) Cup, 1954,
1956, 1957, 1958, 1959, 1960, 1961,
1962, 1964. Captain P.G.A., 1967.
Awarded C.B.E. for services to sport.
Author of *Golf Today* (1962); *Thirty
Years of Championship Golf* (1968).

## REFEREE
"A person who has been appointed
by the Committee to accompany
players to decide questions of fact and
of golf law. He shall act on any
breach of Rule or Local Rule which
he may observe or which may be reported to him by an observer (Definition 19). In stroke play the Committee
may limit a referee's duties. A referee
should not attend the flagstick, stand
at or mark the position of the hole,
or lift the ball or mark its position"
(Rules of Golf Definition). See MAR-
KER; OBSERVER; RULES OF GOLF,
Rule 11.

## REID, John (1840-1916)
Born Dumfermline, Fife. One of
the fathers of American golf. He
probably knew something about golf
before crossing the Atlantic, but his
interest was re-kindled by his friend
and neighbour, Robert Lockhart, who
brought over several sets of clubs
and a supply of balls from a visit to
Scotland, where he had learned the
game as a boy. A meeting was held
on 14th November 1888 at Reid's
house at Yonkers, New York, at which
the St Andrews Club of Yonkers was

formed, with Reid as president. The
first course consisted of three holes in
Reid's cow pasture, followed by one
of six holes laid out on a pasture belonging to Reid's friend, H. O. Tallmadge, who was at the first meeting.
See LOCKHART, ROBERT; ST ANDREWS
GOLF CLUB OF YONKERS; UNITED
STATES, GOLF IN THE.

## REJECTED CLUBS
Among the clubs rejected by the
R. and A. have been adjustable irons
and putters; a putter with a reflex
view-finder, fitted to the upper part of
the blade and designed to assist the
player in getting a true line to the
hole; a mallet-headed putter with a
round face flush with the shaft, taper-
ing away at the back; a ball-bearing
roller-type putter, designed to roll
smoothly over the surface of the
green behind the ball. See ADJUST-
ABLE IRONS; PRESIDENT.

## RENNIE, Mrs J. B. (b 1941)
Born Joan Hastings. Scottish
Ladies' Champion, 1967; runner-up,
1968. Curtis Cup team, 1966.

## REVELL, Roger (b 1951)
Runner-up, English Amateur Cham-
pionship, 1972. English Open Amateur
Stroke Play Championship, 1973

## REVERSE OVERLAPPING GRIP
See GRIP, TYPES OF.

## REVOLTA, Johnny (b 1906)
U.S.P.G.A. Champion, 1935; runner-up, 1945. Ryder Cup, 1935, 1937.

## REYBROECK, Corinne (b 1951)
Belgian. Belgian Ladies' Champion,
1968. Runner-up, British Girls' Championship, 1968, 1969.

## RHODESIA, GOLF IN
One of Rhodesia's 40 clubs—the
Doma Club, Sinoia—deserves special
mention, because they announce:
"Visitors free and very welcome."
Rhodesians have always been keen on
the game, and in remoter places there

are often small but happy clubs with perhaps only 30 or 40 members. At the other end of the scale there are big and long-established clubs like the Bulawayo Club (founded in 1895, only two years after the Matabele War had ended with the capture of Chief Lobengula's Kraal at Bulawayo) and Royal Salisbury, founded in 1888. Salisbury, the capital, has eight clubs. The future of golf in Rhodesia is uncertain, of course.

## RIDGLEY, Harold Brooke (b 1914)

Runner-up, British Amateur Championship, 1957. German Open Amateur Champion, 1957. Runner-up, with Miss Jacqueline Gordon, Worplesdon Mixed Foursomes, 1957. Sergeant Ridgley was stationed in England with the U.S. Air Force for some years.

## RIEBEN, Isabella

See BROMLEY-DAVENPORT, MRS EDWARD.

## RIEGEL, Robert H. ('Skee') (b 1914)

U.S. Amateur Champion, 1947. Turned professional in 1949 and was runner-up in the U.S. Masters, 1951, two strokes behind Ben Hogan, then winning the title for the first time. Walker Cup team, 1947, 1949.

## RILEY, Polly (b 1928)

Runner-up, U.S. Ladies' Championship, 1953. Curtis Cup team, 1948, 1950, 1952, 1954, 1956, 1958; non-playing captain, 1962.

## RIM

See LIP.

## RING (OR WATER) MASHIE

See PRESIDENT.

## RINGER SCORE

An American term for a best-ball score. Used either in, say, a four-ball match or in much wider connotation —as, for instance, in the Ringer Score for the U.S. Masters Tournament, since its inception in 1934, of 38, made up of three ones, ten twos and five threes.

## ROAD HOLE

The 17th on the Old Course, St Andrews. One of the most famous holes in the world, it has been copied many times, but never with complete success. See ST ANDREWS, NAMES OF HOLES AND BUNKERS AT; STATION-MASTER'S GARDEN.

## ROBB, James (b 1871)

British Amateur Champion, 1906; runner-up, 1897, 1900.

## ROBBINS, Hillman (b 1934)

U.S. Amateur Champion, 1957. Walker Cup team, 1957.

## ROBERTS, Jean (Mrs N. Evans) (b 1943)

English Ladies' Champion, 1962. Curtis Cup team, 1962.

## ROBERTS, Pat

Welsh Ladies' Champion, 1956, 1959, 1963, 1969; runner-up, 1952, 1955, 1957, 1958, 1962, 1966.

## ROBERTS, S. B. (b 1909)

Welsh Amateur Champion, 1934, 1947, 1953; runner-up, 1938, 1948. Won *Golf Illustrated* Gold Vase, 1939.

## ROBERTSON, Allan (1815-59)

Born and died at St Andrews. His father was David Robertson, described in George Carnegie's poem, *Golfiana* (1833), as "Davie, oldest of the cads" —i.e. the senior caddie. Davie was in effect a professional golfer, for he was player and teacher as well as caddie for important members and visitors.

Allan was the greatest golfer of his day and was also a renowned maker and supplier of 'feathery' balls. It is recorded that he fell out with Tom Morris, who had been apprenticed to him as a ball-maker, because Tom used the new-fashioned gutta-percha balls that were invented in the late

1840s. Before—and even after—this Allan and Tom played together in many challenge foursomes and were said never to have been beaten. Their most famous match was against the brothers Dunn of Musselburgh in 1849 for £400 (a large sum in those days), the St Andrews men, having lost at Musselburgh and won at St Andrews, just winning the decider at North Berwick, after being four down with eight to play.

Allan set the fashion of using iron clubs through the fairway instead of 'baffing spoons' and other wooden clubs; previously irons had been used almost exclusively for getting out of bad places. He called his favourite iron the 'Frying Pan'. He is said to have been the first player to break 80 on the Old Course, going round in 79 against Mr Bethune, of Blebo in 1858, the year before his death. His score was 4, 4, 4, 5, 5, 6, 4, 4, 4 (40); 4, 3, 5, 6, 4, 5, 5, 4, 3 (39)—a remarkable score considering that the course was far rougher than it is today.

See FEATHERY; 'FRYING PAN', THE; MORRIS, TOM (SENIOR).

## ROBERTSON, Mrs I. C. (b 1936)

Born Belle McCorkindale. Runner-up, British Ladies' Championship, 1959, 1965, 1970. British Women's Stroke Play Champion, 1971. Scottish Ladies' Champion, 1965, 1966, 1971; runner-up, 1959, 1963, 1970. New Zealand Ladies' Champion, 1971. Curtis Cup team, 1960, 1966, 1968, 1970, 1972, 1974, 1976.

## ROBERTSON, Janette

See WRIGHT, MRS INNES.

## RODGERS, Phil (b 1938)

American. Tied, British Open Championship, 1963, with Bob Charles, but lost play-off. Turned professional, 1960.

## ROLLAND, Douglas (1860-1914)

Born Elie, Fife. Famous for his long hitting, he was one of the greatest golfers who never won the Open

Championship. In 1883, as an amateur (he was a stonemason), he played a famous home-and-home challenge match against John Ball, the Hoylake amateur, then aged 22. After 36 holes at Elie Rolland was nine up and then won at Hoylake by 11 and 10. Next day in a further match at Hoylake he won by one hole after being five down and six to play. The first time gate money was charged in Britain was for a match between Rolland and Jack White at Cambridge in 1892. See GATE MONEY, FIRST.

## ROMACK, Barbara (b 1932)

American. U.S. Ladies' Champion, 1954; runner-up, 1958. Canadian Ladies' Champion, 1953. Curtis Cup team, 1954, 1956, 1958.

## ROMANIA, GOLF IN

There are two golf clubs in Romania—at Bucharest, the capital, and Ploesti, the oil centre. The professional at the Bucharest Club is Paul Tomita. Before the Second World War there was also a club at Sinaia, a popular summer resort. It is possible, however, that other courses will be built in Romania soon. See TOMITA, PAUL.

## ROSBURG, Bob (b 1926)

U.S.P.G.A. Champion, 1959. Runner-up, U.S. Open Championship, 1959. Mexican Open Champion, 1957. Author of The Putter Book (1963).

## ROSS, Aleck

U.S. Open Champion, 1907. He had emigrated from Scotland as a young man and was professional at the Brae Burn Club when he won the title. He won the North and South Open at Pinehurst in 1904—in its second year —and again in 1907, 1908, 1910, 1915.

## ROSS, P. Mackenzie (1899-1974)

Scottish. Golf-course architect. Laid out new Turnberry courses (1951), Southerness-on-Solway (1949) and many other courses in Britain and the Continent.

## ROUGH

This is, rather curiously, a term not recognised in the Rules of Golf. It is used to describe all ground on the course that does not come under the heading of fairway, teeing ground, putting green or hazard. In the Badminton Library volume on *Golf* (1890), the 'course' was defined as "that portion of the links on which the game ought to be played, generally bounded on either side by rough ground or other hazards". 'Rough ground' has now been shortened to 'rough' and is not, of course, regarded as a hazard. See SEMI-ROUGH.

## ROUGH, SHORT

See SEMI-ROUGH.

## ROUND ROBIN TOURNAMENT

See AMERICAN TOURNAMENT.

## ROUND, STIPULATED

"The 'stipulated round' consists of playing 18 holes of the course in their correct sequence, unless otherwise authorised by the Committee" (Rules of Golf Definition). One would, of course, play two circuits of a 9-holes course. See EIGHTEEN HOLES, WHY.

## ROYAL ADELAIDE

Tapley's Hill Road, Seaton, South Australia. Founded 1891, the title 'Royal' being conferred by King George V in 1923. Length (championship tees): 6,990 yards (Par 73). Housed Australian Open Championship, 1910, 1923, 1926, 1929, 1932, 1935, 1938, 1958, 1962; Australian Amateur Championship, 1926, 1929, 1932, 1935, 1938, 1947, 1950, 1954, 1958, 1962, 1969, 1975; Australian Ladies' Championship, 1923, 1926, 1929, 1936, 1939, 1947, 1957, 1967.

## ROYAL AIR FORCE CHAMPIONSHIP

Founded in 1922. Decided by stroke play in the first year, then by match play until 1960, and subsequently by stroke play again. In the early years dominated to an extraordinary extent by Squadron Leader Cecil Hayward, who between 1922 and 1935 won the title 12 times, being beaten only twice; later by Air Commodore C. H. Beamish, who between 1949 and 1968 won six times.

## ROYAL AND ANCIENT GOLF CLUB OF ST ANDREWS

A great deal has been written about the R. and A., but these are the salient facts. Golf had been played on the linksland at St Andrews at least from the early sixteenth century—even if it was not much like the modern game—and registers of the kirk sessions from 1580 onwards mention golfers being charged with playing at "tyme of fast and precheing" on Sundays at St Andrews, Perth, Leith and elsewhere.

No club as we know it today, however, existed until the Honourable Company of Edinburgh Golfers formed themselves into a company of friends and held their first Silver Club competition at Leith in 1744. Ten years later, on 14th May 1754, 22 "Noblemen and Gentlemen, being admirers of the antient and healthful exercise of the Golf", met together at St Andrews to subscribe for a silver club, to be played for in a similar way to that of the Edinburgh golfers. The winner became the captain of the club or society—and continues to do so to this day, although winning the Silver Club now consists merely in ceremoniously driving oneself into office from the 1st tee. Other trophies were later added to be played for through the years at the spring and autumn meetings.

Originally the St Andrews golfers had no official premises, but used a room at a tavern until 1835 when more official headquarters were established in the Union Club, near the site of the present R. and A. clubhouse; the foundation stone of this fine old building was laid in 1853, and it was ready for occupation in July 1854.

The old club had become the 'Royal and Ancient Golf Club of St Andrews' in 1834 and had begun to be regarded as one of the leading clubs in Scotland. When the Open Championship Belt was won outright by 'Young Tommy' Morris in 1870, the R. and A. joined with the Prestwick Club and the Honourable Company of Edinburgh Golfers in presenting a new Championship Cup, to be played for in turn on the courses of the three clubs.

The Honourable Company had put out the first code of rules in 1744 for the benefit of players in the Silver Club competition, and in 1754 the St Andrews golfers did the same thing. There were 13 'Articles and Laws' and the two documents were almost word for word. As the years went by, and the rules had to be added to and amended, the R. and A., rather than the Honourable Company, became recognised, although at first unofficially, as the arbiter on golfing matters.

It was not until 1924, however, that the Golf Unions of England, Scotland, Wales and Ireland, at a meeting in York with officials of the R. and A., agreed to make the R. and A. the governing body of the game in the British Isles and throughout the Commonwealth. Thus the old club became the final court of appeal on the rules; the form and make of clubs and balls; amateur status; the management of the Open, Amateur and Boys' Championships and the Walker Cup matches and matches between Great Britain and the Commonwealth countries.

See ROYAL CLUB, OLDEST; RULES, FIRST CODE OF; ST ANDREWS; ST ANDREWS, NAMES OF HOLES AND BUNKERS AT; ST ANDREWS, OLD NAMES FOR HOLES AT; STATION-MASTER'S GARDEN; SWILCAN BURN.

## ROYAL BIRKDALE

Southport, Lancashire. Founded 1889. Traditional links, with massive sandhills and fierce rough. Length: 7,037 yards, S.S.S. 74. Housed Open Championship, 1954, 1961, 1965, 1976. Housed Amateur Championship, 1946; Ladies' Championship, 1909, 1962; English Amateur Championship, 1939, 1953, 1970; English Ladies' Championship, 1935; British Boys' Amateur Championship, 1936; E.G.U. Brabazon Trophy, 1947, 1950; English Open Amateur Stroke Play Championship, 1958, 1963; British Women's Open Stroke Play Championship, 1970. Also Ryder Cup match, 1965, 1969. Became Royal Birkdale in 1951.

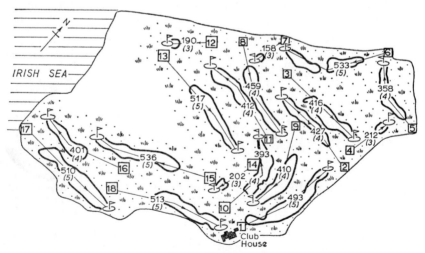

ROYAL BIRKDALE

## ROYAL BLACKHEATH CLUB

In the *Golfer's Handbook* the entry about Royal Blackheath says: "Founded 1608". Unfortunately, this claim has no firm foundation. Even the club historian, the late W. E. Hughes wrote in *Chronicles of Blackheath Golfers* (1897): "In vain we seek for conclusive evidence of the origin of the Blackheath Golf Club. We find an old tradition that King James the First of England, and Sixth of Scotland, played golf on the heath with some of his courtiers when the Court was at Greenwich; that a Society of Golfers at Blackheath was formed in the year 1608, with the royal sanction and authorisation, and that the Society and the game have existed at Blackheath up to the present time." He then adds: "No written evidence of any Society of Blackheath Golfers of earlier date than 1787 has come down to us."

The society was, however, flourish-ing at least as early as 1766, because a Silver Club still in the possession of Royal Blackheath bears the inscription: "August 16 1766, the gift of Mr Henry Foot to the Honourable Company of Goffers at Blackheath." As in the case of the Honourable Company of Edinburgh Golfers, a society existed before anything approaching a club as we know it to-day—with duly elected officers and an official meeting place. A sad thing is that the earliest known records of the Blackheath Society were destroyed in a fire at the end of the eighteenth century, but by 1787 the society had a captain, secretary, treasurer and a committee of six. A portrait of the senior member of this committee, William Innes, painted in 1790 by Lemuel Francis Abbott, R.A., is famous all over the golfing world; it shows him in the club uniform as a past captain, his clubs carried by his 'college man' in the dress of a pen-

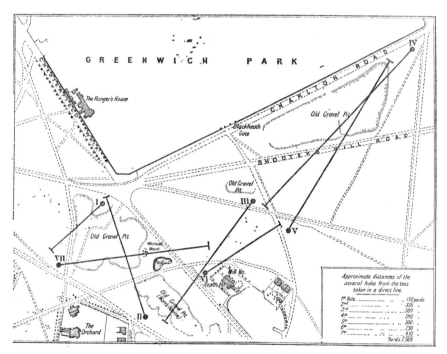

OLD ROYAL BLACKHEATH

sioner of the Royal Naval Hospital, Greenwich.

The original course on Blackheath consisted of only 5 holes, but in 1844 the number was increased to 7; the normal round was either twice or three times round the course. The club had several homes in various parts of Blackheath—including a public house called, successively, the 'Bowling Green' and the 'Green Man'—until it finally settled in 1865 in a house on Blackheath Hill. There the members remained until the hazards of the old heath—which, being common land, had always included pedestrians, children, nursemaids and dogs, to say nothing of lamp-posts, park-benches and railings—became unbearable, and a move was made to completely new surroundings at Eltham. Here the Royal Blackheath Club has a magnificent clubhouse in what was once Eltham Palace, a worthy setting for their collection of historic portraits.

See MANCHESTER CLUB, OLD; MOLESEY HURST, GOLF AT.

## ROYAL BURGESS GOLFING SOCIETY OF EDINBURGH

This ancient golfing society dates from 1773, although it has been claimed that it existed as far back as 1735. Originally its members, like those of the Honourable Company of Edinburgh Golfers, played over the old links at Leith, and then at Bruntsfield, but in the 1830s both societies moved to Musselburgh where conditions were better for golf. When, in turn, Musselburgh became unsuitable, the Royal Burgess Society moved to its present fine course at Barnton; its clubhouse is a former hunting lodge of the Stuart kings called Cramond Regis. See BRUNTSFIELD; LEITH; MUSSELBURGH.

## ROYAL CAPE

Wynberg, Cape Province, South Africa. Founded 1885, at a meeting at the Castle, Cape Town, "for the purpose of introducing the game of golf and starting the game in South Africa". The first course was at Water-

loo Green, then on Rondebosch Common and finally at Wynberg. The club became 'Royal' after a visit of the Duke of Connaught, Queen Victoria's youngest son, in 1910. Length: 6,655 yards. S.A. Golf Union rating, 72. Housed S.A. Open Championship, 1910, 1914, 1923, 1929, 1936, 1947, 1953, 1965; S.A. Amateur Championship, 1910, 1914, 1923, 1929, 1936, 1947, 1953; S.A. Ladies' Championship, 1911, 1921, 1929, 1938, 1955, 1968.

## ROYAL CINQUE PORTS

Deal, Kent. Founded 1892. Natural old-fashioned links. Length: 6,659 yards. S.S.S. 72. Housed Open Championship, 1909, 1920; the 1949 Open should have been held there, but sea-flooding in the spring caused it to be transferred to Royal St George's. Housed Amateur Championship, 1923; Ladies' Championship, 1902; English Amateur Championship, 1936, 1950. English Open Amateur Stroke Play Championship, 1964. Also the permanent home of the Halford Hewitt Cup for public school old boys. See HALFORD HEWITT CHALLENGE CUP.

## ROYAL CLUB, OLDEST

The first golf club to be accorded the honour of calling itself 'Royal' and having royal patronage was the Perth Golfing Society—by King William IV on 4th June 1833. The society, now known as the Royal Perth Golfing Society and County and City Club, still plays on its course on the North Inch. It was founded in 1824.

When the St Andrews Club asked the King, in January 1834, to grant them the same privilege and become the first patron, he approved the title of 'The Royal and Ancient Golf Club of St Andrews', but said that he could not become the club's patron because he had had to decline similar requests. When the case of Royal Perth was raised, however, he changed his mind and agreed, as Duke of St Andrews, to become patron.

See ROYAL AND ANCIENT GOLF CLUB OF ST ANDREWS; ROYAL GOLF CLUBS.

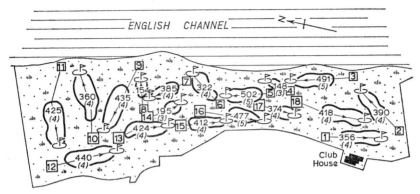

ROYAL CINQUE PORTS

## ROYAL COUNTY DOWN

Newcastle, Co. Down, Northern Ireland. Founded 1889. Beautiful and typical links. Length: 6,651 yards. S.S.S. 72. Housed Amateur Championship, 1970; Ladies' Championship, 1899, 1907, 1920, 1927, 1935, 1950, 1963. Curtis Cup match, 1968.

## ROYAL GOLF CLUBS

The following are the clubs which are entitled to call themselves 'Royal', an honour conferred either by the Sovereign or a member of the Royal Family:

### England and Channel Islands

Royal Ashdown Forest, Forest Row, Sussex.
Royal Birkdale, Southport, Lancashire.
Royal Blackheath, Eltham, London S.E.9.
Royal Cinque Ports, Deal, Kent.
Royal Cromer, Cromer, Norfolk.
Royal Eastbourne, Eastbourne, Sussex.
Royal Epping Forest, Chingford, Essex.
Royal Guernsey, L'Ancresse, Guernsey.
Royal Jersey, Grouville, Jersey.
Royal Liverpool, Hoylake, Cheshire.
Royal Lytham and St Anne's, St Anne's-on-Sea, Lancashire.

Royal Mid-Surrey, Richmond, Surrey.
Royal North Devon, Westward Ho!, Devon.
Royal Norwich, Norwich, Norfolk.
Royal St George's, Sandwich, Kent.
Royal West Norfolk, Brancaster, Norfolk.
Royal Wimbledon, Wimbledon Common, London S.W.19.
Royal Winchester, Winchester, Hampshire.
Royal Worlington, Worlington, Suffolk.
Two other English 'Royal' clubs—Royal Cornwall, Bodmin, and Royal Isle of Wight—have unfortunately vanished.

### Scotland

Royal Aberdeen, Balgownie, Aberdeenshire.
Royal Albert, Montrose, Angus.
Royal and Ancient, St Andrews, Fife.
Royal Burgess Golfing Society, Barnton, Edinburgh.
Royal Dornoch, Dornoch, Sutherland.
Duff House Royal, Banff, Banffshire.
Royal Musselburgh, Prestonpans, Midlothian.
Royal Perth Golfing Society, Perth, Perthshire.
Royal Troon, Troon, Ayrshire.
Royal Craggan is a private course on the Mar Lodge estate, Braemar, Aberdeenshire.

## Ireland

Royal Belfast, Craigavad, Co. Down.
Royal County Down, Newcastle, Co. Down.
Royal Dublin, Dollymount, Dublin.
Royal Portrush, Portrush, Co. Antrim.

## Wales

Royal Porthcawl, Porthcawl, Glamorgan.
Royal St Davids, Harlech, Merioneth.

## Africa

Royal Cape, Wynberg, Cape Province.
Royal Durban, Durban, Natal.
Royal Johannesburg, Johannesburg, Transvaal.
Royal Port Alfred, Kowie West, Cape Province.
Royal Nairobi, Nairobi, Kenya.
Royal Salisbury, Salisbury, Rhodesia.

## Australia

Royal Adelaide, Seaton, South Australia.
Royal Canberra, Canberra, Australian Capital Territory.
Royal Fremantle, Fremantle, West Australia.
Royal Hobart, Hobart, Tasmania.
Royal Melbourne, Black Rock, Victoria.
Royal Perth, South Perth, West Australia.
Royal Queensland, Brisbane, Queensland.
Royal Sydney, Sydney, New South Wales.

## Canada

Royal Colwood, Victoria, British Columbia.
Royal Montreal, Montreal, Quebec.
Royal Ottawa, Ottawa, Quebec.
Royal Quebec, Boischatel, Quebec.

## India

Royal Bombay, Bombay Gymkhana, Bombay.
Royal Calcutta, Tollygunge, Calcutta.
Royal Western India, Nasik.
Other British-created 'Royal' clubs are: Royal Colombo, Sri Lanka;

Royal Hong Kong; Royal Malta. Formerly there was also Royal Singapore.
'Royal' clubs created by other Royal Houses are Royal Johore and Royal Selangor, Malaysia; Royal Bangkok and Royal Dusit, Thailand; and the following nine in Belgium: Royal Antwerp; Royal Golf Club de Belgique and Royal Waterloo, Brussels; Royal Golf Club de Ghent; Royal Zoute; Royal Golf Club du Sart-Tilman, Liège; Royal Golf Club of Hainaut, Mons; Royal Golf Club of Ostend; Royal Golf Club des Fagnes, Spa.

## ROYAL GOLFERS

The first authenticated royal golfers were the later Stuart kings of Scotland. Until the beginning of the sixteenth century, golf had been officially frowned on and indeed banned in Acts of the Scottish Parliament. In the Accounts of the Lords High Treasurers of Scotland, however, there are records of payments made between 1503 and 1506 for "Golf Clubbis and Ballis to the King that he playit with"; "XII Golf Ballis to the King"; and "II Golf Clubbis to the King". This golfing king was the unfortunate James IV, who died at Flodden Field, fighting against the army of his brother-in-law, Henry VIII.

James IV's son, James V, who succeeded at the age of 1, is reputed to have played golf frequently at a place called Godford and his daughter, the ill-fated Mary, Queen of Scots (she succeeded before she was a week old), was the first recorded lady golfer. Mary's son, who became James I of England and VI of Scotland, learnt the game at Perth and in April 1603 appointed William Mayne, "bower burges of Edinburgh, during all dayis of his lyif-tyme, clubmaker to his Hienes". In 1618, realising that "no small quantitie of gold and silver is transported zeirlie out of his Hienes Kingdome of Scotland for bying of golf ballis", he conferred a monopoly of ball making on James Melvill "for the spaice of tuentie-one zeiries" and ordered him to mark all balls with a "stamp of his awin".

When James I came to England, after succeeding in 1603, it is said that he and his Scottish courtiers brought clubs and balls with them and played at Blackheath, where golf was still being played in this century. His eldest son, Prince Henry, who died in 1612 at the age of 18, was certainly a golfer, and a story has come down to us that, in swinging a club, he nearly struck his tutor, who was standing too close. When someone said: "Beware that you hit not Master Newton", the prince, remembering the beatings he had often suffered, remarked: "Had I done so, I had but paid my debts." There is a fine portrait, believed to be of Prince Henry, holding a club and ball.

Prince Henry's brother, Charles I, was playing golf at Leith in 1624 when news was brought of Phelim O'Neale's rebellion in Ireland, causing him to abandon his game and return to Holyrood House. Charles's son, the future James II, played frequently at Leith when he was in Edinburgh as Commissioner to the Scottish Parliament in 1681 and 1682 and on one occasion played a foursome for large stakes against two English noblemen, with a shoemaker named John Patersone as his partner —Patersone building a house in the Canongate with his share of the winnings.

After James II, there is a long gap in royal golfers, until William IV at least began to show interest in the game—even if he never played—by granting the prefix 'Royal' to the Perth Golfing Society in 1833 and to the St Andrews Club in 1834. The Sailor King—he was Duke of St Andrews—became patron of both clubs and in 1837 presented the St Andrews Club with a "Gold Medal and Green Ribband", bearing on one side the Royal Arms and on the other the Arms of St Andrews with the inscription: "Presented by His Majesty King William the Fourth to the Royal and Ancient Golph Club of St Andrews." After his death, later in 1837, his widow, Queen Adelaide, became patroness and gave the club the Royal Adelaide Medal.

In spite of her liking for Scotland, Queen Victoria showed no interest in golf, apart from becoming patron of the R. and A. Her son, the future King Edward VII, was captain in 1863 (without the usual formality of playing himself in) and his younger brother, Prince Leopold, became captain in 1876; this time Tom Morris, the famous professional of the R. and A., teed up a ball and presented the Prince with a new club—with which he had quite a good drive. Next day, partnered by Tom Morris, he played a foursome against John Whyte-Melville and a Mr Lockhart—winning by three holes. Next year Prince Leopold was playing at St Andrews again, but does not seem to have gone back before his death in 1884.

The only mentions I can find of King Edward VII actually playing golf are paragraphs in *Golf Illustrated*. On 17th March 1899 we read: "The latest recruit to the ranks of golf is H.R.H. the Prince of Wales, who has been playing at Cannes under the tuition of the Grand Duke Michael of Russia." And on 31st March: "The Prince is described as being a very promising player with a free and steady swing. Gourlay, the Cannes professional, predicts that he will soon reach proficiency."

The Prince of Wales—the future Duke of Windsor—became an honorary member of the R. and A. in 1913 and captain in 1922—driving himself in as custom demanded; he became patron of the club in 1936. He was the keenest of royal golfers. His brother, the future King George VI, also a keen and good golfer, became captain of the R. and A. in 1930 and was in turn succeeded in 1937 by his younger brother, the Duke of Kent. The present Prince of Wales shows no signs of playing golf, although he was photographed on his third birthday holding a club like an old Mills-type putter.

There is a 9-holes course in the grounds of Balmoral Castle and as far back as 1900 a few holes were laid out in Sandringham Park by the future Queen Alexandra, then Princess of Wales. According to Georgina Battiscombe's *Queen Alexandra* (1969), she "never grasped the rules of the game, regarding it as a kind of hockey allowing of much lighthearted scrummaging, the winner being the player who first succeeded in propelling his or her ball into the hole, regardless of the number of strokes played."

Members of other European royal families have been keen golfers. The Grand Duke Michael, uncle of the last Czar of Russia, was a pioneer of golf on the Riviera and founded the Cannes Golf Club. King Leopold of the Belgians played in the Belgian Open Amateur Championship just before the Second World War at the Zoute Club; his wife, Princess de Rethy, won the 1948 Italian Ladies' Open Championship; and his son, the present King Baudouin, is also a good golfer.

See LADY GOLFER, FIRST; ROYAL CLUB, OLDEST; ROYAL GOLF CLUBS.

## ROYAL LIVERPOOL
Hoylake, Cheshire. Founded 1869.

Historic links, founded partly on former racecourse. Length: 6,995 yards. S.S.S. 73. Housed Open Championship, 1897, 1902, 1907, 1913, 1924, 1930, 1936, 1947, 1956, 1967. Initiated amateur tournament, 1885, that became recognised as the first Amateur Championship; subsequently, 1887, 1890, 1894, 1898, 1902, 1906, 1910, 1921, 1927, 1933, 1939, 1953, 1962, 1969. Housed Ladies' Championship, 1896. Initiated English Amateur Championship, 1925; subsequently, 1957. Housed British Boys' Amateur Championship, 1947, 1954; English Open Amateur Stroke Play Championship, 1961.

## ROYAL LYTHAM AND ST ANNE'S
St Anne's-on-Sea, Lancashire. Founded 1886. Traditional links, but separated from the sea by high dunes; over 200 bunkers. Length: 6,836 yards. S.S.S. 73. Housed Open Championship, 1926, 1952, 1958, 1969. Housed Amateur Championship, 1935, 1955; Ladies' Championship, 1893, 1913, 1948; English Amateur Championship, 1928, 1956, 1966; English Ladies' Championship, 1919, 1921; British Boys' Amateur Championship, 1932, 1950; E.G.U. Brabazon Trophy, 1948. Also Ryder Cup match, 1961.

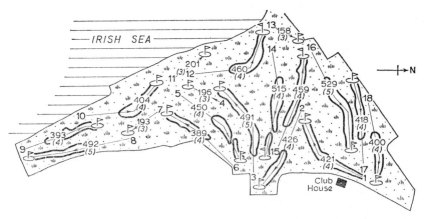

ROYAL LIVERPOOL, HOYLAKE

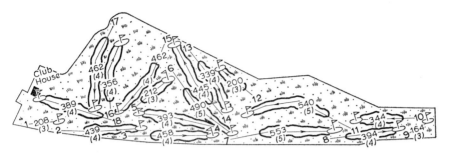

ROYAL LYTHAM AND ST ANNE'S

## ROYAL MELBOURNE

Cheltenham Road, Black Rock, Melbourne, Victoria. Founded 1891, the second oldest in the country. The original course was at Caulfield, but building encroachment caused a move to be made to the present site in 1901. There are two 18-holes courses (West and East) and a special composite course measures 6,946 yards (Par 73). Housed Australian Open Championship, 1905, 1907, 1909, 1912, 1913, 1921, 1924, 1927, 1933, 1939, 1948, 1958, 1963; Australian Amateur Championship, 1907, 1909, 1930, 1933, 1939, 1951, 1961, 1965; Australian Ladies' Championship, 1935, 1958, 1966.

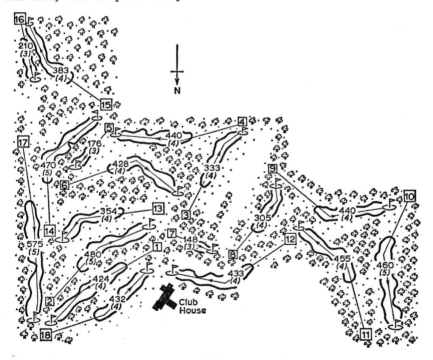

ROYAL MELBOURNE

## ROYAL MID-SURREY
Richmond, Surrey. Founded 1892. Very old parkland, with many bunkers, and humps and hollows, designed by J. H. Taylor, professional there for many years. Length (Outer Course): 6,335 yards. S.S.S. 71. Housed English Amateur Championship, 1946; British Boys' Amateur Championship, 1962. P.G.A. Close Championship, 1961, 1968. Also Inner Course (5,530 yards. S.S.S. 68).

## ROYAL NAVY AND MARINE CHAMPIONSHIP
Founded 1922. A two-round stroke play event, held at different clubs, until 1961, when it went over to match play for three years; four-round stroke play since 1964. In the early days the championship was dominated by a naval chaplain, the Rev. E. S. Ulyat, who won eight times between 1924 and 1938. Later Commander Fell won seven times between 1947 and 1959.

## ROYAL NORTH DEVON (WESTWARD HO!)
Bideford, North Devon. Founded 1864, the oldest English course still on its original site. Length: 6,543 yards. S.S.S. 71. Housed Amateur Championship, 1912, 1925, 1931; Ladies' Championship, 1900, 1910; English Ladies' Championship, 1925, 1933. New E.G.U. West of England Open Amateur Stroke Play Championship, 1970. J. H. Taylor was born there, worked as a caddie before becoming a professional golfer and died there in 1963.

## ROYAL PORTHCAWL
Porthcawl, Glamorgan, South Wales. Founded 1891. Seaside links with constant views of the sea. Length: 6,700 yards. S.S.S. 73. Housed Amateur Championship, 1951, 1965; Ladies' Championship, 1934, 1953. Also Curtis Cup match, 1964.

## ROYAL PORTRUSH
Portrush, Co. Antrim, Northern Ireland. Founded 1888. Traditional seaside links. Length: 6,809 yards. S.S.S. 73. Only course outside England and Scotland to house the Open Championship, 1951, the last time a British golfer (Max Faulkner) won the title before Tony Jacklin's victory in 1969. Housed Amateur Championship, 1960; Ladies' Championship, 1895, 1903, 1911, 1924, 1939, 1955, 1969.

## ROYAL ST DAVID'S
Harlech, Merionethshire, North Wales. Founded 1894. Natural links, some holes menaced by huge sandhills. Length: 6,290 yards. S.S.S. 72. Housed Ladies' Championship, 1926, 1949, 1960, 1967.

## ROYAL ST GEORGE'S
Sandwich, Kent. Founded 1887. Old seaside links, with famous greens. Length: 6,728 yards. S.S.S. 72. First English course to house the Open Championship, 1894; subsequently, 1899, 1904, 1911, 1922, 1928, 1934, 1938, 1949. Housed British Amateur Championship, 1892, 1896, 1900, 1904, 1908, 1914, 1929, 1937, 1948, 1959. English Amateur Championship, 1932, 1954. Also Walker Cup match, 1930, 1967. See ST GEORGE'S CHALLENGE CUP.

## ROYAL SYDNEY
Kent Road, Rose Bay, Sydney, New South Wales. Founded 1893, first at Concord and, in 1899, at its present site between Rose Bay and Bondi. Length: 6,722 yards (Par 72). Housed Australian Open Championship, 1906, 1911, 1922, 1928, 1934, 1946, 1956, 1969; Australian Amateur Championship, 1906, 1908, 1910, 1911, 1912, 1922, 1928, 1930, 1934, 1946, 1949, 1953, 1959, 1964; Australian Ladies' Championship, 1911, 1922, 1928, 1934, 1949, 1955, 1960, 1963.

## RUBBER-CORED BALL
See HASKELL BALL.

## RUB OF THE GREEN
"A 'rub of the green' occurs when

ROYAL BLACKHEATH CLUB. As this picture shows, the hazards of the old heath included gravel pits, lamp-posts, carriages and too-inquisitive pedestrians

(*above left*) ROYAL GOLFERS. King George VI was the best player among the sons of King George V. Here he is practising with the future Queen Elizabeth (now the Queen Mother) while on their honeymoon. (*above right*) The Duke of Windsor (formerly King Edward VIII) was the keenest golfer in the Royal Family and played in many countries of the world. In this picture he is playing himself in as Captain of the R. and A. in 1922. Unfortunately his drive was not a good one!

ROYAL GOLFERS. Tradition has it that Charles I was playing golf at Leith when news was brought of rebellion in Ireland, causing him to abandon the game and return to Holyrood House. This painting is by Sir John Gilbert, R.A. (1875)

ST ANDREWS, NAMES OF HOLES AND BUNKERS AT. This is Hell Bunker on the 14th hole (The Long) on the Old Course, St Andrews—one of the most famous hazards in the world

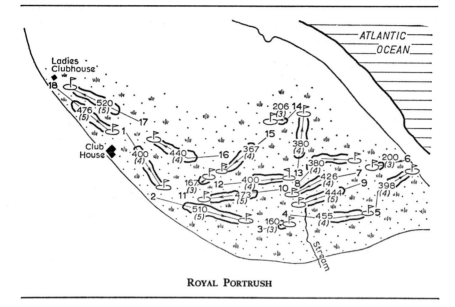

ROYAL PORTRUSH

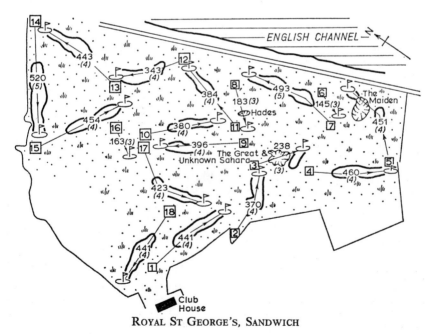

ROYAL ST GEORGE'S, SANDWICH

N

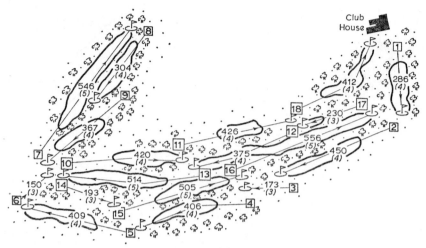

ROYAL SYDNEY

a ball in motion is stopped or deflected by any outside agency" (Rules of Golf Definition). Although not mentioned by name, the earliest code of rules (the Honourable Company of Edinburgh Golfers, 1744) catered for a 'rub of the green' in Rule X, which stated: "If a ball be stop'd by any person, horse, dog or anything else, the ball so stop'd must be played where it lies."

In the 1812 code of the R. and A. the phrase appears for the first time when Rule IX states: "Whatever happens to a ball by accident must be reckoned a rub of the green." By the 1857 code, under which the first Open Championships were played, the wording ran: "Whatever happens to a ball by accident, such as striking any person, or touched with the foot by a third party, or by the forecaddie, must be reckoned a rub of the green, and submitted to."

See RULES, FIRST CODE OF.

## RUDOLPH, Mason (b 1934)

Walker Cup team, 1957. Ryder Cup team, 1971. Turned professional, 1959. See WALKER AND RYDER CUPS, PLAYED IN BOTH.

## RULES, FIRST CODE OF

There were only 13 rules in the first extant code, put out by the 'Gentlemen Golfers' of Leith (the future Honourable Company of Edinburgh Golfers) in 1744. It was identical with the 1754 code of the R. and A., except that in Rule V the ball at St Andrews was dropped, not teed:

I. You must Tee your Ball within a Club length of the Hole.

II. Your Tee must be upon the ground.

III. You are not to change the Ball which you strike off the Tee.

IV. You are not to remove Stones, Bones, or any Break-club for the sake of playing your Ball, except upon the fair Green, and that only within a Club length of your Ball.

V. If your Ball come among Water, or any watery filth, you are at liberty to take out your Ball, and bringing it behind the hazard, and teeing it, you may play it with any club and allow your Adversary a stroke for so getting out your Ball.

VI. If your Balls be found anywhere touching one another, you are to lift the first Ball till you play the last.

VII. At holing, you are to play your ball honestly for the Hole, and not play upon your Adversary's Ball, not lying in your way to the Hole.

XII. He whose Ball lyes farthest from the Hole is obliged to play first.

VIII. If you should lose your Ball by its being taken up, or in any other way, you are to go back to the spot where you struck last, and drop another Ball, and allow your Adversary a stroke for the misfortune.

IX. No man, at Holing his ball, is to be allowed to mark to the Hole with his Club or anything else.

X. If a ball be stop'd by any person, Horse, Dog, or anything else, the Ball so stop'd must be played where it lies.

XI. If you draw your Club in order to strike, and proceed as far in the stroke as to be bringing down your Club—if then your Club shall break in any way, it is to be accounted a stroke.

XIII. Neither Trench, Ditch, nor Dyke made for the preservation of the Links, nor the Scholars' holes, nor the Soldiers' lines, shall be accounted a Hazard, but the Ball is to be taken out, Teed, and played with any iron Club.

See BREAK-CLUB ; GREEN ; RUB OF THE GREEN ; TEEING GROUND.

## RULES OF GOLF

The Rules of Golf, as approved by the Royal and Ancient Golf Club of St Andrews and the United States Golf Association, are reproduced by kind permission of the R. and A.

## Index (Copyright, Royal Insurance Co., Ltd)

## Section I Etiquette (see Etiquette)

## Section II Definitions

*1. Addressing the Ball*

A player has 'addressed the ball' when he has taken his stance and has also grounded his club, except that in a hazard a player has addressed the ball when he has taken his stance.

*2. Advice*

'Advice' is any counsel or suggestion which could influence a player in determining his play, the choice of a club, or the method of making a stroke.

Information on the rules or local rules is not advice.

*3. Ball Deemed to Move*

A ball is deemed to have 'moved' if it leave its position and come to rest in any other place.

*4. Ball Holed*

A ball is 'holed' when it lies within the circumference of the hole and all of it is below the level of the lip of the hole.

*5. Ball in Play, Provisional Ball, Wrong Ball*

a. A ball is 'in play' as soon as the player has made a stroke on the teeing ground. It remains as his ball in play until holed out, except when it is out of bounds, lost or lifted, or another ball has been substituted under an applicable Rule or Local Rule: a ball so substituted becomes the ball in play.

b. A 'provisional ball' is a ball played under Rule 30 for a ball which may be lost outside a water hazard or may be out of bounds. It ceases to be a provisional ball when the Rule provides *either* that the player continue play with it as the ball in play *or* that it be abandoned.

c. A 'wrong ball' is any ball other than the ball in play or a provisional ball or, in stroke play, an alternate ball played in accordance with Rule 11-5.

*6. Ball Lost*

A ball is 'lost' if:

a. It be not found, or be not identified as his by the player, within five minutes after the player's side or his or their caddies have begun to search for it ; *or*

b. The player has put another ball into play under the Rules, even though he may not have searched for the original ball ; *or*

c. The player, having played a provisional ball under Rule 30-1, *either*

(i) abandons his original ball as lost (Rule 29-3), even though he may not have searched for it, *or*

(ii) plays any stroke with the provisional ball from a point beyond the place where the original ball is likely to be,

whereupon the provisional ball becomes the ball in play.

Play of a provisional ball under Rule 30 or of a wrong ball does not constitute abandonment of the ball in play. Time spent in playing a wrong ball is not counted in the five-minute period allowed for search.

*7. Caddie, Forecaddie and Equipment*

a. A 'caddie' is one who carries or handles a player's clubs during play and otherwise assists him in accordance with the Rules.

When one caddie is employed by more than one player, he is always deemed to be the caddie of the player whose ball is involved, and equipment carried by him is deemed to be that player's equipment, except when the caddie acts upon specific directions of another player, in which case he is considered to be that other player's caddie.

Note : *In threesome, foursome, best-ball and four-ball play, a caddie carrying for more than one player should be assigned to the members of one side.*

b. A 'forecaddie' is one employed by the Committee to indicate to players the position of balls on the course, and is an outside agency (Definition 22).

c. 'Equipment' is anything used, worn or carried by or for the player except his ball in play. Equipment includes a golf cart. If such a cart is shared by more than one player, its status under the Rules is the same as that of a caddie employed by more than one player.

*8. Casual Water*

'Casual water' is any temporary accumulation of water which is visible before or after the player takes his stance, and which is not a hazard of itself or is not in a water hazard. Snow and ice are either casual water or loose impediments, at the option of the player.

*9. Committee*

The 'committee' is the committee in charge of the competition.

*10. Competitor*

A 'competitor' is a player in a stroke competition. A 'fellow-competitor' is any player with whom the competitor plays. Neither is partner of the other.

In stroke play foursome and four-ball competitions, where the context so admits, the word 'competitor' or 'fellow-competitor' shall be held to include his partner.

*11. Course*

The 'course' is the whole area within which play is permitted. It is the duty of the authorities in charge of the course to   define its boundaries accurately.

*12. Flagstick*

The 'flagstick' is a movable straight indicator provided by the committee, with or without bunting or other material attached, centred in the hole to show its position. It shall be circular in cross-section.

*13. Ground Under Repair*

'Ground under repair' is any portion of the course so marked by order of the committee concerned or so declared by its authorised representative. It includes material piled for removal and a hole made by a green-keeper, even if not so marked. Stakes and lines defining ground under repair are not in such ground.

*14. Hazards*

A 'hazard' is any bunker or water hazard. Bare patches, scrapes, roads, tracks and paths are not hazards.

a. A 'bunker' is an area of bare ground, often a depression, which is usually covered with sand. Grass-covered ground bordering or within a bunker is *not* part of the hazard.

b. A 'water hazard' is any sea, lake, pond, river, ditch, surface drainage ditch or other open water course (regardless of whether or not it contains water), and anything of a similar nature.

All ground or water within the margin of a water hazard, whether or not it be covered with any growing substance, is part of the water hazard. The margin of a water hazard is deemed to extend vertically upwards.

c. A 'lateral water hazard' is a water hazard or that part of a water hazard running approximately parallel to the line of play and so situated that it is not possible or is deemed by the Committee to be impracticable to drop a ball behind the water hazard and keep the spot at which the ball last crossed the hazard margin between the player and the hole.

d. It is the duty of the committee in charge of a course to define accurately the extent of the hazards and water hazards when there is any doubt. That part of a hazard to be played as a lateral water hazard should be distinctively marked. Stakes and lines defining the margins of hazards are not in the hazards.

## 15. Hole

The 'hole' shall be 4½ inches (108 mm.) in diameter and at least 4 inches (100 mm.) deep. If a lining be used, it shall be sunk at least 1 inch (25 mm.) below the putting green surface unless the nature of the soil makes it impractical to do so; its outer diameter shall not exceed 4¼ inches (108 mm.).

## 16. Honour

The side which is entitled to play first from the teeing ground is said to have the 'honour'.

## 17. Loose Impediments

The term 'loose impediments' denotes natural objects not fixed or growing and not adhering to the ball, and includes stones, not solidly embedded, leaves, twigs, branches and the like, dung, worms and insects and casts or heaps made by them.

Snow and ice are either casual water or loose impediments, at the option of the player.

Sand and loose soil are loose impediments on the putting green, but not elsewhere on the course.

## 18. Marker

A 'marker' is a scorer in stroke play who is appointed by the committee to record a competitor's score. He may be a fellow-competitor. He is not a referee.

A marker should not lift the ball or mark its position and, unless he is a fellow-competitor, should not attend the flagstick or stand at the hole or mark its position.

## 19. Observer

An 'observer' is appointed by the committee to assist a referee to decide questions of fact and to report to him any breach of a rule or local rule. An observer should not attend the flagstick, stand at or mark the position of the hole, or lift the ball or mark its position.

## 20. Obstructions

An 'obstruction' is anything artificial, whether erected, placed or left on the course, except:—

a. Objects defining out of bounds, such as walls, fences, stakes and railings;

b. Artificial surfaces and sides of roads and paths;

c. In water hazards, artificially surfaced banks or beds, including bridge supports when part of such a bank. Bridges and bridge supports which are not part of such a bank are obstructions;

d. Any construction declared by the committee to be an integral part of the course.

## 21. Out of Bounds

'Out of bounds' is ground on which play is prohibited.

When out of bounds is fixed by stakes or a fence, the out of bounds line is determined by the nearest inside points of the stakes or fence posts at ground level; the line is deemed to extend vertically upwards. When out of bounds is fixed by a line on the ground, the line itself is out of bounds.

A ball is out of bounds when all of it lies out of bounds.

**22. Outside Agency**

An 'outside agency' is any agency not part of the match or, in stroke play, not part of a competitor's side, and includes a referee, a marker, an observer, or a forecaddie employed by the committee.

**23. Partner**

A 'partner' is a player associated with another player on the same side. In a threesome, foursome or a four-ball where the context so admits, the word 'player' shall be held to include his partner.

**24. Penalty Stroke**

A 'penalty stroke' is one added to the score of a side under certain rules. It does not affect the order of play.

**25. Putting Green**

The 'putting green' is all ground of the hole being played which is specially prepared for putting or otherwise defined as such by the committee.

**26. Referee**

A 'referee' is a person who has been appointed by the committee to accompany players to decide questions of fact and of golf law. He shall act on any breach of rule or local rule which he may observe or which may be reported to him by an observer (Definition 19).

In stroke play the committee may limit a referee's duties. A referee should not attend the flagstick, stand at or mark the position of the hole, or lift the ball or mark its position.

**27. Rub of the Green**

A 'rub of the green' occurs when a ball in motion is stopped or deflected by any outside agency.

**28. Sides and Matches**

Side: A player, or two or more players who are partners.

Single: A match in which one plays against another.

Threesome: A match in which one plays against two, and each side plays one ball.

Foursome: A match in which two play against two, and each side plays one ball.

Three-Ball: A match in which three play against one another, each playing his own ball.

Best-Ball: A match in which one plays against the better ball of two or the best ball of three players.

Four-Ball: A match in which two play their better ball against the better ball of two other players.

*Note: In a best-ball or four-ball match, if a partner be absent for reasons satisfactory to the committee, the remaining member(s) of his side may represent the side.*

**29. Stance**

Taking the 'stance' consists of a player placing his feet in position for and preparatory to making a stroke.

**30. Stipulated Round**

The 'stipulated round' consists of playing eighteen holes of the course in their correct sequence, unless otherwise authorised by the committee. The number of holes in a stipulated round is 18 unless a smaller number is authorised by the committee.

**31. Stroke**

A 'stroke' is the forward movement of the club made with the intention of fairly striking at and moving the ball.

**32. Teeing**

In 'teeing' the ball may be placed on the ground or on sand or other substance in order to raise it off the ground.

**33. Teeing Ground**

The 'teeing ground' is the starting place for the hole to be played. It is a rectangular area two club-lengths in depth, the front and the sides of which are defined by the outside limits of two markers. A ball is outside the teeing ground when all of it lies outside the stipulated area.

**34. Terms Used in Reckoning**

The reckoning of holes is kept by the terms:—so many 'holes up' or 'all square', and so many 'to play'.

A side is 'dormie' when it is as many holes up as there are holes remaining to be played.

(*above left*) SCOTT, LADY MARGARET. This remarkable golfer won the first three British Ladies' Championships. Here she is (on the right), with Miss Issette Pearson (left), the runner-up and Miss Starkie-Bence, the semi-finalist. (*above right*) THOMSON, PETER W. The first Australian to win the British Open Championship

TREVINO, LEE. In the space of five years, twice winner of the U.S. and British Open Championships, as well as many other tournaments

TRIUMVIRATE. Vardon is seated right, Braid seated left, Taylor standing right, with their friend and rival, Sandy Herd, standing left

WATSON, TOM. This talented young man is threatening the supremacy of Nicklaus, Player and their peers. He has already won the British Open twice, in 1975 and 1977, and the U.S. Masters in 1977, and played in the 1977 Ryder Cup team

WIMBLEDON COMMON, GOLF ON. Golf has been played on this London common since 1865, with the windmill as a landmark through the years

ZAHARIAS, MILDRED ("BABE"). This famous American golfer and athlete (1915–56) won both the British and U.S. Ladies' Championships

*35. Through the Green*
'Through the green' is the whole area of the course except:—
a. Teeing ground and putting green of the hole being played;
b. All hazards on the course.

## Section III   The Rules of Play

### Rule 1   The Game
The Game of Golf consists in playing a ball from the teeing ground into the hole by successive strokes in accordance with the rules.

Penalty for breach of rule: match play—loss of hole; stroke play—disqualification.

### Rule 2   The Club and the Ball
*The Royal and Ancient Golf Club and the United States Golf Association reserve the right to change the Rules and the interpretations regulating clubs and balls at any time.*
*1. Legal Clubs and Balls*
The player shall use clubs and balls which conform with Clauses 2 and 3 of this rule.
*2. Form and Make of Clubs*
*a. General Characteristics.* The golf club shall be composed of a shaft and a head, and all of the various parts shall be fixed so that the club is one unit: the club shall not be designed to be adjustable, except for weight.
*Note: Playing characteristics not to be changed during a round—Rule 2-2b.*

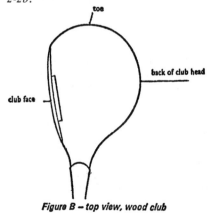

*Figure B – top view, wood club*

O

The club shall not be substantially different from the traditional and customary form and make.

An 'iron' club is one with a head which usually is relatively narrow from face to back, and usually is made of steel.

A 'wood' club is one with a head relatively broad from face to back (see Figure B), and usually is made of wood, plastic or a light metal.

A 'putter' is a club designed primarily for use on the putting green.

*b. Playing Characteristics Not to be Changed.* The playing characteristics of a club shall not be purposely changed during a round: foreign material shall not be added to the club face at any time.

*c. Shape of Head.* The length of a clubhead shall be greater than the breadth. Length shall be determined on a horizontal line, 0.625 inches (16 mm.) above the sole, from the back of the heel to the end of the toe or a vertical projection thereof.

Breadth shall be determined on a horizontal line between the outermost points of the face and the back of the head or vertical projections thereof.

*d. Face of Head.* The club shall have only one face designed for striking the ball, except that a putter may have two faces if the loft of both faces is substantially the same and does not exceed ten degrees.

Club faces shall not embody any degree of concavity on the hitting surface.

Club faces shall not have any lines, dots or other markings with sharp or rough edges, or any type of finish, for the purpose of unduly influencing the movement of the ball.

Markings on the face of an iron club shall conform with the specifications in Appendix II (see note to this rule). The face of an iron club shall not contain an inset or attachment.

*e. Shaft.* The shaft shall be designed to be straight from the top to a point not more than five inches (127 mm.) above the sole. The shaft, including any inserted plug, shall be generally circular in cross-section and shall extend to the upper end of the grip.

The shaft shall be fixed to the clubhead at the heel (as illustrated in Figure A). The shaft may be attached directly to the clubhead or to a neck or socket of the clubhead; any neck or socket shall not be more than five inches (127 mm.) in length meas-

**Iron**                              **Wood**

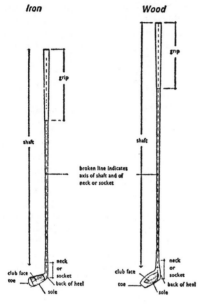

*Figure A – front view*

ured from the top of the neck or socket to the sole. The shaft and the neck or socket shall remain in line with the heel, or with a point to right or left of the heel, when the club is soled at address. The distance between the axis of the shaft (or the neck or socket) and the back of the heel shall not exceed 0.625 inches (16 mm.) in wood clubs and 0.3125 inches (8 mm.) in iron clubs.

Exception for putters: The shaft or neck or socket of a putter may be fixed at any point in the head and need not remain in line with the heel. The axis of the shaft from the top to a point **not** more than five inches

(127 mm.) above the sole shall diverge from the vertical by at least ten degrees in relation to the horizontal line determining length of head under Rule 2-2c. The shaft in cross-section shall be generally circular or otherwise symmetrical.

*f. Grip.* The grip shall be a continuation of the shaft to which material may be added for the purpose of obtaining a firm hold. The grip shall be substantially straight and plain in form, may have flat sides, but shall not have a channel or furrow or be moulded for any part of the hands. (See diagrams on page 235).

A device designed to give the player artificial aid in gripping the club, other than a plain glove, shall be deemed to violate this rule even though it be not part of the club.

(Other artificial devices—Rule 37-9)

*Note: Players in doubt as to the legality of clubs are advised to consult the Royal and Ancient Golf Club. Specifications for markings on iron clubs have been issued to manufacturers and appear on pages 231-3.*

*If a manufacturer is in doubt as to the legality of a club which he proposes to manufacture, he should submit a sample to the Royal and Ancient Golf Club for a ruling, such sample to become the property of the Royal and Ancient Golf Club for reference purposes.*

*3. The Ball*

*a. Specifications.* The weight of the ball shall be *not greater than* 1·620 ounces avoirdupois (45.9 gm.) and the size *not less than* 1.620 inches (41.2 mm.) in diameter.

*Note: Under the Rules of the United States Golf Association, the weight of the ball shall not be greater than 1.620 ounces avoirdupois (45.9 gm.) and the size not less than 1.680 inches (42.7 mm.) in diameter, but in international team competitions the size of the ball shall be not less than 1.620 inches (41.2 mm.) in diameter.*

*b. Foreign Material Prohibited.* Foreign material shall not be applied to a ball for the purpose of changing its playing characteristics.

Penalty for breach of rule: disqualification.

## Rule 3   Maximum of Fourteen Clubs

*1. Selection and Replacement of Clubs*

The player shall start a stipulated round with not more than fourteen clubs. He is limited to the clubs thus selected for that round except that, without unduly delaying play, he may:

a. If he started with fewer than fourteen, add as many as will bring his total to that number:

b. Replace a club which becomes unfit for play in the normal course of play.

The addition or replacement of a club or clubs may not be made by borrowing from any other person playing on the course.

*2. Side May Share Clubs*

Partners may share clubs provided that the total number of clubs carried by the side does not exceed fourteen.

Penalty for breach of Rule 3-1 or 3-2, regardless of number of wrong clubs carried; Match play—loss of one hole for each hole at which any violation occurred; maximum penalty per round: loss of two holes. The penalty shall be applied to the state of the match at the conclusion of the hole at which the violation is discovered, provided all players in the match have not left the putting green of the last hole of the match.

Stroke play—two strokes for each hole at which any violation occurred; maximum penalty per round: four strokes.

*Note: A serious breach of this rule should be dealt with by the committee under Rule 1.*

*3. Wrong Club Declared Out of Play*

Any club carried or used in violation of this rule shall be declared out of play by the player immediately upon discovery and thereafter shall not be used by the player during the round *under penalty of disqualification.*

## Rule 4   Agreement to Waive Rules Prohibited

Players shall not agree to exclude the operation of any rule or local rule or to waive any penalty incurred.

Penalty for breach of rule: match play—disqualification of both sides; stroke play—disqualification of competitors concerned.

## Rule 5   General Penalty

Except when otherwise provided for, the penalty for a breach of a rule or local rule is:

Match play—loss of hole; stroke play—two strokes.

## Rule 6   Match Play

*1. Winner of Hole*

In match play the game is played by holes.

Except as otherwise provided for in the rules, a hole is won by the side which holes its ball in the fewer strokes. In a handicap match the lower net score wins the hole.

A hole is halved if each side holes out in the same number of strokes.

*2. Halved Hole*

When a player has holed out and his opponent has been left with a stroke for the half, nothing that the player who has holed out can do shall deprive him of the half which he has already gained; but if the player thereafter incur any penalty, the hole is halved.

*3. Winner of Match*

A match (which consists of a stipulated round, unless otherwise decreed by the committee) is won by the side which is leading by a number of holes greater than the number of holes remaining to be played.

## Rule 7   Stroke Play

*1. General Rule*

The rules for match play, so far as they are not at variance with specific rules for stroke play, shall apply to stroke competitions. The converse is not true.

## 2. Winner

The competitor who holes the stipulated round or rounds in the fewest strokes is the winner.

## Rule 8   Practice

### 1. During Play of Hole

During the play of a hole, a player shall not play any practice stroke.

Penalty for breach of Rule 8-1: match play—loss of hole; stroke play—two strokes.

### 2. Between Holes

Between the play of two holes, a player shall not play a practice stroke from any hazard, or on or to a putting green other than that of the hole last played.

Penalty for breach of Rule 8-2: match play—loss of hole; stroke play —two strokes. The penalty applies to the next hole.

### 3. Stroke Play

On any day of a stroke competition or play-off, a competitor shall not practise on the competition course before a round or play-off. When a competition extends over consecutive days, practice on the competition course between rounds is prohibited.

*Note: The committee may, at its discretion, waive or modify these prohibitions in the conditions of the competition (Appendix 1-3).*

Penalty for breach of Rule 8-3: disqualification. (Duty of committee to define practice ground—Rule 36-4b.)

*Note 1: A practice swing is not a practice stroke and may be taken at any place on the course provided the player does not violate the rules.*

*Note 2: Unless otherwise decided by the committee, there is no penalty for practice on the course on any day of a match play competition.*

## Rule 9   Advice (Def 2) and Assistance

### 1. Giving or Asking for Advice; Receiving Assistance

a. *Advice.* A player may give advice to, or ask for advice from, only his partner or either of their caddies.

b. *Assistance.* In making a stroke, a player shall not seek or accept physical assistance or protection from the elements.

### 2. Indicating Line of Play

Except on the putting green, a player may have the line of play indicated to him by anyone, but no mark shall be placed on the line, nor shall anyone stand on or close to the line while the stroke is being played. (Indicating line of play on putting green—Rule 35-1e)

Penalty for breach of rule: match play—loss of hole; stroke play—two strokes.

## Rule 10   Information as to Strokes Taken

### 1. General

A player who has incurred a penalty shall state the fact to his opponent or marker as soon as possible. The number of strokes a player has taken shall include any penalty strokes incurred.

### 2. Match Play

A player is entitled at any time during the play of a hole to ascertain from his opponent the number of strokes the latter has taken. If the opponent give wrong information as to the number of strokes he has taken and correct his mistake before the player has played his next stroke, he shall incur no penalty; if he fail to do so, *he shall lose the hole.*

## Rule 11   Disputes, Decisions and Doubt as to Rights

### 1. Claims and Penalties

a. *Match Play.* In match play, if a dispute or doubt arise between the players on any point, in order that a claim may be considered it must be made before any player in the match plays from the next teeing ground, or, in the case of the last hole of the match, before all players in the match leave the putting green. Any later claim based on newly discovered facts cannot be considered unless the player making the claim had been given wrong information by an opponent.

b. *Stroke Play.* In stroke play no penalty shall be imposed after the competition is closed unless wrong information had been given by the competitor. A competition is deemed to have closed:—

In stroke play only—when the result of the competition is officially announced ;

In stroke play qualifying followed by match play—when the player has teed off in his first match.

*2. Referee's Decision*

If a referee has been appointed by the committee, his decision shall be final.

*3. Committee's Decision*

In the absence of a referee, the players shall refer any dispute to the committee, whose decision shall be final.

If the committee cannot come to a decision, it shall refer the dispute to the Rules of Golf Committee of the Royal and Ancient Golf Club of St Andrews, whose decision shall be final.

If the point in dispute or doubt has not been referred to the Rules of Golf Committee, the player or players have the right to refer an agreed statement through the Secretary of the Club to the Rules of Golf Committee for an opinion as to the correctness of the decision given. The reply will be sent to the secretary of the club or clubs concerned.

If play be conducted other than in accordance with the Rules of Golf, the Rules of Golf Committee will not give a decision on any question.

*4. Decision by Equity*

If any point in dispute be not covered by the rules or local rules, the decision shall be made in accordance with equity.

*5. Stroke Play: Doubt as to Procedure*

In stroke play only, when a competitor is doubtful of his rights or procedure, he may play out the hole with the ball in play and, at the same time, complete the play of the hole with an alternate ball. Before playing a stroke with either ball, the competitor must announce to his marker his intention to proceed under this rule and

must announce which ball he wants to score with if the rules permit.

On completing the round the competitor must report the facts immediately to the committee. If it be found that the rules allow the procedure selected in advance by the competitor, the score with the ball selected shall be his score for the hole. Should the competitor fail to announce in advance his procedure or selection, the ball with the higher score shall count if played in accordance with the rules.

*Note 1: The sole purpose of this rule is to enable a competitor to avoid disqualification when doubtful of his rights or procedure ; a competitor is not permitted to play in two ways and then choose his score.*

*Note 2: The privilege of playing a second ball does not exist in match play. A second ball played under Rule 11-5 is not a provisional ball under Rule 30.*

## Rule 12    The Honour (Def 16)

*1. The Honour*

*a. Match Play.* A match begins by each side playing a ball from the first teeing ground in the order of the draw. In the absence of a draw, the option of taking the honour shall be decided by lot.

The side which wins a hole shall take the honour at the next teeing ground. If a hole has been halved, the side which had the honour at the previous teeing ground shall retain it.

*b. Stroke Play.* The honour shall be taken as in match play.

*2. Second Ball from Tee*

If a player has to play a second ball from the tee, he shall do so after the opponent or the fellow-competitor has played his first stroke.

*3. Playing out of Turn*

*a. Match Play.* If, on the teeing ground, a player play when his opponent should have played, the opponent may immediately require the player to abandon the ball so played and to play a ball in correct order, without penalty.

*b. Stroke Play.* If, on the teeing

ground, a competitor by mistake play out of turn, no penalty shall be incurred and the ball shall be in play.

## Rule 13 Playing Outside Teeing Ground (Def 33)

### 1. Match Play

If a player, when starting a hole, play a ball from outside the teeing ground, the opponent may immediately require the player to replay the stroke, in which case the player shall tee a ball and play the stroke within the teeing ground, without penalty.

### 2. Stroke Play

If a competitor, when starting a hole, play his first stroke from outside the teeing ground, he shall count that stroke and any subsequent stroke so played and then play from within the teeing ground with the privilege of teeing his ball. If the competitor fail to rectify his mistake before making a stroke on the next teeing ground or, in the case of the last hole of the round, before leaving the putting green, *he shall be disqualified*.

Penalty for breach of Rule 13-2: disqualification.

*Note: Stance. A player may take his stance outside the teeing ground to play a ball within it.*

## Rule 14 Ball Falling off Tee

If a ball, when not in play, fall off a tee or be knocked off a tee by the player in addressing it, it may be re-teed without penalty, but if a stroke be made at the ball in these circumstances, whether the ball be moving or not, the stroke shall be counted but no penalty shall be incurred.

## Rule 15 Order of Play in Three-some or Foursome

### 1. General

In a threesome or a foursome, the partners shall strike off alternatively from the teeing grounds, and thereafter shall strike alternatively during the play of each hole. Penalty strokes (Definition 24) do not affect the order of play.

### 2. Match Play

During a match (which may, if authorised by the committee, consist of more than one stipulated round), if a player play when his partner should have played, *his side shall lose the hole*.

### 3. Stroke Play

If the partners play a stroke or strokes in incorrect order, such stroke or strokes shall be cancelled, and *the side shall be penalised two strokes*. A ball shall then be put in play as nearly as possible at the spot from which the side first played in incorrect order. This must be done before a stroke has been played from the next teeing ground, or, in the case of the last hole of the round, before the side has left the putting green. If they fail to do so, *they shall be disqualified*. If the first ball was played from the teeing ground, a ball may be teed anywhere within the teeing ground; if from through the green or a hazard, it shall be dropped; if on the putting green, it shall be placed.

## Rule 16 Ball Played as it Lies and Not Touched

The ball shall be played as it lies and shall not be purposely moved or purposely touched except that the player may, without penalty, touch his ball with his club in the act of addressing it and except as otherwise provided in the rules or local rules.

Penalty for breach of rule: match play—loss of hole; stroke play—two strokes.

(Ball moved accidentally by player —Rule 27-1c.)

(Ball moved accidentally after address—Rule 27-1d.)

## Rule 17 Improving Lie or Stance and Influencing Ball Prohibited

### 1. Improving Line of Play or Lie Prohibited

A player shall not improve, or allow to be improved, his line of play or the position or lie of his ball or the area of his intended swing by moving, bending or breaking anything fixed or growing, or by removing or pressing down sand, loose soil, cut turf placed in position or other irregularities of surface which could in any way affect a player's lie except:

a. As may occur in the course of fairly taking his stance;

b. In making the stroke or the backward movement of his club for the stroke;

c. When teeing a ball;

d. In repairing damage to the putting green under Rule 35-1c. The club may be grounded only lightly and not be pressed on the ground.

(Removal of obstructions—Rule 31-1.)

*Note: Things fixed include objects defining out of bounds.*

*2. Long Grass and Bushes*

If a ball lie in long grass, rushes, bushes, whins, heather or the like, only so much thereof shall be touched as will enable the player to find and identify his ball; nothing shall be done which may in any way improve its lie.

The player is not of necessity entitled to see the ball when playing a stroke.

*3. Building of Stance Prohibited*

A player is always entitled to place his feet firmly on the ground when taking his stance, but he is not allowed to build a stance.

*4. Exerting Influence on Ball*

No player or caddie shall take any action to influence the position or the movement of the ball except in accordance with the rules.

Penalty for breach of rule: match play—loss of hole; stroke play—two strokes.

*Note: In the case of a serious breach of Rule 17-4, the committee may impose a penalty of disqualification.*

## Rule 18    Loose Impediments (Def 17)

*1. Removal of Impediments*

Any loose impediments may be removed without penalty except when both the impediment and the ball lie in or touch a hazard. When a ball is in motion, a loose impediment shall not be removed.

Penalty for breach of Rule 18-1: match play—loss of hole; stroke play —two strokes.

(Finding ball in hazard—Rule 33-1e.)

*2. Ball Moved*

Through the green, if the ball move after any loose impediment lying within a club-length of it has been touched by the player, his partner or either of their caddies, the player shall be deemed to have caused the ball to move. *The penalty shall be one stroke,* and the ball shall be played as it lies.

(Loose impediments on putting green—Rule 35-1b.)

## Rule 19    Striking at Ball

*1. Ball to be Fairly Struck at*

The ball shall be fairly struck at with the head of the club and must not be pushed, scraped or spooned.

Penalty for breach of Rule 19-1: match play—loss of hole; stroke play —two strokes.

*2. Striking Ball Twice*

If the player strike the ball twice when making a stroke, he shall count the stroke and *add a penalty stroke,* making two strokes in all.

(Playing a moving ball—Rule 25.)

## Rule 20    Ball Farther from the Hole Played First

*1. General*

When the balls are in play, the ball farther from the hole shall be played first. If the balls are equidistant from the hole, the option of playing first shall be decided by lot.

A player or a competitor incurs no penalty if a ball is moved in measuring to determine which ball is farther from the hole. A ball so moved shall be replaced.

*2. Match Play*

Through the green or in a hazard, if a player play when his opponent should have done so, the opponent may immediately require the player to replay the stroke. In such a case, the player shall drop a ball as near

as possible to the spot from which his previous stroke was played, and play in correct order without penalty.
Penalty for breach of Rule 20-2: loss of hole.
(Playing out of turn on putting green—Rule 35-2b.)
3. *Stroke Play*
If a competitor play out of turn, no penalty shall be incurred. The ball shall be played as it lies.

## Rule 21 Playing a Wrong Ball (Def 5) or from a Wrong Place

*1. General*
A player must hole out with the ball driven from the teeing ground unless a Rule or Local Rule permit him to substitute another ball.
*2. Match Play*
a. *Wrong Ball.* If a player play a stroke with a wrong ball (Def. 5) except in a hazard, *he shall lose the hole.* There is no penalty if a player play any strokes in a hazard with a wrong ball provided he then play the correct ball; the strokes so played with a wrong ball do not count in the player's score.
If the wrong ball belong to another player, it shall be replaced where it originally lay.
When the player and the opponent exchange balls during the play of a hole, the first to play the wrong ball shall lose the hole; when this cannot be determined the hole shall be played out with the balls exchanged.
b. *Ball Played from Wrong Place.* If a player play a stroke with a ball which has been dropped or placed under an applicable Rule but in a wrong place, *he shall lose the hole.*
*Note: For a ball played outside tee-ing ground, see Rule 13-1.*
*3. Stroke Play*
a. *Wrong Ball.* If a competitor play any strokes with a wrong ball (Def. 5) except in a hazard, *he shall add two penalty strokes* to his score for the hole and shall then play the correct ball. Strokes played by a competitor with a wrong ball do not count in his score. There is no penalty if a com-

petitor play any strokes in a hazard with a wrong ball, provided he then play the correct ball.
If the wrong ball belong to another player, it shall be replaced where it originally lay.
b. *Rectification after Holing Out.* If a competitor hole out with a wrong ball, he may rectify his mistake by proceeding in accordance with Clause 3a of this Rule, subject to the prescribed penalty, provided he has not made a stroke on the next teeing ground, or, in the case of the last hole of the round, has not left the putting green. *The competitor shall be disqualified* if he does not so rectify his mistake.
c. *Ball Played from Wrong Place.* If a competitor play a stroke with a ball which has been dropped or placed under an applicable Rule but in a wrong place, *he shall add two penalty strokes* to his score for the hole and shall then play out the hole with that ball.
*Note 1: For a ball played outside teeing ground, see Rule 13-2.*
*Note 2: A serious breach of Rule 21-3c should be dealt with by the Committee under Rule 1.*

## Rule 22 Lifting, Dropping and Placing

*1. Lifting*
a. *By Whom.* A ball to be lifted under the rules or local rules may be lifted by the owner, his partner or either of their caddies, or by another person authorised by the owner. In any such case the owner shall be responsible for any breach of the rules or local rules.
b. *Before Holing Out in Stroke Play.* If a competitor's ball be lifted before it is holed out, except as provided for in the rules or local rules, the competitor shall replace it *under a penalty of two strokes* provided he does so before he has played a stroke from the next teeing ground, or, in the case of the last hole of the round, before he has left the putting green. If he fail so to replace it, *he shall be disqualified.*

(Procedure in discontinuing play—Rule 37-6b.)

(Ball moved by outside agency—Rule 27-1a.)

2. *Dropping*

a. *How to Drop.* A ball to be dropped under the rules or local rules shall be dropped by the player himself. He shall face the hole, stand erect, and drop the ball behind him over his shoulder. If a ball be dropped in any other manner and remain the ball in play (Definition 5), *the player shall incur a penalty stroke.*

If the ball touch the player before it strikes the ground, the player shall re-drop without penalty. If the ball touch the player after it strikes the ground, or if it come to rest against the player and move when he then moves, there is no penalty, and the ball shall be played as it lies.

b. *Where to drop.* When a ball is to be dropped, it shall be dropped as near as possible to the spot where the ball lay, but not nearer the hole, except when a Rule permits it to be dropped elsewhere or placed. In a hazard, the ball must come to rest in that hazard ; if it roll out of the hazard, it must be re-dropped, without penalty.

c. *Rolling into Hazard, Out of Bounds, Two Club-Length or Nearer the Hole.* If a dropped ball roll into a hazard, out of bounds, more than two club-lengths from the point where it first struck the ground, or come to rest nearer the hole than its original position, it shall be re-dropped, without penalty. If the ball again roll into such a position, it shall be placed where it was last dropped, without penalty.

Penalty for Breach of Rule 22-2: *Match play—Loss of hole ; Stroke play—Two strokes.*

3. *Placing*

a. *How and Where to Place.* A ball to be placed or replaced under the Rules or Local Rules shall be placed by the player, his partner or either of their caddies on the spot where the ball lay, except when a Rule permits it to be placed elsewhere.

b. *Lie of Ball to be Placed or Re-placed Altered.* If the original lie of a ball to be placed or replaced has been altered, the ball shall be placed in the nearest lie most similar to that which it originally occupied, not more than two club-lengths from the original lie and not nearer the hole.

c. *Spot Not Determinable.* If it be impossible to determine the spot where the ball is to be placed, through the green or in a hazard the ball shall be dropped, or on the putting green it shall be placed, as near as possible to the place where it lay, but not nearer the hole.

d. *Ball Moving.* If a ball when placed fail to remain on the spot on which it was placed, it shall be replaced without penalty. If it still fail to remain on that spot, it shall be placed at the nearest spot not nearer the hole where it can be placed at rest.

Penalty for Breach of Rule 22-3: *Match play—Loss of hole ; Stroke play—Two strokes.*

4. *Ball in Play when Dropped or Placed*

A ball dropped or placed under a Rule governing the particular case is in play (Definition 5) and shall not be lifted or re-dropped or replaced except as provided in the Rules.

5. *Lifting Ball Wrongly Dropped or Placed.*

A ball dropped or placed but not played may be lifted without penalty if :

a. It was dropped or placed under a Rule governing the particular case but not in the right place or otherwise not in accordance with that Rule. The player shall then drop or place the ball in accordance with the governing Rule.

b. It was dropped or placed under a Rule which does not govern the particular case. The player shall then proceed under a Rule which governs the case. However, in match play, if, before the opponent plays his next stroke, the player fail to inform him that the ball has been lifted, *the player shall lose the hole.*

*Note : In stroke play a serious*

*breach of Rule 22 should be dealt with by the Committee under Rule 1.*

## Rule 23   Identifying or Cleaning Ball

*The responsibility for playing the proper ball rests with the player. Each player should put an identification mark on his ball.*

*1. Identifying Ball*

Except in a hazard, the player may, without penalty, lift his ball in play for the purpose of identification and replace it on the spot from which it was lifted provided this is done in the presence of his opponent in match play or marker in stroke play.

(Touching grass, etc., for identification—Rule 17-2.)

*2. Cleaning Ball*

A ball may be cleaned when lifted as follows:—

> From an unplayable lie under Rule 29-2;
> For relief from an obstruction under Rule 31;
> From casual water, ground under repair, or otherwise under Rule 32;
> From a water hazard under Rule 33-2 or 33-3;
> On the putting green under Rule 35-1d.

Otherwise, during the play of a hole a player may not clean a ball, except to the extent necessary for identification or if permitted by local rule.

Penalty for breach of rule: match play—loss of hole; stroke play—two strokes.

## Rule 24   Ball Interfering with Play

Through the green or in a hazard, a player may have any other ball lifted if he consider that it might interfere with his play. A ball so lifted shall be replaced after the player has played his stroke.

If a ball be accidentally moved in complying with this rule, no penalty shall be incurred and the ball so moved shall be replaced.

(Lie of lifted ball altered—Rule 22-3b.)

(Putting green—Rule 35-2a and 35-3a.)

Penalty for breach of rule: match play—loss of hole; stroke play—two strokes.

## Rule 25   A Moving Ball

*1. Playing Moving Ball Prohibited*

A player shall not play while his ball is moving.

> Exceptions:— Ball falling off tee— Rule 14.
> Striking ball twice—Rule 19-2.
> As hereunder—Rule 25-2.
> As hereunder—Rule 25-2.

When the ball only begins to move after the player has begun the stroke or the backward movement of his club for the stroke, he shall incur no penalty under this rule, but he is not exempted from the provisions for:

Ball moving after removal of loose impediment—Rule 18-2 and 27-1e.

Ball moved accidentally by player —Rule 27-1c.

Ball moving after it has been addressed—Rule 27-1d.

*2. Ball Moving in Water*

When a ball is in water, the player may, without penalty, make a stroke at it while it is moving, but he must not delay to make his stroke in order to allow the wind or current to better the position of the ball.

Penalty for breach of rule: match play—loss of hole; stroke play—two strokes.

## Rule 26   Ball in Motion Stopped or Deflected

*1. General*

*a. By Outside Agency.* If a ball in motion be accidentally stopped or deflected by an outside agency, it is a rub of the green and the ball shall be played as it lies, without penalty. Exception: On putting green—Rule 35-1h.

*b. Lodging in Outside Agency.* If a ball lodge in anything moving, the player shall, through the green or in a hazard, drop a ball, or on the putting green place a ball, as near as possible to the spot where the object was when the ball lodged in it, without penalty.

## 2. Match Play

*a. By Player.* If a player's ball be stopped or deflected by himself, his partner or either of their caddies or equipment, *he shall lose the hole.*

*b. By Opponent.* If a player's ball be stopped or deflected by an opponent, his caddie or equipment, *the opponent's side shall lose the hole.*

(Ball striking opponent's ball—Rule 27-2b). Exceptions: Ball striking person attending flagstick—Rule 34-3b.

## 3. Stroke Play

*a. By Competitor.* If a competitor's ball be stopped or deflected by himself, his partner or either of their caddies or equipment, *the competitor shall incur a penalty of two strokes.* The ball shall be played as it lies, except when it lodges in the competitor's, his partner's or either of their caddies' clothes or equipment, in which case the competitor shall, through the green or in a hazard, drop the ball, or on the putting green place the ball, as near as possible to where the article was when the ball lodged in it.

*b. By Fellow-Competitor.* If a competitor's ball be accidentally stopped or deflected by a fellow-competitor, his caddie, ball or equipment, it is a rub of the green and the ball shall be played as it lies. Exceptions:

Ball lodging in fellow-competitor's clothes, etc.—Clause 1b of this rule.

Ball striking fellow-competitor's ball on the putting green—Rule 35-1h and 35-3c.

Ball striking person attending flagstick—Rule 34-3b.

Penalty for breach of rule: match play—loss of hole; stroke play—two strokes.

*Note: If the referee or the committee determine that a ball has been deliberately stopped or deflected by an outside agency, including a fellow-competitor or his caddie, further procedure should be prescribed in equity under Rule 11-4.*

## Rule 27    Ball at Rest Moved (Def 3)

## 1. General

*a. By Outside Agency.* If a ball at rest be moved by any outside agency except wind, the owner shall incur no penalty and shall replace the ball before playing another stroke.

(Opponent's ball moved by player's ball—Rule 27-2b.)

*Note: If the ball moved is not immediately recoverable, another ball may be substituted.*

*b. During Search.* During search for a ball, if it be moved by an opponent, a fellow-competitor or the caddie of either, no penalty shall be incurred. The player shall replace the ball before another stroke.

*c. By Player, Accidentally.* When a ball is in play, if a player, his partner, or either of their caddies accidentally move it, or by touching anything cause it to move (except as otherwise provided for in the rules), *the player shall incur a penalty stroke* and the ball shall be played as it lies.

(Ball purposely moved or purposely touched—Rule 16.)

*d. Ball Moving Accidentally After Address.* If a ball in play move after the player has addressed it (Definition 1), he shall be deemed to have caused it to move and *shall incur a penalty stroke,* and the ball shall be played as it lies.

(Ball purposely moved or puposely touched—Rule 16.)

*e. Touching Loose Impediment.* If a player has touched a loose impediment (Rules 18 and 35-1b) and the ball move, but not until the player has addressed it (Definition 1), he shall be deemed to have caused it to move under paragraph d above, and *shall incur a penalty stroke.* The ball shall be played as it lies.

## 2. Match Play

*a. By Opponent.* If a player's ball be touched or moved by an opponent, his caddie or equipment (except as otherwise provided in the rules), *the opponent shall incur a penalty stroke.* The player shall replace the ball before playing another stroke.

*b. Opponent's Ball Moved by Player's Ball.* If a player's ball move an opponent's ball, no penalty shall be incurred. The opponent may either play his ball as it lies or, before another stroke is played by either side, he may replace the ball.

If the player's ball stop on the spot formerly occupied by the opponent's ball and the opponent declare his intention to replace the ball, the player shall first play another stroke, after which the opponent shall replace his ball.

(Putting green—Rule 35-2c.)

(Three-Ball, Best-Ball and Four-Ball Match play—Rule 40-1c.)

*3. Stroke Play*

*Ball Moved by a Fellow-Competitor.* If a competitor's ball be moved by a fellow-competitor, his caddie, ball or equipment, no penalty shall be incurred. The competitor shall replace his ball before playing another stroke.

Exception to Penalty: Ball striking fellow-competitor's ball on putting green—Rule 35-3c.

Penalty for breach of rule: match play—loss of hole; stroke play—two strokes.

(Playing a wrong ball—Rule 21.)

*Note: A serious breach of this rule should be dealt with by the committee under Rule 1.*

## Rule 28 Ball Unfit for Play

If the ball become so damaged as to be unfit for play, the player may substitute another ball, placing it on the spot where the original ball lay. Substitution may only be made on the hole during the play of which the damage occurred and in the presence of the opponent in match play or the marker in stroke play.

Penalty for breach of rule: match play—loss of hole; stroke play—two strokes.

(Ball unplayable—Rule 29-2.)

*Note 1: Mud or loose impediment adhering to the ball do not make it unfit for play.*

*Note 2: Where the existence of* mud could become an encumbrance to play, the committee should frame a local rule providing for the removal of mud.

## Rule 29 Ball Lost (Def 6), Out of Bounds (Def 21), or Unplayable

*1. Lost or Out of Bounds*

*a. Procedure.* If a ball be lost outside a water hazard or be out of bounds, the player shall play his next stroke as nearly as possible at the spot from which the original ball was played or moved by him, *adding a penalty stroke* to his score for the hole. If the original stroke was played from the teeing ground, a ball may be teed anywhere within the teeing ground; if from through the green or a hazard, it shall be dropped; if on the putting green, it shall be placed.

(Ball lost in casual water, ground under repair, etc.—Rule 32-3.)

*b. Ascertaining Location.* A player has the right at any time of ascertaining whether his opponent's ball is out of bounds.

A person outside the match may point out the location of a ball for which search is being made.

*c. Standing Out of Bounds.* A player may stand out of bounds to play a ball lying within bounds.

*2. Unplayable*

*a. Player Sole Judge.* The player is the sole sole judge as to whether his ball is unplayable. It may be declared unplayable at any place on the course except in a water hazard (Rule 33-2, 3).

*b. Procedure.* If the player deem his ball to be unplayable, he shall either:—

(i) Play his next stroke as provided in Clause 1a of this Rule *(stroke-and-distance penalty).*

*or*

(ii) Drop a ball, *under penalty of one stroke,* either (a) within two club-lengths of the point where the ball lay, but not nearer the hole, or (b) behind the point where the ball lay, keeping that point between

himself and the hole, with no limit to how far behind that point the ball may be dropped. If the ball lay in a bunker, a ball must be dropped in the bunker.
(Ball in casual water, etc.—Rule 32.)
(Ball unfit for play—Rule 28.)
*3. Ball Abandoned as Lost*
Before his ball has been found, a player may abandon it as lost, whereupon:
a. If he has already played a provisional ball, he shall continue play with that ball as his ball in play ; or
b. If no provisional ball has been played, he shall put another ball into play in accordance with Clause 1a of this rule.
Penalty for breach of rule: match play—loss of hole ; stroke play—two strokes.
*Note 1: A serious breach of this rule should be dealt with by the committee under Rule 1.*
*Note 2: The penalty stroke provided for in Rule 29-1 and 29-2 may not be remitted by local rule.*

## Rule 30   Provisional Ball (Def. 5)
*1. Procedure*
If a ball may be lost outside a water hazard or may be out of bounds, to save time the player may at once play another ball provisionally as nearly as possible from the spot at which the original ball was played. If the original ball was played from the teeing ground, a ball may be teed anywhere within the teeing ground ; if from through the green or a hazard, it shall be dropped; if on the putting green, it shall be placed.
a. The player must inform his opponent or marker that he intends to play a provisional ball, and he must play it before he or his partner goes forward to search for the original ball: if he fail to do so, and play another ball, such ball is not a provisional ball and becomes the ball in play *under penalty of stroke and distance* (Rule 29-1) ; the original ball must be abandoned.

b. Play of a provisional ball from the teeing ground does not affect the order in which the sides play (Rule 12-2).
c. A provisional ball is never an outside agency.
*2. Play of a Provisional Ball*
a. The player may play a provisional ball until he reaches the place where the original ball is likely to be. If he play any strokes with the provisional ball from a point beyond that place, the original ball is deemed to be lost (Def. 6c).
b. If the original ball be lost outside a water hazard or be out of bounds, the provisional ball becomes the ball in play, *under penalty of stroke and distance* (Rule 29-1).
c. If the original ball be neither lost outside a water hazard nor out of bounds, the player shall abandon the provisional ball and continue play with the original ball. Should he fail to do so, any further strokes played with the provisional ball shall constitute playing a wrong ball and the provisions of Rule 21 shall apply.
Penalty for Breach of Rule: *Match Play—Loss of hole ; Stroke Play—Two strokes.*
*Note: If the original ball be unplayable or lie or be lost in a water hazard, the player must proceed under Rule 29-2 or Rule 33-2 or 33-3, whichever is applicable.*

## Rule 31   Obstructions (Def. 20)
*1. Movable Obstruction may be Removed*
Any movable obstruction may be removed. If the ball be moved in so doing, it shall be replaced on the exact spot from which it was moved, without penalty. If it be impossible to determine the spot or to replace the ball on the exact spot from which it was moved, the ball shall, through the green or in a hazard, be dropped, or on the putting green be placed, as near as possible to the spot from which it was moved but not nearer the hole, without penalty.
When a ball is in motion, an obstruction other than an attended flag-

stick and equipment of the players shall not be removed.

## 2. Interference by Immovable Obstruction

*a. Interference.* Interference by an immovable obstruction occurs when the ball lies in or on the obstruction, or so close to the obstruction that the obstruction interferes with the player's stance or the area of his intended swing. The fact that an immovable obstruction intervenes on the line of play is not, of itself, interference under this Rule.

*b. Relief.* A player may obtain relief from interference by an immovable obstruction, without penalty, as follows:

(i) THROUGH THE GREEN:
Through the green, the player may lift and drop the ball, not nearer the hole, within two club-lengths of that point on the edge of the obstruction nearest which the ball originally lay; the two club-lengths must not be measured over, through or under the obstruction.
*Exception:* If the ball lie in such a position in or on the obstruction, or between the obstruction and the hole, that it be impossible for the player to obtain relief under Clause b (i) without dropping the ball nearer the hole, he may drop the ball, not nearer the hole, within two club-lengths of the nearest point on the edge of the obstruction from which relief from interference is obtainable; the two club-lengths must not be measured over, through or under the obstruction.

(ii) IN A HAZARD:
In a hazard, the player may lift and drop the ball in accordance with Clause (i) above, or with the Exception to that Clause if applicable, but the ball must be dropped in the hazard.

(iii) ON THE PUTTING GREEN:
On the putting green, the

player may lift and place the ball in the nearest position to where it lay which affords relief from interference, but not nearer the hole.

*c. Re-dropping.* If a dropped ball roll into a position covered by this Rule, or nearer the hole than its original position, it shall be re-dropped without penalty. If it again roll into such a position, it shall be placed where it was last dropped.

Penalty for Breach of Rule: *Match play—Loss of hole; Stroke play—two strokes*

## Rule 32    Casual Water (Def. 8), Ground under Repair (Def. 13), Hole Made by Burrowing Animal

*1. Ball Lying in or Touching*

If a player's ball lie in or touch casual water, ground under repair, or a hole, cast or runway made by a burrowing animal, a reptile or a bird, or if any of these conditions interfere with the player's stance or the area of his intended swing, the player may either play the ball as it lies or take relief as provided in Clause 2 of this Rule.

*2. Relief*

If the player elect to take relief, he shall proceed as follows:

a. *Through the Green.* Through the green, the player shall drop the ball without penalty on ground which avoids these conditions, within two club-lengths of the point on the margin of such area nearest to which the ball originally lay, but not nearer the hole.

*Exceptions:*

(i) If the player cannot comply with Clause 2a of this Rule without dropping the ball in a hazard, he may drop the ball at the nearest place outside the hazard which is not nearer the hole than the ball's original position.

(ii) If the player cannot comply with Clause 2a of this Rule without dropping the ball on a putting green, he shall drop the ball at the nearest place off the putting green which is not nearer the hole than the ball's original position.

*b. In a Hazard.* In a hazard, the player may lift and drop the ball either:

Without penalty, in the hazard as near as possible to the spot where the ball lay, but not nearer the hole, on ground which affords maximum relief from these conditions,

*or*

*Under penalty of one stroke,* outside the hazard, but not nearer the hole, keeping the spot where the ball lay between himself and the hole.

*c. On the Putting Green.* On the putting green, or if such conditions intervene between a ball lying on the putting green and the hole, the player may lift the ball and place it without penalty in the nearest position to where it lay which affords maximum relief from these conditions, but not nearer the hole.

*3. Ball Lost*

*a. Outside a Hazard.* If a ball be lost under a condition covered by this Rule, except in a hazard, a ball may be dropped without penalty as near as possible to the spot at which the ball last crossed the margin of the area, on ground which avoids these conditions, but not nearer the hole.

*b. In a Hazard.* If a ball be lost in a hazard under a condition covered by this Rule, the player may drop a ball either: —

Without penalty, in the hazard, but not nearer the hole than the spot at which the ball last crossed the margin of the area, on ground which affords maximum relief from these conditions,

*or*

*Under penalty of one stroke,* outside the hazard, but not nearer the hole, keeping the spot at which the ball last crossed the margin of the hazard between himself and the hole.

In order that a ball may be treated as lost, there must be reasonable evidence to that effect.

*4. Re-dropping*

If a dropped ball roll into the area from which relief was taken, or come to rest in such a position that that area still affects the player's stance or the area of his intended swing, the ball shall be re-dropped, without penalty. If the ball again roll into such a position, it shall be placed where it was last dropped.

Penalty for Breach of Rule: *Match play—Loss of hole ; Stroke play— Two strokes.*

## Rule 33  Hazards and Water Hazards (Def 14)

*1. Touching Hazard Prohibited*

When a ball lies in or touches a hazard or a water hazard, nothing shall be done which may in any way improve its lie. Before making a stroke, the player shall not touch the ground in the hazard or water with a club or otherwise, nor touch or move a loose impediment lying in or touching the hazard, nor test the condition of the hazard or any similar hazard ; subject to the following considerations:—

*a. Stance* The player may place his feet firmly in taking his stance.

*b. Touching Fixed or Growing Object.* In addressing the ball or in the stroke or in the backward movement for the stroke, the club may touch any wooden or stone wall, paling or similar fixed object or any grass, bush, tree, or other growing substance (but the club may not be soled in the hazard).

*c. Obstructions.* The player is entitled to relief from obstructions under the provisions of Rule 31.

*d. Loose Impediment Outside Hazard.* Any loose impediment not in or touching the hazard may be removed.

*e. Finding Ball.* If the ball be covered by sand, fallen leaves or the like, the player may remove as much thereof as will enable him to see the top of the ball ; if the ball be moved in such removal, no penalty shall be incurred, and the ball shall be replaced.

If the ball is believed to be lying in water in a water hazard, the player may probe for it with a club or otherwise. If the ball be moved in such search, no penalty shall be incurred; the ball shall be replaced, unless the player elects to proceed under clause 2 or 3 of this rule.

The ball may not be lifted for identification.

*f. Placing Clubs in Hazard.* The player may, without penalty, place his clubs in the hazard prior to making a stroke, provided nothing is done which may improve the lie of the ball or constitute testing the soil.

*g. Smoothing Irregularities.* There is no penalty should soil or sand in the hazard be smoothed by the player after playing a stroke, or by his caddie at any time without the authority of the player, provided nothing is done that improves the lie of the ball or assists the player in his subsequent play of the hole.

*h. Casual Water, Ground under Repair.* The player is entitled to relief from casual water, ground under repair, and otherwise as provided for in Rule 32.

*i. Interference by a Ball.* The player is entitled to relief from interference by another ball under the provisions of Rule 24.

**2. Ball in Water Hazard**

If a ball lie or be lost in a water hazard (whether the ball lie in water or not), the player may drop a ball, *under penalty of one stroke,* either:—

a. Behind the water hazard, keeping the spot at which the ball last crossed the margin of the water hazard between himself and the hole, and with no limit to how far behind the water hazard the ball may be dropped.

*or*

b. As near as possible to the spot from which the original ball was played; if the stroke was played from the teeing ground, the ball may be teed anywhere within the teeing ground.

*Note: If a ball has been played from within a water hazard and has not crossed any margin of the hazard, the player may drop a ball behind the hazard under Rule 33-2a.*

**3. Ball in Lateral Water Hazard (Def. 14c)**

If a ball lie or be lost in a lateral water hazard, the player may, *under penalty of one stroke,* either:—

a. Play his next stroke in accordance with Clause 2a or 2b of this rule.

*or*

b. Drop a ball within two club-lengths of the margin of either side of the lateral water hazard, opposite the point where the ball last crossed the hazard margin. The ball must come to rest not nearer the hole than that point.

*Note: If a ball has been played from within a lateral water hazard and has not crossed any margin of the hazard, the player may drop a ball outside the hazard under Rule 33-3b.*

Penalty for breach of rule: match play—loss of hole; stroke play—two strokes.

*Note 1: A serious breach of this rule should be dealt with by the committee under Rule 1.*

*Note 2: It is a question of fact whether a ball lost after having been struck towards a water hazard is lost inside or outside the hazard. In order to treat the ball as lost in the hazard, there must be reasonable evidence that the ball lodged therein. In the absence of such evidence, the ball must be treated as a lost ball and Rule 29-1 applies.*

**Rule 34   The Flagstick (Def 12)**

*1. Flagstick Attended, Removed or Held up*

The player may have the flagstick attended, removed or held up to indicate the position of the hole. This may be done only on the authority of the player before he plays his stroke. If the flagstick be attended or removed by an opponent, a fellow-competitor or the caddie of either with the knowledge of the player and no objection is made, the player shall be deemed to have authorised it.

If a player or caddie attend or remove the flagstick or stand near the hole while a stroke is being played, he shall be deemed to attend the flagstick until the ball comes to rest.

If the flagstick be not attended before the stroke is played, it shall not be attended or removed while the ball is in motion.

**2. Authorised Attendance**

*a. Match Play.* In match play, an opponent or his caddie shall not attend or remove the flagstick without the knowledge or authority of the player.

*b. Stroke Play.* In stroke play, if a fellow-competitor or his caddie attend or remove the flagstick without the knowledge or authority of the competitor, and if the ball strike the flagstick or the person attending it, it is a rub of the green, there is no penalty, and the ball shall be played as it lies.

Penalty for breach of Rule 34-1 and 34-2: match play—loss of hole; stroke play—two strokes.

**3. Ball Striking Flagstick or Attendant**

The player's ball shall not strike either:—

a. The flagstick when attended or removed by the player's caddie, his partner or his partner's caddie, or by another person with the knowledge or authority of the player; or

b. The player's caddie, his partner or his partner's caddie when attending the flagstick, or another person attending the flagstick with the knowledge or authority of the player, or equipment carried by any such person; or

c. The flagstick in the hole, unattended, when the ball has been played from the putting green.

Penalty for breach of Rule 34-3: match play—loss of hole; stroke play —two strokes, and the ball shall be played as it lies.

**4. Ball Resting Against Flagstick**

If the ball rest against the flagstick when it is in the hole, the player shall be entitled to have the flagstick removed, and if the ball fall into the hole the player shall be deemed to have holed out at his last stroke.

*Note: A referee, observer, marker, steward, gallery marshal or other outside agency should not attend the flagstick.*

P

## Rule 35   The Putting Green (Def 25)

*1. General*

*a. Touching Line of Putt.* The line of the putt must not be touched except as provided in Clauses 1b, 1c, and 1d of this rule, or in measuring (Rule 20-1), but the player may place the club in front of the ball in addressing it without pressing anything down.

*b. Loose Impediments.* The player may move any loose impediment on the putting green by picking it up or brushing it aside with his hand or a club without pressing anything down. If the ball be moved, it shall be replaced, without penalty.

*c. Repair of Ball Marks.* The player may repair damage to the putting green caused by the impact of a ball. The ball may be lifted to permit repair and shall be replaced on the spot from which it was lifted; in match play the ball must be replaced immediately if the opponent so requests.

If a ball be moved during such repair, it shall be replaced, without penalty.

*d. Cleaning Ball.* A ball lying on the putting green may be lifted and cleaned, without penalty, and replaced on the spot from which it was lifted; in match play the ball must be replaced immediately if the opponent so requests.

*e. Direction for Putting.* When the player's ball is on the putting green the player's caddie, his partner or his partner's caddie may, before the stroke is played, point out a line for putting, but the line of the putt shall not be touched in front of, to the side of, or behind the hole.

No mark shall be placed anywhere on the putting green to indicate a line for putting.

*f. Testing Surface.* During the play of a hole, a player shall not test the surface of the putting green by rolling a ball or roughening or scraping the surface.

*g. Other Ball to be at Rest.* While the player's ball is in motion after a stroke on the putting green, an opponent's or a fellow-competitor's ball shall not be played or touched.

*h. Ball in Motion Stopped or Deflected.* If a ball in motion after a stroke on the putting green be stopped or deflected by any outside agency, the stroke shall be cancelled and the ball shall be replaced.

*i. Ball Overhanging Hole.* When any part of the ball overhangs the edge of the hole, the owner of the ball is not allowed more than a few seconds to determine whether it is at rest. If by then the ball has not fallen into the hole, it is deemed to be at rest.

*j. Ball on a Wrong Putting Green.* A ball lying on a putting green other than that of the hole being played must be lifted and dropped off the putting green as near as possible to where the ball lay but not nearer the hole and not in a hazard, without penalty.

*Note: Unless otherwise stipulated by the committee, the term a putting green other than that of the hole being played includes a practice putting or pitching green lying within the boundaries of the course.*

*k. Ball Played as it Lies and Not Touched.* For ball purposely moved or purposely touched, see Rule 16.

*l. Standing Astride or on Line of Putt Prohibited.* The player shall not make a stroke on the putting green from a stance astride, or with either foot touching, the line of the putt or an extension of that line behind the ball.

Penalty for breach of Rule 35-1: match play—loss of hole ; stroke play —two strokes.

*Note: When a ball on the putting green is to be lifted, its position should be marked by placing an object, such as a small coin, immediately behind the ball ; if the object interfere with another player, it should be moved one or more putter-head-lengths to one side.*

2. *Match Play*

*a. Ball Interfering with Play.* When the ball nearer the hole lies on the putting green, if the player consider that the opponent's ball might either be struck by his ball or interfere with his stance or stroke, the player may require the opponent to lift his ball without penalty. The opponent shall replace his ball after the player has played his stroke. If the player's ball stop on the spot formerly occupied by the lifted ball, the player shall first play another stroke before the lifted ball is replaced.

If the player's ball be accidentally touched or moved in complying with this rule, no penalty shall be incurred and the ball if moved shall be replaced.

*b. Playing out of Turn.* If a player play when his opponent should have done so, the opponent may immediately require the player to replay the stroke, in which case the players shall replace his ball and play in correct order, without penalty.

*c. Opponent's Ball Displaced.* If the player's ball knock the opponent's ball into the hole, the opponent shall be deemed to have holed out at his last stroke.

If the player's ball move the opponent's ball, the opponent may replace it, but this must be done before another stroke is played by either side. If the player's ball stop on the spot formerly occupied by the opponent's ball, and the opponent declare his intention to replace his ball, the player shall first play another stroke, after which the opponent shall replace his ball. (Three-Ball, Best-Ball and Four-Ball match play—Rule 40-1c.)

*d. Conceding Opponent's Next Stroke.* When the opponent's ball has come to rest, the player may concede the opponent to have holed out with his next stroke and may remove the opponent's ball with a club or otherwise. If the player does not concede the opponent's next stroke and the opponent's ball fall into the hole, the opponent shall be deemed to have holed out with his last stroke.

If the opponent's next stroke has been conceded, the opponent shall play without delay in correct order.

Penalty for breach of Rule 35-2: loss of hole.

### 3. Stroke Play

*a. Ball Interfering with Play.* When the ball nearer the hole lies on the putting green, if the competitor consider that the fellow-competitor's ball might either be struck by his ball or interfere with his stance or stroke, the competitor may require the fellow-competitor to lift or play his ball, at the option of its owner, without penalty.

*Note: It is recommended that the ball nearer the hole be played rather than lifted, unless the subsequent play of a fellow-competitor is likely to be affected.*

*b. Ball Assisting Play.* If the fellow-competitor consider that his ball lying on the putting green might be of assistance to the competitor, the fellow-competitor may lift or play first, without penalty.

*c. Ball Striking Fellow-Competitor's Ball.* When both balls lie on the putting green, if the competitor's ball strike a fellow-competitor's ball, *the competitor shall incur a penalty of two strokes* and shall play his ball as it lies. The fellow-competitor's ball shall be at once replaced.

*d. Ball Lifted Before Holed Out.* For ball lifted before holed out, see Rule 22-1b.

## Rule 36   The Committee (Def 9)

### 1. Conditions

The committee shall lay down the conditions under which a competition is to be played.

Certain special rules governing stroke play are so substantially different from those governing match play that combining the two forms of play is not practicable and is not permitted. The results of matches played and the scores returned in these circumstances shall not be accepted.

### 2. Order and Times of Starting

*a. General.* The committee shall arrange the order and times of starting, which, when possible, shall be decided by lot.

*b. Match Play.* When a competition is played over an extended period, the committee shall lay down the limit of time within which each round shall be completed.

When players are allowed to arrange the date of their match within these limits, the committee should announce that the match must be played at a stated hour on the last day of the period unless the players agree to a prior date.

*c. Stroke Play.* Competitors shall play in couples unless the committee authorises play by threes or fours. If there be a single competitor, the committee shall provide him with a player who shall mark for him, or provide a marker and allow him to compete alone, or allow him to compete with another group.

### 3. Decision of Ties

The committee shall announce the manner, day and time for the decision of a halved match or of a tie, whether played on level terms or under handicap.

A halved match shall not be decided by stroke play. A tie in stroke play shall not be decided by a match.

### 4. The Course

*a. New Holes.* New holes should be made on the day on which a stroke competition begins, and at such other times as the committee considers necessary, provided all competitors in a single round play with each hole cut in the same position.

*b. Practice Ground.* Where there is no practice ground available outside the area of a competition course, the committee should lay down the area on which players may practise on any day of a competition, if it is practicable to do so. On any day of a stroke competition, the committee should not normally permit practice on or to a putting green or from a hazard of the competition course.

*c. Course Unplayable* If the committee or its authorised representative consider that the course is not in a playable condition, or that insufficient light renders the proper playing of the game impossible, it shall have the power in match and stroke play to order a temporary suspension of play, or in stroke play to declare play null and void and to cancel all scores for the round in question.

When a round is cancelled, all penalties incurred in that round are cancelled.

When play has been temporarily suspended, it shall be resumed from where it was discontinued, even though resumption occur on a subsequent day.

(Procedure in discontinuing play—Rule 37-6b.)

*5. Modification of Penalty*

The committee has no power to waive a Rule of Golf. A penalty of disqualification, however, may, in exceptional individual cases, be waived or be modified or be imposed under Rule 1 if the committee consider such action warranted.

*6. Defining Bounds and Margins*

The committee shall define accurately:

a. The course and out of bounds.

b. The margins of hazards, water hazards, and lateral water hazards, where there is any doubt.

c. Ground under repair.

d. Obstructions.

*7. Local Rules*

*a. Policy.* The committee shall make and publish local rules for abnormal conditions, having regard to the policy of the governing authority of the country concerned as set forth in Appendix I attached to these rules.

*b. Waiving Penalty Prohibited.* A penalty imposed by a Rule of Golf shall not be waived by a local rule.

## Rule 37    The Player

*1. Conditions*

The player shall be responsible for acquainting himself with the Conditions under which the competition is to be played.

*2. Caddie and Forecaddie*

For any breach of a rule or local rule by his caddie, the player incurs the relative penalty.

The player may have only one caddie, *under penalty of disqualification.*

The player may send his own caddie forward to mark the position of any ball.

If a forecaddie be employed by the committee, he is an outside agency (Definition 22).

*3. Infringement Assisting Partner*

If the player infringe a rule or local rule so as to assist his partner's play, *the partner incurs the relative penalty in addition to any penalty incurred by the player.*

*4. Handicap*

Before starting in a handicap competition, the player shall ensure that his current handicap is recorded correctly on the official list, if any, for the competition and on the card issued to him by the committee. In the case of match play or bogey, par or Stableford competitions, he shall inform himself of the holes at which strokes are given or taken.

If a player play off a higher handicap than his current one, *he shall be disqualified* from the handicap competition. If he play off a lower one, the score, or the result of the match, shall stand.

*5. Time and Order of Starting*

The player shall start at the time and in the order arranged by the committee.

Penalty for breach of Rule 37-5: disqualification.

*6. Discontinuance of Play*

*a. When Permitted.* The player shall not discontinue play on account of bad weather or for any other reason, unless: he considers that there be danger from lightning.

There be some other reason, such as sudden illness, which the committee considers satisfactory.

If the player discontinue play without specific permission from the committee, he shall report to the committee as soon as possible.

General Exception: Players discontinuing match play by agreement are not subject to disqualification unless by so doing the competition is delayed.

Penalty for breach of Rule 37-6a: disqualification.

*b. Procedure.* When play is discontinued in accordance with the rules, it should, if feasible, be discontinued after the completion of the play of a hole. If this is not feasible, the player should lift his ball after marking the spot on which it lay; in such case he shall replace the ball on that spot when play is resumed.

Penalty for breach of Rule 37-6b: match play—loss of hole; stroke play —two strokes.

*Note: A serious breach of this rule should be dealt with by the committee under Rule 1.*

*7. Undue Delay*

The player shall at all times play without undue delay. Between the completion of a hole and driving off the next tee, the player may not delay play in any way.

Penalty for breach of Rule 37-7: match play—loss of hole; stroke play —two strokes.

*For repeated offence—disqualification.*

If the player delay play between holes, he is delaying the play of the next hole, and the penalty applies to that hole.

*8. Refusal to Comply with Rule*

If a competitor in stroke play refuse to comply with a rule affecting the rights of another competitor, *he shall be disqualified.*

*9. Artificial Devices*

Except as provided for under the rules, the player shall not use any artificial device:

a. Which might assist him in making a stroke or in his play,

*or*

b. For the purpose of gauging or measuring distance or conditions which might affect his play.

Penalty for breach of Rule 37-9: disqualification.

## Rule 38    Scoring in Stroke Play

*1. Recording Scores*

The committee shall issue to each competitor's marker a score card containing the date and the competitor's name.

After each hole the marker shall check the score with the competitor. On completion of the round the marker shall sign the card and hand it to the competitor; should more than one marker record the scores, each shall sign the part of which he is responsible.

*2. Checking Scores*

The competitor shall check his score for each hole, settle any doubtful points with the committee, ensure that the marker has signed the card, countersign the card himself, and return it to the committee as soon as possible.

Penalty for breach of Rule 38-2: disqualification.

The competitor is solely responsible for the correctness of the score recorded for each hole. The committee is responsible for the addition of scores and application of the correct handicap.

*3. No Alteration of Scores*

No alteration may be made on a card after the competitor has returned it to the committee.

If the competitor return a score for any hole lower than actually played, *he shall be disqualified.*

A score higher than actually played must stand as returned.

Exception: Four-ball stroke play— Rule 41-6a.

## Rule 39    Bogey, Par or Stableford Competitions

*1. Conditions*

A bogey, par or Stableford competition is a form of stroke competition in which play is against a fixed score at each hole of the stipulated round or rounds.

a. The reckoning for bogey or par competitions is made as in match play. The winner is the competitor who is most successful in the aggregate of holes.

b. The reckoning in Stableford competitions is made by points awarded in relation to a fixed score at each hole as follows:

For hole done in one over fixed score—1 point

For hole done in fixed score—
2 points
For hole done in one under fixed
score—3 points
For hole done in two under fixed
score—4 points
For hole done in three under fixed
score—5 points
The winner is the competitor who
scores the highest number of points.

2. *Rules for Stroke Play apply*
The rules for stroke play shall
apply with the following exceptions:

*a. No Return at any Hole.* Any
hole for which a competitor makes no
return shall be regarded as a loss in
bogey or par competitions and as
scoring no points in Stableford competitions.

*b. Scoring Cards.* The holes at which
strokes are to be given or taken shall
be indicated on the card issued by
the committee.

*c. Recording Scores.* In bogey and
par competitions the marker shall be
responsible for marking only the
gross number of strokes at each hole
where the competitor makes a net
score equal to or less than the fixed
score. In Stableford competitions the
marker shall be responsible for marking only the gross number of strokes
at each hole where the competitor's
net score earns one or more points.

3. *Disqualification Penalties*
*a. From the Competition.* A competitor shall be disqualified from the
competition for a breach of any of the
following:—

Rule 2—The Club and the Ball.
Rule 3—Agreement to Waive Rules
Prohibited.
Rule 8-3—Practice before Round.
Rule 24—Ball Interfering with
Play: Stroke Play.
Rule 35-3a—Putting Green: Stroke
Play. Ball Interfering with Play.
Rule 37-2—Caddie and Forecaddie.
Rule 37-5—Time and Order of
Starting.
Rule 37-6a—Discontinuance of
Play.
Rule 37-7—Undue Delay (repeated
offence).

Rule 37-8—Refusal to Comply with
Rule.
Rule 37-9—Artificial Devices.
Rule 38-2—Checking Scores.
Rule 38-3—No Alteration of
Scores, except that the competitor
shall not be disqualified when a
breach of this rule does not affect
the result of the hole.

*b. For a Hole.* In all other cases
where a breach of a rule would entail
disqualification, *the competitor shall
be disqualified only for the hole at
which the breach occurred.*
(Modification of penalty—Rule
36-5.)

## Rule 40   Three-Ball, Best-Ball and Four-Ball Match Play

1. *General*
*a. Rules of Golf Apply.* The Rules
of Golf, so far as they are not at
variance with the following special
rules, shall apply to all three-ball,
best-ball and four-ball matches.

*b. Ball Influencing Play.* Any player
may have any ball (except the ball
about to be played) lifted, if he consider that it might interfere with or be
of assistance to a player or side, but
this may not be done while any ball
in the match is in motion.

*c. Ball Moved by Another Ball.* If
a player's ball move any other ball in
the match, the owner of the moved
ball shall replace the ball, without
penalty.

*d. Playing out of Turn.* Through the
green or in a hazard, a player shall
incur no penalty when an opponent
should have done so. The stroke shall
not be replayed.

On the putting green, if a player
play when an opponent should have
done so, the opponent may immediately require the player to replay the
stroke in correct order, without
penalty.

2. *Three-Ball Match Play*
In a three-ball match, each player
is playing two distinct matches.

*a. Ball Stopped or Deflected by an
Opponent.* If a player's ball be stopped or deflected by an opponent, his

caddie or equipment, *that opponent shall lose the hole in his match with the player*. The other opponent shall treat the occurrence as a rub of the green (Definition 27).

Exception: ball striking person attending flagstick—Rule 35-3b.

*b. Ball at Rest Moved by an Opponent*. If the player's ball be touched or moved by an opponent, his caddie or equipment (except as otherwise provided in the rules), Rule 27-2a applies. *That opponent shall incur a penalty stroke in his match with the player*, but not his match with the other opponent.

*3. Best-Ball and Four-Ball Match Play*

*a. Order of Play*. Balls belonging to the same side may be played in the order the side considers best.

*b. Ball Stopped by Player's Side*. If a player's ball be stopped or deflected by the player, his partner or either of their caddies or equipment, *the player is disqualified for the hole*. His partner incurs no penalty.

*c. Ball Stopped by Opponent's Side*. If a player's ball be stopped or deflected by an opponent, his caddie or equipment, *the opponent's side shall lose the hole*.

Exception: ball striking person attending flagstick—Rule 34-3b.

*d. Partner's Ball Moved by Player Accidentally*. If a player, his partner, or either of their caddies accidentally move a ball owned by their side or by touching anything cause it to move (except as otherwise provided in the rules), *the owner of the ball shall incur a penalty stroke*, but the penalty shall not apply to his partner. The ball shall be played as it lies.

*e. Ball Moved by Opponent's Side*. If a player's ball be touched or moved by an opponent, his caddie or equipment (except as otherwise provided for in the rules), *that opponent shall incur a penalty stroke*, but the penalty shall not apply to the other opponent. The player shall replace the ball, without penalty.

*f. Maximum of Fourteen Clubs*. The *side shall be penalised* for a violation of Rule 3 by either partner.

*g. Disqualification Penalties. A player shall be disqualified from the match* for a breach of Rule 37-5 (Time and Order of Starting), but, in the discretion of the committee, the penalty shall not necessarily apply to his partner (Definition 28—Note).

*A side shall be disqualified* for a breach of any of the following:

Rule 2—The Club and the Ball.
Rule 4—Agreement to Waive Rules Prohibited.
Rule 37-2—Caddie and Forecaddie.
Rule 37-7—Undue Delay (repeated offence).
Rule 37-9—Artificial Devices.

*A player shall be disqualified for the hole in question and from the remainder of the match* for a breach of Rule 37-6a (Discontinuance of Play), but the penalty shall not apply to his partner.

*(Modification of penalty—Rule 36-5.)*

*h. Infringement Assisting Partner or Affecting Opponent*. If a player's infringement of a rule or local rule might assist his partner's play or adversely affect an opponent's play, *the partner incurs the relative penalty in addition to any penalty incurred by the player*.

*i. Penalty Applies to Player Only*. In all other cases where, by the Rules of Golf, a player would incur a penalty, the penalty shall not apply to his partner.

*j. Another Form of Match Played Concurrently*. In a best-ball or a four-ball match when another form of match is played concurrently, the above special rules shall apply.

## Rule 41   Four-Ball Stroke Play

*1. Conditions*

a. The Rules of Golf, so far as they are not at variance with the following special rules, shall apply to four-ball stroke play.

b. In four-ball stroke play two competitors play as partners, each playing his own ball.

c. The lower score of the partners is the score of the hole.

If one partner fail to complete the play of a hole, there is no penalty. (Wrong score—Rule 41-6a.)

d. The marker is required to record at each hole only the gross score of whichever partner's score is to count. The partners are responsible for the correctness of only their gross scores for each hole. The committee is responsible for recording the better-ball score for each hole, the addition and the application of the correct handicap.

e. Only one of the partners need be responsible for complying with Rule 38.

2. *Ball Influencing Play*

Any competitor may have any ball (except the ball about to be played) lifted or played, at the option of the owner, if he consider that it might interfere with or be of assistance to a competitor or side, but this may not be done while any ball in the group is in motion.

If the owner of the ball refuse to comply with this rule when required to do so, *his side shall be disqualified.*

3. *Balls to be at Rest*

While the competitor's ball is in motion after a stroke on the putting green, any other ball shall not be played or touched.

4. *Ball Struck by Another Ball*

When the balls concerned lie on the putting green, if a competitor's ball strike any other ball, *the competitor shall incur a penalty of two strokes* and shall play his ball as it lies. The other ball shall be at once replaced.

In all other cases, if a competitor's ball strike any other ball, the competitor shall play his ball as it lies. The owner of the moved ball shall replace his ball, without penalty.

5. *Order of Play*

Balls belonging to the same side may be played in the order the side considers best.

6. *Disqualification Penalties*

a. *From the Competition. A competitor shall be disqualified* from the competition for a breach of any of the following, but the penalty shall not apply to his partner:

Rule 8-3—Practice before Round.
Rule 37-5—Time and Order of Starting.

*A side shall be disqualified* from the competition for a breach of any of the following:

Rule 2—The Club and the Ball.
Rule 4—Agreement to Waive Rules Prohibited.
Rule 37-2—Caddie and Forecaddie.
Rule 37-7—Undue Delay (repeated offence).
Rule 37-8—Refusal to Comply with Rule.
Rule 37-9—Artificial Devices.
Rule 38-2—Checking Scores.
Rule 38-3—No alternation of scores, i.e. when the recorded lower score of the partners is lower than actually played. If the recorded lower score of the partners is higher than actually played, it must stand as returned.
Rule 41-2—Ball Influencing Play, Refusal to Lift.

By both partners, at the same hole, of a rule or rules the penalty for which is disqualification either from the competition or for a hole.

b. *From the Remainder of the Competition. A competitor shall be disqualified for the hole in question and from the remainder of the competition for a breach of Rule 37-6a* (Discontinuance of Play), but penalty shall not apply to his partner.

c. *For the Hole only.* In all other cases where a breach of a rule would *entail disqualification, the competitor shall be disqualified only for the hole at which the breach occurred.*

*(Modification of penalty—Rule 36-5.)*

7. *Infringement Assisting Partner*

If a competitor infringe a rule or local rule so as to assist his partner's play, *the partner incurs the relative penalty in addition to any penalty incurred by the competitor.*

8. *Penalty Applies to Competitor Only*

In all other cases where, by the Rules of Golf, a competitor would incur a penalty, the penalty shall not apply to his partner.

## Appendix I  Local Rules

Committees in charge of courses shall, when considered necessary,

*1.* Make local rules for such abnormal conditions as:

a. Existence of mud.

b. Accumulation of leaves.

c. Unusual damage to course.

d. Local conditions which could be held to interfere with the proper playing of the game. If this necessitates modification of a Rule of Golf the approval of the governing authority must be obtained.

e. Conditions which make a local rule necessary for the preservation of the course; this includes prohibition, where necessary, of playing a ball lying in ground under repair.

f. Obstructions, their limits and the extent of relief if the application of Rule 31 is impracticable or inequitable.

g. Any construction which the committee considers an integral part of the course (Def. 20d), and defines as not an obstruction.

h. Subject to the approval of the governing authority, permitting play of a provisional ball for a ball which may be in a water hazard of such character that it would be impracticable to determine whether the ball is in the hazard or to do so would unduly delay play.

*Note: The play of a provisional ball will automatically disallow the procedure under Rule 33-2 or 33-3.*

i. Roads and Paths.—Relief of the type afforded under Rule 32 may be provided from surfaces and sides of roads and paths or similar conditions which could unfairly affect play.

*2.* Frame regulations governing Priority on the Course.

*3.* Frame regulations governing practice during stroke competitions. (Rules 8-3, 36-4b.)

## Appendix II  Design of Clubs (Def. 36)

Rule 2-2d provides in part:

"Club faces ... shall not have any lines, dots or other markings with sharp or rough edges, or any type of finish, for the purpose of unduly influencing the movement of the ball ... Markings on the face of an iron club shall conform with the specifications."

Sharp or rough edges of markings may be determined by the finger test. A different problem is presented, however, by the detailed Specifications for Markings on Iron Clubs. These are manufacturing specifications. For the guidance of players and committees, following are a layman's interpretation of some essential parts of the specifications:

In general it is required that the face of an iron club shall present a smooth, flat surface on which a limited percentage of the area may be depressed by markings.

When the depressed area is in the form of grooves, each groove may not be wider than .035 inch (0.889 mm.) (approximately one thirty-second of an inch), the angle between the flat surface of the club face and the side of the groove may not be less than 135 degrees, and the distance between grooves may not be less than three times the width of the groove.

When the depressed area is in the form of punch marks, the markings must not exceed a slight amount over one-sixteenth of an inch (1.6 mm.) in diameter.

The complete specifications follow:

*SPECIFICATIONS*

In general a definite area of the surface is reserved for scoring. All the sections contained in this specification shall refer to this particular scored area. For reference purposes see illustrations of "Golf Head Scorings" on next page.

This specification is divided into three sections: Section 1 refers to golf clubs where grooves are used; Section 2 refers to golf clubs with punch marks; Section 3 includes a combination of groove and punch markings.

*Section 1-a Wood Clubs*

On wood clubs scoring designs are unrestricted provided the loft or face angle does not exceed 24 degrees.

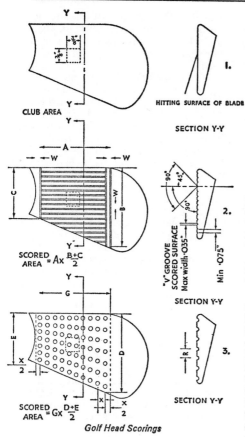

CLUB AREA

HITTING SURFACE OF BLADE

SECTION Y-Y

$$\text{SCORED AREA} = Ax \frac{B+C}{2}$$

"V" GROOVE SCORED SURFACE
Max width ·035"

Min ·075"

SECTION Y-Y

$$\text{SCORED AREA} = Gx \frac{D+E}{2}$$

SECTION Y-Y

*Golf Head Scorings*

Where the loft or face angle is greater than 24 degrees, the specifications for iron clubs (Section 1-b) shall apply.

*Section 1-b Iron Clubs*
*Section 1*
*1.* A series of straight grooves in the form of V's may be put in the face of the club. The side walls of the grooves shall be essentially flat and the included angle shall be equal to or greater than 90 degrees. The bisector of the angle shall be normal to the face of the club. (See Figure 2.)
*2.* The width of the groove shall not exceed .035 inch (0.889 mm.) along its full length. This width shall be measured in the plane of the face of the club and shall be between the two points where the planes of the groove meet the face of the club.

*3.* At no place on the face of the club shall the distances between grooves be less than three times the width of the grooves; i.e. 25 per cent of the area reserved for scoring may be grooved.

In the event that grooves are used with a width less than .025 inch (0.635 mm.), the minimum distance between the edges of the grooves shall be .075 inch (1.905 mm.).

The scored area shall be considered as that portion between the outer vertical lines shown in Figure 2. If only two vertical lines are used and these lines intersect the grooves, it shall be permissible to add to the length of the groove the distance between three grooves (2W) in determining the scored area. In no case can the total length be greater than 2W plus the length of the groove. The total length multiplied by the average width shall be the scored area.

The area of metal removed from the vertical lines or grooves shall not be counted in determining the percentage of area scored.
*4.* The centre of the scored area may be indicated by any design provided it does not exceed the boundary set up a square whose sides are 0.375 inch (9.525 mm.) (See Figure 1.) If manufacturers have no particular design or trade mark, any arrangement of lines or grooves may be used within the square to designate the centre of the scored area shall not be counted to removed area, when added to the area removed by grooving, as described in Section 1-1, does not exceed in total 25 per cent of the scoring area. Further, the method of scoring as found in Sections 1-1 and 1-2 must be used.
*5.* The total length of grooves in any one square inch of surface area cannot exceed fourteen inches (350 mm.). The vertical grooves found to right and left of the scored area and the grooves which mark the centre of scored area shall not be counted to make the fourteen inches (55 mm.) of length.
*6.* The face of the club shall be smooth and flat over the full surface. No sharp edges or lips due to die impression of any type will be per-

mitted. For decorative purposes only, it is permissible to sandblast with fine sand.

The above conditions for smoothness apply also to Sections 2 and 3.

## Section 2

*1.* If punch markings are used instead of grooves, the removed area cannot exceed 18 per cent; i.e., 82 per cent of the scored area must remain after the depressions have been made. The maximum diameter of circular punch marks cannot exceed 0.75 inch (1.905 mm.) and must be so adjusted that the total area, of all punch markings, does not exceed 18 per cent of the scored area. (See Figure 3.) The punch markings shall be spaced uniformly over the scored area. No concentration of punch marks in the scored areas will be permitted.

If punch markings are not circular they shall be acceptable if the maximum width is not greater than 1·25 the maximum allowable for circular punch marks. Further, the boundary length of the non-circular punch marks cannot exceed 3·75 times the maximum allowable diameter for circular punch marks.

The scored area shall be considered as that portion between the outer vertical lines shown in Figure 3. If no vertical lines are used, the scored area shall be determined by adding the distance between the centreline of the two holes (X) to the distance between the outer centrelines of the punch mark and multiplying this imaginary distance by the average width of the iron.

*2.* Punch marks shall be essentially uniform and symmetrical in the plane of the face of the club. The centreline of all punch marks shall be normal to the hitting face.

The punch marking may be conical or circular in cross-section. If a conical cross-section is used, the included angle (apex) cannot be less than 90 degrees. If a circular cross-section is used, the depth of penetration cannot be greater than the radius of the circle.

## Section 3

*1.* If grooves and punch marks are used in combination, the total removed area cannot exceed 25 per cent of the area reserved for scoring; the shortest distance between the centreline of any two adjacent punch marks must be 2·5 the diameter of the punch mark. (See X and R of Figure 3.) The minimum distance on the surface of the club between the edges of the groove shall be .075 inch (1.905 mm.) and further, only fourteen inches (350 mm.) in any one square inch (6.45 sq. cm.) of scored surface may be used, i.e. 55 mm. of grooves may be used in any one square centimetre of surface.

## Appendix III    Nature of Grip

Rule 2-2f

Following are examples of grips which have been approved and some which have been disapproved:

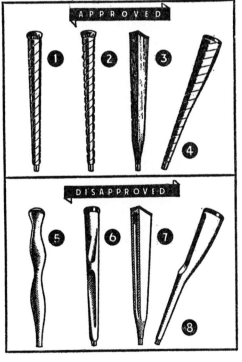

## Handicaps in General Use

*Match Play*
   *Singles.* ¾ of the difference between the full handicap of the two players.
   *Foursomes.* ⅜ of the difference between the aggregate handicaps on either side.
   *Four-ball.* Back marker to concede strokes to other three players based on ¾ of the difference between the full handicaps.
   Strokes to be taken according to the Stroke Table.

*Bogey or Par Competitions*
   *Singles.* ¾ of full handicap.
   *Foursomes.* ⅜ of the aggregate handicaps of the partners.
   *Four-ball.* Each partner receives ¾ of a full handicap.
   Strokes to be taken according to the Stroke Table.

*Stroke Play*
   *Singles.* Full handicap.
   *Foursomes.* ½ of aggregate handicaps of the partners.
   *Four-ball.* Each partner receives ¾ of the full handicap and strokes to be taken according to the Stroke Table.

*Stableford Competitions*
   *Singles.* ⅞ of full handicap.
   *Foursomes.* ⁷⁄₁₆ of aggregate handicap.
   *Four-ball.* Each partner receives ⅞ of full handicap.
   Strokes to be taken according to the Stroke Table and not added to the points scored.

NOTES:
1. *Half Strokes*
   Half strokes or over to be counted as one; smaller fractions to be disregarded.
2. *Handicaps*
   Detailed methods of handicapping are not covered by the Rules of Golf and must be laid down by the Committee in the Conditions of the Competition (Rule 36-1).
3. *36 hole competitions*
   In handicap competitions over 36 holes, strokes should be given or taken in accordance with the 18 hole Stroke Table unless the Committee introduces a special Stroke Table.
4. *Sudden-death play-off*
   When extra holes are played in handicap competitions, strokes should be taken in accordance with the Stroke Table.

## RULES OF AMATEUR STATUS

See AMATEUR STATUS, RULES OF.

## RULES OF GOLF COMMITTEE, R. AND A.

What may be regarded as the first Rules of Golf Committee dates back to 1828, when a special committee of the R. and A. produced a new code of rules, but it was not until 1896 that a permanent and powerful R. and A. committee was established to deal with all matters pertaining to the rules. Many of the most distinguished amateurs of the day were elected members. One of their first and most important tasks was to co-operate with the newly-formed United States Golf Association on matters concerning both countries; although there have been some differences of opinion, this close co-operation has continued.

All queries on the rules are answered by the Rules Committee, but they must be submitted by club secretaries or other officials, and not by individual club members.

## RUN

A ball's 'run' is the final part of its journey after being struck, when it stops bouncing and runs along the ground. The phrase 'There is a lot of run on the ball' indicates that the ball runs a long way after landing.

## RUN-UP SHOT

A stroke to the putting green in which allowance is made for the run of the ball after it has landed on the ground; also called 'pitch-and-run'. The opposite type of stroke to the green is a pitch, in which the ball is struck with a higher trajectory and/or with backspin, causing it to fall near the hole without any, or with very little run. See CHIP; PITCH.

## RUNYAN, Paul (b 1909)

U.S.P.G.A. Champion, 1934, 1938, on the first occasion defeating Craig Wood in the final at the 38th and on the second young Sam Snead by eight and seven. Argentine Open Champion, 1938. U.S. Senior Professional Champion, 1961, 1962, both times defeating S. L. King in the World Senior Championship. Ryder Cup team, 1933, 1935.

## RUSSIA, GOLF IN

The game was played in Russia before the First World War, but was always restricted by the vagaries of the Russian climate. In *The Spirit of the Links* (1907), Henry Leach wrote:

> They have had two courses in Russia for a long time past—one near Moscow and the other at Murino, a small village a few versts out from St. Petersburg. The men who play here are a hardy, determined strain, fine men for pioneers. To get their golf they have to drive 13 miles out from the capital over bad roads; and in order to obtain a fair amount of satisfaction from their game they have to returf their putting greens almost every year, owing to the extreme sandiness of the soil.

The Murino course had nine holes and there were both boy and girl caddies. Bob Randall, who was professional at Herne Bay for 50 years, was professional at Murino from 1906 to 1908.

Unfortunately, neither course survived the Revolution and golf is no longer played in Russia. One might have thought that a good course could have been constructed near the Crimean seaside resorts, where the weather conditions would be more favourable, but it was not to be. The Russian official paper, *Pravda,* once reported that golf was "a game which the Caucasian shepherds played with enthusiasm about 1,000 years ago".

Curiously enough, it was a Russian —the Grand Duke Michael—who was a pioneer of golf on the French Riviera; it was he who also tried to interest the Prince of Wales (the future King Edward VII) in golf when he was staying at Cannes in 1899. The Grand Duke and his morganatic wife, the Countess Zia Torby, played at St Andrews and other courses in Britain. In the summer of 1978 it was rumoured that a full-length course was to be built on a site about ten miles from Moscow. SEE ROYAL GOLFERS.

## RUT IRON

A club with a small round head used for getting out of ruts, cart-tracks or similar difficult places. Also called Track Iron. See NIBLICK; PRESIDENT.

## RYDER, Samuel (1859-1936)

Son of a nurseryman and founder of the prosperous seed-merchants business in St Albans, Hertfordshire. After the unofficial match between British and American professionals at Wentworth in 1926, he presented the Ryder Cup to be played for every other year between teams representing the British and American Professional Golfers' Associations. He also contributed largely towards the expenses of the British teams during his lifetime. See RYDER CUP.

## RYDER AND WALKER CUPS, PLAYED IN BOTH

See WALKER AND RYDER CUPS, PLAYED IN BOTH.

## RYDER CUP

The Ryder Cup matches, between members of the British and U.S. Professional Golfers' Associations, grew out of an unofficial match played at the then new club, Wentworth, Surrey, in 1926. The British team, which included Abe Mitchell, George Duncan and Ted Ray, won by the staggering total of 13 matches to one, with one halved, against a rather un-American American team, which included Walter Hagen, but also Jim Barnes, Tommy Armour and Cyril Walker, all born in Britain, and Australian-born Joe Kirkwood.

Seeing how popular the match was,

the P.G.A. committee approached Samuel Ryder, the wealthy St Albans seed-merchant, who had Abe Mitchell as his private professional. Mr Ryder presented a gold cup—it cost £750 then but is worth far more now— for a biennial contest between the two countries. The first was held in 1927 at Worcester, Massachusetts, and the Americans had their revenge for the 1926 match, winning by nine matches to two with one halved. The redoubtable Walter Hagen led the Americans, while Ted Ray captained the British team.

Britain won the 1929 match at Moortown, Leeds, and again at Southport and Ainsdale in 1933, but our only other win was at Lindrick in 1957. In 1969, at Royal Birkdale, however, the match ended in a draw after one of the most thrilling finishes in the history of golf, everything depending on the last putt in the game between Jack Nicklaus and Tony Jacklin. The British team has never won on American soil.

The following are the results of the Ryder Cup matches since 1927:

*1927 (Worcester, Massachusetts)*
U.S.A. 9 matches; Britain 2 matches; 1 halved.

*1929 (Moortown, Leeds)*
Britain 6 matches; U.S.A. 4 matches; 2 halved.

*1931 (Scioto, Columbus, Ohio)*
U.S.A. 9 matches; Britain 3 matches.

*1933 (Southport and Ainsdale)*
Britain 6 matches; U.S.A. 5 matches; 1 halved.

*1935 (Ridgewood, New Jersey)*
U.S.A. 8 matches; Britain 2 matches; 2 halved.

*1937 (Southport and Ainsdale)*
U.S.A. 7 matches; Britain 3 matches; 2 halved.

*1947 (Portland, Oregon)*
U.S.A. 11 matches; Britain 1 match.

*1949 (Ganton, Scarborough)*
U.S.A. 7 matches; Britain 5 matches.

*1951 (Pinehurst, North Carolina)*

U.S.A. 9 matches; Britain 2 matches; 1 halved.

*1953 (Wentworth, Surrey)*
U.S.A. 6 matches; Britain 5 matches; 1 halved.

*1955 (Thunderbird, Palm Springs)*
U.S.A. 8 matches; Britain 4 matches.

*1957 (Lindrick, Yorkshire)*
Britain 7 matches; U.S.A. 4 matches; 3 halved.

*1959 (Palm Desert, California)*
U.S.A. 7 matches; Britain 2 matches; 3 halved.

*1961 (Royal Lytham and St Anne's)*
U.S.A. 13 matches; Britain 8 matches; 3 halved.

*1963 (Atlanta, Georgia)*
U.S.A. 20 matches; Britain 6 matches; 6 halved.

*1965 (Royal Birkdale)*
U.S.A. 18 matches; Britain 11 matches; 3 halved.

*1967 (Houston, Texas)*
U.S.A. 21 matches; Britain 6 matches; 5 halved.

*1969 (Royal Birkdale)*
U.S.A. 13 matches; Britain 13 matches; 6 halved.

*1971 (Old Warson, St Louis)*
U.S.A. 16 matches; Britain 11 matches; 5 halved.

*1973 (Muirfield)*
U.S.A. 16 matches; Britain 10 matches; 6 halved.

*1975 (Laurel Valley, Pennsylvania)*
U.S.A. 18 matches; Britain 8 matches; 6 halved.

*1977 (Royal Lytham and St. Anne's)*
U.S.A. 12 matches; Britain 7 matches; 1 halved.

## RYE

Camber, Rye, Sussex. Founded 1894. Typical links among the sand dunes, with famous greens. Length: 6,483 yards. S.S.S. 72. Housed English Ladies' Championship, 1970. Permanent home of the Oxford and Cambridge Golfing Society's President's Putter, played for in January, and many times venue of the Oxford and Cambridge match.

## SABINE, Mrs N. (1913-73)
As Diana Plumpton, runner-up, British Ladies' Championship, 1933. Curtis Cup team, 1934.

## SADDLER, A. C. ('Sandy') (b 1935)
Runner-up, Scottish Amateur Championship, 1960. Walker Cup team, 1963, 1965, 1967. World Cup (formerly Eisenhower Trophy) team, 1962.

## ST ANDREWS
St Andrews, Fife. Earliest records of the Royal and Ancient Golf Club of St Andrews go back to 1754. Traditional links, with innumerable bun-kers, many hidden from the teeing ground, and unique double greens. Length (Old Course): 6,951 yards S.S.S. 72. Housed Open Championship, 1873, 1876, 1879, 1882, 1885, 1888, 1891, 1895, 1900, 1905, 1910, 1921, 1927, 1933, 1939, 1946, 1955, 1957, 1960, 1964, 1970; Amateur Championship, 1886, 1889, 1891, 1895, 1901, 1907, 1913, 1924, 1930, 1936, 1950, 1958, 1963; Ladies' Championship, 1908, 1929, 1965. British Boys' Amateur Championship, 1949; Walker Cup match, 1923, 1926, 1934, 1938, 1947, 1955, 1971; Eisenhower Trophy (later World Cup), 1958. Also New Course (6,612 yards: S.S.S. 72), Eden Course (6,250 yards: S.S.S. 70), Jubilee Course (6,005 yards: S.S.S. 69). See ROYAL AND ANCIENT GOLF CLUB OF ST ANDREWS.

## ST ANDREWS, NAMES OF HOLES AND BUNKERS AT
Many of the bunkers on the Old Course have names, often of obscure origin going back into the past. The following are the chief ones to be encountered at the various holes:

1st (Burn): No bunkers, the only hazard being the Swilcan Burn. Halket's Bunker now filled in.

2nd (Dyke): Cheape's Bunker, Wig Bunker.

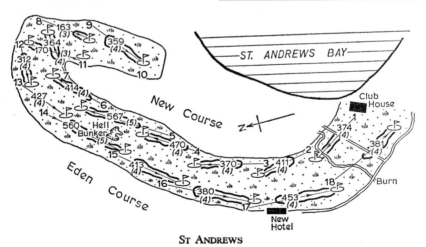

ST ANDREWS

3rd (Cartgate Going Out): Cartgate Bunker.

4th (Ginger Beer): Sutherland Bunker, Students' Bunkers, Ginger Beer Bunkers.

5th (Hole o' Cross Going Out): Pulpit Bunker.

6th (Heathery): Nick's Bunker.

7th (High Going Out): Cockle Bunker.

8th (Short): Short Hole Bunker.

9th (End): Kruger and Mrs Kruger Bunkers, End Hole Bunker.

10th (Bobby Jones): Boase's Bunker.

11th (High Coming Home): Strath Bunker, Shelly Bunker, Cockle Bunker, Hill Bunker.

12th (Heathery Coming Home): Stroke Bunker.

13th (Hole o' Cross Coming Home): Coffin Bunker, Walkinshaw's Grave, Cat's Trap, Hole o' Cross Bunker.

14th (Long): Beardies, Benty Bunker, Kitchen Bunker, Hell Bunker, Grave Bunker.

15th (Cartgate Coming Home): Cottage Bunker, Sutherland Bunker, Rob's Bunker.

16th (Corner of the Dyke): Principal's Nose, Deacon Sime, Grant's Bunker, Wig Bunker.

17th (Road Hole): Cheape's Bunker, Scholar's Bunker, Progessing Bunker, Road Bunker.

18th (Tom Morris): No bunkers here.

Several of the old named bunkers have now been filled in, including Halket's Bunker at the 1st, Hull's Bunker at the 15th and Tam's Coo at the 16th. The 10th hole, previously the only one without a name, was officially called the 'Bobby Jones Hole' in 1972.

See ROYAL AND ANCIENT GOLF CLUB OF ST ANDREWS; ST ANDREWS, OLD NAMES FOR HOLES AT; SWILCAN BURN.

## ST ANDREWS, OLD NAMES FOR HOLES AT

The first hole on the Old Course, now known as the Burn, was once called the Hole of Leslie. The 7th (High Hole Going Out) was the Hole of Rhi. A more mysterious one was the Hole of Craig, which is difficult to locate exactly, although it must have been named after the rock called Doo (or Dhu) Craig in St Andrews bay. See ST ANDREWS, NAMES OF HOLES AND BUNKERS AT.

## ST ANDREWS GOLF CLUB OF YONKERS

This, the first American golf club, was founded on 14th November 1888 at a dinner given at his house at Yonkers-on-Hudson, New York, by a Scot named John Reid. His four guests—who had already been knocking balls about—were his near neighbours, Henry O. Tallmadge, Harry Holbrook, John B. Upham and Kingman Putnam. That night Reid became the first president and Upham the first secretary and treasurer, the others forming the first board of governors. The first member was a fellow Scot from Dunfermline, Robert Lockhart, who had brought back clubs and balls from a visit to St Andrews and taught the game to Reid, who oddly enough hadn't played in Scotland.

The first course of the St Andrews Club, as they piously called it, consisted of three holes laid out in John Reid's cow pasture. After about four years they moved to a bigger pasture and constructed six holes and later to an apple orchard where they became known as the 'Apple Tree Gang'; they hung their coats on one of the trees and ate their lunch under its shade. In 1894, when they had some 20 members, they moved to Grey Oaks, with a 9-holes lay-out and, for the first time, a clubhouse. Finally, in 1897, they settled in the present home of the club at Mount Hope, Westchester County, where 18 holes were possible and there was a comfortable clubhouse.

See LOCKHART, ROBERT; REID, JOHN; UNITED STATES, GOLF IN THE.

## ST ANDREWS TROPHY

A biennial meeting between amateur teams representing the British Isles and the Continent of Europe. Play, over two days, is by eight foursomes and 16 singles. The venue alternates between a British course and a Continental one. Although there have been some close finishes, the British Isles have won each of the nine matches so far played.

## ST GEORGE'S CHALLENGE CUP

One of the oldest open amateur competitions, founded in 1888, the year after the St George's (later Royal St George's) course was laid out on Sandwich Bay. It is a 36-holes stroke-play competition.

The winner in the first four years was the great Hoylake amateur, John Ball, and his club-mate, Harold Hilton, won in 1893, 1894. Most of the country's leading players—and several foreigners—have won the St George's Cup through the years.

See ROYAL ST GEORGE'S.

## ST HELENA, GOLF ON

The Longwood Club—with the romantic address of 'Longwood, South Atlantic Ocean'—was founded in 1903. It has 9 holes and a length of 2,363 yards. Napoleon died in exile at Longwood, which is about three miles inland from Jamestown, the capital.

## ST VINCENT, GOLF IN

There is a new 9-holes course on this Windward Island, in the West Indies, lying about 95 miles west of Barbados. Called the Aquaduct, it has been built in consultation with Freddie George, professional at the Belham River Valley Club, Montserrat, in the Leeward Islands.

## SAMMY

A now vanished iron club with a shallow face and rounded back used mainly for run-up shots to the green. Francis Ouimet used one in winning the 1913 U.S. Open.

## SANDERS, Doug (b 1933)

Runner-up (with Dave Thomas), British Open Championship, 1966, 1970 (after tie with Jack Nicklaus). Runner-up (with Jerry Barber), U.S.P.G.A. Championship, 1959.

Q

Canadian Open Champion (as amateur) 1956, after which he turned professional. Ryder Cup team, 1967. Author of *Compact Golf* (1967). Famous for his gay and elegant golf clothes and very short swing.

## SAND IRON

Also called Sand Wedge or Blaster. A deep-faced club with a thicker sole or flange at the bottom than other clubs, used for getting the ball out of bunkers or, sometimes, heavy rough. In the sand iron the back part of the sole is lower than the front edge, to enable the club to get under the ball better. The term began to be used as far back as the 1890s. See BLASTER ; NIBLICK ; WEDGE.

## SANDS, Charles E.

Runner-up to Charles B. Macdonald in the first U.S. Amateur Championship, 1895, at the Newport Club, Rhode Island. Over 36 holes Macdonald won by 12 and 11. See MACDONALD, CHARLES B.

## SARAZEN, Gene (b 1902)

Born Eugene Saraceni. One of the few golfers to have won both the American and British Open Championships and, with Bobby Jones and Ben Hogan, the only player to have held both titles in one year. U.S. Open Champion, 1922, 1932 ; tied with Lawson Little, 1940, but lost play-off ; runner-up, 1934. British Open Champion, 1932 ; runner-up, 1928. U.S.P.G.A. Champion, 1922, 1923, 1933. Won U.S Masters, 1935. Australian Open Champion, 1936. Ryder Cup team, 1927, 1929, 1931, 1933, 1935, 1937.

In winning the 1935 Masters Sarazen had what was called a 'golden eagle' at the par-5 15th in the last round. At this point he was three shots behind the leader, Craig Wood. His drive of 260 yards still left him some 240 yards from the green, but a No 4 wood shot cleared the lake in front of the green, bounced a couple of times and rolled into the hole. This albatross two wiped out the three-stroke deficit and he did the last three holes in par figures to tie with Craig Wood, beating him in the play-off.

Bobby Jones, who was standing at the back of 15th green, said years later; "It is not difficult at all to name the most dramatic finish of the Masters, a finish which I think would be the choice of everyone. It is that provided by Gene Sarazen in 1935 when he holed the double eagle at the 15th hole in the final round." A plaque at Augusta commemorates this shot, like Bobby Jones's at Royal Lytham and Arnold Palmer's at Royal Birkdale.

Gene Sarazen returned to St Andrews for the centenary Open Championship in 1960—and at the age of 58 did a 69 on the Old Course! He also played in the 1970 Open at St. Andrews.

## SARDINIA, GOLF IN

Golf has been slow to reach the large Italian island of Sardinia. However, an 18-holes course has recently been opened near Porto Cervo, capital of the developing district called the Costa Smeralda—the emerald coast. Called Pevero, it has been created by Robert Trent Jones. Another club, Is Molas, was opened in 1975.

## SARGENT, George (b 1880)

U.S. Open Champion, 1909, defeating Tom McNamara by one stroke with a score of 290 that was not to be equalled until Walter Hagen's first Open in 1914 and not bettered until 'Chick' Evans's 286 in 1916. Sargent had come to America from England and was professional at the Hyde Manor Club.

## SAUNDERS, Vivien (b 1946)

Runner-up, British Ladies' Championship, 1966. Curtis Cup team, 1968. Turned professional, 1969.

## SAUNTON

Braunton, North Devon. Founded 1891. Typical links, recreated after damage in the Second World War. Length: 6,673 yards. S.S.S. 72. Housed Ladies' Championship, 1932; English Amateur Championship, 1937; English Open Amateur Stroke Play Championship, 1967.

## SAYERS, Bernard ('Ben') (1857-1924)

Born Leith. One of the smallest of the famous old-time professionals, he was only 5ft 3in in height and weighed only $9\frac{1}{2}$ stone. Played in every British Open Championship from 1880 to 1923 and was runner-up to Jack Burns in 1888. A great putter, he used to say: "If a man can putt, he can play anybody." He was the author of a famous golfing saying, attributed to many other golfers; after being beaten by the popular young amateur, Lieutenant 'Freddie' Tait, at North Berwick, he said: "Beaten by eight holes on my own green; it's no' possible, but it's a fac'!" Founder of the North Berwick club-making firm that still bears his name.

## SCHENECTADY PUTTER

This type of centre-shafted putter was invented by a man named Wright, who worked for the General Electric Company at the great plant at Schenectady, a town in New York State. It had always been allowed in the United States, but was banned in Britain in 1909 and made legal only in January 1952. There is still a good deal of misinformation about the banning.

The first time that the name became familiar in Britain was in 1904, although a club with the shaft inserted in the middle of the head had been used in the old French game of Crosse; about 1870 a centre-shafted mid-iron was patented by a man named Anderson, of Edinburgh; and in the early twentieth century a centre-shafted putter called the 'Simplex' was on the market.

In 1904, however, the British Amateur Championship was won for the first time by an American, Walter J. Travis, already three-times U.S. Amateur Champion. The 'Old Man', as he was called, was putting very badly in practice at the Royal St George's Club, Sandwich, and on the day before the first round he borrowed a Schenectady from an American friend, Edward Phillips. The result was that, as Horace Hutchinson wrote in his reminiscences, everybody at Sandwich went round saying: "Have you seen that American who is putting with an extraordinary thing like a croquet mallet?" 'That American' beat Hutchinson with it, too, and Harold Hilton and, in the final, the mighty-hitting Edward Blackwell.

As may be imagined, there was a rush for Schenectadies—although Travis stopped using one as soon as he returned to America—and they went on being used in England for the next five years. In 1906 Spaldings were advertising a Schenectady for 7s. 6d. "as used by Mr W. J. Travis" and there was no question of the Schenectady being banned by the R. and A. because of its use by Travis. In 1909, however, a letter reached St Andrews from the Nga Moto Club, New Zealand, asking the Rules of Golf Committee: "With regard to the form and make of golf clubs, is it permissible to use a small croquet mallet to putt with?" The reply was: "A small croquet mallet is not a golf club and is inadmissible."

The question now was: "Is a Schenectady putter a small croquet mallet?" Yes, said the R. and A. No, said the U.S.G.A. So it was banned in Britain and allowed in the United States.

Forty years later one of the sensations of the 1949 British Open Championship at Sandwich was the disqualification of Charles Rotar, an American, for using a Schenectady in the first round. And when 'Babe' Zaharias arrived in England in 1951 with her team of woman professionals, she brought only a centre-shafted putter and had to borrow an ordinary one. Told about the ban, she said: "Schenectady putters? What are they?" In America they were just

putters—as they are now in Britain.

See CROSSE ; SIMPLEX.

## SCHWEIZER, Hans (b 1913)

One of Switzerland's leading amateurs. Swiss Open Amateur Champion, 1931, 1938 ; runner-up, 1936. Swiss National Amateur Champion, 1933, 1934, 1936, 1937, 1942, 1943, 1944, 1945, 1947, 1948.

## SCILLY ISLES, GOLF IN THE

The 9 holes of the Isles of Scilly course, on St Mary's, were laid out in 1904 and opened next year by the famous amateur golfer, Horace Hutchinson. In the late 1930s aircraft, linking the islands with the mainland, used to land on the fairways, golfers being warned by a bell. During the Second World War the course almost vanished, but it was brought back to life by a group of enthusiasts and in 1969 a fine new clubhouse was opened.

## SCLAFF

A Scottish word for a light slap. In golf it had the same meaning as 'baff'—a stroke in which the sole of the club scrapes the ground before striking the ball. See BAFFY.

## SCORE-CARDS, FIRST

The first time that official printed score cards were used was in the 1865 British Open Championship at Prestwick, the winner being Andrew Strath with a 36-holes score of 162. The originals have been preserved by the club.

## 'SCOTCH CROQUET'

A derogatory name given to golf by its detractors—particularly in the United States—when the game was booming in the 1890s. See 'HOCKEY AT THE HALT'.

## SCOTCH FOURSOME

An American term for the game merely called foursome in England, in which the two partners on each side play the one ball alternately ; also jocularly called a 'one-ball twosome'. In America foursome has the same meaning as four-ball. See MATCHES, TYPES OF.

## SCOTT, Lady Margaret (b 1875)

Daughter of the Earl of Eldon and sister of the Hon. Osmund, Denys and Michael Scott, all fine golfers. British Ladies' Champion for the first three years, 1893-5, after which she retired from competitive golf. She learned her golf on a course laid out in the grounds of her home, Stowell Park, Wiltshire, playing with her father and brothers. Photographs show Lady Margaret's remarkable swing; she was so supple that at the top of her backswing the shaft of her club was in a direct line to the ball, her right elbow, of course, flying up in the air. On her marriage, she became Lady Margaret Hamilton Russell. See SCOTT, HON. MICHAEL.

## SCOTT, Hon. Michael (b 1878)

British Amateur Champion, 1933—the oldest winner. Australian Open Champion, 1904, 1907. Australian Amateur Champion, 1905, 1907, 1909, 1910. French Open Amateur Champion, 1912, 1922. First amateur in British Open Championship, 1912, 1922. Won Worplesdon Mixed Foursomes, with Miss Joyce Wethered, 1931. Walker Cup team, 1924, 1934 (captain).

## SCOTT, Sydney S. (b 1913)

Runner-up (with Dai Rees and Bobby Locke), British Open Championship, 1954. British Senior Professional Champion, 1964, losing to Sam Snead in the World Senior Championship. Ryder Cup team, 1955

## SCOTTISH AMATEUR CHAMPIONSHIP

This championship was founded in 1922, three years earlier than its English counterpart, but many years later than the Irish and Welsh Championships. It is open to those of Scottish birth or at least one of whose parents is Scottish; no one is eligible who has played for England, Ireland or Wales or taken part in the close championships of these countries.

Jack M'Lean won the event three times running (1932, 1933, 1934), but no golfer dominated it to the same extent as Ronnie Shade in recent years; before turning professional in 1968, he won the championship five times in succession (1963-7), having been runner-up in 1962.

## SCOTTISH GOLF UNION

The Scottish Union, founded in 1920, embraces over 515 clubs. Its chief objects are:

1. To foster and maintain a high standard of amateur golf in Scotland.

2. To organise an annual Scottish Amateur Championship.

3. To administer the Standard Scratch Score and Handicapping Scheme.

4. To deal with any other matters of Scottish interest that may arise.

## SCOTTISH OPEN CHAMPIONSHIP

A tournament revived in 1972, the first winner being Neil Coles, at the Downfield Club, Dundee. The 1973 winner, at St Andrews, was Graham Marsh.

## SCRATCH

The word used to describe a golfer who is supposed to play to the scratch score of the course; he gives strokes to all players with a higher handicap but receives them from a player with a plus handicap. Hence 'scratch man'.

According to *The Standard Scratch Score and Handicapping Scheme,* prepared by the Council of National Golf Unions, a scratch player

is expected consistently to return cards equalling or bettering the standard scratch score of the day of his own and other courses. A player may only be given or allowed to retain a handicap of scratch if his performances fully justify the rating, and then only with the prior approval of the County Union or District Committee. The minimum requirement for a player to obtain or retain a handicap of scratch is that he should have played to that handicap in at least five competitions during the calendar year then current by returning a gross score equal to or lower than the standard scratch score of the day for the competition concerned. At least two of these scores must be returned on a course other than that of the player's home club. See COUNCIL OF NATIONAL GOLF UNIONS; PLUS; STANDARD SCRATCH SCORE.

## SEGARD, Mme Patrick (b 1921)

French. Born Lally Vagliano. British Ladies' Champion, 1950. French Ladies' Open Champion, 1948, 1950, 1951, 1952. French Ladies' Close Champion, 1939, 1946, 1949, 1950, 1951, 1954; runner-up, 1952, 1953. Italian Ladies' Open Champion, 1949, 1951. Spanish Ladies' Open Champion, 1951. Benelux Ladies' Open Champion, 1953, 1954, 1955. Swiss Ladies' Open Champion, 1949. British Girls' Champion, 1937.

## 'SELECTIVE SCOTCH BALL'

See GREENSOME.

## SEMI-ROUGH

The term used for the grass area often found between the closely-cut fairway and the thick, uncut rough; such area is usually kept half-cut. Rough and semi-rough are not officially recognised in the Rules of Golf. See ROUGH.

## SENIOR GOLFERS' SOCIETY OF GREAT BRITAIN

This famous society, limited to 750 members, was founded in 1926 for golfers who have reached the age of 55. The idea originated in the United States in 1917 and was brought across the Atlantic by Frederick Snare, one-time American Seniors' Champion, who persuaded Colonel Francis ('Pops') Popham, F. W. Ashe, J. A. (Jack) Milne and other seniors to start a British society. Milne invented the Seniors' tie—whose colours are a blend of port and the sere and yellow—which is now worn by seniors in all countries where there is a society.

A triangular match between the seniors of the United States, Canada and Britain, held annually since 1927 for a cup presented by Lord Derby—then president of the British society—has now developed into a World Senior Amateur Team Championship. See UNITED STATES SENIORS' GOLF ASSOCIATION.

## SET

A full complement of clubs; hence 'matched set', indicating clubs of a uniform design. A full set of clubs is limited to 14, the United States Golf Association ruling dating from 1st January 1938 and the R. and A. ruling from 1st May 1939. In announcing their decision, the U.S.G.A. said: "We have come to the conclusion that the limitation of the number of clubs would tend to restore the making of individual shots, and increase the skill of the player." At first the U.S.G.A. decided on 16, but changed to 14.

Before the limit was set, many golfers—particularly some Americans—carried over 20 clubs. Lawson Little at one time carried 23 or 24, including eight niblicks of various kinds; and a golfer named Campbell played in the U.S. Amateur Championship with no fewer than 29. See LOW, JOHN LAING.

## SEWELL, Douglas N. (b 1929)

English Amateur Champion, 1958, 1960. English Open Amateur Stroke Play Champion, 1957, 1959 (after tie with Michael Bonallack). Walker Cup team, 1957, 1959. World Cup (formerly Eisenhower Trophy) team, 1960. Turned professional, 1960.

## SEWGOLUM, Susunker

Born in Durban, Natal, of Indian parents, 'Papwa' Sewgolum, as he is called, is one of the world's best known 'coloured' golfers. He has played in the British Open Championship and various professional tournaments and was Dutch Open Champion, 1959, 1960, 1964. He plays with his left hand below his right on the shaft. See LEFT HAND BELOW RIGHT.

## SEYMOUR, Mark (b 1897)

Won *Golf Illustrated* Gold Vase, 1921, and turned professional, 1922. Scottish Professional Champion, 1931, 1933, 1934. Runner-up, Irish Open Championship, 1931. Runner-up, British Professional Match Play Championship, 1931, 1933.

## SHADE, R. D. B. M. ('Ronnie') (b 1938)

Runner-up, British Amateur Championship, 1966. Scottish Amateur Champion, 1963, 1964, 1965, 1966, 1967; runner-up, 1962. English Open Amateur Stroke Play Champion, 1961, 1963, 1967. Scottish Open Amateur Stroke Play Champion, 1968. Scottish Professional Champion, 1970; runner-up, 1972. Walker Cup team, 1961, 1963, 1965, 1967. World Cup (formerly Eisenhower Trophy) team, 1962, 1964, 1966, 1968. World (formerly Canada) Cup team, 1970. Turned professional, 1968.

## SHANKING

See SOCKETING.

## SHEARER, Bob (b 1948)

Australian Amateur, 1969.

## SHORT

A term used to describe any shot that fails to reach its intended target. You can be short of the green, short of the bunker, short of the hole—or just short all the way. The opposite of 'too short' is 'too strong'.

## SHUT-TO-OPEN

A stroke in which the wrists are allowed to turn, as far as is physically possible, to the left on the backswing and then brought back to square on the downswing. Actually the wrists cannot be rolled much to the left on the backswing, but this method of swinging is often recommended to chronic slicers. See OPEN-TO-SHUT.

## SHUTE, Densmore (1904-74)

British Open Champion, 1933, after tie with Craig Wood—his score of 73, 73, 73, 73 being a model of con-

sistency. Tied U.S. Open Championship, 1939, with Byron Nelson and Craig Wood, but lost second play-off to Nelson after tie in first play-off; runner-up to Craig Wood, 1941. U.S.P.G.A. Champion, 1936, 1937. Ryder Cup team, 1931, 1933, 1937.

## SHUTTING THE FACE

See HOODING THE CLUB.

## SIAM, GOLF IN

See THAILAND, GOLF IN.

## SICILY, GOLF IN

The game has never flourished on the Italian island of Sicily, although before the Second World War there was a 9-holes course at Palermo.

## SIDE

"A player, or two or more players who are partners" (Rules of Golf Definition).

## SIDEROWF, Richard (b 1937)

British Amateur Champion, 1973. Walker Cup team, 1969, 1973, 1975, 1977. Played for America in World Cup (formerly Eisenhower Trophy) team, 1968.

## SIERRA LEONE, GOLF IN

The Freetown Club, in the capital, was founded as long ago as 1904. It originally had 9 holes, but now has 12. There is another course at Yengema.

## SIGEL, Helen (Mrs Wilson) (b 1919)

Runner-up, U.S. Ladies' Championship, 1931, 1948. Curtis Cup team, 1950

## SIKES, Dan (b 1930)

U.S. Public Links Champion, 1958. Ryder Cup team, 1969.

## SIKES, Richard H. (b 1940)

Runner-up, U.S. Amateur Championship, 1963. U.S. Public Links Champion, 1961, 1962. Walker Cup team, 1963.

## 'SILVER SCOT, THE'

See ARMOUR, THOMAS DICKSON.

## SILVERTOWN

In the 1890s the Silvertown India-rubber Co. produced a popular, if rather hard, gutty ball called the Silvertown. See BALL, MAKES OF.

## SIMONS, James B. (b 1950)

Runner-up, British Amateur Championship, 1971. Leading amateur, U.S. Open Championship, 1971. Walker Cup team, 1971.

## SIMPLEX

A type of centre-shafted putter—of the Schenectady pattern—put on the market about 1904 or 1905. When Andrew Kirkaldy, the famous St Andrews professional, was shown a Simplex, he said: "I wad suner play wi' a tay spune!" See SCHENECTADY PUTTER.

## SIMPSON, Jack

Born Elie, Fife, one of six brothers, of whom Jack and Archie were the best players. British Open Champion, 1884. For their golf the Simpsons were more closely connected with Carnoustie, Angus, than with Elie.

## SINGAPORE, GOLF IN

The Prime Minister of Singapore has stated that "in no city in South-East Asia are there so many golf courses—a legacy of British colonisation". Three 18-holes courses—Bukit, Island and Sime—comprise the Singapore Island Country Club; there are the 9-holes Keppel and Warren Clubs; and three 9-holes R.A.F. clubs—Changi, Seletar and Tengah.

The Singapore Open Championship has been held since 1957 either on the Island or Bukit courses. The Island Club housed the World (formerly Canada) Cup, 1969.

## SINGLE

See MATCHES, TYPES OF.

## SISTER GOLFERS

Among the best known golfing sisters have been the following:

Barton: Pamela and Mervyn (Mrs Sutherland-Pilch).

Curtis: Margaret and Harriot.

Hezlet: May, Florence and Violet.

Leitch: Cecil, Edith (Mrs Guedalla) and May (Mrs Millar).

Orr: Miss Orr, E. C. and A. L.

## SLICE

"To strike or play so as to send the ball curving to the right" (Chambers's Dictionary). A slice can be caused by bringing the club across the ball from right to left. With a left-handed player, of course, the ball curves to the left. Also used as a noun. See FADE, CONTROLLED ; PULL.

## SMALLEST GOLF COURSE

On the Isle of May, in the Firth of Forth, is a golf course consisting of three holes. On the island of Benbecula, in the Outer Hebrides, is one of six holes. The Dalmunzie Club, Glenshee, Perthshire, also has six holes, and 20 members.

## SMITH, Mrs Frances ('Bunty') (1924-78)

Born Frances Stephens. British Ladies' Champion, 1949, 1954 ; runner-up, 1951, 1952. English Ladies' Champion, 1948, 1954, 1955 ; runner-up, 1959. Runner-up, British Women's Open Stroke Play Championship, 1970. French Ladies' Open Champion, 1949. Won Worplesdon Mixed Foursomes, with Leonard Crawley, 1949, 1950 ; with W. A. Slark, 1954 ; with Bruce Critchley, 1961. Curtis Cup team, 1950, 1952, 1954, 1956, 1958, 1960 ; non-playing captain, 1962, 1972.

## SMITH, Horton (b 1908)

Won U.S. Masters in its first year, 1934, and again in 1936. Ryder Cup team, 1929, 1933, 1935. Of Horton Smith in his heyday, Bernard Darwin wrote: "The United States have sent us a number of great putters from whom to choose models, but I am disposed to doubt if they have sent a better than Horton Smith."

## SMITH, Joan (b 1947)

Scottish Ladies' Champion, 1968. Scottish Girls' Champion, 1964, 1965.

## SMITH, Lancy (b 1950)
American Curtis Cup team, 1972.

## SMITH, Macdonald (1890-1949)
Born Carnoustie, Angus. Younger brother of Willie and Alex Smith, both U.S. Open Champions. Tied U.S. Open Championship, 1910, with Alex Smith and John McDermott, but lost play-off; runner-up to Bobby Jones, 1930. Runner-up, also to Bobby Jones, British Open Championship, 1930, and to Gene Sarazen, 1932. Canadian Open Champion, 1926.

In the 1925 British Open at Prestwick, MacSmith, as he was called, finally needed a 78 to win and a 79 to tie. Unfortunately for him the huge crowds were very unruly and, so he later told J. H. Taylor, "not once was he allowed the opportunity of seeing the result of his longer shots or given the quiet meditative period between strokes, which is so essential when one is trying to build up a respectable score". The result was that he finished in 82, being beaten into fourth place. This was the last time that the Open was staged at historic Prestwick.

See SMITH, WILLIE AND ALEX.

## SMITH, Margaret ('Wiffi') (b 1937)
American. British Ladies' Champion, 1956. French Ladies' Open Champion, 1956. U.S. Girls' Amateur Champion, 1954. Curtis Cup team, 1956. Her nickname, given to her as a child in Mexico, is a Mexican-Indian word meaning roughly 'Felicity'.

## SMITH, William Dickson (b 1918)
Scottish Amateur Champion, 1958. Portuguese Open Amateur Champion, 1967, 1970. Won Worplesdon Mixed Foursomes, with Mrs Betty Singleton, 1957; runners-up, 1958. Walker Cup team, 1959.

## SMITH, Willie and Alex
Two Carnoustie-born professionals who figured in the early U.S. Open Championships; their younger brother was Macdonald Smith. Willie won the 1899 championship and was runner-up to brother Alex, 1906 and to Fred McLeod, 1908. Alex was runner-up, 1898, 1901 (after a tie with Willie Anderson) and 1905 (again to Willie Anderson) and champion in 1906 (Willie being runner-up) and 1910 (after a tie with brother Macdonald and John J. McDermott, the native-born professional who was to win the next two U.S. Opens).

Alex Smith was noted as a very quick putter and is said to have coined the famous phrase 'Miss 'em quick!' also attributed to George Duncan, another celebrated quick putter.

## SMOLLETT ON GOLF
Tobias Smollett (1721-1771) has this to say about golf at Leith, Edinburgh, in his famous novel, *Humphrey Clinker* (1771):

In the fields called the Links, the citizens of Edinburgh divert themselves at a game called Golf, in which they use a curious kind of bats tipped with horn, and small elastic balls of leather, stuffed with feathers. . . . These they strike with such force and dexterity from one hole to another, that they fly to an incredible distance. Of this diversion the Scots are so fond that, when the weather will permit, you may see a multitude of all ranks, from the senator of justice to the lowest tradesman, mingled together, in their shirts, and following the balls with the utmost eagerness.

## SMOTHER
A ball is said to be smothered when the player—usually by swaying forward—causes it to be struck feebly along the ground. The ball is, as it were, stifled or suffocated—the normal meaning of the word.

## SNAP HOOK
See DUCK HOOK.

## SNEAD, Jesse Carlyle (b 1941)
Nephew of Sam Snead (*below*).
Runner-up, U.S. Masters, 1973. Ryder
Cup team, 1971, 1973, 1975.

## SNEAD, Samuel Jackson (b 1912)
One of golf's great characters, who
has won practically everything except
the U.S. Open Championship; runner-
up, 1937, 1947 (after tie with Lew
Worsham), 1949 (with Clayton Heaf-
ner), 1953. British Open Champion,
1946. Won U.S. Masters, 1949, 1952,
1954 (after tie with Ben Hogan);
runner-up, 1939, 1957. U.S.P.G.A.
Champion, 1942, 1949, 1951; runner-
up, 1938, 1940. World Senior Champion, 1964, 1965, 1970. Canadian Open
Champion, 1938, 1940, 1941; tied,
1969 (with Tommy Aaron), but lost
play-off. Ryder Cup team, 1937, 1947,
1949, 1951 (captain), 1953, 1955, 1959,
1969 (captain). Won World (formerly
Canada) Cup, 1956 (with Ben Hogan),
1960 (with Arnold Palmer), 1961 (with
Jimmy Demaret), 1962 (with Arnold
Palmer); runner-up, 1959 (with Cary
Middlecoff). Author of *How To Hit a
Golf Ball* (1950); *Natural Golf* (1954);
*Sam Snead on Golf* (1966).

## SNELL, David (b 1933)
British Professional Match Play
Champion, 1959. World (formerly
Canada) Cup team, 1965.

## 'SNIELER' NIBLICK
See RAY, EDWARD.

## SOCKETING
Also called shanking, this is one of
golf's deadliest ailments. It means
hitting the ball on the socket or
shank, where the shaft joins the clubhead, sending it off at an acute angle
to the right. One can speak (but not
too loud) of having a socket or a
shank. Chambers's Dictionary just
says "a stroke with the socket of a
golf club" and "an act of shanking
a golf ball"—but this is putting it
mildly. In rhyming slang, socket has
become 'Lucy Lockit'.

## SOMERVILLE, Charles Ross (b 1903)
U.S. Amateur Champion, 1932, the
only Canadian winner until Gary
Cowan (1966, 1971). Canadian Amateur Champion, 1926, 1928, 1930, 1931,
1935, 1937; runner-up, 1924, 1925,
1934, 1938.

## SORENSEN, Carol
See FLENNIKEN, MRS W. W.

## SOTA, Ramon (b 1940)
Spanish. French Open Champion,
1965. Portuguese Open Champion,
1963, 1969, 1970; tied with Angel
Miguel, 1964, but lost play-off. Spanish
Open Champion, 1963. Italian Open
Champion, 1971. Dutch Open Cham-
pion, 1971.

## SOUCHAK, Mike (b 1927)
Runner-up, U.S. Open Championship, 1960. Ryder Cup team, 1959,
1961.

## SOUTH AFRICA, GOLF IN
South Africa is one of the world's
keenest golfing countries and has
produced some fine golfers. Altogether in the Union there are some
200 clubs, great and small. The oldest
clubs are Royal Cape, founded at
Waterloo Green, Wynberg, in 1885,
and the Maritzburg Club at Pieter-
maritzburg, Natal, established in 1886.
Many other clubs were founded early
in the twentieth century, including the
9-holes course at Mafeking, which
dates from 1903, only three years after
the famous 'Relief of Mafeking' in
1900 during the Boer War.
Both the South African Open and
Amateur Championships began rather
unofficially in 1899 and, after being
interrupted by the Boer War, settled
down from 1902 onwards. The Ladies'
Championship dates from 1909 and
the Professional Match Play Championship from 1923, becoming the
South African Stroke Play Masters'
Tournament from 1960.
The name of A. D. ('Bobby')
Locke first appeared in the Amateur
Championship list in 1935, when he

was 18. It appeared again in 1937, while he won the Open Championship in the same two years as an amateur and then, as a professional, in 1938, 1939, 1940, 1946, 1950, 1951, 1955. From 1956 his natural successor was Gary Player, and other South African-born golfers who have made their mark include Clarence Olander, Jock Verwey (Gary Player's father-in-law), Harold Henning and his brothers, Graham and Alan, Dennis Hutchinson, and such new stars as Cobie Legrange, Teinie Britz and Dale Hayes, son of Otway Hayes.

Golfing affairs are looked after by the South African Golf Union, the South African Ladies' Golf Union and the South African Professional Golfers' Association.

## SOUTHERLY COURSE, WORLD'S MOST

See FALKLAND ISLANDS, GOLF IN THE.

## SOUTHERN HEMISPHERE, OLDEST CLUB IN THE

The Otago Club, Dunedin, in New Zealand's South Island, founded in 1871, can claim to be the oldest golf club in the Southern Hemisphere. See NEW ZEALAND, GOLF IN; OTAGO.

## SOUTHPORT AND AINSDALE

Southport, Lancashire. Founded 1907. Linksland with high sand hills and deep bunkers, including a famous one called 'Gumbleys'. Length: 6,883 yards. S.S.S. 74. Housed Ladies' Championship, 1936, and Ryder Cup matches, 1933, 1937.

## SOUTH YEMEN, PEOPLE'S REPUBLIC OF, GOLF IN

See ADEN, GOLF IN.

## SPADE MASHIE

The name formerly given to the club now called a No 6 Iron. See MASHIE.

## SPAIN, GOLF IN

When other continental countries were enjoying a golf boom in the years between the wars, Spain had the mis-

fortune to experience a devastating Civil War. Between 1936 and 1941 not only were no new courses built, but some were destroyed and very little golf played at all. Since the end of the Second World War, however, some old clubs have been re-established and new ones formed. Among the latter are the fine Costa del Sol courses—Sotogrande, Marbella (Golf Rio Real, Nueva Andalucia and Atalaya Park) and Guadalmina. Altogether there are some 40 clubs, golf affairs being run by the Spanish Golf Union.

The Spanish Open Amateur and Ladies' Open Championships date back to 1911; the Spanish Open Championship from 1912, the first winner being the ubiquitous Frenchman, Arnaud Massy. All the earlier championships were played at Madrid, but now Sotogrande and other new courses are being used. Spain has produced some fine golfers, among the amateurs being Javier and Luis Arana, who won eight amateur titles between them, and among the professionals Angel de la Torre, the brothers Sebastian and Angel Miguel, the Gallardo brothers and Ramon Sota and his nephews, Manuel and Severiano Ballesteros.

See CANARY ISLANDS, GOLF IN THE.

## SPEARMAN, Mrs Marley

See HARRIS, MRS MARLEY.

## SPLIT-HAND PUTTING METHOD

A putting style in which the hands are well separated on the shaft. The position of the right hand (in a right-handed golfer) can vary according to the personal preference of the player or according to the length of the putt, usually the shorter the putt the nearer the right hand to the head of the club. This is not a new method, but has been popularised in recent years by Paul Trevillion, the sports writer and cartoonist.

## SPOON

Robert Browning, the golf historian, says in *A History of Golf* (1955) that 'spoon', 'cleek' and 'bunker' are "taken from names familiar to Scottish domesticity". With the spoon—the equivalent of the modern No 3 or 4 wood—you 'spooned' the ball from a close lie on the fairway. In the old days there were several varieties of spoon. See BAFFY ; NAMES OF WOODEN CLUBS.

## SQUARE

A stroke that is played with the face of the club held, as far as physically possible, at right-angles to the line of flight before impact, at impact and through the ball.

## SQUARE STANCE

See STANCE.

## SQUIRRELL, Hew C. (b 1932)

Welsh Amateur Champion, 1958, 1959, 1960, 1964, 1965 ; runner-up, 1962, 1971.

## SRI LANKA, GOLF IN

In May, 1971, Ceylon became the Independent Republic of Sri Lanka after 157 years' link with Britain. Golf has been established there a long time, for the Royal Colombo Club was founded in 1882. The Amateur and Ladies' Championships date from 1920 and have continued to be held more or less alternately at Royal Colombo and Nuwara Eliya, familiar to generations of tea-planters.

W. P. Fernando has had a remarkable Amateur Championship record, winning nine times between 1947 and 1962 and being runner-up another seven times. The Sri Lanka Golf Union operates from Colombo.

## STABLEFORD

The Stableford system of scoring was invented by Dr Frank Stableford (1870-1959), a member of the Royal Liverpool and Wallasey Clubs, in 1931 and first used in a competition at Wallasey in May, 1932. It is a variation of the older bogey competition, players scoring points for each hole instead of counting the number

of holes up or down against bogey. The reckoning is as follows:

For hole done in one over fixed score—1 point.

For hole done in fixed score—2 points.

For hole done in one under fixed score—3 points.

For hole done in two under fixed score—4 points.

For hole done in three under fixed score—5 points.

No points are scored for any hole done in more than one over the fixed score. Any hole for which a competitor makes no return is regarded as scoring no points.

In a Stableford single each player receives 7/8ths of his handicap, taken at the appropriate holes. In a Stableford foursome, the partners received 7/16ths of their combined handicaps.

In all other respects, the rules for stroke play apply.

See BOGEY (OR PAR) COMPETITION.

## STACY, Hollis (b 1954)

U.S. Girls' Junior Amateur Champion, 1969, 1970, 1971. Curtis Cup team, 1972.

## STANCE

"Taking the 'stance' consists in a player placing his feet in position for and preparatory to making a stroke" (Rules of Golf Definition).

There are only three basic stances —the square, the open and the closed. Ben Hogan summarises them as simply as possible in *Power Golf* (1949): "In the square stance both feet are equidistant from an imaginary line which should parallel the intended line of flight. In the open stance your left foot is slightly withdrawn from the imaginary line parallel to the intended line of flight. For a closed stance your right foot is dropped back slightly from the imaginary line parallel to the intended line of flight."

One also talks of an uphill stance, with the left foot higher than the right, and a downhill stance, with the left foot lower than the right.

## STANDARD SCRATCH SCORE

"The score in which a scratch player is expected to go round the course, playing from the medal tees, in summer conditions" *(The Standard Scratch Score and Handicapping Scheme,* prepared by the Council of National Golf Unions). "The Standard Scratch Score is fixed for the round and must not be allocated among the individual holes, but should be printed as a total on the card. In addition, the par figures for each hole should be printed on the card ... The total of the par figures for each hole of a course will not necessarily coincide with the Standard Scratch Score, although in many cases it will." Par is "the score in which a first-class player should play a hole in summer conditions".

The basic Standard Scratch Score of each course is fixed according to the length of the course. For a normal course of 6,300 yards, the basic Standard Scratch Score is 70. One stroke will be added or one stroke will be deducted for each 200 yards by which the length of a course exceeds or falls short of 6,300 yards. As all courses are not of these standard lengths, the basic Standard Scratch Scores for these standard lengths will apply also to courses which measure within 100 yards more or within 100 yards less than the standard lengths mentioned.

The following table will fix the basic Standard Scratch Score of each course:

| Standard Length of Course Yards | Lengths Included in Standard Length Yards | Basic Standard Scratch Score |
|---|---|---|
| 7,100 | 7,001-7,200 | 74 |
| 6,900 | 6,801-7,000 | 73 |
| 6,700 | 6,601-6,800 | 72 |
| 6,500 | 6,401-6,600 | 71 |
| 6,300 | 6,201-6,400 | 70 |
| 6,100 | 6,001-6,200 | 69 |
| 5,900 | 5,801-6,000 | 68 |
| 5,700 | 5,601-5,800 | 67 |
| 5,500 | 5,401-5,600 | 66 |
| 5,300 | 5,201-5,400 | 65 |
| 5,100 | 5,001-5,200 | 64 |
| 4,900 | 4,801-5,000 | 63 |

Measurements are taken "by chain along the middle of the fairways from a point six feet in front of the back of the standard medal tee to the centre of the green of each hole. In the case of holes with steep slopes or where a deep valley is crossed, the measurement shall be by projection (plan measurement). It is recommended that on all courses permanent markers be placed six feet from the back of each medal tee to mark the point from which the measurement has been taken."

See COURSE VALUE ; PAR.

## STATION-MASTER'S GARDEN

For many years, golfers on the Old Course at St Andrews sliced their drives at the 17th (Road Hole) over a fence into the St Andrews Station-Master's garden. Eventually the garden disappeared, to be replaced by a number of ugly black sheds. Now these have also gone to make room for a British Railways hotel, the windows being guarded by wire netting, so that instead of going out of bounds the slicer has a chance of bouncing back into play. See ROYAL AND ANCIENT GOLF CLUB OF ST ANDREWS.

## STEAL

A term no longer in use, meaning to hole an unexpected putt, the ball only just reaching the hole. The word was also used as a noun in such phrases as "he holed a long steal." A ball that went in travelling fast was called a 'gobble'.

## STEAMY

A word indicating that a putt has been hit too hard and the ball has run well past the hole, in such phrases as: "That was a bit steamy, wasn't it?" See MERRY.

## STEEL SHAFTS

In November 1929 steel shafts were made legal in Britain by the R. and A.

in these words: "The Rules of Golf Committee have decided that steel shafts, as approved by the Rules of Golf Committee, are declared to conform with the requirements of the clause in the Rules of Golf on the form and make of golf clubs." The R. and A. followed the example of the U.S.G.A., which had allowed steel-shafted putters in 1924.

Experiments with steel shafts were going on in the 1890s, particularly by Thomas Horsburgh, an amateur, and Willie Dunn, Jun., a professional. Horsburgh, an Edinburgh blacksmith, forged himself a set of steel-shafted clubs and played with them at the Baberton Club, of which he had become a founder member in 1893. He found them so good that he took out a patent in 1894 for an invention relating "to the use of steel shafts for golf clubs for the purpose of giving strength and elasticity". Although professionals and clubmakers showed interest, steel shafts were not allowed, and by the time they were, 35 years later, Thomas Horsburgh had let his patent lapse—so possibly lost a fortune. Several of his clubs are in a showcase in the Baberton clubhouse.

A little later than Horsburgh's experiments, Willie Dunn had tried inserting thin steel rods into split-cane shafts, to give them added strength, but nothing came of it.

An article in the Tube Investments' magazine, January-February, 1972, tells how Sidney Alphonse Saunders, in 1912 'in an obscure corner' of Accles and Pollock's works, produced the first tapered, seamless steel shafts. War intervened after specification was accepted on 27th November, 1913, and only a few clubs were made. The R. and A. refused to recognise them, but exports were successfully made to the United States and Canada.

In 1929 the Sandwell Park Club, West Bromwich, permitted the use of steel shafts in competitions and a set of steel-shafted clubs were presented to the then Prince of Wales, who played with them on the Old Course, St Andrews. The R. and A. either had

to disqualify the Prince or legalise steel shafts. By the end of the year the battle was over, by which time Americans were using them freely, partly through the shortage of hickory.

See ALUMINIUM SHAFTS ; DUNN, WILLIE.

### STEPHEN, Alexander R, ('Sandy') (b 1954)

Scottish Amateur Champion, 1971, the youngest winner. Scottish Boys' Champion, 1970.

### STEPHENS, Frances

See SMITH, MRS FRANCES.

### STEWART, John Campbell

Captain J. C. Stewart of Fasnacloich, partnered by George Glennie, won for the Royal Blackheath Club the first inter-club foursomes competition in 1857 at St Andrews, beating the R. and A. pair in the final. In 1853 he played a halved match on level terms with the great professional, Allan Robertson. In the same year his score of 90 beat the previous record of 99 in the R. and A. King William IV Gold Medal, being beaten two years later by the 88 of his partner, George Glennie.

When he went to India with his regiment, an old St Andrews member exclaimed: "It is a shame for a man with such powers to go out to India!"

See GLENNIE, GEORGE ; INTER-CLUB FOURSOMES, FIRST.

### STEWART, Rufus (b 1893)

Australian Open Champion, 1927 ; runner-up, 1926, 1928, 1929, 1930. Australian Professional Champion, 1929 ; runner-up, 1930.

### STILL, Ken (b 1935)

Ryder Cup team, 1969.

### STIRLING, Alexa

See FRASER, ALEXA STIRLING.

## STOCKTON, DAVID ('DAVE') (b 1942)

U.S.P.G.A. Champion, 1970, 1976. Ryder Cup team, 1971.

## STOREY, Edward Francis ('Eustace') (b 1901)

Runner-up, British Amateur Championship, 1924. Won Worplesdon Mixed Foursomes, with Mrs Percy Garon, 1938, and with Miss Wanda Morgan, 1948. Walker Cup team, 1924, 1926, 1928.

## STOUGHTON

An improved type of gutta-percha ball, pink in colour, introduced early in the twentieth century. Soon all 'gutties', however, were superseded by the rubber-cored Haskell ball. See BALL, MAKES OF ; HASKELL BALL.

## STOWE, Charles (b 1909)

Runner-up, English Amateur Championship, 1937, 1949. English Open Amateur Stroke Play Champion (Brabazon Trophy), 1948, 1953. Walker Cup team, 1938, 1947.

## STRANAHAN, Frank R. (b 1922)

British Amateur Champion, 1948, 1950; runner-up, 1952. Runner-up, British Open Championship, 1947, 1953. Runner-up, U.S. Amateur Championship, 1950. Canadian Amateur Champion, 1947, 1948. Mexican Amateur Champion, 1948, 1951. Walker Cup team, 1947, 1949, 1951. Turned professional, 1954.

## STRATH, Andrew (1836-68) and David (1840-79)

Andrew was born at St Andrews. British Open Champion, 1865 ; runner-up, 1864. His younger brother, David, was born at St Andrews, but died in Melbourne, where he had gone on a voyage for his health. Tied British Open Championship in 1876 with Bob Martin, but after it was alleged that he had played to the 17th green before the players in front had left it, he refused to compete in the play-off and the title went to Martin.

David Strath was a close friend of 'Young Tommy' Morris and played a number of challenge matches both against him and in partnership with him. Andrew was professional and greenkeeper at Prestwick, David at North Berwick. Another brother, George, was professional at Troon from 1881 to 1887.

## STREIT, Mrs Marlene Stewart (b 1934)

Born Marlene Stewart. British Ladies' Champion, 1953. U.S. Ladies' Champion, 1956. She was the first Canadian to win either title. Canadian Ladies' Open Champion, 1951, 1954, 1955, 1956, 1958, 1959, 1963, 1968, 1969, 1972, 1973. Canadian Ladies' Close Champion, seven years running between 1951 and 1957 and again in 1963, 1968. Australian Ladies' Champion, 1963.

## STROKE

"The forward movement of the club made with the intention of fairly striking at and moving the ball" (Rules of Golf Definition). Also the handicapping system in golf—i.e. the better player gives the less good player one, two or more 'strokes' in the round, the holes where strokes are given or received being set out on the score-card. See STROKE INDEX.

## STROKE HOLE

A hole at which a player either gives or receives a stroke.

## STROKE INDEX

On the card of the course, the stroke index shows the holes at which strokes are given or received in match play, from one stroke upwards. The sequence is decided by the club committee with the object of apportioning the strokes as fairly as possible ; in most cases the strokes are divided evenly between the two halves of 9 holes.

## STROKE PLAY

Also called Medal Play. The form of golf in which the winner is the player who holes the course in the least number of strokes. See MATCH PLAY.

## STROKE PLAY, FIRST RECORDS OF

Originally golf was purely a match-play game, man against man or, in foursomes, two men against two men. In the first recorded competition—in April 1744 for the Silver Club of the Honourable Company of Edinburgh Golfers—the conditions provided that the players should go out in parties of two or "of threes if their number should be great", the winner being the player who had won the greatest number of holes.

Some idea of how the competition was actually decided is given in the following clause taken from the Minute Book of the St Andrews Club, which in 1754 followed the Edinburgh golfers in arranging a Silver Club competition: "After the figures are drawn, the set or match beginning with No 1, etc., shall go out first, with a clerk to mark down every stroke each of them shall take to every hole...And when the match is ended... then a scrutiny of the whole clerks' books or jottings is to be made, and the player who shall appear to have won the greatest number of holes shall be declared the winner."

Clearly this method of scoring was very complicated and in a Minute dated 9th May 1759 we find: "In order to remove all disputes and inconveniences with regard to the gaining of the Silver Club, it is enacted and agreed by the captain and the gentlemen golfers present, that in all time coming whoever puts in the ball at the fewest strokes over the field, being 22 holes, shall be declared and sustained victor." This was stroke (or medal) play as we know it today. The first winner was Sir James Carnegie. See EIGHTEEN HOLES, WHY; MATCH PLAY; STROKE PLAY.

## STUART, Hugh B. (b 1942)

Scottish Amateur Champion, 1972; runner-up, 1970. Scottish Boys' Champion, 1959. Walker Cup team, 1971.

## STYLE

A golfer's style is the way in which he plays; it may be good, bad or indifferent, but is peculiar to him alone.

## STYMIE

A stymie occurs when your opponent's ball lies on the green between your ball and the hole, the balls being more than 6 inches apart; a half-stymie occurs when your line is partly blocked. Apart from a year between 1833 and 1834, stymies were allowed until 1951, when the R. and A. and U.S.G.A. abolished them. The stymie rule held good for match play only.

Probably derived from the old Scottish word 'styme', meaning a minimum, as in the phrase 'not to see a styme'—not to be able to see at all. In one of his poems Robert Burns wrote:

I've seen me daez't upon a time
I scarce could wink or see a styme.

Another suggested derivation is the Dutch phrase *stuit mij*, meaning 'it stops me', but there is no evidence that it was used in any Dutch game; compare also the Gaelic *stigh mi*, meaning 'inside me'.

The '6 inches apart' qualification dates from 1789 at St Andrews, a Minute of 8th October reading: "The Society resolve that in all time coming, in the course of playing over the links, any ball shall lye in the way of his opponent at the distance of six inches upon the hole green [*sic*], it shall be in the power of the party playing to cause his opponent to remove said ball. And this resolution to continue in force till altered by the Society."

## STYMIES, FAMOUS

Before they were abolished in 1951, stymies have often influenced match-play results. In Bobby Jones's 'Grand Slam' year of 1930, his opponent in the semi-final of the British Amateur Championship at St Andrews, Cyril Tolley, laid himself a stymie at the 19th hole. In the final of the 1936

American Amateur Championship at Garden City, Johnny Fischer laid Jack M'Lean, who was one up, a dead stymie on the 34th green—and went on to win at the 37th. G. P. Roberts won the 1951 English Amateur Championship at Hunstanton by laying Harry Bennett a stymie at the 39th after they had been all square coming off the 38th green. In the 1951 Walker Cup match at Royal Birkdale, Ronnie White, laid a stymie by Charles Coe on the 7th green, successfully lofted the ball into the hole. There have, of course, been many more instances.

## SUCKER
See PLUGGED BALL.

## 'SUCKER'S SIDE'
See PROFESSIONAL SIDE OF THE HOLE.

## SUDAN, GOLF IN THE
Although not to the same extent as it was during the British occupation, golf is still played in the Sudan. The Khartoum Club was established as long ago as 1904 and there is also a club at Atbara, on the Nile north of Khartoum.

The Sudan has bred some fine golfers, one of whom, Hassan Hassanein, won the French Open Championship, 1951, played in the British Open Championship and other tournaments in the 1950s and won the Egyptian Open Championship four times running, 1949-52.

## SUDDEN DEATH
See PLAY-OFF.

## SUGGS, Louise (b 1923)
U.S. Ladies' Champion, 1947. U.S. Women's Open Champion, 1949, 1952; runner-up, 1951, 1955, 1958, 1959, 1963. British Ladies' Champion, 1948. Curtis Cup team, 1948. Turned professional, 1948. Author of *Par Golf For Women* (1953); editor of *Golf For Women* (1960).

## SUMATRA, GOLF IN
See INDONESIA, GOLF IN.

## SUNNINGDALE
Sunningdale, Berkshire. Old Course founded 1900. One of England's finest pine, heather and gorse courses. Length: 6,490 yards. S.S.S. 70. In qualifying for the 1926 Open Championship, Bobby Jones had his famous round of 33:33-66 at Sunningdale. Housed Ladies' Championship, 1956; E.G.U. Brabazon Trophy, 1953. Also Sunningdale Open Foursomes annually since 1934. Also New Course (6,527 yards: S.S.S. 71).

## SUNNINGDALE OPEN FOURSOMES
This popular match-play tournament was founded at the Sunningdale Club, Berkshire, in 1934. Professionals play off plus two, amateurs off scratch and ladies off six. Any combination of players is allowed.

Ladies have often done well. The first winners were Miss Diana Fishwick (Mrs Critchley) and Noel Layton, and in the next two years (1935, 1936) the winners were Miss Joyce Wethered (Lady Heathcoat-Amory) and J. S. F. Morrison.

Perhaps the most remarkable win was that of 15-year-old Warren Humphreys and 19-year-old John Davies, of the Royal Mid-Surrey Club, who beat Max Faulkner and Brian Barnes in the 1968 final by 6 and 4.

## SUNNINGDALE SCORING
This is a system of scoring in informal match play, intended to make the game as close as possible. The players start level, but if one becomes two holes up, he gives his opponent a stroke at the next hole. If they halve this hole, a stroke is again given at the next hole; if the receiver of the stroke wins, they play the next hole level; if the giver of the stroke wins again, he still gives one stroke at the next hole. He never gives more than one stroke. Normally, when using the Sunningdale system, the game goes to the last hole—but it should not really be necessary if both players are play-

ing reasonably to their respective handicaps. See SUNNINGDALE.

## SWAZILAND, GOLF IN

There are seven clubs in this former High Commission Territory, in South Africa, now an independent kingdom. Three are near the capital, Mbabane, including the 18-holes Royal Swazi Club.

## SWEDEN, GOLF IN

Golf came to Sweden in the early years of the twentieth century, as it did to many other countries. The Gothenburg Club was founded in 1902, the Stockholm Club in 1904, the Falsterbo Club in 1909. Many of Sweden's 90 clubs were born between the wars and there have been many new ones since the end of the Second World War, including several more Stockholm courses.

The most northerly course is that of the Boden Club, founded in 1936, but not completed until after the war; it holds an annual 'Midnight Sun' tournament.

The Swedish Open Amateur Championship dates from 1909 and the Ladies' Open Championship from 1910. From 1956 they were incorporated in the Scandinavian Open Amateur and Ladies' Open Championships respectively. Mrs Michael Bonallack has the distinction of winning both the last Swedish Ladies' and the first Scandinavian Ladies' Championships. Miss Liv Forsell has won the event six times in the last nine years. The Swedish Golf Union operates from Stockholm.

## SWEENY, Robert (b 1911)

American. British Amateur Champion, 1937; runner-up, 1946. Runner-up, to Arnold Palmer, U.S. Amateur Championship, 1954. Won *Golf Illustrated* Gold Vase, 1937.

## SWEET SPOT

Every club is said to have a 'sweet spot' in its hitting surface; if you can hit the ball exactly with this spot, the chances are that the shot will be a good one. It really means hitting the ball in the middle of the club-face and not towards the toe or heel.

## SWEETSER, Jess W. (b 1898)

American. U.S. Amateur Champion, 1922; runner-up, 1923. British Amateur Champion, 1926. Walker Cup team, 1922, 1923, 1924, 1926, 1928, 1932.

## SWILCAN BURN

This most famous of golf links burns—also spelt Swilkin or Swilken in the old days—runs in front of the first green on the Old Course, St Andrews, and has to be crossed again at the beginning of the 18th fairway.

Under the name of the "Swilcanthe burn", it is mentioned in a book as early as 1863, and W. T. Linkskill, referring to the early 1870s, when he played with 'Young Tommy' Morris, said: "The historic Swilcan burn formerly swept almost into the centre of the links before it turned into the sea, and one often drove into this bed from the first tee. It was then a sandy natural hazard, but now is a concrete walled channel."

In *The Golf Courses of the British Isles* (1910), Bernard Darwin wrote:

It is an inglorious little stream enough: we could easily jump over it were we not afraid of looking foolish if we fell in, and yet it catches an amazing number of balls. It is now part of golfing history that when Mr Leslie Balfour-Melville won the Amateur Championship he beat successively at the 19th hole Mr W. Greig, Mr Laurence Auchterlonie and Mr John Ball, and all three of these redoubtable persons plumped the ball into this apparently paltry little streamlet with their approach shots.

In modern times one's ball is at least easy to find in the clear water—and long-poled nets are handy for the purpose of fishing the ball out. From the earliest days, however, to lift and drop behind the Swilcan entails a penalty stroke.

R

See LINKSKILL, W. T.; ROYAL AND ANCIENT GOLF CLUB OF ST ANDREWS.

## SWING

"The sweep of a golf club" (Chambers's Dictionary). A golfer refers to his 'swing' or is said to have a good (or bad) swing; or be a good (or bad) swinger.

## SWING WEIGHT

A term used by golf club manufacturers to indicate the constancy of weight, balance and any other factors that might contribute towards an exactly matched set. See SET.

## SWIPE

An old-fashioned word originally meaning a full shot with a driver, but later adapted to mean a violent blow with any club. As far back as the mid-eighteenth century, Dr Alexander Carlyle was described as 'a mighty swiper'. See MOLESEY HURST, GOLF AT.

## SWITZERLAND, GOLF IN

In spite of the fact that golf on many courses is restricted to a season between May or even June to September or October, the game is firmly established. And there are courses—at the Lugano Club, the Basle Country Club, the Golf de Geneve, the Dolder and Zurich Clubs at Zurich, etc.—where golf is possible almost all the year. Altogether there are 30 clubs, 11 of which are actually situated in the Alps, including the Engadine Club, St Moritz, and the Crans-sur-Sierre Club, over 5,000 feet above sea level, where the Swiss Open Championship has been held since 1948.

The Swiss Open Amateur and Ladies' Open Championships both date from 1907, the winner of the latter in its first three years being the famous Lady Margaret Scott (by then Lady Margaret Hamilton Russell), winner of the first three British Ladies' Championships, 1893-5. The Swiss Open Championship dates from 1923, the National Amateur Championship from 1925, the Professional Championship from 1926 and the National Ladies' Championship from 1958. Golf affairs are run by the Swiss Golf Association. See BARRAS, OLIVIER.

## 'SYNDICATE'

American golfers sometimes add to the gambling in a four-ball match by playing 'syndicates'—a 'syndicate' being won by the player who has the lowest score in his playing group on a single hole. See 'GREENIE'; 'NASSAU'.

## TAIT, Frederick Guthrie (1870-1900)

British Amateur Champion, 1896, 1898 ; runner-up, 1899. Leading amateur in the British Open Championship, 1894, 1896, 1899 ; he was third overall in the 1896 and 1897 Opens. Killed in Boer War, leading his company of the Black Watch.

'Freddie' Tait, as everybody called him, was a great match-player and one of the most popular golfers in the country. His father, Professor of Natural Philosophy at Edinburgh University, made many experiments into the flight—he called it the 'dynamics'—of the golf ball ; 'Freddie' was a valuable helper as he had driven a gutty ball at St Andrews 280 yards, all carry, and was said to have driven a ball at the 14th hole 341 yards. John Low wrote a book about him entitled *F. G. Tait: A Record* (1901). See DRIVES WITH 'GUTTY', LONGEST ; GOLF BALL, VELOCITY OF.

## TAIWAN, GOLF IN

This is the island that used to be known as Formosa, some 90 miles east of the Chinese mainland, and on which General Chiang Kai-shek set up the 'Government of the Republic of China' in 1949. Before this time golf was unknown on the island, but now there are 15 courses and some 15,000 golfers.

In a remarkably short space of time Taiwan has produced some world-class players. In the 1968 World (formerly Canada) Cup, at Olgiata, Rome, the Taiwan couple—Hsieh Yung-Yo and Lu Liang-Huan —filled fourth place behind Canada, the United States and Italy. Hsieh's individual score was 70, 75, 71, 74 and Lu's 69, 69, 72, 76, for a total of 576, only seven strokes behind Canada's winning total.

In 1964 Hsieh's cousin, Hsieh Min-Nam, won the Italian Open Amateur Championship and in the same year had the best individual score in the World Cup (formerly Eisenhower Trophy), which was also played at Olgiata. In 1971 Lu Liang-Huan ('Mr Lu') was runner-up to Lee Trevino in the British Open Championship. See LU LIANG-HUAN.

## TAKE-AWAY

The initial movement, normally made with the hands, in taking the club back in the back-swing. In Ben Hogan's words, "the hands start the clubhead back a split second before the arms start back, and the arms begin their movement a split second before the shoulders begin to turn".

## TAKE TURF

To remove a small quantity of turf in making a stroke, normally with an iron club, off the fairway. A stroke that removed more turf than was necessary would be called 'taking too much turf'. A stroke with an iron club could, of course, be made without taking any turf at all, but this is more commonly done with a wooden club. See DIVOT.

## TAKOURA

T'hami el Glaoui, the famous Pasha of Marrakesh, in the Atlas Mountains of Morocco—he was a friend of Winston Churchill—was a keen golfer and built a course at Marrakesh. According to Gavin Maxwell's book, *Lords of the Atlas* (1966), when visitors expressed surprise at his skill as a golfer, he would reply: "Golf is not a new game to me. When

I was a boy in the mountains I used to play a game called takoura, which was very much the same. We used to play it on *jol* (pebble desert) with a stick whittled from an oak branch and a wooden ball." See CAMBUCA ; CHOLE ; CROSSE ; MOROCCO, GOLF IN ; PAGANICA.

## TANZANIA, GOLF IN

Since the union of Tanganyika and Zanzibar in 1962, golf has continued to be very popular. There are 18-holes courses at the Dar-es-Salaam and Tabora Clubs and 9-holes courses at the Bukoba Club (Lake Victoria), the English Club (Zanzibar), the Iringa Club and the Tanga Gymkhana Club, from which the Tanzania Golf Union operates. The Tanzania (formerly Tanganyika) Amateur Championship has been played for since 1950. See VICTORIA FALLS, BALL DRIVEN ACROSS.

## TAYLOR, Dr Frank (b 1926)

Runner-up, U.S. Amateur Championship, 1957. Walker Cup team, 1957, 1959, 1961.

## TAYLOR, John Henry (1871-1963)

Born and died at Northam, North Devon. One of the immortal Triumvirate of Vardon, Taylor and Braid, who won 16 British Open Championships between them. British Open Champion, 1894, 1895, 1900, 1909, 1913 ; runner-up, 1896 (after tie with Harry Vardon), 1904, 1905, 1906, 1907, 1914. Runner-up, U.S. Open Championship, 1900. French Open Champion, 1908, 1909. German Open Champion, 1912. British Professional Match Play Champion, 1904, 1908 ; runner-up, 1907. Non-playing captain, Ryder Cup team, 1933.

He was a moving spirit in the foundation of the Professional Golfers' Association in 1901 ; he was also largely responsible for the creation of the two public courses in Richmond Park, both of which he designed ; and —looking back to his early days as a member of the Northam Working Men's Golf Club—he did much to encourage artisan golf clubs. He was the first chairman of the National Association of Public Golf Courses.

Of J. H. Taylor, while he was still alive, Bernard Darwin wrote: "There has been no more remarkable man and golfer. The story of J. H.'s life might be called, like that of the Mayor of Casterbridge, the 'Story of a Man of Character'. For almost innumerable years he has been the acknowledged head of his profession and it is due to him, more than to any other man, that the profession has climbed so far above its old unsatisfactory condition. He is a natural speaker, a natural fighter, a natural leader, who would have made his mark in any walk of life." As a golfer he was renowned for his iron play, particularly with the mashie (now called the No 5 iron), of which he was the virtual inventor.

He did a good deal of golf-course architecture, including Royal Birkdale's present course. He was professional in his early days at Burnham and Winchester, but his name was mainly associated with the Royal Mid-Surrey Club, Richmond, Surrey, to which he was attached from 1899 until his retirement. Author of *Taylor on Golf* (1902) ; *Golf: My Life's Work* (1943).

See BRAID, JAMES ; VARDON, HARRY.

## TEE, ORIGIN OF WORD

This is one of golf's mysteries. In his *Concise Etymological Dictionary,* Professor Ernest Weekley says that the golf 'tee' is apparently distinct from other meanings of the word, including the "mark aimed at (curling, bowls, quoits)". The golf historian, Robert Browning, points out in *A History of Golf* (1955), however, that the original codes of rules laid down that "your tee must be upon the ground" and that "you must tee your ball not nearer the hole than two club-lengths, nor further distance from it than four".

In other words, the putting green was also the teeing ground and the player had to tee his ball in the space between two imaginary circles drawn round the hole. "This," he says, "presents an obvious similarity to the *tee* in curling, though there the tee is the centre of the concentric circles which curlers call 'the house', and which is the target in which they try to bring their stones to rest. The curling *tee* is almost certainly from the Gaelic *tigh,* meaning a house, and I imagine that the golf tee is the same." The difference is that in curling you enter the house, in golf you leave it!

Originally, therefore, the golfer's tee did not refer to the pinch of sand or the modern peg on which the ball is placed, but only to the area from which the player drove off.

Another suggested derivation is from the Dutch word 'tuitje', meaning a small heap of earth ; it is known that in the old Belgian and French game of Chole, the ball was placed for the first stroke on a heap of earth or, in winter, hard snow.

See CHOLE ; PEG TEES ; RULES, FIRST CODE OF (clauses I and II).

## TEEING

"In 'teeing', the ball may be placed on the ground or on sand or other substance to raise it off the ground" (Rules of Golf Definition). Normally, of course, nowadays a plastic or wooden peg tee is used.

### TEEING GROUND

"The starting place for the hole to be played. It is a rectangular area of two club-lengths in depth, the front and the sides of which are defined by the outside limits of two markers. A ball is outside the teeing ground when all of it lies outside the stipulated area" (Rules of Golf Definition).

The phrase is shortened to 'tee'.

See RULES OF GOLF, Rules 12, 13 ; RULES, FIRST CODE OF, clauses I and II ; TEE, ORIGIN OF WORD.

### TELEVISION, FIRST USE IN OPEN CHAMPIONSHIPS

The first year that there was television coverage of the U.S. Open Championship was 1954, when Jack Fleck beat Ben Hogan in a play-off at the Olympic Country Club, San Francisco. The first British coverage was in 1957, when Bobby Locke won at St Andrews.

## TEMPO

A term meaning the correct timing and rhythm that make for a successful shot. It is Tony Jacklin's watchword that he always tries to keep in mind. On the last day of the 1970 U.S. Open Championship, which he won, when he opened his locker he found that his American friends, Bert Yancey and Tom Weiskopf, had pinned a note inside consisting of the one word— 'Tempo'.

## TERMS USED IN RECKONING

"The reckoning of holes is kept by the terms: so many 'holes up' or 'all square', and so many 'to play'. A side is 'dormie' when it is as many holes up as there are holes remaining to be played" (Rules of Golf Definition). See DORMIE ; MATCH PLAY.

## TEXAS WEDGE

The putter, when used for approaching, is so called after its successful employment by Ben Hogan and other famous American golfers from Texas. See MUSSELBURGH IRON.

## THAILAND, GOLF IN

Golf has been played a surprisingly long time in Thailand, the Royal Bangkok Sports Club having been founded in 1890 ; its first clubhouse was adapted from an ancient temple.

Bangkok has two other clubs— Royal Dusit and the Royal Thai Air Force Club—and there is the Hua Hin Country Club at a seaside resort some 140 miles from the capital.

In the 1969 World (formerly Canada) Cup at the Singapore Island Club, the Thai pair, Sukree Onsham and Suchin Suwanapong, finished equal fourth with Taiwan (Nationalist China) on 562. In the individual scores Sukree Onsham shared third place on 277 with Orville Moody, Hsieh Yung-Yo of Taiwan and Takaaki Kono of Japan.

### THIRLWELL, Alan (b 1928)
Runner-up, British Amateur Championship, 1958, 1972. English Amateur Champion, 1954, 1955; runner-up, 1963. Walker Cup team, 1957.

### THOM, Kenneth Gordon (b 1922)
Runner-up, English Amateur Championship, 1946. Runner-up, British Boys' Championship, 1939. Walker Cup team, 1949. Now runs a golf school in London.

### THOMAS, David C. (b 1934)
Tied, British Open Championship, 1958, with Peter Thomson, losing play-off; joint runner-up, with Doug Sanders, 1966. French Open Champion, 1959. Belgian Open Champion, 1955. Dutch Open Champion, 1958. British Professional Match Play Champion, 1963. Ryder Cup team, 1959, 1963, 1965, 1967. Represented Wales in World (formerly Canada) Cup, 1957, 1958, 1959, 1960, 1961, 1962, 1963, 1966, 1967, 1969. Turned professional, 1949. Author of *Instructions to Young Golfers* (1959); *Modern Golf* (1967).

### THOMPSON, Bertha (Mrs Walker) (b 1881)
British Ladies' Champion, 1905; runner-up, 1906.

### THOMSON, Hector (b 1913)
British Amateur Champion, 1936. Scottish Amateur Champion, 1935; runner-up, 1939. Irish Open Amateur Champion, 1934, 1935. Scottish Professional Champion, 1953; runner-up, 1950. Walker Cup team, 1936, 1938. Turned professional, 1940.

### THOMSON, James (b 1908)
Son of Wilfred Thomson, the North Berwick professional. Went to America and was runner-up, U.S. Open Championship, 1935. Runner-up,

U.S.P.G.A. Championship, 1936. Runner-up, Canadian Open Championship, 1936. Famous as the longest hitter of his day.

### THOMSON, Lena (Mrs Charles Towne) (b 1875)
British Ladies' Champion, 1898; runner-up, 1896.

### THOMSON, Peter W. (b 1929)
British Open Champion—the first winner from Australia—1954, 1955. 1956, 1958 (after tie with David Thomas), 1965; runner-up, 1952, 1957. He was the first to win three times running since Bob Ferguson in 1880-82, Jamie Anderson in 1877-79 and Tommy Morris in 1868-70. Australian Open Champion, 1951, 1967, 1972; runner-up, 1950. Australian Professional Champion, 1967; runner-up, 1957, 1959, 1966. New Zealand Open Champion, 1950, 1951, 1953, 1959, 1960, 1961, 1965, 1971, 1972. New Zealand Professional Champion, 1953. Italian Open Champion, 1959. Spanish Open Champion, 1959. Runner-up, German Open Championship, 1971. British Professional Match Play Champion, 1954, 1961, 1966, 1967. With Kel Nagle, won World (formerly Canada) Cup, 1954, 1959; runners-up, 1961. Turned professional, 1949. Awarded M.B.E. for services to sport. Author of *This Wonderful World of Golf* (1969).
See BRITISH OPEN CHAMPION MORE THAN ONCE.

### THREE-BALL
See MATCHES, TYPES OF.

### THREESOME
See MATCHES, TYPES OF.

### THROUGH THE GREEN
See GREEN, THROUGH THE.

### TIES
See PLAY-OFF.

### TIGER
A complimentary name for a good

golfer; the opposite of rabbit. Hence 'tiger tees' for teeing grounds set well back to give the maximum length to the hole. See RABBIT; TIGER COUNTRY.

## TIGER COUNTRY
Any area of the course where the rough is particularly thick and like the jungle where, had it been in India, you might have expected to meet a tiger. The phrase has really no connection with the 'tiger', or expert player, because the inexperienced golfer, or 'rabbit', would be just as likely to get into 'tiger country'. Also just called 'jungle'. See RABBIT; TIGER.

## TIMING
A rather loose term used to indicate the combination of mind and muscle that brings about the best possible stroke under various circumstances. A well-timed shot is normally a good one, an ill-timed shot a bad one.

## TITTERTON, Maud (Mrs Jock Gibb)
British Ladies' Champion, 1908. Although born in England, she learnt her golf at Musselburgh in Scotland. She did not defend her title next year because of the illness of her fiancé and took little part in competitive golf again.

## TOBAGO, GOLF IN
The Tobago Club, Mount Irvine Bay, designed by John Harris, was opened in 1971. See WEST INDIES, GOLF IN THE.

## TOLLEY, Cyril James Hastings (1896-1978)
British Amateur Champion, 1920, 1929. French Open Champion, 1924, 1928. Welsh Open Amateur Champion, 1921, 1923. Won Golf Illustrated Gold Vase, 1923, 1926 (with T. A. Torrance), 1928. Won Worplesdon Mixed Foursomes, with Miss Joyce Wethered, 1923. Walker Cup team, 1922, 1923, 1924, 1926, 1930, 1934. Captain R. and A., 1948.

As a golfer Cyril Tolley was famous for his tremendous hitting—including driving the 18th green at St Andrews (370 yards) and the 1st at Troon (350 yards), holing the putt for an eagle two. In the 1950 Amateur Championship at St Andrews, at the age of 54, he was the only British semi-finalist, being beaten by the ultimate winner, Frank Stranahan, 30 years his junior. Author of The Modern Golfer (1924).

## TOMITA, Paul (b 1913)
Professional at the Bucharest Club, Romania, who played in the 1968 World (formerly Canada) Cup at Olgiata, Rome. As he was his country's sole representative, he was unable to play in the two-man team event, but was allowed to compete in the individual event. In the 1970 World Cup at Buenos Aires he played with Dmitriu Munteanu—and the fact that they were last does nothing to lessen their sporting spirit. He is helping to build Bulgaria's first course, some ten miles from Sofia, the capital. See ROMANIA, GOLF IN.

## TOP
To hit the ball above its centre, so that, in most cases, it runs along the ground instead of rising into the air. Also used as a noun—'a bad top', etc.

## TOPSPIN
Natural topspin is imparted to the ball by hitting it correctly with the flatter-faced wooden clubs (driver or brassey), causing it to revolve in a downwards direction during the course of its flight. Topspin can also be imparted by mistake by topping the ball. A ball so struck naturally rolls forward on landing. Also called overspin. See GOLF BALL, VELOCITY OF.

## TORRANCE, Thomas Arthur (1891-1978)
British. Irish Open Amateur Champion, 1925. German Open Amateur Champion, 1927, 1929. Won Worplesdon Mixed Foursomes, with Miss E. E. Helme, 1921, and with Miss Molly

Gourlay, 1934. Walker Cup team, 1924, 1928, 1930, 1932 (captain), 1934.

## TORSION

The shafts of all clubs have a degree of torsion—or twist—during the course of a stroke as well as a degree of bend or 'give'.

## TOWNSEND, Peter M. P. (b 1946)

British Boys' Amateur Champion, 1962, 1964. English Open Amateur Stroke Play Champion, 1966. Dutch Open Champion, 1967. Swiss Open Champion, 1971, in the third round of which he finished in 61 strokes. British P.G.A. Close Champion, 1968. Won *Golf Illustrated* Gold Vase, 1966, after tie with Bobby Cole. Walker Cup team, 1965; Ryder Cup team, 1969; one of the few to have played in both Walker and Ryder Cups. Played for British Isles in World Cup (formerly Eisenhower Trophy) team, 1966; played for England in World (formerly Canada) Cup, 1969; one of the few to have played in both World Cups. Turned professional, 1966. See WALKER AND RYDER CUPS, PLAYED IN BOTH.

## TOYE, Jeffrey L. (b 1940)

Welsh Amateur Champion, 1969; runner-up, 1961, 1972.

## TRACK IRON

See NIBLICK; PRESIDENT; RUT IRON.

## TRADESMAN'S ENTRANCE

See BACK DOOR.

## TRAJECTORY

As in the case of a missile, the trajectory of a golf ball merely means its flight through the air. Various factors influence the ball's trajectory and one speaks of a high trajectory, a low trajectory, etc. See QUAIL HIGH.

## TRAP

A bunker to a British golfer is a trap to an American; both are

hazards. Its origin goes back at least to the 1920s because Bernard Darwin, writing in *Green Memories* (1933) of a visit to the United States in 1922, says: "There is some small difference in language, as they call traps what we call bunkers." To many Americans Sand Trap corresponds to Bunker and Bunker to Grass Bunker.

## TRAVERS, Jerome Dunstan (1887-1951)

One of the greatest of the early American-born golfers. U.S. Open Champion, 1915, the second amateur winner. U.S. Amateur Champion, 1907, 1908, 1912, 1913; runner-up to Francis Ouimet, 1914. He never did himself justice during his visits to Britain, 1909, 1914. His great rival was his near namesake, Walter J. Travis.

Of American golf he wrote in 1924:

I believe that many of us here are prone to take the game too seriously, which doesn't help in the slightest to mould the proper mental attitude towards it. For another, we have a tendency to be too deliberate. That is a real handicap. Step out on any golf course and watch the average American golfer as he fiddles around before swinging the club . . . . I do not suggest that every golfer try to emulate the methods of Duncan and Mitchell, but I am convinced that the average player would get more enjoyment and better scores if he abandoned the national habit of overemphasising the care necessary in every shot.

Author of *Travers' Golf Book* (1913); *The Fifth Estate* (1926). See TRAVIS, WALTER J.

## TRAVIS, Walter J. (1862-1927)

Born Victoria, Australia, died New York. U.S. Amateur Champion, 1900, 1901, 1903; semi-finalist, 1898, 1899, 1906, 1908, 1914. Runner-up, U.S. Open Championship, 1902. British Amateur Champion, 1904—the first American winner and the only time he competed.

The 'Old Man', as he was called in

America, did not take up golf until he was 34, but soon became a formidable competitor. His putting was a great feature of his game. At Sandwich in the 1904 Amateur he putted with a borrowed Schenectady putter—and many British golfers followed his example until Schenectadies were banned by the R. and A. some five years later; meanwhile, Travis took to a 'Braid Aluminium' the moment he got home—and putted better than ever with it! Of the Schenectady he wrote: "I have never been able to do anything with it since. I have tried it repeatedly, but it seems to have lost all its virtue."

Unfortunately, his aggresive spirit and unsmiling face, with a more-or-less permanent cigar in his mouth, did not make him a popular figure in England and, for his part, he freely criticised British golf and golfers on his return to America.

See SCHENECTADY PUTTER; TRAVERS, JEROME DUNSTAN.

## TREDINNICK, Pamela (Mrs Peter Benka) (b 1946)

British Girls' Champion, 1964. Runner-up, English Girls' Championship, 1964. Portuguese Ladies' Champion, 1970. Curtis Cup team, 1966.

See BROTHER AND SISTER GOLFERS.

## TREVINO, Lee (b 1939)

A Texan of Mexican descent. U.S. Open Champion, 1968, 1971, after tie with Jack Nicklaus. The first player to break par in all four rounds—69, 68, 69, 69: 275. In his first Open Championship, 1967, he finished in fifth place, eight strokes behind Jack Nicklaus, runner-up in 1968. British Open Champion, 1971, 1972. Canadian Open Champion, 1971, 1977. U.S.-P.G.A. Champion, 1974. Ryder Cup team, 1969. With Orville Moody, won World (formerly Canada) Cup for the United States at Singapore, 1969; with Jack Nicklaus, 1971. Author of *I Can Help Your Game* (1972).

## TRINIDAD, GOLF IN

One of the world's many St Andrews Clubs is at Port of Spain, Trinidad. It has one of this West Indian island's two 18-holes courses, the other being the Pointe-à-Pierre Club. There are also three 9-holes courses —the Brighton Club, La Brea, the Clifton Hall Club, Point Fortin, and the Brechin Castle Club, Couva.

## TRIUMVIRATE

The name given to the three great British professionals whose dominance stretched from the mid-1890s to the outbreak of war in 1914—Harry Vardon (1870-1937), J. H. Taylor

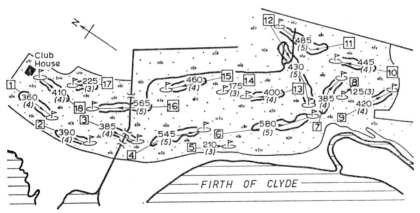

ROYAL TROON

(1871-1963) and James Braid (1870-1950). Between them they won the British Open Championship 16 times in the space of 21 years. See BRAID, JAMES; TAYLOR, J. H; VARDON, HARRY.

## TROLLEY
See CADDIE-CAR.

## TROON
Troon, Ayrshire. Founded 1878. One of Britain's longest courses, on typical linksland. Length: 7,045 yards. S.S.S. 74. Housed Open Championship, 1923, 1950, 1962, 1973; Amateur Championship, 1938, 1956, 1968; Ladies' Championship, 1904, 1925, 1952; British Boys' Amateur Championship, 1955. In 1962 Arnold Palmer set up a four-round Open Championship record score of 276, equalled by T. Weiskopf, also at Troon, in 1973. It became Royal Troon in 1978.

## TRUCIAL STATES, GOLF IN THE
Seven independent Arab sheikhdoms, having treaty relations with Britain, make up what are known as the Trucial States; they lie on the south side of the Persian Gulf and are rich in oil. The largest in area of the Trucial States is Abu Dhabi, which has a golf club, the Tarif Club, used mainly by employees of the local oil companies. The par of the two rounds of the 9-holes course is 72.

## TRUNDLER
See CADDIE-CAR.

## TUNISIA, GOLF IN
A course of 7,000 yards is being created at Sousse.

## TURN, REACH THE
When 9 holes have been played, the players are said to have 'reached the turn'. Hence such phrases as: "He took 36 to the turn."

## TURNBERRY
Turnberry, Ayrshire. Founded 1903. Fine links, reconstructed after the

Second World War when runways were built across it. Length (Ailsa Course): 7,025 yards. S.S.S. 74. Housed Amateur Championship, 1961; Ladies' Championship, 1937; Walker Cup match, 1963; Open Championship, 1977. Also Arran Course (6,653 yards. S.S.S. 72).

## TURNESA, William P. (b 1914), Joe (b 1901) and Jim (1913-71)
William, the son of a professional and with five professional brothers. U.S. Amateur Champion, 1938, 1948. British Amateur Champion, 1947; runner-up, 1949. Walker Cup team, 1947, 1949, 1951 (captain).

His elder brother, Joe, was runner-up to Bobby Jones in the U.S. Open (1926) and to Walter Hagen in the U.S.P.G.A. Championship (1927). Ryder Cup team, 1927, 1929. Another brother, Jim, was runner-up in the U.S.P.G.A. Championship, 1942, on his way to the final with Sam Snead defeating Ben Hogan and Byron Nelson. Ryder Cup team, 1953.

## TUTWILER, Edward M.
Runner-up, U.S. Amateur Championship, 1964. Walker Cup team, 1965, 1967.

## TWEDDELL, Dr William (b 1897)
British Amateur Champion, 1927; runner-up, 1935. Walker Cup team, 1928 (captain), 1936 (non-playing captain). Captain R. and A., 1961. In the 1935 final Dr Tweddell was beaten by only one hole by the formidable Lawson Little, who in the previous year had annihilated James Wallace by 14 and 13.

## TWITCH, PUTTING
An affliction that attacks many golfers, particularly the older ones, and causes them to miss the shortest of putts because they find it almost impossible to take the club back and bring it down again smoothly. Also

called the yips, the jitters and various other names.

## TWO UP AND FIVE TO PLAY NEVER WON A MATCH

An old golf saying of obscure origin, disproved countless times, of course, but still often quoted jocularly.

## TWOSOME

Has the same meaning as a Single. See MATCHES, TYPES OF.

## UGANDA, GOLF IN

Like its neighbours, Kenya and Tanzania, Uganda has thriving golf clubs. There are 18-holes courses at the Uganda Club, Kampala, and the Kilembe Club, and 9-holes courses at Entebbe, Jinja, Mbale and several other places.

There is a Uganda Golf Union, operating from Kampala. One of the local rules at Jinja reads: "On the green, a ball interfered with by a hippo footmark may be lifted and placed not nearer the hole, without penalty." It is feared that recent troubles in the country will interfere with golf.

## UNDERSPIN

See GOLF BALL, VELOCITY OF.

## UNIFORMS WORN BY GOLFERS

From earliest times red coats have been associated with golf—but not necessarily as a sign of danger to passers-by. Many of the fine portraits of old-time golfers show them in their red uniform coats—St Clair of Roslin, for instance, painted in 1771 when captain of the Honourable Company of Edinburgh Golfers; William Innes, captain of Blackheath in 1778 ; Henry Callender, also of Blackheath, in his Field Marshal's uniform; John Whyte-Melville of St Andrews, with the bridge over the Swilcan Burn in the background.

John Whyte-Melville is painted wearing a red coat with dark blue lapels ; much the same as the St Andrews uniform agreed upon in 1784, although by 1820 the R. and A. had decided on a plain blue coat with the society button.

The Edinburgh Burgess Society in 1790 resolved, apparently for the first time, to have a uniform "and that the uniform be a scarlet jacket, black neck and badge, as presently worn by some of the members". By 1837 they also had "a dress coat, colour dark claret, with black velvet collar".

The Blackheath golfers wore a uniform coat, "with buff waistcoat", at least as early as 1831 and were instructed in 1856 to wear the club uniform when playing on Summer Medal day.

One famous club that dared to be different was Prestwick. A suggestion put forward at a committee meeting in 1869 that members should wear a scarlet uniform coat was defeated.

Even the Oxford and Cambridge golfers in the early University matches wore uniform. Bernard Darwin said that the Cambridge team wore "a light blue cap, bearing a device of crossed clubs in silver, and a red coat with a light blue collar, on the pocket of which blazed the University arms, a miracle of gold and ermine". Later the red coat was succeeded by a sober grey one.

A red dress coat is still worn by some club captains at evening functions, but the once universal red coat for playing in has almost died out except on Wimbledon Common and the course of the Royal Epping Club at Chingford, Essex.

## UNITED ARAB REPUBLIC, GOLF IN THE

See EGYPT, GOLF IN.

## UNITED STATES, EARLY REFERENCES TO GOLF CLUBS IN THE

Although there is no record of golf having been played in the United States in the eighteenth century, there were a number of 'Golf Clubs', which held dinners, balls and other functions. From contemporary newspapers we learn, for instance, that a 'Golf Club' was formed at Charleston, South Carolina, in 1786 and held social meetings in 1791 and 1794; and that the Savannah Golf Club, Georgia, held an anniversary meeting in 1796 and a ball in 1811. Many years earlier there had been some rather mysterious references to a game that sounded more like the Dutch Kolven.

Coming to the late nineteenth century, a rather shadowy Oakhurst Golf Club was formed at White Sulphur Springs, West Virginia, in 1884, its land later being taken over by the Greenbriar Club, of which the famous professional is Sam Snead.

See KOLVEN; ST ANDREWS GOLF CLUB OF YONKERS; UNITED STATES, GOLF IN THE.

## UNITED STATES, GOLF IN THE

Golf in the United States really dates from 1888, when the first club —the St Andrews Golf Club of Yonkers, New York—was founded by two Scotsmen, John Reid and Robert Lockhart, and a group of American friends. A little earlier, the famous British amateur Horace Hutchinson, on a visit to America, had tried to interest American friends in the game. "We cut some holes in the soil," he wrote in *Fifty Years of Golf* (1919), "probably with carving knives, and I proceeded to instruct them by precept and example, as to what golf meant." The only reaction he received was that "it might be a good game for Sundays".

Golf had already reached the American continent, for Canada's first club at Montreal, which later became Royal Montreal, had been founded in 1873, and still in the 1870s several other clubs had begun.

Once the modern game had been established in 1888, it spread like a prairie fire. By the time that the Open, Amateur and Ladies' Championships were founded in 1895, there were over 80 clubs and courses of various kinds throughout the country. America was lucky to have such enthusiastic pioneers as Reid and Lockhart; Charles Blair Macdonald, creator of the Chicago Club; Theodore Havemeyer, first president of the United States Golf Association; and Henry O. Tallmadge, its first secretary.

As might be expected, although American amateurs and ladies held their own in their early championships, foreign-born professionals— particularly Scots—at first dominated the Open Championships. It was not until 1911 that a homebred player, John J. McDermott, won the title, winning again in the following year. In 1913 a terrific fillip was given to American golf when a 20-year-old amateur, Francis Ouimet, not only tied with the great English professionals, Harry Vardon and Ted Ray, at the Country Club, Brookline, but beat them in the play-off.

After that American golfers kept a firm grip on their championship, apart from 1920 when Ted Ray avenged his 1913 defeat, right up until 1965 when South African Gary Player won the title. In those years the U.S. Open Champions included such brilliant amateurs as Jerome Travers, 'Chick' Evans and the immortal Bobby Jones, and such famous professionals as Walter Hagen, Gene Sarazen, Ralph Guldahl, Byron Nelson, Craig Wood, Lloyd Mangrum, Ben Hogan, Cary Middlecoff, Julius Boros, Billy Casper, Arnold Palmer, Gene Littler, Jack Nicklaus and Lee Trevino. Perhaps the three whose personalities most appealed to the golfing public were Walter Hagen, Bobby Jones and Arnold Palmer—the latter perhaps attracting the greatest amount of hero-worship.

Golf has grown into big business in America, with the leading players becoming dollar millionaires both from the heavily sponsored tournament circuits and exhibition matches and from goods of all kinds that they sponsor. Golf in America has come a long way since John Reid and

Robert Lockhart and their friends of the 'Apple Tree Gang' played over the three holes laid out in John Reid's pasture at Yonkers-on-Hudson. Now the number of clubs approaches 11,500, increasing by some 300 a year, with some 10,500,000 players.

See individual golfers and AMERICA, EARLY REFERENCES TO GOLF CLUBS IN; AMERICAS CUP MATCHES; CURTIS, RYDER AND WALKER CUPS; GOLF BOOK, FIRST AMERICAN; KOLVEN; PROFESSIONAL GOLFERS' ASSOCIATION OF AMERICA; ST ANDREWS GOLF CLUB OF YONKERS; U.S. AMATEUR CHAMPION MORE THAN ONCE; U.S. AMATEUR CHAMPIONSHIP; U.S. GIRLS' JUNIOR CHAMPIONSHIP; U.S. GOLF ASSOCIATION; U.S. LADIES' CHAMPIONSHIP; U.S. OPEN CHAMPION MORE THAN ONCE; U.S. OPEN CHAMPIONSHIP; U.S. OPEN CHAMPIONSHIP COURSES; U.S. PUBLIC LINKS CHAMPIONSHIP; U.S. SENIORS' ASSOCIATION; U.S. WOMEN'S OPEN CHAMPIONSHIP.

## UNITED STATES AMATEUR CHAMPION MORE THAN ONCE

The following players have won the U.S. Amateur Championship more than once:

### Five times
Bobby Jones (1924, 1925, 1927, 1928, 1930).

### Four times
Jerome Travers (1907, 1908, 1912, 1913).

### Three times
Walter Travis (1900, 1901, 1903).

### Twice
Deane Beman (1960, 1963).
Charles Coe (1949, 1958).
Gary Cowan (1966, 1971).
H. Chandler Egan (1904, 1905).
Charles ('Chick') Evans (1916, 1920).
Robert Gardner (1909, 1915).
Lawson Little (1934, 1935).
Jack Nicklaus (1959, 1961).
Francis Ouimet (1914, 1931).

W. P. Turnesa (1938, 1948).
E. Harvie Ward (1955, 1956).
Marvin H. Ward (1939, 1941).
H. J. Whigham (1896, 1897).

## UNITED STATES AMATEUR CHAMPIONSHIP

The first U.S. National Amateur Championship was held, under the auspices of the new-formed U.S.G.A., in October 1895 at the Newport Club, Rhode Island, on the three days before the first U.S. Open Championship. The winner was Charles Blair Macdonald, who had done much to encourage the spread of golf in America and who had been runner-up in two unofficial amateur championships in 1894. There were only 32 entries and matches were over 18 holes with a 36-holes final. One player, Richard Peters, insisted on putting with a billiard cue until barred by the committee.

Next year, at the Shinnecock Hills Club, New York, there were 58 entries and a qualifying round was played to reduce the field to 16 for match play. The winner was H. J. Whigham, C. B. Macdonald's son-in-law, and he won again in 1897. The first non-American-born winner was Walter Travis (1900), who was born in Australia, and the first and only English winner was Harold Hilton (1911), who was also the current British Amateur Champion. The only other non-American winners were C. Ross Somerville, six times Canadian Amateur Champion, and another Canadian, Gary Cowan.

The U.S. Amateur continued to be a match-play event until 1965, when it went over to four rounds of stroke play. Among the winners who have gone on to make their names in the professional ranks are W. Lawson Little (1934, 1935), Gene Littler (1953), Arnold Palmer (1954), Jack Nicklaus (1959, 1961).

The following are the winners and runners-up in match play:

| Year | Winner | Runner-up | Venue | By |
|---|---|---|---|---|
| 1895 | C. B. Macdonald | Charles Sands | Newport, R.I. | 12 and 11 |
| 1896 | H. J. Whigham | J. G. Thorp | Shinnecock Hills, N.Y. | 3 and 2 |
| 1897 | H. J. Whigham | W. R. Betts | Chicago, Ill. | 8 and 6 |
| 1898 | Findley Douglas | W. B. Smith | Morris County, N.J. | 5 and 3 |
| 1899 | H. M. Harriman | Findley Douglas | Onwentsia, Ill. | 3 and 2 |
| 1900 | Walter Travis | Findley Douglas | Garden City, N.Y. | 2 holes |
| 1901 | Walter Travis | Walter Egan | Atlantic City, N.J. | 5 and 4 |
| 1902 | Louis N. James | Eben Byers | Glen View, Ill. | 4 and 2 |
| 1903 | Walter Travis | Eben Byers | Nassau, N.Y. | 5 and 4 |
| 1904 | Chandler Egan | Fred Herreshoff | Baltusrol, N.J. | 8 and 6 |
| 1905 | Chandler Egan | D. E. Sawyer | Chicago, Ill. | 6 and 5 |
| 1906 | Eben Byers | G. S. Lyon | Englewood, N.J. | 2 holes |
| 1907 | Jerome Travers | Archibald Graham | Euclid, Ohio | 6 and 5 |
| 1908 | Jerome Travers | Max Behr | Garden City, N.Y. | 8 and 7 |
| 1909 | Robert Gardner | Chandler Egan | Chicago, Ill. | 4 and 3 |
| 1910 | W. C. Fownes | Warren Wood | Brookline, Mass. | 4 and 3 |
| 1911 | Harold Hilton | Fred Herreshoff | Apawamis, N.Y. | 37th |
| 1912 | Jerome Travers | Chick Evans | Chicago, Ill. | 7 and 6 |
| 1913 | Jerome Travers | John Anderson | Garden City, N.Y. | 5 and 4 |
| 1914 | Francis Ouimet | Jerome Travers | Ekwanok, Vt. | 6 and 5 |
| 1915 | Robert Gardner | John Anderson | Detroit, Mich. | 5 and 4 |
| 1916 | Chick Evans | Robert Gardner | Merion, Pa. | 4 and 3 |
| 1917-18 | No Championships | | | |
| 1919 | S. Davidson Herron | Bobby Jones | Oakmont, Pa. | 5 and 4 |
| 1920 | Chick Evans | Francis Ouimet | Engineers, N.Y. | 7 and 6 |
| 1921 | Jesse Guilford | Robert Gardner | St. Louis, Mo. | 7 and 6 |
| 1922 | Jess Sweetser | Chick Evans | Brookline, Mass. | 3 and 2 |
| 1923 | Max Marston | Jess Sweetser | Flossmoor, Ill. | 38th |
| 1924 | Bobby Jones | George Von Elm | Merion, Pa. | 9 and 8 |
| 1925 | Bobby Jones | Watts Gunn | Oakmont, Pa. | 8 and 7 |
| 1926 | George Von Elm | Bobby Jones | Baltusrol, N.J. | 2 and 1 |
| 1927 | Bobby Jones | Chick Evans | Minikahda, Minn. | 8 and 7 |
| 1928 | Bobby Jones | Philip Perkins | Brae Burn, Mass. | 10 and 9 |
| 1929 | Harrison Johnston | Dr O. F. Willing | Del Monte, Cal. | 4 and 3 |
| 1930 | Bobby Jones | Eugene Homans | Merion, Pa. | 8 and 7 |
| 1931 | Francis Ouimet | Jack Westland | Beverley, Ill. | 6 and 5 |
| 1932 | Ross Somerville | Johnny Goodman | Baltimore, Md. | 2 holes |
| 1933 | George Dunlap | Max Marston | Kenwood, Ohio | 6 and 5 |
| 1934 | Lawson Little | David Goldman | Brookline, Mass. | 8 and 7 |
| 1935 | Lawson Little | Walter Emery | Cleveland, Ohio | 4 and 2 |
| 1936 | Johnny Fischer | Jack M'Lean | Garden City, N.Y. | 37th |
| 1937 | Johnny Goodman | Ray Billows | Alderwood, Ore. | 2 holes |
| 1938 | W. P. Turnesa | Buell P. Abbott | Oakmont, Pa. | 8 and 7 |
| 1939 | Marvin Ward | Ray Billows | North Shore, Ill. | 7 and 5 |
| 1940 | Richard Chapman | W. B. McCullough | Winged Foot, N.Y. | 11 and 9 |
| 1941 | Marvin Ward | Buell P. Abbott | Omaha, Nebr. | 4 and 3 |
| 1942-45 | No Championships | | | |
| 1946 | Stanley Bishop | Smiley Quick | Baltusrol, N.J. | 37th |
| 1947 | Robert Riegel | John Dawson | Pebble Beach, Cal. | 2 and 1 |
| 1948 | W. P. Turnesa | Ray Billows | Memphis, Tenn. | 2 and 1 |
| 1949 | Charles Coe | Rufus King | Oak Hill, N.Y. | 11 and 10 |
| 1950 | Sam Urzetta | Frank Stranahan | Minneapolis, Minn. | 39th |
| 1951 | Billy Maxwell | J. F. Gagliardi | Saucon Valley, Pa. | 4 and 3 |
| 1952 | Jack Westland | Al Mengert | Seattle, Wash. | 3 and 2 |

| Year Winner | Runner-up | Venue | By |
|---|---|---|---|
| 1953 Gene Littler | Dale Morey | Oklahoma, Okla. | 1 hole |
| 1954 Arnold Palmer | Robert Sweeny | Detroit, Mich. | 1 hole |
| 1955 Harvie Ward | Bill Hyndman | James River, Va. | 9 and 8 |
| 1956 Harvie Ward | Charles Kocsis | Knollwood, Ill. | 5 and 4 |
| 1957 Hillman Robbins | Dr. Frank Taylor | Brookline, Mass. | 5 and 4 |
| 1958 Charles Coe | Tommy Aaron | Olympic, Cal. | 5 and 4 |
| 1959 Jack Nicklaus | Charles Coe | Broadmoor, Colo. | 1 hole |
| 1960 Deane Beman | Robert W. Gardner | St. Louis, Mo. | 6 and 4 |
| 1961 Jack Nicklaus | Dudley Wysong | Pebble Beach, Cal. | 8 and 6 |
| 1962 Labron Harris | Downing Gray | Pinehurst, N.C. | 1 hole |
| 1963 Deane Beman | Richard Sikes | Wakonda, Iowa | 2 and 1 |
| 1964 W. C. Campbell | Edward Tutwiler | Canterbury, Ohio | 1 hole |

The following are the winners since going over to stroke play:

| Year Winner | Venue | Score |
|---|---|---|
| 1965 Robert Murphy | Tulsa, Okla. | 291 |
| 1966 Gary Cowan | Ardmore, Penn. | 285 |
| 1967 Robert Dickson | Broadmoor, Colo. | 285 |
| 1968 Bruce Fleischer | Columbus, Ohio | 284 |
| 1969 Steve Melnyk | Oakmont, Pa. | 286 |
| 1970 Lanny Wadkins | Portland, Ore. | 280 |
| 1971 Gary Cowan | Wilmington, Del. | 280 |
| 1972 Marvin Giles | Charlotte, N.C. | 285 |

## UNITED STATES GIRLS' JUNIOR AMATEUR CHAMPIONSHIP

Like the U.S. Boys' Junior Championship, this is one of the few American events still decided by match play, after qualifying rounds of stroke play. It was founded in 1949, a year after the boys' championship, and has the same age limit of 18. Similarly, it has produced a number of well-known amateur and professional golfers, including Pat Lesser (1950), 1955 U.S. Ladies' Champion; Mary ('Mickey') Wright (1952), four times U.S. Women's Open Champion; Margaret ('Wiffi') Smith (1954), British Ladies' Champion, 1956; JoAnne Gunderson (1956), five times U.S. Ladies' Champion.

## UNITED STATES GOLF ASSOCIATION

On 22nd December 1894 one of America's pioneer golfers, Harry O. Tallmadge, organised a dinner at the Calumet Club, New York, to which he invited two representatives from five of the earliest American golf clubs. Winthrop Rutherford of the Newport Club was absent, but those present were: Mr Tallmadge and John Reid (St Andrews Club of Yonkers); General Barber and Samuel Parrish (Shinnecock Hills); Theodore Havemeyer (Newport); Charles B. Macdonald and Arthur Ryerson (Chicago Club); Laurence Curtis and P. Sears (The Country Club of Brookline).

Out of this meeting grew the United States Golf Association in 1894, its stated objects being "to promote interest in the game of golf; the protection of the mutual interests of its members; to establish and enforce uniformity in the rules of the game by creating a representative authority; its Executive Committee to be a Court of Reference as a final authority in matters of controversy; to establish a uniform system of handicapping; to decide on what links the Amateur and Open Championships shall be played". Theodore Havemeyer was the first president, until his death in 1897, and Tallmadge the first secretary.

The association soon grew in stature and every properly constituted club in the United States is a member. It now conducts the following annual championships: The U.S. National Open, the U.S. National Amateur, the U.S. Ladies' Amateur, the U.S. Women's Open, the Public Links, the U.S. Junior Amateur, the U.S. Girls' Junior, the U.S. Seniors' Amateur, the Walker Cup Matches, the Curtis Cup Matches, the Americas Cup Matches.

The association makes and interprets the Rules of Golf in the United States (in close collaboration with the R. and A.), gives decisions and information on the rules, controls the standards for amateur status and, in general, creates and maintains uniformity in the game. The headquarters, including the museum and library, are at U.S.G.A. Golf House, Far Hills, New Jersey 07931.

See MACDONALD, CHARLES BLAIR.

## UNITED STATES JUNIOR AMATEUR CHAMPIONSHIP

This event, founded in 1948, corresponds to the British Boys' Amateur Championship, the age limit being 18. It is decided by match play after qualifying by stroke play.

The first runner-up (1948) was Ken Venturi, U.S. Open Champion, 1964. The youngest qualifier that year was Mason Rudolph, aged 14, who was runner-up in 1949 and winner in 1950, and later a well-known professional. The 1949 winner was Gay Brewer, U.S. Masters winner, 1967, and the 1951 winner Tommy Jacobs, who tied with Brewer and Jack Nicklaus in the 1966 Masters. The 1954 runner-up, Al Geiberger, was 1966 U.S.P.G.A. Champion.

## UNITED STATES LADIES' CHAMPIONSHIP

As soon as the United States Golf

S

Association was formed in December 1894, it proceeded with plans for American Open, Amateur and Ladies' Championships. The first Amateur was held on 1st-3rd October 1895 at the Newport Club, Rhode Island, the Open on the following day, and the Ladies' on 9th November at the Meadowbrook Club, Hempstead, New York.

The first Ladies' Championship differed from the men's Amateur in that it was decided, like the Open Championship, by stroke play and not match play. There were only 13 entries and the winner, Mrs Charles S. Brown, turned in what at first glance looks a very respectable score —69, 63: 132—until one realises that she had played two rounds of a 9-holes course; the runner-up, Miss N. C. Sargeant, was two strokes more. A contemporary account said: "Mrs Brown did not start off with very good prospects as she took 11 strokes to make the first hole. The second she made in 4 and the third in 9."

Next year the event went over to match play, as it has been ever since. The winner was Beatrix Hoyt, at 16 the youngest champion, and she won again in 1897 and 1898. Two of the early champions were the Curtis sisters, Harriot (1906) and Margaret (1907, 1911, 1912), donors of the Curtis Cup.

The first non-American champion was Dorothy Campbell (Mrs J. V. Hurd), who won in 1909, 1910, 1924, and was British Champion in 1909, 1911. Others have been Gladys Ravenscroft (1913) and Pam Barton (1936), both also British Champions. All other winners have been American except Marlene Stewart (Mrs Streit) of Canada (1956) and Catherine Lacoste of France (1969).

The Championship was conducted by the U.S.G.A. Championship Committee until the Women's Committee took over in 1926.

The following are the winners and runners-up of the championship since its inception:

| Year | Winner | Runner-up | Venue | Score |
|---|---|---|---|---|
| 1895 | Mrs. Charles Brown | N. C. Sargeant | Meadowbrook, N.Y. | 132 |
| 1896 | Beatrix Hoyt | Mrs. A. Turmore | Morris County, N.J. | 2 and 1 |
| 1897 | Beatrix Hoyt | N. C. Sargeant | Essex, Mass. | 5 and 4 |
| 1898 | Beatrix Hoyt | Maud Wetmore | Ardsley, N.Y. | 5 and 3 |
| 1899 | Ruth Underhill | Mrs. C. Fox | Philadelphia, Pa. | 2 and 1 |
| 1900 | Frances Griscom | Margaret Curtis | Shinnecock Hills, N.Y. | 6 and 5 |
| 1901 | Genevieve Hecher | Lucy Herron | Baltusrol, N.J. | 5 and 3 |
| 1902 | Genevieve Hecher | Louisa Wells | Brookline, Mass. | 4 and 3 |
| 1903 | Bessie Anthony | J. A. Carpenter | Chicago, Ill. | 7 and 6 |
| 1904 | Georgianna Bishop | Mrs. E. F. Sanford | Merion, Pa. | 5 and 3 |
| 1905 | Pauline Mackay | Margaret Curtis | Morris County, N.J. | 1 hole |
| 1906 | Harriot Curtis | Mary Adams | Brae Burn, Mass. | 2 and 1 |
| 1907 | Margaret Curtis | Harriot Curtis | Midlothian, Ill. | 7 and 6 |
| 1908 | Katherine Harley | Mrs. T. H. Polhemus | Chevy Chase, Md. | 6 and 5 |
| 1909 | Dorothy Campbell | Mrs. R. H. Barlow | Merion, Pa. | 3 and 2 |
| 1910 | Dorothy Campbell | Mrs. G. M. Martin | Homewood, Ill. | 2 and 1 |
| 1911 | Margaret Curtis | Lillian Hyde | Baltusrol, N.J. | 5 and 3 |
| 1912 | Margaret Curtis | Mrs. R. H. Barlow | Essex, Mass. | 3 and 2 |
| 1913 | Gladys Ravenscroft | Marion Hollins | Wilmington, Del. | 2 holes |
| 1914 | Mrs. H. A. Jackson | Elaine Rosenthal | Nassau, N.Y. | 1 hole |
| 1915 | Mrs. C. H. Vanderbeck | Mrs. W. A. Gavin | Onwentsia, Ill. | 3 and 2 |
| 1916 | Alexa Stirling | Mildred Caverly | Belmont, Mass. | 2 and 1 |
| 1917-18 | No Championships | | | |
| 1919 | Alexa Stirling | Mrs. W. A. Gavin | Shawnee, Pa. | 6 and 5 |
| 1920 | Alexa Stirling | Mrs. J. V. Hurd | Mayfield, Ohio | 5 and 4 |
| 1921 | Marion Hollins | Alexa Stirling | Hollywood, N.J. | 5 and 4 |
| 1922 | Glenna Collett | Mrs. W. A. Gavin | Greenbrier, Va. | 5 and 4 |
| 1923 | Edith Cummings | Alexa Stirling | Westchester, N.Y. | 3 and 2 |
| 1924 | Mrs. J. V. Hurd | Mary K. Browne | Rhode Island, R.I. | 7 and 6 |
| 1925 | Glenna Collett | Mrs. Alexa Fraser | St. Louis, Mo. | 9 and 8 |
| 1926 | Mrs. G. H. Stetson | Mrs. W. G. Goss | Merion, Pa. | 3 and 1 |
| 1927 | Mrs. Miriam Horn | Maureen Orcutt | Cherry Valley, N.Y. | 5 and 4 |
| 1928 | Glenna Collett | Virginia Van Wie | Hot Springs, Va. | 13 and 12 |
| 1929 | Glenna Collett | Mrs. L. Pressler | Oakland Hills, Mich. | 4 and 3 |
| 1930 | Glenna Collett | Virginia Van Wie | Los Angeles, Cal. | 6 and 5 |
| 1931 | Helen Hicks | Mrs. Glenna Vare | Buffalo, N.Y. | 6 and 5 |
| 1932 | Virginia Van Wie | Mrs. Glenna Vare | Salem, Mass. | 10 and 8 |
| 1933 | Virginia Van Wie | Helen Hicks | Exmoor, Ill. | 4 and 3 |
| 1934 | Virginia Van Wie | Dorothy Traung | Whitemarsh, Pa. | 2 and 1 |
| 1935 | Mrs. Glenna Vare | Petty Berg | Interlachen, Minn. | 3 and 2 |
| 1936 | Pamela Barton | Mrs. J. D. Crews | Canoe Brook, N.J. | 4 and 3 |
| 1937 | Mrs. Julius Page | Patty Berg | Memphis, Tenn. | 7 and 6 |
| 1938 | Patty Berg | Mrs. Julius Page | Westmoreland, Ill. | 6 and 5 |
| 1939 | Betty Jameson | Dorothy Kirby | Wee Burn, Conn. | 3 and 2 |
| 1940 | Betty Jameson | Jane Cochran | Pebble Beach, Cal. | 6 and 5 |
| 1941 | Mrs. Frank Newell | Helen Sigel | Brookline, Mass. | 5 and 3 |
| 1942-45 | No Championships | | | |
| 1946 | 'Babe' Zaharias | Mrs. Clara Sherman | Southern Hills, Okla. | 11 and 9 |
| 1947 | Louise Suggs | Dorothy Kirby | Franklin Hills, Mich. | 2 holes |
| 1948 | Grace Lenczyk | Helen Sigel | Pebble Beach, Cal. | 4 and 3 |
| 1949 | Mrs. Mark Porter | Dorothy Kielty | Merion, Pa. | 3 and 2 |
| 1950 | Beverly Hanson | Mae Murray | East Lake, Ga. | 6 and 4 |
| 1951 | Dorothy Kirby | Claire Doran | St. Paul, Minn. | 2 and 1 |
| 1952 | Mrs. J. Pung | Shirley McFedters | Waverly, Ore. | 2 and 1 |

| Year Winner | Runner-up | Venue | By |
|---|---|---|---|
| 1953 Mary Lena Faulk | Polly Riley | Rhode Island, R.I. | 3 and 2 |
| 1954 Barbara Romack | Mary Wright | Allegheny, Pa. | 4 and 3 |
| 1955 Pat Lesser | Jane Nelson | Myers Park, N.C. | 7 and 6 |
| 1956 Marlene Stewart | JoAnne Gunderson | Meridian Hills, Ind. | 2 holes |
| 1957 JoAnne Gunderson | Ann Johnstone | Del Paso, Cal. | 8 and 6 |
| 1958 Anne Quast | Barbara Romack | Wee Burn, Conn. | 3 and 2 |
| 1959 Barbara McIntire | Joanne Goodwin | Congressional, D.C. | 4 and 3 |
| 1960 JoAnne Gunderson | Jean Ashley | Tulsa, Okla. | 6 and 5 |
| 1961 Mrs. (Anne Quast) Decker | Phyllis Preuss | Tacoma, Wash. | 14 and 13 |
| 1962 JoAnne Gunderson | Ann Baker | Rochester, N.Y. | 9 and 8 |
| 1963 Mrs. (Anne Quast) Welts. | Pat Conley | Taconic, Conn. | 2 and 1 |
| 1964 Barbara McIntire | JoAnne Gunderson | Prairie Dunes, Kan. | 3 and 2 |
| 1965 Jean Ashley | Mrs. (Anne Quast) Welts | Denver, Colo. | 5 and 4 |
| 1966 Mrs. JoAnne Carner | Mrs. J. D. Streit | Pittsburg, Pa. | 41st |
| 1967 Mary Lou Dill | Jean Ashley | Annandale, Cal. | 5 and 4 |
| 1968 Mrs. JoAnne Carner | Mrs. (Anne Quast) Welts | Birmingham, Mich. | 5 and 4 |
| 1969 Catherine Lacoste | Shelly Hamlin | Dallas, Tex. | 3 and 2 |
| 1970 Martha Wilkinson | Cynthia Hill | Darien, Conn. | 3 and 2 |
| 1971 Laura Baugh | Beth Barry | Atlanta, Ga. | 1 hole |
| 1972 Mary Ann Budke | Cynthia Hill | St. Louis, Mo. | 5 and 4 |
| 1973 Carol Semple | Mrs. A. Sander | Montclair, N.J. | 1 hole |
| 1974 Cynthia Hill | Carol Semple | Broadmoor, Seattle | 5 and 4 |
| 1975 Beth Daniel | D. Horton | Brae Burn, Mass. | 3 and 2 |
| 1976 D. Horton | Mrs. M. Bretton | Del Paso, Cal. | 2 and 1 |
| 1977 Beth Daniel | Mrs. C. Sherek | Cincinnati, Ohio | |

## UNITED STATES MASTERS TOURNAMENT

See MASTERS TOURNAMENT.

## UNITED STATES OPEN CHAMPION MORE THAN ONCE

The following players have won the U.S. Open Championship more than once:

### Four times

Willie Anderson (1901, 1903, 1904, 1905).

Ben Hogan (1948, 1950, 1951, 1953).

Bobby Jones (1923, 1926, 1929, 1930).

### Three Times

Jack Nicklaus (1962, 1967, 1972).

### Twice

Julius Boros (1952, 1963).
Billy Casper (1959, 1966).
Ralph Guldahl (1937, 1938).
Walter Hagen (1914, 1919).
J. J. McDermott (1911, 1912).
Cary Middlecoff (1949, 1956).
Gene Sarazen (1922, 1932).
Alex Smith (1906, 1910).
Lee Trevino (1968, 1971).

## UNITED STATES OPEN CHAMPIONSHIP

The first official championship followed soon after the formation of the United States Golf Association in December 1894. But the first National Open was held in October 1895 at the Newport Club, Rhode Island. The winner was a young Englishman of 19 named Horace Rawlins, who had been in America, as assistant professional at Newport, for only nine months. His 36-holes total, an undistinguished 173 (91, 83), was two strokes better than that of the far more experienced Willie Dunn.

In 1898 the U.S. Open was extended to 72 holes, when eight rounds were played over the 9-holes course of the Myopia Hunt Club, Hamilton, Massachusetts. Either Scottish-born or English-born professionals—including Harry Vardon (1900), when on a tour of the United States with J. H. Taylor, the runner-up—went on winning until John J. McDermott became champion in 1911, after surviving a three-way play-off.

The first amateur to win the title was 20-year-old Francis Ouimet, who won a dramatic play-off with Harry Vardon and Ted Ray in 1913. There were 165 entries, causing a qualifying round to be played for the first time. Amateurs were to win seven more times (including Bobby Jones's four victories), the last one being Johnny Goodman in 1933.

The only champion of neither American nor British birth was South African Gary Player, who won the title in 1965 after being runner-up in 1958.

Prize money has risen from the 335 dollars available in 1895, of which the winners received 150 dollars, to the 200,000 dollars available in 1972, of which the winner received 30,000 dollars.

The following are the winners of the U.S. Open since its inception:

| Year | Winner | Venue | Score |
|------|--------|-------|-------|
| 1895 | Horace Rawlins | Newport, R.I. | 173 |
| 1896 | James Foulis | Shinnecock Hills, N.Y. | 152 |
| 1897 | Joe Lloyd | Chicago, Ill. | 162 |
| 1898 | Fred Herd | Myopia Hunt, Mass. | 328 |
| 1899 | Willie Smith | Baltimore, Md. | 315 |
| 1900 | Harry Vardon | Chicago, Ill. | 313 |
| 1901 | Willie Anderson | Myopia Hunt, Mass. | 331 |
| 1902 | Laurence Auchterlonie | Garden City, N.Y. | 307 |
| 1903 | Willie Anderson | Baltusrol, N.J. | 307 |
| 1904 | Willie Anderson | Glen View, Ill. | 303 |
| 1905 | Willie Anderson | Myopia Hunt, Mass. | 314 |
| 1906 | Alex Smith | Onwentsia, Ill. | 295 |
| 1907 | Aleck Ross | Philadelphia, Pa. | 302 |
| 1908 | Fred McLeod | Myopia Hunt, Mass. | 322 |
| 1909 | George Sargent | Englewood, N.J. | 290 |
| 1910 | Alex Smith | Philadelphia, Pa. | 298 |
| 1911 | J. J. McDermott | Chicago, Ill. | 307 |
| 1912 | J. J. McDermott | Buffalo, N.Y. | 294 |
| 1913 | Mr. Francis Ouimet | Brookline, Mass. | 304 |
| 1914 | Walter Hagen | Midlothian, Ill. | 290 |
| 1915 | Mr. Jerome Travers | Baltusrol, N.J. | 297 |
| 1916 | Mr. Charles Evans | Minikahda, Minn. | 286 |
| 1917-18 | No Championships | | |
| 1919 | Walter Hagen | Brae Burn, Mass. | 301 |
| 1920 | Edward Ray | Inverness, Ohio | 295 |
| 1921 | Jim Barnes | Columbia, Md. | 289 |
| 1922 | Gene Sarazen | Skokie, Ill. | 288 |
| 1923 | Mr. R. T. Jones | Inwood, N.Y. | 296 |
| 1924 | Cyril Walker | Oakland Hills, Mich. | 297 |
| 1925 | Willie MacFarlane | Worcester, Mass. | 291 |
| 1926 | Mr. R. T. Jones | Scioto, Ohio | 293 |
| 1927 | Tommy Armour | Oakmont, Pa. | 301 |

| Year | Winner | Venue | Score |
|------|--------|-------|-------|
| 1928 | Johnny Farrell | Olympia Fields, Ill. | 294 |
| 1929 | Mr. R. T. Jones | Winged Foot, N.Y. | 294 |
| 1930 | Mr. R. T. Jones | Interlachen, Minn. | 287 |
| 1931 | Billy Burke | Inverness, Ohio | 292 |
| 1932 | Gene Sarazen | Fresh Meadow, N.Y. | **286** |
| 1933 | Mr. Johnny Goodman | North Shore, Ill. | 287 |
| 1934 | Olin Dutra | Merion, Pa. | 293 |
| 1935 | Sam Parks | Oakmont, Pa. | 299 |
| 1936 | Tony Manero | Baltusrol, N.J. | 282 |
| 1937 | Ralph Guldahl | Oakland Hills, Mich. | 281 |
| 1938 | Ralph Guldahl | Cherry Hills, Colo. | 284 |
| 1939 | Byron Nelson | Philadelphia, Pa. | 284 |
| 1940 | W. Lawson Little | Canterbury, Ohio | 287 |
| 1941 | Craig Wood | Colonial, Tex. | 284 |
| 1942-45 | No Championships | | |
| 1946 | Lloyd Mangrum | Canterbury, Ohio | 284 |
| 1947 | Lew Worsham | St. Louis, Mo. | 282 |
| 1948 | Ben Hogan | Riviera, Cal. | 276 |
| 1949 | Cary Middlecoff | Medinah, Ill. | 286 |
| 1950 | Ben Hogan | Merion, Pa. | 287 |
| 1951 | Ben Hogan | Oakland Hills, Mich. | 287 |
| 1952 | Julius Boros | Northwood, Tex. | 281 |
| 1953 | Ben Hogan | Oakmont, Pa. | 283 |
| 1954 | Ed Furgol | Baltusrol, N.J. | **284** |
| 1955 | Jack Fleck | Olympic, Cal. | 287 |
| 1956 | Cary Middlecoff | Oak Hill, N.Y. | 281 |
| 1957 | Dick Mayer | Inverness, Ohio | 282 |
| 1958 | Tommy Bolt | Southern Hills, Okla | 283 |
| 1959 | Billy Casper | Winged Foot, N.Y. | 282 |
| 1960 | Arnold Palmer | Cherry Hills, Colo. | 280 |
| 1961 | Gene Littler | Oakland Hills, Mich. | 281 |
| 1962 | Jack Nicklaus | Oakmont, Pa. | 283 |
| 1963 | Julius Boros | Brookline, Mass. | 293 |
| 1964 | Ken Venturi | Congressional, D.C. | **278** |
| 1965 | Gary Player | Bellerive, Miss. | 282 |
| 1966 | Billy Casper | Olympic, Cal. | 278 |
| 1967 | Jack Nicklaus | Baltusrol, N.J. | 275 |
| 1968 | Lee Trevino | Oak Hill, N.Y. | 275 |
| 1969 | Ray Floyd | Dayton, Ohio | 276 |
| 1970 | Tony Jacklin | Hazeltine, Minn. | 281 |
| 1971 | Lee Trevino | Pebble Beach, Cal. | 290 |
| 1972 | Jack Nicklaus | Merion, Pa. | 280 |
| 1973 | Johnny Miller | Oakmont, Pa. | 279 |
| 1974 | Hale Irwin | Winged Foot, N.Y. | 287 |
| 1975 | Lou Graham | Medinah, Ill. | 287 |
| 1976 | Jerry Pate | Atlanta, Ga. | 277 |
| 1977 | Hubert Green | Southern Hills, Tulsa | 278 |
| 1978 | Andy North | Cherry Hills, Colo. | 285 |

## UNITED STATES OPEN CHAMPIONSHIP COURSES

The following courses have been chosen since the first event in 1895:

Baltimore, Maryland: 1899.

Baltusrol, Springfield, New Jersey: 1903, 1915, 1936, 1954, 1967.

Bellerive, St Louis, Missouri: 1965.
Brae Burn, West Newton, Massachusetts: 1919.
Brookline, Massachusetts: 1913, 1963.
Buffalo, New York: 1912.
Canterbury, Cleveland, Ohio: 1930, 1946.
Champions' Club, Houston, Texas: 1969.
Cherry Hills, Denver, Colorado: 1938, 1960, 1978.
Colonial, Fort Worth, Texas: 1941.
Columbia, Chevy Chase, Maryland: 1921.
Congressional, Washington, D.C.: 1964.
Englewood, New Jersey: 1909.
Fresh Meadow, Flushing, New York: 1932.
Garden City, New York: 1902.
Glen View, Illinois: 1904.
Hazeltine National, Chaska, Minnesota: 1970.
Interlachen, Minneapolis, Minnesota: 1930.
Inverness, Toledo, Ohio: 1920, 1931, 1957.
Inwood, New York: 1923.
Medinah, Illinois, 1949.
Merion, Ardmore, Pennsylvania: 1933, 1950, 1971.
Midlothian, Blue Island, Illinois: 1914.
Minikahda, Minneapolis, Minnesota: 1916.
Myopia, Hamilton, Massachusetts: 1898, 1901, 1905, 1908.
Newport, Rhode Island: 1895.
North Shore, Glen View, Illinois: 1933.
Northwood, Dallas, Texas: 1952.
Oak Hill, Rochester, New York: 1956, 1968.
Oakland Hills, Birmingham, Michigan: 1924, 1937, 1951, 1961.
Oakmont, Pennsylvania: 1927, 1935, 1953, 1962, 1973.
Olympia Fields, Mateson, Illinois, 1928.
Olympic, San Francisco, California: 1955, 1966.
Onwentsia, Lake Forest, Illinois: 1906.

Pebble Beach, California: 1972.
Philadelphia, Pennsylvania: 1907, 1910, 1939.
Riviera, Los Angeles, California: 1948.
St Louis, Clayton, Missouri: 1947.
Scioto, Columbus, Ohio: 1926.
Shinnecock Hills, Southampton, New York: 1896.
Skokie, Glencoe, Illinois: 1922.
Southern Hills, Tulsa, Oklahoma: 1958, 1977.
Wheaton, Illinois: 1897, 1900, 1911.
Winged Foot, Mamaroneck, New York: 1929, 1959, 1974.
Worcester, Massachusetts: 1925.

## UNITED STATES OPEN CHAMPIONSHIP CUP

The original cup was presented by the U.S. Golf Association for the first championship in 1895. Unfortunately it was destroyed in a fire in 1946 while in the custody of the Tam O' Shanter Club, Chicago. The exact specifications, however, were still available and another cup was ready for the 1947 championship. On one side are the names of all the winners and on the other an engraved scene of early golfers, surrounded by a laurel wreath; on top is the figure of a Winged Victory.

## UNITED STATES OPEN CHAMPIONSHIP, RECORD ENTRY FOR

See BRITISH OPEN CHAMPIONSHIP, RECORD ENTRY FOR.

## UNITED STATES PROFESSIONAL GOLFERS' ASSOCIATION CHAMPIONSHIP

See PROFESSIONAL GOLFERS ASSOCIATION OF AMERICA.

## UNITED STATES PROFESSIONAL MATCH-PLAY TOURNAMENT

In this new event, at Pinehurst, North Carolina, eight players qualify for match play after 36 holes of stroke play. In the 1972 final Jack Nicklaus beat Frank Beard by 2 and 1.

## UNITED STATES PROFESSIONAL TOUR

The American professional tour has been increasing steadily in recent years both in prize money and in the number of sponsored tournaments available. For the 1971 U.S. and Caribbean season a total of about £2,950,000 was at stake for 63 tournaments, approximately a 10 per cent increase in winnings over the previous season. 43 of the tournaments offered prizes worth £42,000 or more. The Jackie Gleason Classic alone offers prize money of $260,000, with a first prize of $52,000 (£21,000).

## UNITED STATES PUBLIC LINKS CHAMPIONSHIP

Until 1967 this was one of the few major American championships still decided by match play. In 1967 it went over to four rounds of stroke play. It was founded in 1922 by the United States Golf Association, largely through the efforts of James D. Standish, of Detroit, who presented a championship trophy. In the first year there were 140 entries: 30 years later there were 4,015.

Entries are restricted to amateurs who, since 1st January of the current year, have been *bona fide* public course players and have not held privileges of any course from which the general public is excluded. It is run by the U.S.G.A.

The first notable winner was Carl F. Kauffmann, who was runner-up in 1926 and then won the next three championships. Buell Patrick Abbott (1936) was runner-up in the U.S. Amateur Championship (1938, 1941); Smiley Quick (1946) was runner-up in the U.S. Amateur Championship (1946) and was in the 1947 Walker Cup team; Dan Sikes (1958) turned professional and was in the 1969 Ryder Cup team; Richard H. Sikes (1961, 1962) was in the 1963 Walker Cup team and turned professional in 1964; William A. Wright (1959) was the first Negro to win an American national championship.

See NATIONAL ASSOCIATION OF PUBLIC GOLF COURSES.

## UNITED STATES SENIORS' GOLF ASSOCIATION

The idea for this association grew out of a Seniors' Tournament arranged at the Apawamis Club, Rye, New York, in 1905, largely through the efforts of a member, Horace L. Hotchkiss. Members had to be 55 or over and their motto was "Once a Senior, always a Senior; sometimes venerable but never aged." The Seniors' Tournament has always been held at the Apawamis Club and decided over two rounds of stroke play.

The association was officially formed in 1917 and led in the following spring to a Canadian Senior Golfers' Association. The first international match was held in September 1918 at the Royal Montreal Club, the Canadians winning by 23 points to 19. Encouraged by Frederick Snare, Seniors' Champion, 1922, 1925, and a former president of the association, the idea spread across the Atlantic and the Senior Golfers' Society of Great Britain was formed in 1926.

In 1927 the first International Triangular Match between the three countries was held at the Sunningdale Club, Berkshire, being won by the British team. It has become an annual event, held in each country in turn, teams consisting of 12 players.

Among the winners of the U.S. Seniors' Championship have been Findley S. Douglas (1932), U.S. Amateur Champion, 1898, and runner-up, 1899, 1900, and Jack Westland (1963), U.S. Amateur Champion, 1952, and Walker Cup team captain, 1961.

See SENIOR GOLFERS' SOCIETY OF GREAT BRITAIN.

## UNITED STATES SENIOR WOMEN'S AMATEUR CHAMPIONSHIP

This championship is restricted to women amateurs who have reached the age of 50 and whose handicaps are 15 or less. The first event was decided by 54 holes of stroke play, spread over three days, but next year it went over to match play. The first winner and runner-up were both famous golfers—Miss Maureen Orcutt and Mrs Glenna Collett Vare.

## UNITED STATES (U.S.G.A.) SENIORS AMATEUR CHAMPIONSHIP

This is a newer tournament than the U.S. Seniors' Association Championship, having been founded only in 1955. Players must be 55 or over. It is decided by match play and among the winners have been Frederick J. Wright (1956), who played in the 1923 Walker Cup team; and Merril L. Carlsmith (1962), the first Hawaiian (apart from 'Jackie' Pung, the 1952 U.S. Ladies' Champion) to win a U.S.G.A. championship.

## UNITED STATES WOMEN'S OPEN CHAMPIONSHIP

The championship for women professionals—although amateurs can, of course, compete—was founded in 1946. In its first year only it was decided by match play, after 36 holes of qualifying stroke play, the winner being Patty Berg, who had been a professional since 1940.

Since 1947 the championship has been decided by four rounds of stroke play, the 1947 winner being Betty Jameson, who had been runner-up in 1946. The winner in 1948, 1950 was 'Babe' Zaharias and she won again in 1954, making a brave comeback after a cancer operation, two years before her death. Both Betsy Rawls and 'Mickey' Wright have won the event four times. The only non-American champion has been the well-known French amateur, Mme Catherine De Prado (1967), who also won the U.S. Ladies' Championship, 1969.

## UNIVERSITY MATCH

See OXFORD AND CAMBRIDGE MATCH.

## UP AND DOWN PLAYER

One who goes in and out of bunkers or traps.

## UPDEGRAFF, Dr Edgar R. (b 1922)

American. Walker Cup team, 1963, 1965, 1969.

## UPRIGHT SWING

See FLAT SWING.

## URUGUAY, GOLF IN

The leading club is the Club de Golf del Uruguay, about ten miles from the centre of the capital, Montevideo. It is an 18-holes course of 6,340 yards and there is a very large membership. Uruguay also has several other courses, including the Quilmes and Tlahualilo Clubs.

## URZETTA, Sam (b 1926)

U.S. Amateur Champion, 1950. Walker Cup team, 1951, 1953.

**VAGLIANO, André (1896-1971)**
French Open Amateur Champion, 1925. French Amateur Native Champion, 1923, 1924, 1926, 1930, 1931; runner-up, 1927. Donor of the Vagliano Cup for matches between teams of women golfers representing the British Isles and the rest of Europe. Father of Mlle Lally Vagliano (Mme Patrick Segard). See SEGARD, MME PATRICK; VAGLIANO CUP MATCHES.

**VAGLIANO CUP MATCHES**
This cup, given in 1931 by M. André Vagliano, the well-known French golfer and administrator, was originally intended for a biennial match between women golfers of the British Isles and France, but since 1959 between the British Isles and the Continent of Europe. The match consists of five foursomes in the morning and ten singles in the afternoon over two days and is played on a British and a Continental course alternately.

**VALENTINE, Mrs George (b 1915)**
Born Jessie Anderson, daughter of a Scottish professional, Joe Anderson. British Ladies' Champion, 1937, 1955, 1958; runner-up, 1950, 1957. French Ladies' Champion, 1936. Scottish Ladies' Champion, 1938, 1939, 1951, 1953, 1955, 1956; runner-up, 1934, 1954. New Zealand Ladies' Champion, 1935. Won Worplesdon Mixed Foursomes, with J. E. Behrend, 1963, 1964, 1965. Curtis Cup team, 1936, 1938, 1950, 1952, 1954, 1956, 1958.

**VALLEY OF SIN**
The wide dip immediately in front of the 18th green on the Old Course, St Andrews. If you don't play your second shot firmly enough, your ball is apt to roll back into the bottom of the Valley of Sin—a fate that has befallen many distinguished golfers.

**VAN DONCK, Flory (b 1912)**
Runner-up, British Open Championship, 1956, 1959. Belgian Open Champion, 1939, 1946, 1947, 1953, 1956; runner-up, 1935, 1951. Belgian Professional Champion, 1935, 1938, 1949, 1952, 1953, 1954, 1955, 1956, 1957, 1959, 1960, 1963, 1964. Dutch Open Champion, 1936, 1937, 1946, 1951, 1953; runner-up, 1957. French Open Champion, 1954, 1957, 1958; runner-up, 1946, 1956. German Open Champion, 1953, 1956. Portuguese Open Champion, 1955. Swiss Open Champion, 1953, 1955; runner-up, 1947, 1952, 1956, 1957. Played for Belgium in World (formerly Canada) Cup every year, 1954-64.

**VAN WIE, Virginia (b 1909)**
U.S. Ladies' Champion, 1932, 1933, 1934; runner-up, 1928, 1930. Curtis Cup team, 1932, 1934.

**VARANGOT, Brigitte (b 1940)**
Born in Biarritz. British Ladies' Champion, 1963, 1965, 1968. French Ladies' Open Champion, 1961, 1962, 1964, 1965, 1966; runner-up, 1960, 1963, 1967, 1970. French Ladies' Close Champion, 1959, 1961, 1962, 1963, 1966, 1970; runner-up, 1960, 1965, 1968, 1969. Runner-up, Italian Ladies' Open Championship, 1961; won Italian title, 1970. British Girls' Champion, 1957; runner-up, 1958.

**VARDON, Harry (1870-1937)**
Born Grouville, Jersey; died Totteridge, Hertfordshire. One of the

greatest golfers who ever lived and a member of the Triumvirate, with J. H. Taylor and James Braid, who dominated British golf between the mid-1890s and the outbreak of the 1914-18 war.

British Open Champion for the record number of six times—1896, 1898, 1899, 1903, 1911, 1914. His first win was after a tie with J. H. Taylor, preventing his hat-trick. Runner-up, 1900, 1902, 1912. U.S. Open Champion, 1900; lost in 1913 after tie with Francis Ouimet and Ted Ray. German Open Champion, 1911. British Professional Match Play Champion, 1912. Played many famous challenge matches, including his defeat in 1899 of Willie Park, Jun, at North Berwick and Ganton; with J. H. Taylor, his defeat in 1905 of James Braid and Sandy Herd in an England-Scotland match at St Andrews, Troon, Lytham and St Anne's and Deal; and with James Braid his defeat in 1906 of George Duncan and C. H. Mayo at Walton Heath and Timperley.

He was one of the seven sons (two of whom, Tom and Fred, also became professionals) of a gardener; the master at the village school at Gorey, where they all went, was the father of two other famous golfers, Aubrey and Percy Boomer. When he was about 7, the Royal Jersey Golf Club was laid out over Grouville Common and young Harry's first introduction to the game was as a caddie. His younger brother, Tom, was the first member of the family to become a professional and with his help Harry—then 20—was appointed professional and greenkeeper at a new course, the Studley Royal Club at Ripon, Yorkshire. From there he went to the Bury Club, Lancashire, where he played the first professional match of his life, against Sandy Herd, who won easily.

Vardon played in his first British Open Championship in 1893 at Prestwick—J. H. Taylor also making his first appearance. Taylor won the next two Opens in 1894 and 1895 and tied with Vardon at Muirfield in 1896, losing the play-off by four strokes.

By then Vardon had become professional at Ganton, near Scarborough, where he stayed until he moved to the South Herts Club, Totteridge, early in 1903.

Of Vardon as a golfer, Harold Hilton, the great Hoylake amateur, wrote in 1912:

Never in recent times has a player stood out by himself as did Harry Vardon at one period in his career, some eleven or twelve years ago. During the seasons of 1898 and 1899, until he departed from these shores for his tour in America, not only did he win nearly every event he entered for, but he won the majority of them with sufficient ease to suggest that his opponents were not, as golfers, quite in the same class as himself. This all happened in the last few years of the gutta-percha ball, and many critics have dated his gradual descent from the exalted position he then held to the incoming of the rubber-cored ball.

There is no doubt, too, that Vardon's strenuous tour of the United States in 1900—he travelled over 20,000 miles, played scores of exhibition matches, won the U.S. Open and played a major part in popularising the game in America—contributed towards his breakdown in health in 1903, causing him to spend many months in a sanatorium in Norfolk. That he was able to go on winning major events after his recovery was due both to his fighting spirit and his supreme skill as a golfer. Author of *The Complete Golfer* (1905); *How to Play Golf* (1912); *My Golfing Life* (1933). See VARDON GRIP.

## VARDON, Tom (b 1872)

Born Grouville, Jersey. Younger brother of Harry Vardon. Runner-up to Harry in British Open Championship, 1903. Runner-up, British Professional Match Play Championship, 1905.

## VARDON GRIP

In his book, *The Complete Golfer* (1905), Harry Vardon wrote: "My grip is one of my own inventions." What is called the 'Vardon Grip', however, is essentially the now almost universal overlapping grip—and this grip was used by a number of leading players before Vardon's time. In particular, the famous Scottish amateur, Leslie Balfour-Melville (born 1854 and British Amateur Champion, 1895), always used an overlapping grip. J. H. Taylor, too, an almost exact contemporary of Vardon, although he won his first Open Championship two years earlier, employed a similar grip. In his book, *Taylor on Golf* (1902), he wrote: "Harry Vardon's style is very similar to mine, with this exception—my thumb is placed over the club."

This is Vardon's own description of his grip: "The right hand is brought up so high that the palm of it covers over the left thumb, leaving very little of the latter to be seen. The first and second fingers of the right hand just reach round to the thumb of the left and the third finger completes the overlapping process, so that the club is held in the grip as if it were in a vice. The little finger of the right hand rides on the first finger of the left."

This is Taylor's description: "When I have the club in my hands, the thumb of my left hand is kept down the shaft, and it is entirely covered by the palm of my right hand; then the little finger of the last-mentioned hand is over the forefinger of the left hand, with the thumb of the other hand curled around the shaft, and not upon it."

See GRIP, TYPES OF ; HOGAN, BEN.

## VARE, Glenna Collett (b 1903)

Glenna Collett (Mrs Edwin H. Vare) was for many years one of America's greatest lady golfers. U.S. Ladies' Champion, 1922, 1925, 1928, 1929, 1930, 1935—a record number of victories ; runner-up, 1931, 1932. Canadian Ladies' Open Champion, 1923, 1924. Runner-up British Ladies' Championship, 1929, 1930, taking part in exciting finals against Joyce Wethered (Lady Heathcoat-Amory) and Diana Fishwick (Mrs A. C. Critchley). Curtis Cup team, 1932, 1934 (captain), 1936, 1938, 1948 (captain) ; non-playing captain, 1950. Author of *Ladies in the Rough* (1929).

## VAUGHAN, Sheila (Mrs Maher) (b 1942)

British Girls' Champion, 1959. Curtis Cup team, 1962, 1964.

## VENEZUELA, GOLF IN

Much of the terrain is unsuitable for golf but there are some 10 courses. The oldest club is the Caracas Country Club, near the capital city, and the other clubs include the Maracaibo Country Club and the La Salina Club, run by the Shell Company.

## VENTURI, Ken (b 1931)

U.S. Open Champion, 1964. Runner-up, U.S. Junior Amateur Championship, 1948. As an amateur, was runner-up in the U.S. Masters, 1956, being beaten by Jack Burke by one stroke after taking 80 in the final round; also runner-up, 1960. Walker Cup team, 1953. Ryder Cup team, 1965. Turned professional, 1956.

See WALKER AND RYDER CUPS, PLAYED IN BOTH.

## VICTORIA FALLS, BALL DRIVEN ACROSS

The first man to drive a ball across the Victoria Falls on the Zambezi— 160 yards—was Professor John Milne, the seismologist, during a meeting of the British Association in South Africa. Professor Sims Woodhead, the Cambridge pathologist, was so impressed that he, too, tried—and succeeded. Both professors then tried again—and failed. This was in the 1890s.

## VON ELM, George (b 1901)

Runner-up, U.S. Open Championship, 1931. U.S. Amateur Champion, 1926, beating Bobby Jones in the final; runner-up, 1924, being beaten by Bobby Jones. Walker Cup team, 1926, 1928, 1930.

## VON NIDA, Norman George (b 1917)

At 15 Queensland Amateur Champion. Australian Open Champion, 1950, 1952, 1953. Australian Professional Champion, 1946, 1948, 1950, 1951; runner-up, 1938, 1960. Won many tournaments in Britain after the Second World War, including Dunlop Masters, 1948; tied with Arthur Lees, 1947, but lost play-off. Has done much for golf in Australia and to encourage young professionals. Author of *Golf Isn't Hard* (1949); *Golf is My Business* (1956).

## VON SZLAVY, Erzsebet (Elizabeth) (b 1902)

Born Budapest. Hungary's greatest lady golfer. Hungarian Ladies' Champion, 1922, 1923, 1924, 1925, 1926, 1927, 1928, 1931, 1932, 1933, 1935, 1936, 1937, 1938, 1939; runner-up, 1929. Austrian Ladies' Open Champion, 1927, 1928, 1929, 1936. Czechoslovak Ladies' Open Champion, 1932, 1933, 1935, 1937. German Ladies' Open Champion, 1926.

## Vs

The v-shaped divisions between one's thumb and fingers. When a club is gripped correctly the Vs point almost exactly in the same direction. Golfers have slight variations, but with most players the Vs point towards the right shoulder at the address position.

## WADKINS, Jerry Lanston ('Lanny') (b 1949)

U.S. Amateur Champion, 1970. Walker Cup team, 1969, 1971. World Cup (formerly Eisenhower Trophy) team, 1970. His brother, Bobby (b 1951), won the first European Open Championship, 1978.

## WAGGLE

The to-and-fro movement of the hands and clubhead preparatory to making a stroke. The degree of waggle varies enormously among golfers. To take one example, Charles Whitcombe, one of three famous golfing brothers, just put the clubhead down behind the ball and took it straight back for the stroke without any waggle ; Sandy Herd, on the other hand, often had as many as 16 waggles ; J. H. Taylor had only two or three waggles, but very aggressive ones. In the final of the 1931 British Amateur Championship, the runner-up, John De Forest, suffered so violently from 'waggling' that he could hardly get the club back at all ; next year he won the title, although, according to Bernard Darwin, "his waggling symptoms were as pronounced as ever." See MORRIS, TOM (JUNIOR).

## WALKER AND RYDER CUPS, PLAYED IN BOTH

The following British golfers have played in both Walker and Ryder Cup matches:

Norman Drew: 1953 ; 1959.
Peter Townsend: 1965 ; 1969.
Mark James: 1975; 1977.
The following have played for the United States in both matches:
Tommy Aaron: 1959 ; 1969.
Fred Haas: 1938 ; 1953.
Gene Littler: 1953 ; 1961, 1963, 1965, 1967, 1969.
Jack Nicklaus: 1959, 1961 ; 1969.
Ken Venturi: 1953 ; 1965.
Almost more remarkable was the case of Tommy Armour—he played for Britain in the 1921 match that led to the Walker Cup series and for the United States in the 1926 match that was the forerunner of the Ryder Cup series.

## WALKER, Arthur (b 1929)

English Amateur Champion, 1957. Although born in Johannesburgh, qualified because his mother was English. In the same year reached the semi-final of the British Amateur Championship. South African Amateur Champion, 1959.

## WALKER, Cyril (b 1892)

U.S. Open Champion, 1924, defeating the holder, Bobby Jones, by three strokes. An Englishman from Lancashire, he played for America in the unofficial match at Wentworth, 1926, that led next year to the Ryder Cup series.

## WALKER, George Herbert

See WALKER CUP.

## WALKER, James (b 1921)

Runner-up, British Amateur Championship, 1961. Scottish Amateur Champion, 1961. Walker Cup team, 1961.

## WALKER, Mrs J. B. (b 1896)

Irish Ladies' Champion, 1930; runner-up, 1934. Australian Ladies' Champion, 1935. Runner-up, New Zealand Ladies' Championship, 1935. Curtis Cup team, 1934, 1936, 1938.

## WALKER, Maureen (b 1955)

British Girls' Champion, 1972; runner-up 1971. Scottish Girls' Champion, 1971.

## WALKER, Michelle (b 1952)

British Ladies' Champion, 1971, 1972; runner-up, 1973. English Ladies' Champion, 1973. Runner-up, British and English Girls' Championship, 1970. Portuguese Ladies' Champion, 1972. Curtis Cup team, 1972.

## WALKER CUP

In 1913 Charles B. Macdonald, the famous American golfer and administrator, had offered to donate a cup for competition between teams of four amateurs from any country; but, although the matter was discussed by the R. and A., the outbreak of the war in 1914 caused it to be shelved.

The Walker Cup series began after the war, like the Ryder Cup, with an unofficial match between teams of British and American amateurs, on the day before the 1921 British Amateur Championship at Royal Liverpool Club, Hoylake. The leading spirit on the American side was William C. Fownes, who had captained two teams against Canadian golfers, 1919, 1920. Early in 1921 the United States Golf Association had invited all golfing countries to send teams to compete for a trophy in America, but, partly owing to post-war difficulties, none was able to accept. Instead, Fownes raised a team, including the youthful Bobby Jones, 'Chick' Evans and Francis Ouimet, and succeeded in beating a British team which included Cyril Tolley, Roger Wethered, Ernest Holderness—and Tommy Armour, then an amateur.

George H. Walker, President of the U.S.G.A., had already agreed to donate an International Challenge Trophy. Newspapers called it the Walker Cup, and this was the name given to the series when it became a contest limited to Britain and the United States. It was originally intended to be an annual event, but after being played in 1922, 1923, 1924, it became biennial.

The first meeting, at the National Links, Long Island, was rather a casual affair. The British team comprised only eight players, and when the captain, Robert Harris, was taken ill just before the match, his place was filled, as captain and player, by Bernard Darwin, who was reporting the match for *The Times*; he lost his foursome playing with Cyril Tolley in the top match against Francis Ouimet and Jesse Guilford, but won his single against the American captain, William Fownes.

Matches were played in the same way—four 36-holes foursomes and eight 36-holes singles spread over two days—until 1963, when the method was changed to eight 18-holes foursomes and sixteen 18-holes singles played over two days.

Two players—one on each side—have an outstanding record in the Walker Cup matches. The late Francis Ouimet was in the American team, 1922, 1923, 1924, 1926, 1928, 1930, 1932, 1934, being playing captain in the last two years, and then non-playing captain, 1936, 1938, 1949. Joe Carr was in the British team, 1947, 1949, 1951, 1953, 1955, 1957, 1959, 1961, 1963, 1967, being captain in 1963, and then non-playing captain in 1965.

The following are the results of the Walker Cup matches since 1922:

*1922 (National Links, Long Island)*
U.S.A. 8 matches; Britain 4 matches.
*1923 (Old Course, St Andrews)*
U.S.A. 6 matches; Britain 5 matches; one halved.
*1924 (Garden City, New York)*
U.S.A. 9 matches; Britain 3 matches.
*1926 Old Course, St Andrews*
U.S.A. 6 matches; Britain 5 matches; one halved.
*1928 (Chicago Club, Wheaton)*
U.S.A. 11 matches; Britain 1 match.
*1930 (Royal St George's Sandwich)*

U.S.A. 10 matches; Britain 2 matches.

*1932 (The Country Club, Brookline)*
U.S.A. 8 matches; Britain 1 match; 3 halved.

*1934 (Old Course, St Andrews)*
U.S.A. 9 matches; Britain 2 matches; 1 halved.

*1936 (Pine Valley, New Jersey)*
U.S.A. 9 matches; Britain 0 matches; 3 halved.

*1938 (Old Course, St Andrews)*
Britain 7 matches; U.S.A. 4 matches; 1 halved.

*1947 (Old Course, St Andrews)*
U.S.A. 8 matches; Britain 4 matches.

*1949 (Winged Foot, New York)*
U.S.A. 10 matches; Britain 2 matches.

*1951 (Royal Birkdale, Southport)*
U.S.A. 6 matches; Britain 3 matches; 3 halved.

*1953 (Kittansett, Marion, Mass.)*
U.S.A. 9 matches; Britain 3 matches.

*1955 (Old Course, St Andrews)*
U.S.A. 10 matches; Britain 2 matches.

*1957 (Minikahda, Minneapolis)*
U.S.A. 8 matches; Britain 3 matches; 1 halved.

*1959 (Muirfield, East Lothian)*
U.S.A. 9 matches; Britain 3 matches.

*1961 (Seattle, Washington)*
U.S.A. 11 matches; Britain 1 match.

*1963 (Turnberry, Ayrshire)*
U.S.A. 12 matches; Britain 8 matches, 4 halved.

*1965 (Baltimore, Maryland)*
U.S.A. 11 matches; Britain 11 matches; 2 halved.

*1967 (Royal St George's, Sandwich)*
U.S.A. 13 matches; Britain 7 matches; 4 halved.

*1969 (Milwaukee, Wisconsin)*
U.S.A. 10 matches; Britain 8 matches; 6 halved.

*1971 (Old Course, St Andrews)*
Britain 12 matches; U.S.A. 10 matches; 2 halved.

*1973 (Brookline, Mass.)*

U.S.A. 12 matches; Britain 8 matches; 4 halved.

*1975 (Old Course, St. Andrews)*
U.S.A. 14 matches; Britain 8 matches; 2 halved.

*1977 (Shinnecock Hills, New York)*
U.S.A. 16 matches, Britain 8 matches.

### WALL, Art (b 1923)
Won U.S. Masters, 1959. Canadian Open Champion, 1960. Mexican Open Champion, 1964. Ryder Cup team, 1957, 1959, 1961. Turned professional 1949, after winning the Pennsylvania Amateur Championship. Is said to have done 37 holes-in-one. See HOLES-IN-ONE, GREATEST NUMBER OF.

### WALTON HEATH
Tadworth, Surrey. Founded 1904. Fine and very testing heathland course. Length (Old Course): 6,834 yards. S.S.S. 73. Housed English Amateur Championship 1926, 1958; English Ladies' Championship, 1914, 1928. English Open Amateur Stroke Play Championship, 1968. Also Professional Match Play Championship, 1905, 1909, 1911, 1913, 1919, 1923, 1927, 1934, 1938, 1945, 1949, 1952, 1955. 1958, 1961, 1962, 1964-69. Also New Course (6,612 yards. S.S.S. 72).

### WARD, Charles H. (b 1911)
P.G.A. Champion, 1956. British Senior Professional Champion, 1965, losing to Sam Snead in the World Senior Championship. Won Dunlop Masters (after tie with John Burton), 1949; runner-up, 1950. Ryder Cup team, 1947, 1949, 1951.

### WARD, E. Harvie (b 1926)
American. U.S. Amateur Champion, 1955, 1956. British Amateur Champion, 1952; runner-up, 1953. Might have won the U.S. Championship three times running but for the fact that he was suspended for a year by the U.S. Golf Association. Walker Cup team, 1953, 1955, 1959.

### WARD, Marvin H. ('Bud') (1913-67)
U.S. Amateur Champion, 1939, 1941. Walker Cup team, 1938, 1947,

## WARDLAW, Mrs A. M. H. (b 1911)

Born Nan Baird. British Girls' Champion, 1929. Scottish Ladies' Champion, 1934; runner-up, 1935. Curtis Cup team, 1938.

## WARM BALL, ADVANTAGES OF A

Many golfers believe that a warm ball will travel at least a few yards further than a cold one and, therefore, they use two balls at alternate holes, keeping one warm in a trouser pocket. This theory is considered in *The Search for the Perfect Swing* (1968), an account of the Golf Society of Great Britain Scientific Study, and the authors, Alastair Cochran and John Stobbs, write:

A ball's coefficient of restitution—the liveliness, that is, with which it springs away again after being flattened against the clubface—is directly affected by its temperature; and keeping it warm can make it start off quite a bit faster from impact and thus fly quite a bit further from the tee. A drive which will carry 200 yards with the ball at 70°F (21°C) will carry only 185 yards when the ball is at freezing point.

The effect upon a ball's temperature of keeping it in your trouser pocket for ten minutes on a cold day, though, is very much less than the optimist may believe. Rubber is a poor conductor of heat, and it may take several hours for a ball to heat up all the way through, however warm it feels on its surface. But it loses heat only very slowly too; and it will thus have quite an effect on the length of a player's drive on a cold day for him to store a few balls in the boiler-house the night before, and then to use a different one every three or four holes, keeping the others in his trouser pockets.

See GOLF BALL, VELOCITY OF; HITTING THE BALL, STATISTICS.

## WATER HAZARD

See HAZARDS.

## WATROUS, Al (b 1899)

Runner-up, British Open Championship, 1926, the first year that Bobby Jones won. Canadian Open Champion, 1922. U.S. Senior Professional Champion, 1950, 1951, 1957. Ryder Cup team, 1927, 1929.

## WATSON, Tom (b 1949)

American. British Open Champion, 1975, 1977. U.S. Masters, 1977. Ryder Cup team, 1977.

## WEDGE

The most modern of the golfer's armoury of clubs. "Before 1932", writes Doug Ford in *The Wedge Book* (1963), "the niblick performed the services the wedge does now ... During the winter of 1932 Gene Sarazen fashioned a club with a heavily flanged sole. With this club he was able to 'blast' out of a sand trap within ten feet of the pin. This newly-developed sand iron was the forerunner of the present-day wedge." The wedge is heavier and more lofted than the No 9 iron and is intended for shots to the green of up to about 90 yards. Bobby Locke was one of the first masters of the wedge. See NIBLICK; SAND IRON.

## WEETMAN, Harry (1920-72)

British Professional Match Play Champion, 1951, 1958; runner-up, 1956, 1959, 1960. German Open Champion, 1957. Won Dunlop Masters, 1952, 1958. Ryder Cup team, 1951, 1953, 1955, 1957, 1959, 1961, 1963; non-playing captain, 1965. Represented England in World (formerly Canada) Cup, 1953, 1954, 1956, 1960. Killed in a car accident.

## WEISKOPF, Tom (b 1942)

Won Piccadilly Match Play Tournament, 1972, beating Lee Trevino in the final. British Open Champion, 1973. Canadian Open, 1973.

## WELSH AMATEUR NATIVE CHAMPIONSHIP

Although just behind Ireland and Scotland, Wales started its Amateur Championship 30 years before England. Competitors must be of Welsh birth or have one Welsh parent and must not have played for any of the other three countries or in their Close Championship for at least 15 years.

In the 1920s and 30s, H. R. Howell had a remarkable record, winning eight times, including three in a row (1922, 1923, 1924) and four in a row (1929, 1930, 1931, 1932). In more recent times, Hew Squirrell has won five times between 1958-65, including a hat-trick (1958, 1959, 1960).

## WELSH GOLFING UNION

Founded in 1895, the W.G.U. is an association of Welsh golf clubs and organisations, at present numbering 100. Its chief objects are:

1. To take any necessary steps for furthering the interests of golf in Wales and Monmouthshire.
2. To organise the annual Welsh Amateur Championship.
3. To encourage inter-club, inter-county and international matches.
4. To help to maintain a uniform system of handicapping.
5. To help to maintain the Sports Turf Research Institute.
6. To co-operate with the R. and A. through the medium of the Council of National Golf Unions.

## WELTS, Mrs Anne Quast (b 1937)

Born Anne Quast. U.S. Ladies' Champion, 1958, 1961 (as Mrs J. D. Decker), 1963 (as Mrs Welts); runner-up, 1965, 1968. Curtis Cup team, 1958, 1960, 1962, 1964, 1966, 1968. Now Mrs S. Sander.

## WENTWORTH

Virginia Water, Surrey. Founded 1924. Length (West Course): 6,997 yards. S.S.S. 73. Cut out of pine, heather and gorse land and, for its toughness, called the 'Burma Road'. Housed English Amateur Championship, 1961. Also Ryder Cup match, 1953; Canada (now World) Cup, 1956; annual Piccadilly World Match Play Tournament. Also East Course (6,202 yards. S.S.S. 70). See BURMA ROAD; PICCADILLY WORLD MATCH PLAY TOURNAMENT.

## WESLOCK, Nick K. (b 1930)

Canadian Amateur Champion, 1957, 1963, 1964, 1966; runner-up, 1950. Member of Canadian teams that were runners-up in World Cup (formerly Eisenhower Trophy), 1962, 1964.

## WEST INDIES, GOLF IN THE

Golf is booming in the various West Indian islands. Apart from those listed below, courses are being developed in St Kitts and St Lucia.

See separately under BARBADOS, GRENADA, JAMAICA, MONTSERRAT, ST VINCENT, TOBAGO, TRINIDAD.

## WESTLAND, Jack (b 1905)

American. U.S. Amateur Champion, 1952—at 47 the oldest winner of the title; runner-up, to Francis Ouimet, 1931. Walker Cup team, 1932, 1934, 1953; non-playing captain, 1961.

## WESTWARD HO!

See ROYAL NORTH DEVON CLUB.

## WETHERED, Joyce

See HEATHCOAT-AMORY, LADY.

## WETHERED, Roger (b 1899)

Elder brother of Miss Joyce Wethered (Lady Heathcoat-Amory). Tied for British Open Championship, 1921, but lost play-off to Jock Hutchison. British Amateur Champion, 1923; runner-up, 1928, 1930. Won *Golf Illustrated* Gold Vase, 1927; President's Putter of the Oxford and Cambridge Golfing Society, 1926, 1927, 1928, 1935, 1936; runner-up, 1933, 1949. Won Worplesdon Mixed Foursomes, with Miss Joyce Wethered, 1922. Wal-

T

ker Cup team, 1922, 1923, 1926, 1930, 1934. Captain R. and A., 1946.

In the 1921 Open at St Andrews Roger Wethered was the victim of a famous unlucky incident. In his third round of 72—a fine score in those days when the Old Course was much rougher than it is now—he walked forward to spy out the land at the long 14th, menaced by Hell Bunker, and in returning accidentally trod on his ball, incurring a penalty stroke. In the end Hutchison's final round of 70 and Wethered's 71 caused a tie, Hutchison winning the 36 holes play-off by nine strokes. Author (with his sister) of *Golf From Two Sides* (1922).

### WHIFF
See AIR SHOT.

### WHIGHAM, H. J. (b 1868)
U.S. Amateur Champion, 1896, 1897. An American-born member of an Ayrshire family, educated at Oxford, Whigham was a professional journalist and, among other assignments, covered the American-Spanish war in Cuba. He married a daughter of C. B. Macdonald, one of the pioneers of golf in America.

### WHIPPING
The twine or waxed thread used— more in the old days than now—for binding round a golf club at the point where the head meets the shaft and at the bottom of the grip. With modern methods of fixing, whipping has almost disappeared.

### WHITCOMBE, Charles Albert (b 1895)
British Professional Match Play Champion, 1928, 1930; runner-up, 1934. Ryder Cup team, 1927, 1929, 1931 (captain), 1933, 1935 (captain), 1937 (captain); non-playing captain, 1949. Author of *Golf* (1949). See BROTHER GOLFERS.

### WHITCOMBE, Ernest (1890-1971)
The eldest of three well-known golfing brothers. Runner-up, British Open Championship, 1923, one stroke behind Walter Hagen. Irish Open Champion, 1928, 1935. Dutch Open Champion, 1928. French Open Champion, 1930. British Professional Match Play Champion, 1924. Ryder Cup team, 1929, 1931, 1935 (in this year all three Whitcombes played).

### WHITCOMBE, Reginald Arthur (1898-1958)
British Open Champion, 1938; runner-up, 1937. Irish Open Champion, 1936; runner-up, 1935, 1939. Ryder Cup team, 1935. Won £500 36-holes challenge match, with Henry Cotton against Bobby Locke and Sid Brews of South Africa, Walton Heath, 1938. Author of *Golf's No Mystery* (1938).

### WHITE, Jack (1875-1949)
Born near Edinburgh, a nephew of Ben Sayers; died Musselburgh. British Open Champion, 1904—when he was the first player to break 300 for the four rounds, with a score of 296. Runner-up to Harry Vardon, 1899.

He began his golf career as a caddie, at one time regularly carrying the clubs of the well-known Scottish amateur, John Laidlay. He was professional at York, Newmarket and Seaford and in 1901 became the first professional at the newly-made Sunningdale Club, Berkshire, where he remained for the rest of his working life, retiring in 1926.

Like his friend, the younger Willie Park, he was a great putter, and in his book, *Putting* (1921), he said that the winner of the Open Championship was "the man who is holing his putts". Also author of *Easier Golf* (1924). With Park he designed a number of golf courses, including West Hill, Surrey.

### WHITE, Ronald James (b 1921)
English Amateur Champion, 1949; runner-up, 1953. English Open Ama-

teur Stroke Play Champion, 1950, 1951. Won *Golf Illustrated* Gold Vase, 1949. Walker Cup team, 1947, 1949, 1951, 1953, 1955, 1961. Author of *Golf As I Play It* (1953).

### WHYTE-MELVILLE, John (1797-1883)

Born near St Andrews. A familiar figure in many early photographs of St Andrews golfers, he was a member of the R. and A. from 1816. He was captain in 1823 and had just been re-elected in 1883 when he died and the captaincy was left vacant for that year.

His son, George, the Victorian novelist, was captain of the R. and A. in 1851. He was killed in the hunting-field in 1878.

There is a fine portrait of John Whyte-Melville, painted by Sir Francis Grant, P.R.A., in the R. and A. clubhouse. He is wearing his red jacket, with the bridge over the Swil-can Burn behind him.

### WILKINSON, Martha

See KIROUAC, MRS MARTHA.

### WILL, George (b 1937)

British Youths' Champion, 1957. Assistant Professionals' Champion, 1963. British Army Champion, 1959, 1960. Ryder Cup team, 1963, 1965, 1967. Played for Scotland in World (formerly Canada) Cup, 1963, 1969, 1970. Author of *Golf: The Modern Way* (1969).

### WILLING, Dr Oscar F. (b 1899)

Runner-up, U.S. Amateur Championship, 1929. Walker Cup team, 1923, 1924, 1930.

### WILSON, Enid (b 1910)

British Ladies' Champion, 1931, 1932, 1933—the only player, apart from Cecil Leitch and Lady Margaret Scott, to win the championship three times running. English Ladies' Champion, 1928, 1930; runner-up, 1927. Won Girls' Championship and the Derbyshire Ladies' Championship in

1925 at the age of 15. Curtis Cup team, 1932. A distinguished golf writer. Author of *A Gallery of Women Golfers* (1961).

### WILSON, James

A St Andrews clubmaker who was assistant to the great Hugh Philp, 1845-52, when he set up his own business. For some years he turned out clubs—particularly cleeks—as fine as his old master's, his trade-mark being a bent carpenter's nail. One of his apprentices was Andrew Strath. See PHILP, HUGH; STRATH, ANDREW.

### WILSON, James C. (b 1920)

Runner-up, Scottish Amateur Championship, 1951, 1952. Walker Cup team, 1947, 1953.

### WILSON, John (b 1892)

Scottish Amateur Champion, 1922, 1931. Walker Cup team, 1923.

### WIMBLEDON COMMON, GOLF ON

Golf has been played on Wimbledon Common, to the south-west of London, since 1865, thus making it the oldest English golfing ground where the game is still played, after Westward Ho!, founded a year earlier. The original club on Wimbledon Common was that of the London Scottish Volunteers, but in 1880 some civilian members broke away and formed their own club, with a separate clubhouse, each club starting the round from its own end of the course. The Wimbledon Club became Royal Wimbledon in 1882 and in 1908 opened a separate course of its own on good golfing terrain at nearby Caesar's Camp. Its place on the Common was taken by a new Wimbledon Common Club, which still shares the old course with the London Scottish Club. The old windmill is a famous landmark. Red coats or pullovers have to be worn by all players on the Common.

The first 15 Oxford and Cambridge matches were held on Wimbledon Common, from 1878 onwards, and the foundation of the Ladies' Golf Union in 1893 owes much to Miss Issette Pearson and other lady members of Royal Wimbledon. See LADIES' GOLF UNION; OXFORD AND CAMBRIDGE MATCH.

## WINGED FOOT

Mamaroneck, New York. Founded 1923, to the design of A. W. Tillinghast. Length (East Course): 6,614 yards (Par 71). Housed U.S. Open Championship, 1929. (West Course), 1959; U.S. Amateur Championship, 1940; U.S. Women's Open Championship, 1957. Also Walker Cup Match, 1949. West Course: 6,445 yards (Par 70).

## WINTER RULES

See PREFERRED LIES.

## WOLSTENHOLME, Guy B. (b 1933)

English Amateur Champion, 1956, 1959. English Open Amateur Stroke Play Champion, 1960. Dutch Open Champion, 1969. German Open Amateur Champion, 1956. P.G.A. Champion, 1966. Won *Golf Illustrated* Gold Vase, 1957. Walker Cup team, 1957, 1959. Turned professional 1961. Now an Australian citizen.

## WOOD, Craig R. (1901-68)

Like Jimmy Adams in Britain, he was famous as a runner-up; he took part in some exciting finishes, particularly with Densmore Shute. U.S. Open Champion, 1941 (runner-up being Shute); runner-up, 1939, to Byron Nelson after tie with him and Shute. Tied for British Open Championship, 1933, with Shute; lost play-off. Won U.S. Masters, 1941; runner-up in first two years, 1934, 1935. Runner-up, U.S.P.G.A. Championship, 1934. Canadian Open Champion, 1942. Ryder Cup team, 1931, 1933, 1935.

In the 1933 British Open at St Andrews, Wood played a remarkable and much-discussed drive at the long 5th, the 'Hole o' Cross Going Out'. As Bernard Darwin put it, he "drove his ball from the tee into one of the bunkers in the face of the hill in front of the green. The hole as played that day was 530 yards long and the ball ended about 100 yards from the hole. That this happened there is no shadow of doubt, as to how it happened I give it up".

## WOODEN CLUBS, COVERS FOR

The now almost universal covers, or hoods, for protecting the heads of

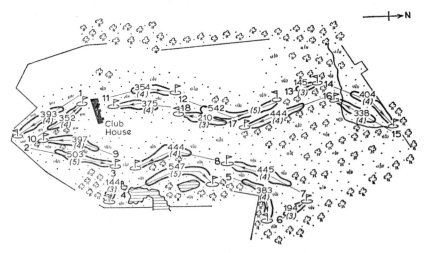

WINGED FOOT

wooden clubs were invented in 1916 by a young Japanese golfer named Seiichi Takahata, later a leading figure in Japanese golf. According to George Houghton's *Golf Addict Goes East* (1967), young Takahata, while working in England, became a member of the Addington Club and commissioned Jack Ross, the local professional, to make him a driver. "So lovely, in the eyes of the young Japanese, was this piece of polished persimmon that, rather than risk scratching the head of the club, Takahata asked a lady friend to make a protective covering. This prototype was knitted in heavy yellow yarn and attracted great attention from fellow members at Addington, who promptly followed suit and got their ladies working."

Owing to the war, no further steps were taken and it was not until the late 1920s that club covers, in various materials, began to be popular both in Britain and the United States. Jimmy Demaret reached a peak with a mink set.

## WOODHALL SPA
Woodhall Spa, Lincolnshire. Founded 1905. Heathland, with pine and heather. Length: 6,823 yards. S.S.S. 73. Housed English Amateur Championship, 1967; English Ladies' Championship, 1926, 1954, 1962; E.G.U. Brabazon Trophy, 1954; English Open Amateur Stroke Play Championship, 1962.

## WOODS USED IN CLUBMAKING
In the old days, shafts and heads of clubs were all made of wood, apart from such primitive clubs as 'rut irons'. For shafts, before the coming of American hickory, many woods were used, including ash, greenheart, purpleheart, lancewood, lemonwood, orangewood and blue-mahoo ('bloo-mahoo'). Golfers even tried malacca and other types of cane. All other shaft woods, however, were superseded by hickory, from the Tennessee Hickory Belt, which reached Britain in the mid-19th century.

For wooden-club heads, thorn, apple, pear, dogwood and beech were the main woods used, with beech perhaps the most suitable. The coming from America of persimmon, with its hardness and enduring qualities, however, ousted the other woods. Nowadays, of course, many club heads are made of laminated woods.

## WOOFS
A variation on the normal method of handicapping, in which the less good player is allowed 'woofs' instead of strokes. He is allowed to use his 'woofs'—by shouting 'woof' or pretending that he is about to do so—at any time during the game; the strain is on the better player because he never knows when a 'woof' is coming. 'Woofs' are, of course, used only in light-hearted games; and are not often met with at all these days.

## WORLD AMATEUR GOLF TEAM CHAMPIONSHIP
See WORLD CUP (FORMERLY EISENHOWER TROPHY).

## WORLD CUP (FORMERLY EISENHOWER TROPHY)
During his term of office as President of the United States, General Dwight D. Eisenhower, always a keen golfer, gave a trophy for a World Amateur Golf Team Championship, to be played for every other year. The teams consist of four players from each country and the three best four-round medal scores count.

The first meeting was held on the Old Course, St Andrews, in 1958, the winners being the Australian team, after a tie with the United States team. Since then the venue has been widely spread, to such countries as Japan and Singapore as well as the United States and Australia.

## WORLD (FORMERLY CANADA) CUP
This annual international professional team tournament was founded by the late John Jay Hopkins in 1953.

Each participating country is represented by a team of two, the winners being the team with the best four-round aggregate. The first winners were the Argentinians, Antonio Cerda and Roberto De Vicenzo.

John Jay Hopkins, a Canadian businessman, hoped that the idea of a World Cup would help towards international goodwill. "In golf," he said, "I have found a common meeting-ground for all men of genuine goodwill. The knave, the cheat, the boor—all soon find themselves playing alone, or not at all. The men you see strolling together down a fairway share a mutual regard for the integrity of each other and for the game that offers them a zestful form of recreation."

The World Cup has been held in countries as wide apart as Japan, Mexico, Puerto Rico and Spain.

## WORLD SERIES OF GOLF

This exclusive annual invitation tournament was inaugurated at the Firestone Country Club, Akron, Ohio, in 1962. It is confined to the holders of the four chief professional titles—the U.S. and British Open Champions, the U.S. Masters winner and the U.S. P.G.A. Champion—and a few more chosen players. It is decided over 36 holes of stroke play, the winner receiving £20,830 (50,000 dollars) and the runner-up £6,250 (15,000 dollars). As 1969 British Open Champion, Tony Jacklin was the first British golfer to qualify.

## WORLD WOMEN'S AMATEUR TEAM CHAMPIONSHIP

This international event, played every other year, was inaugurated in 1964. The first winners were the French team and the United States won in 1966, 1968, 1970, 1972. Play is for the Espirito Santo Trophy.

## WORPLESDON MIXED FOURSOMES

This famous annual tournament was inaugurated at the Worplesdon Club, near Woking, Surrey, in 1921. In the final at the first meeting, Miss Eleanor Helme, well-known as a golf journalist, and T. A. Torrance beat Miss Joyce Wethered and her brother, Roger. Next year the Wethereds won and thereafter for many years Miss Wethered, with a variety of partners, dominated the tournament. Her final appearance was in 1948 when, as Lady Heathcoat-Amory, she and her husband lost in the final.

## WORSHAM, Lewis ('Lew') (b 1922)

U.S. Open Champion, 1947, after tie with Sam Snead. Ryder Cup team, 1947.

## WRIGHT, Mrs Innes (b 1935)

Born Janette Robertson. Scottish Ladies' Champion, 1959, 1960, 1961; runner-up, 1958. British Girls' Champion, 1950; runner-up, 1951. Won Worplesdon Mixed Foursomes, with Innes Wright, 1959. Curtis Cup team, 1954, 1956, 1958, 1960.

## WRIGHT, Mary Kathryn ('Mickey') (b 1935)

Runner-up, U.S. Ladies' Championship, 1954. Turned professional, 1954. U.S. Women's Open Champion, 1958, 1959, 1961, 1964. U.S. Girls' Amateur Champion, 1952; runner-up, 1950.

## WRY-NECKED PUTTER

See GOOSE-NECKED PUTTER.

## WYLIE, Mrs John (b 1911)

Born Phyllis Wade. English Ladies' Champion, 1934; runner-up, 1936. Curtis Cup team, 1938.

## WYSONG, Dudley

Runner-up, U.S. Amateur Championship, 1961. Turned professional, 1962. Runner-up, U.S.P.G.A. Championship, 1966.

## YATES, Charles Richardson (b 1913)

British Amateur Champion, 1938, after taking part in the Walker Cup match at St Andrews; also Walker Cup team, 1936, and non-playing captain, 1953.

## YIPS, THE

See FREEZE; TWITCH, PUTTING.

## YOUNGEST AMATEUR CHAMPIONS

The youngest winners of the British Amateur Championship were John Beharrell and South African, Bobby Cole. They were both 18 and the same age to the day when they won, respectively, at Troon, 1956, and Carnoustie, 1966.

The youngest winner of the U.S. Amateur Championship was Robert A. Gardner, who was 19 and 5 months when he won at the Chicago Club, Wheaton, 1909. The next youngest—all at 19—were Jack Nicklaus, when he won the first of his two titles at the Broadmoor Club, Colorado, 1959; Bruce Fleischer, at the Scioto Country Club, Ohio, 1968; Louis James, at Glen View, Illinois, 1902; Lanny Wadkins, 1970.

## YOUNGEST LADY CHAMPIONS

The youngest winner of the British Ladies' Championship was Miss May Hezlet, member of a well-known Irish golfing family, who was 17 when she won at Newcastle, Co. Down, 1899. She celebrated her 17th birthday a week earlier on the day she won the Irish Ladies' Championship.

The youngest winner of the U.S. Ladies' Championship was Miss Beatrix Hoyt, who was 16 when she won the first of her three championships at the Morris Country Club, Morristown, New Jersey, 1896.

## YOUNGEST OPEN CHAMPIONS

The youngest winner of the British Open Championship was 'Young Tommy' Morris, who was 18 when he won the first of his four championships at Prestwick in 1868. The next youngest was Willie Auchterlonie, who was 21 when he became champion in 1893.

The youngest U.S. Open Champion was an Englishman, Horace Rawlins, who was 19 when he won the first championship at Newport, Rhode Island, 1895. The second youngest was the first American-born champion, John J. McDermott, also 19 when he won at the Chicago Club, Wheaton, 1911.

## YUGOSLAVIA, GOLF IN

The first club was founded in 1930 at Zagreb and was followed in 1936 by one near Belgrade, both of 9 holes. In 1938 an 18-holes course was established at Bled. None survived the war, but the Golf Club Bled was rebuilt in 1974 and the Open Amateur and Ladies' championships were begun again in 1977. A new full-length course is planned near Belgrade. A Golf Union was founded in 1939.

# Z

## ZAHARIAS, Mildred ('Babe') (1915-56)

Born Mildred Ella Didrikson. U.S. Ladies' Champion, 1946. British Ladies' Champion, 1947—the first American winner. U.S. Women's Open Champion, 1948, 1950, 1954.

Before becoming a golfer 'Babe' Zaharias was a noted athlete. In the 1932 Olympic Games at Los Angeles, limited by the rules to three events, she won gold medals for the javelin and 80 metres high hurdles and broke the high jump record, only to be disqualified for using the style called the 'western roll', since allowed. She was an expert swimmer, rifle shot and tennis player—indeed, as someone put it, she was capable of winning everything except the Kentucky Derby.

Shortly after winning the Texas Open Championship in 1935, she was banned as an amateur by the U.S. Golf Association, but after her marriage to George Zaharias in 1938 she applied for reinstatement, and this was allowed in 1943. After winning the British Ladies' Championship in 1947, she turned professional again. Author of *Championship Golf* (1949); *This Life I've Led* (1956).

## ZAIRE, GOLF IN REPUBLIC OF

In spite of the troubles of recent years, golf is still played in the Congo, now known as Zaire, although some courses have vanished. There are about six clubs, including the Royal Club at Lubumbashi, formerly Elizabethville, founded in 1934.

## ZAMBIA, GOLF IN

Plenty of golf is still played in what was formerly called Northern Rhodesia until it gained independence under Dr Kenneth Kaunda in 1964. The Livingstone Club, founded in 1908, is the oldest and there are nine others at Broken Hill and Roan Antelope, in the big mining areas, at Bancroft, Choma, Kasama, Lusaka, the capital (a fine course with a length of 6,990 yards), Mufulira, Nchanga and Ndola. A new course has recently been designed for Dr Kaunda by Frank Pennink.

## ZOELLER, Frank Urban ('Fuzzy') (b 1952)

Won U.S. Masters, 1979, after tie with Ed. Snead and Tom Watson.

# Index